Behavior, Society, and International Conflict

BEHAVIOR, SOCIETY, AND INTERNATIONAL CONFLICT
A Series of Review Volumes

Edited by Philip E. Tetlock, Jo L. Husbands,
Robert Jervis, Paul C. Stern, and Charles Tilly

Committee on International Conflict and Cooperation
(formerly, Committee on Contributions of Behavioral and Social Science
to the Prevention of Nuclear War)
Commission on the Behavioral and Social Sciences and Education
National Research Council/National Academy of Sciences

BEHAVIOR, SOCIETY, AND INTERNATIONAL CONFLICT

VOLUME THREE

Philip E. Tetlock
Jo L. Husbands
Robert Jervis
Paul C. Stern
Charles Tilly
Editors

Committee on International Conflict and Cooperation
Commission on Behavioral and Social Sciences and Education
National Research Council

New York   Oxford
OXFORD UNIVERSITY PRESS
1993

Oxford University Press

Oxford   New York   Toronto
Delhi   Bombay   Calcutta   Madras   Karachi
Kuala Lumpur   Singapore   Hong Kong   Tokyo
Nairobi   Dar es Salaam   Cape Town
Melbourne   Auckland

and associated companies in
Berlin   Ibadan

Copyright © 1993 by Oxford University Press, Inc.

Published by Oxford University Press, Inc.,
200 Madison Avenue, New York, New York 10016

Oxford is a registered trademark of Oxford University Press

Library of Congress Cataloging-in-Publication Data
(Revised for volume 3)
Behavior, society, and nuclear war.
"Committee on Contributions of Behavioral and Social Science to the
Prevention of Nuclear War, Commission on Behavioral and Social Sciences
and Education, National Research Council."
Vol. 3 has title: Behavior, society, and international conflict.
   Includes bibliographical references and indexes.
1. Nuclear warfare—Psychological aspects.   2. Nuclear warfare—Social
aspects.   I. Tetlock, Philip.
U263.B45   1989   355.02'17   88-33043
ISBN 0-19-505765-1 (v. 1)
ISBN 0-19-505766-X (v. 1 : pbk.)
ISBN 0-19-505767-8 (v. 2)
ISBN 0-19-505768-6 (v. 2 : pbk.)
ISBN 0-19-505769-4 (v. 3)
ISBN 0-19-505770-8 (v. 3 : pbk.)

9 8 7 6 5 4 3 2 1

Printed in the United States of America
on acid-free paper

Foreword

The National Academy of Sciences/National Research Council has long been concerned with the contributions of the social and behavioral sciences to the understanding of major problems facing the United States. In the past four decades, few problems have loomed as large as the danger of nuclear war. In response to a belief that many of the issues associated with the prevention of nuclear war were human and social issues, the Research Council established, in 1985, the Committee on Contributions of Behavioral and Social Science to the Prevention of Nuclear War to supplement its long-standing commitment to studies of the technical aspects of the subject. The committee brought together scientists from across a wide range of disciplines—anthropology, economics, psychology, history, sociology, and political science—to improve our understanding of the social and psychological forces that might affect decisions to develop, deploy, and use nuclear weapons.

The purposes of the committee were to foster multi-disciplinary research on the subject, to develop collaborative relations between American and Soviet scholars working on relevant subjects, and to disseminate the results of its own work as well as existing knowledge to those who could use such materials. One of the committee's main tasks has been to survey existing social science research relating to nuclear war, aggression, and other topics, such as decision making, negotiation, and domestic influences on foreign policy, that are indirectly relevant to the potential for international conflict.

The present book is the third in a series that contains the fruits of that effort. As in the first two volumes of the series, the authors attempt to distill the best knowledge from various parts of the social sciences. They highlight what we know, and they are sensitive to the vast amount we do not know. They find much that helps to understand the forces that lead to international conflict but are appropriately cautious in their conclusions. The volumes are steps in an ongoing social science discussion of these issues. They help us understand where we are and, thereby, should help us to move forward more effectively.

As is always the case in relation to long-term enterprises dealing with contemporary issues—but is even more the case for such enterprises in the past few years—the world changes as we study it. One of the goals of the committee was to collaborate with Soviet scholars. We continue the collaboration, but they are no longer "Soviet." (At the present writing, the appellation is not certain.)

In addition, the threat of nuclear war—at least the threat of a major war between the United States and the Soviet Union, if not the threat of the proliferation of nuclear weapons into dangerous parts of the world—has diminished. The series, of which this is the third volume, began as *Behavior, Society, and Nuclear War*. Over time, the series has evolved in a more general direction, which is reflected in its broader title. Indeed, the committee that sponsors these volumes has become the Committee on International Conflict and Cooperation. If the chances of a superpower nuclear war have diminished, the chances of international conflict in its many other deadly forms, alas, have not. We hope that this volume and the continuing work of the committee will contribute to a better understanding of conflict and cooperation and, thereby, in some small measure add to the chances of a peaceful future.

The series is edited by committee member Charles Tilly, former members Philip E. Tetlock and Robert Jervis, and staff members Jo L. Husbands and Paul C. Stern. The editors have been responsible for developing ideas for chapters, selecting the authors, and managing the review process. Each chapter has been reviewed by the editors, additional members of the committee, and scholars and practitioners who brought diverse perspectives to the topics. The views expressed in the chapters, however, are those of the authors.

We are indebted to the Carnegie Corporation of New York, the John D. and Catherine T. MacArthur Foundation, and the National Research Council Fund for their support of the committee. We wish also to acknowledge the important role of the Commission on Behavioral and Social Sciences and Education of the National Research Council, which was responsible for organizing this committee. Special thanks are due former committee chairs William K. Estes, Herbert A. Simon, and Charles Tilly, and to David A. Goslin, former executive director of the commission, for their leadership and support of the committee's efforts from its inception.

Sidney Verba, *Chair*
Committee on International Conflict and Cooperation

Engineering in providing services to the government, the public, and the scientific and engineering communities. The Council is administered jointly by both academies and the Institute of Medicine. Dr. Frank Press and Dr. Robert M. White are chairman and vice chairman, respectively, of the National Research Council.

Committee on International Conflict and Cooperation 1991–1992*

SIDNEY VERBA
Chair, Department of Government, Harvard University

GEORGE W. BRESLAUER
Department of Political Science, University of California, Berkeley

JOHN L. COMAROFF
Department of Anthropology, University of Chicago

LYNN R. EDEN
Department of History, Carnegie-Mellon University

BARRY EICHENGREEN
Department of Economics, University of California, Berkeley

ROBERT FOGEL
Center for Population Economics, University of Chicago

WILLIAM A. GAMSON
Department of Sociology, Boston College

ALBERT O. HIRSCHMAN
Institute for Advanced Study, Princeton, N.J.

ROBERT KEOHANE
Department of Government, Harvard University

GAIL LAPIDUS
Department of Political Science, University of California, Berkeley

*formerly, Committee on Contributions of Behavioral and Social Science to the Prevention of Nuclear War

Contents

Behavior, Society, and International Conflict

Introduction

PHILIP E. TETLOCK, JO L. HUSBANDS, ROBERT JERVIS, PAUL C. STERN, AND CHARLES TILLY

"**M**ay you live in interesting times," runs the legendary Chinese curse. These are interesting times: almost anything can happen except a return to the delicate but enduring balance between two blocs that marked international relations for nearly half a century after World War II. The possibilities include nuclear war, not in the form of the long-feared mutual destruction of the Soviet Union and the United States, but as a last resort in the course of escalating regional conflicts in the Middle East or South Asia. In the aftermath of the 1991 Gulf War, United Nations inspectors found evidence of strong steps toward the production of nuclear arms in Iraq, a country whose leaders did not hesitate to rain missiles on noncombatant Israel during their struggle to hold Kuwait; the same science is available to many other small, rich despots throughout the world. While the chances that two of the world's largest countries would annihilate each other simultaneously have surely receded, the risk of nuclear war has by no means vanished.

We began the adventure of *Behavior, Society, and Nuclear War* at a time of mixed dread and hope: dread of the mutual threat between the United States and the Soviet Union, with its many risks of missteps and calculated accelerations, hope that changes in the international system could finally occur. Although we took the Cold War as a durable reality, we thought that heavy concentration on strategic analyses of hypothetical Soviet-American conflicts was a mistake, for several reasons: first, because wars have frequently resulted from errors in strategic calculations or their execution rather than from the simple rational calculation of interests; second, because those errors often flowed from the very organization of military and diplomatic decision making; third, because a nuclear war could begin elsewhere than in the threat and counterthreat of Washington and Moscow, either because peripheral segments of the superpowers' military forces deployed the arms or because third parties did so. Thinking primarily of policy discussions within the United States, we decided to survey and publicize the possible contributions of current behavioral and social sciences to the analysis of these problems. Our central idea was to locate subjects that were in principle applicable to questions of war and peace, where a well-developed scientific literature already existed whose relevance to the analysis of international relations had not been widely recognized or pursued. Our secondary object was to draw specialists in those subjects more explicitly into applying their theories and findings to war and peace.

With those objectives in mind, we solicited synthetic papers from leading theorists and researchers on crisis decision making, negotiations, the causes of war, third-party intervention in conflict, arms races, and similar topics. They varied in how much they focused on nuclear conflict and the nuclear age: some intensely, some hardly at all. Almost all of them, however, turned out to be relevant to meeting the challenges of the post–Cold War world. The ways in which human beings process information (Fischhoff, 1991) remain central, and we will still need to take account of the effects of stress on the quality of decision making (Holsti, 1989). Arms races (Downs, 1991) are likely to recur even if they do not involve the United States and what was the Soviet Union. The role for third-party intervention (Wallensteen, 1991) and negotiation (Druckman and Hopmann, 1989) may increase, as is likely to be the case for the use of reassurances (J. Stein, 1991).

The outlines of the post–Cold War international system are still indistinct. In such a time of flux, we have become even more concerned to draw on scholars who can put particular conflicts into historical, comparative, and global perspective or who can analyze the potential to restructure the conditions of war and peace by forging new relationships and institutional arrangements between states. The present volume should forward that effort.

In this volume, perspectives on conflict are offered in chapters on the strategy of conflict (Shubik, Chapter 4), learning in international relations (Jarosz and Nye, Chapter 3), and influence techniques among nations (Leng, Chapter 2). Analyses of the opportunities for and barriers to structural change in the international system are provided by Robert Hinde (Chapter 1), who examines the relevance for war of human tendencies toward aggression, William Jarosz and Joseph Nye (Chapter 3), who assess the potential for states to learn; and Arthur Stein (Chapter 5), who analyzes the peace-generating potential of international economic interdependencies.

As with earlier volumes of *Behavior, Society, and Nuclear War*, a central purpose remains to help disentangle the factual and moral issues that underlie disagreements about how best to prevent nuclear war. The behavioral and social sciences contribute toward this goal in two categories: methodological and theoretical. On the methodological side, the behavioral and social sciences can identify the dangers of making vague causal claims that are difficult to falsify and that rest on superficial and subjective readings of the historical record. For instance, the discussion of international politics and conflicts that accompanies policy debates is often analytically weak. One rarely hears policy advocates specify the types of evidence that would induce them to change their minds, clearly articulate the causal assumptions that undergird their policy recommendations, or dispassionately assess the strengths and weaknesses of alternative research methods for testing their causal assumptions. Although the contributors to this series are asked to explore the policy implications of the research literatures they review, they are also asked not to slip into roles of policy advocacy. We encourage contributors to be methodologically self-conscious—to make careful note of both the strengths and weaknesses of the data and methods that underlie their theoretical and policy conclusions.

On the theoretical side, the behavioral and social sciences can identify the dangers of making undifferentiated, sweeping claims concerning the causes of war and peace. Simple theoretical generalizations tend to have poor empirical track records in the arena of public policy. The causes of international conflict are extremely complex; variables operating at a number of levels of analysis appear to play key causal roles (Tetlock, 1989). Moreover, the effects of these variables appear to be both interactive (the effects of variable A on war depend on levels of variables B, C, D, . . .) and probabilistic (variables influence the likelihood of various types of war and peace but rarely make a particular outcome inevitable).

The behavioral and social sciences have established lines of research and theory that promise to clarify the factors affecting the likelihood of war in general and of nuclear war in particular. Although there is no well-accepted theory of the conditions that promote nuclear war, there is knowledge about important parts of the problem, including the behavior of decision makers under uncertainty, the effects of different kinds of organizations on their members, the circumstances under which threats do or do not deter dangerous behavior, and the processes of negotiation when stakes are high. There is also knowledge about parts of the problems of the causes of war in general (in this series, Levy, 1989) and of change in specific policies or broader social systems that may decrease the likelihood of war (e.g., Evangelista, 1991; J. Stein, 1991; Jarosz and Nye, Chapter 3; A. Stein, Chapter 5).

Our strategy in developing this series has been to identify existing work that bears on these issues and then to persuade a well-informed researcher to summarize the current state of the literature and reflect on its implications for reducing the risk of nuclear war and enhancing international security. Given the difficulties of conducting research on these issues—the limited number of observations, the large number of confounding variables, and the fallibility of the research methods at our disposal—it is impressive, as Tetlock argues (1989), that we have achieved as much as we have. Given the magnitude of the problem, it is discouraging, as Tetlock also argues, that so much remains to be accomplished.

As recent international events reemphasize, the behavioral and social sciences do not offer short-term predictions or decisive solutions for the international predicaments confronting the world today; they do, however, identify considerations that prudent policymakers should take into account in choosing among policies aimed at reducing the risk of nuclear war. They can help illuminate and specify for the policy community the dangers of cognitive conceit (of thinking we know more than we do); the limitations of deterrence theory, the most widely accepted theory of international influence, and the strengths and limitations of the alternatives; the impact of crisis-induced stress on human thought and the difficult trade-offs in crisis management; the pitfalls of international communications; and the egregious errors that can arise from relying on selective and superficial readings of the historical record.

In brief, we draw on the behavioral and social sciences to make a case for new intellectual approaches to the subject of international security. The approaches need to be conceptually rigorous, with key ideas well defined and their links to reality explicitly noted; theoretically eclectic in drawing upon a broad range of interacting levels of analysis, from the psychological to the international; and methodologically self-conscious, with careful scrutiny of the distinctive strengths and weaknesses of the different research methods that underlie claims to knowledge about the sources of war and peace. Taking a new approach, to be sure, is not easy; it requires increased tolerance of ambiguity and complexity. There are no neatly packaged answers to the pressing policy dilemmas posed by the multifaceted and rapidly changing international environment. To contribute to policy deliberations, researchers must try to understand and take account of the complex interactions of human and societal processes. Appreciating the difficulties, we attempt here to mobilize new resources for the task.

References

Downs, G.W. 1991. Arms race and war. In P.E. Tetlock, J.L. Husbands, R. Jervis, P.C. Stern, and C. Tilly, eds., *Behavior, Society, and Nuclear War*, Vol. 2. New York: Oxford University Press.

Druckman, D., and P.T. Hopmann. 1989. Behavioral aspects of negotiations on mutual security. In P.E. Tetlock, J.L. Husbands, R. Jervis, P.C. Stern, and C. Tilly, eds., *Behavior, Society, and Nuclear War*, Vol. 1. New York: Oxford University Press.

Evangelista, M. 1991. Sources of moderation in Soviet security policy. In P.E. Tetlock, J.L. Husbands, R. Jervis, P.C. Stern, and C. Tilly, eds., *Behavior, Society, and Nuclear War*, Vol. 2. New York: Oxford University Press.

Fischhoff, B. 1991. Nuclear decisions: Cognitive limits to the thinkable. In P.E. Tetlock, J.L. Husbands, R. Jervis, P.C. Stern, and C. Tilly, eds., *Behavior, Society, and Nuclear War*, Vol. 2. New York: Oxford University Press.

Holsti, O.R. 1989. Crisis decision making. In P.E. Tetlock, J.L. Husbands, R. Jervis, P.C. Stern, and C. Tilly, eds., *Behavior, Society, and Nuclear War*, Vol. 1. New York: Oxford University Press.

Levy, J. 1989. The causes of war: A review of theories and evidence. In P.E. Tetlock, J.L. Husbands, R. Jervis, P.C. Stern, and C. Tilly, eds., *Behavior, Society, and Nuclear War*, Vol. 1. New York: Oxford University Press.

Stein, J.G. 1991. Deterrence and reassurance. In P.E. Tetlock, J.L. Husbands, R. Jervis, P.C. Stern, and C. Tilly, eds., *Behavior, Society, and Nuclear War*, Vol. 2. New York: Oxford University Press.

Tetlock, P.E. 1989. Methodological themes and variations. In P.E. Tetlock, J.L. Husbands, R. Jervis, P.C. Stern, and C. Tilly, eds., *Behavior, Society, and Nuclear War*, Vol. 1. New York: Oxford University Press.

Wallensteen, P. 1991. Is there a role for third parties in the prevention of nuclear war? In P.E. Tetlock, J.L. Husbands, R. Jervis, P.C. Stern, and C. Tilly, eds., *Behavior, Society, and Nuclear War*, Vol. 2. New York: Oxford University Press.

1

Aggression and War: Individuals, Groups, and States

ROBERT A. HINDE

Introduction

In everyday speech we often use the same terms to describe phenomena at different levels of social complexity. We speak of two individuals being friendly with or hostile to each other and yet use precisely the same terms when speaking of two nations or states each with a population of many million individuals. We use the same terms to describe strategies whether we are referring to a game or a military campaign. The question therefore arises, are these really comparable phenomena? Are the factors that increase the likelihood of aggression between individuals similar to those that increase the likelihood of war between states? Are similar processes involved? These are the issues with which this paper is concerned. It will consider the nature and bases of aggression at different levels of social complexity, asking whether the phenomena at increasing levels of social complexity remain similar, incorporate new elements, or are fundamentally different from those at lower levels.

To anticipate the argument, to understand human social behavior, it is necessary both to distinguish successive levels of social complexity—individuals, interactions, relationships, groups, societies—and to understand the relations between them. Each level of social complexity involves elements of lower levels and also additional properties arising only at that level, and each level both influences and is influenced by adjacent ones. While the phenomena at any one level often have a heuristic value for understanding behavior at others, different issues become important as we move up the levels. A physical fight between two individuals and the societal phenomenon of war can be described using similar words, yet the two differ in many respects. Although the phenomena differ between levels, there are links between them. Thus to understand aggression at one level of social complexity, it is necessary to understand its relations with others, and for that it is necessary to cross and recross between the levels. Aggression between groups involves individual propensities, but also issues of group dynamics, irrelevant to the behavior of individuals. War involves issues of group dynamics but is also an institution that must be analyzed in terms of its constituent roles and the relations between them. Because of the increase in complexity with successive levels, and because new properties arise and new explanatory concepts are needed, simple analogies between one level and another tell us little or nothing about causation. As we move up the levels, we must come to terms not only with increasing complexity, but also with the relations between levels.

The importance of these dialectical influences between levels for understanding the phenomena of war depends on the precise question being asked. Analyses of the causes of war in sociological, political, and economic terms, and rough predictions concerning its probability in particular circumstances, may be possible through consideration only of the higher levels of social complexity. Understanding of the causes and courses of particular wars demands also analyses of both the group processes and the individual personalities involved, and how these affect each other. And the ultimate question of what maintains war as an institution for the solution of international conflict will require detailed analyses of the dialectical relations between levels. Seen from this perspective, the arguments both of those who claim that the causes of war can be traced to fundamental properties of human nature and of those who assume models of individual human nature to be irrelevant, appealing rather to "rational actors" adapting to the threats and opportunities presented to them, seem in each case but partial pictures.

In the following sections the bases of aggression at different levels of social complexity will be discussed, the focus being on their relevance, or lack of relevance, to international war. It is logically and heuristically preferable to start with individual aggression. But before proceeding, it is necessary to come to terms with some definitional issues. What exactly do we mean by "levels of social complexity"? And what are we to include within the category of "aggression"?

Levels of Social Complexity

Social behavior involves at least two individuals. We may define an interaction as involving two individuals and lasting only a brief span of time. Thus individual A may show behavior X to individual B, and B may respond with Y, and a similar sequence may be repeated a number of times—though there is no implication here that the interaction involves linear causal sequences. During an interaction, the behavior of each is influenced by that of the other, and also by the other's appearance and by the circumstances of the meeting. Just how each affects the other will depend on the personality and other characteristics of the individuals concerned, including the norms of behavior that each brings to the encounter, and all these in turn depend on their past experience of interactions and relationships.

If we seek to describe an interaction, we must describe properties that would be simply irrelevant to the behavior of an individual in isolation: for instance, a complete description would involve reference to the extent to which the behavior of each individual meshed with that of the other, whether one initiated each interchange or whether they played similar roles, and so on.

In terms of the behavior involved, a relationship involves a series of interactions over time between the same individuals, such that each interaction is affected by previous ones and perhaps by expectations concerning future interactions. That there is no clear dividing line between an interaction and a relationship is an issue that need not detain us. Full description of a relationship would involve properties that would be simply irrelevant to individual interactions. For instance, some relationships involve only one or a few types of interaction—A and B meet to play squash or drink beer together but do not meet in other contexts. Other relationships, such as those between marital partners, involve many types of interaction. This property of "uniplex" versus "multiplex" is irrelevant to individual interactions.

Of course relationships, and for that matter interactions, do not involve only behavior. Relationships may persist in the absence of interactions and are accompanied by emotions, judgments, wishes, and expectations that are usually important for their future course. More important in the present context, the behavior of each participant is guided and evaluated by beliefs, values, expectations, and so on acquired from the group or society in which he or she lives. The behavior of the individuals is determined not only by their individual idiosyncrasies, but also by the rights and duties conventionally associated with the role they see themselves as occupying. For instance, in most societies there is an institution of marriage, with component roles of husband and wife. How husbands and wives behave is influenced in part by conventions concerning the behavior appropriate for husbands and wives in the society in question. These values, beliefs, institutions, roles, and so on are referred to here as the sociocultural structure of the group or society.

Relationships are usually set within groups containing three or more individuals. This introduces new complexities. First, the several relationships within the group may affect one another: A's relationship with B may be influenced by B's relationship with C. And again, new properties are present, concerned especially with the patterning of the relationships, which are irrelevant to the description of particular ones. Thus the group may consist of a number of individuals all of whom have relationships with a central individual but none with each other (centrifocal), or each may have relationships with all others, or the relationships may be hierarchically organized, and so on.

Most societies consist of overlapping groups of various sorts—the detailed possibilities need not concern us here. But it will be apparent that yet again the society will have properties consequent upon the degree of segregation between its constituent groups and other aspects of their patterning that are simply not relevant to the constituent groups.

We have, then, a series of levels of social complexity—individuals, interactions, relationships, groups, and societies. The properties at each level

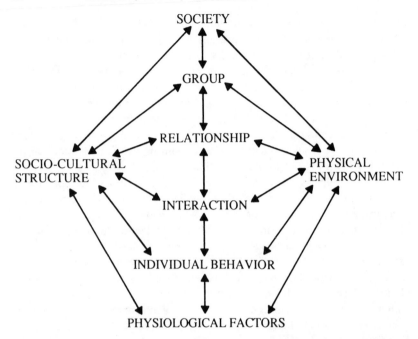

FIGURE 1.1. Dialectical relations between successive levels of (social) complexity.

depend in part on dialectical relations with the adjacent levels and with the sociocultural structure (Figure 1.1). For example, the nature of an interaction is affected by the characteristics of the participating individuals and of the relationship in which it is embedded; the nature of individuals affects and is affected by the interactions and relationships they experience and have experienced; the nature of a relationship depends on its component interactions and on the characteristics of the groups to which the members belong. Thus the successive levels of social complexity are to be seen not as entities but in terms of processes, maintained or changed through their mutual influences upon each other. And each affects, or is affected by, the sociocultural structure—and also, though not mentioned so far, by the physical environment (see Hinde, 1979, 1987a, 1990, 1991; Hinde and Stevenson-Hinde, 1987 for further discussion of their issues).

In harmony with these considerations, we shall see in subsequent sections that, at successive levels of social complexity, aggression has different properties and requires different explanatory concepts, and yet aggression at any one level cannot be understood without reference to others. First, however, exactly what do we mean by "aggression"?

Aggression

It is generally agreed that behavior directed toward causing physical or psychological injury to another should be labeled "aggressive." Accidental injury to another is not normally called aggressive, though the boundary between accident and intent is often hard to determine. Furthermore, the intentional infliction of harm that is held to be justified, as in punishment, is often not seen as aggressive: again, the boundary is shady, and even when the harm is justified, the motivation may have much in common with aggression.

In any case, the intent to harm may or may not be primary; the harm may be inflicted in the pursuit of another goal, such as the acquisition of an object or status. This raises another problem: in everyday speech individuals who single-mindedly pursue a given goal are often described as "aggressive," as when we speak of an "aggressive salesman" or "aggressive driving." In such cases there is no intent to injure others, though injury may result. The motivation is usually quite different: there is no evidence that an aggressive salesman is especially likely to get involved in a punch-up. In such cases "assertive" would be a better term.

Aggression usually involves risk of injury for the attacker. It is therefore rarely single-minded and is associated with self-protective and/or withdrawal responses. At the individual level these include threat postures, apparently irrelevant behavior (displacement activities—see below), aggression redirected onto a different object, submissive behavior, and so on. Since these all seem to involve tendencies to attack and flee from a rival, and because the boundary between attack and threat is not always easy to specify, the whole spectrum is often labeled "agonistic behavior" (Scott and Fredericson, 1951).

It will be apparent that "aggressive behavior" is a concept with a hard core but extremely shady at the edges. For some purposes it needs to be distinguished from the more general concept of "hostility," which embraces vindictiveness, greed, lack of cooperation, and so on, and for others a broader concept is acceptable. The difficulties of definition apply equally to group and state levels: for instance, is the building of a dam by one state, resulting in harm to another by reducing its water supplies, an aggressive act?

Conflict of Motivation

Many aggressive acts involve considerable ambivalence. We may start with a consideration of display postures in animals and humans. Those that accentuate size and weapons and often elicit withdrawal are referred to as threat displays, those with the opposite characteristics as submissive displays, and those with a primarily reproductive function as courtship: it is with the first two that we are concerned here.

Displays were formerly considered merely as expressions of emotion (Darwin, 1872). However, the complexity of animal displays provoked detailed study by ethologists, leading to the hypothesis that they could be better understood if they were seen as based on conflicting motivations—to attack the rival, to flee from the rival, and, in some cases, to stay put. Evidence for this view lay in the fact that many threat postures consist of a mosaic of elements of attack and defense, they are accompanied by incipient movements of attacking or fleeing, they are often followed by one or the other, and they are given especially in situations in which tendencies to attack, to flee, and/or to stay put are just in balance (Baerends, 1975; Tinbergen, 1948, 1952). Displays also often include elements of other types of behavior seen in situations in which motivations conflict. These include both "displacement activities," that is, behavior apparently irrelevant to the context in which it occurs, as when a threatening bird suddenly preens its feathers, or a human, engaged in a course of action, stops to scratch his or her head; and also redirected activities, such as aggression elicited by a strong opponent and redirected onto a weaker one (Tinbergen, 1952; van Iersel and Bol, 1958).

Ethologists have also noted that threat displays often involve movements that make the individual appear larger or more dangerous. Structures have been evolved to make the movements more effective in communication (Tinbergen, 1948; Eibl Eibesfeldt, 1975). Comparable issues, though not on an evolutionary time scale, arise in the use by humans of decorations or dress to emphasize aspects of their physique: the epaulets on military uniforms are a classic example (Eibl Eibesfeldt, 1975).

Extending this view, Dawkins and Krebs (1979) have suggested that, rather than being evolved to convey to the reactor information about the actor's current state, displays have been selected to deceive the reactor and to manipulate his or her behavior. In support of this view, Caryl (1979, 1982) reanalyzed data on the sequelae of some avian displays and found that, while some could predict the escape of the actor fairly well, the best predictors of attack were only followed by attack in less than 50 percent of the occurrences. However, other workers have produced evidence that other intraspecific signals are "honest" indicators of the signaler's current capacities and intentions (Halliday and Houston, 1978; Clutton-Brock and Albon, 1979). A further approach is to regard threat postures as contributing to a process of negotiation. Although they do not predict attack with great precision, they do predict "attack or stay" or "escape or stay." A possible suggestion, therefore, is that the sequelae of threat depend on the behavior of the rival (Hinde, 1981); the threat is in effect saying "if you do so and so, I will attack, but if you do something else, I will not." Some evidence in favor of this view is provided by a study of the threat postures of jays: what the actor did after threatening depended both on its current posture and on the behavior of the reactor (Bossema and Burgler, 1980). Furthermore, some displays do involve long periods of interaction between two individuals, leading to a more or less sudden resolution (e.g., Simpson, 1968).

This issue is not yet resolved in general, but it seems that signals range from those whose sequelae are relatively independent of the behavior of the reactor and that can be regarded as more or less pure expressions of emotion, to signals that can be regarded as reflecting a process of deception and/or negotiation, in the latter case the sequelae depending on what the reactor does. Deception, and especially negotiation, often appear to involve complicated motivations.

Analyses of threat postures have principally concerned animals. There are obvious parallels with human aggression at all levels of social complexity. For instance, the following principle is equally applicable to humans: If you are certain you are going to attack, you do best to do so without hesitation; but you will do better to threaten if you feel that thereby you can weaken the nerve of the opposition and avoid the risks inherent in launching an attack. It is important to note, however, that the parallels lie in the functional consequences of actions and not in their causation. While threat may serve to deter the opponents of both birds and superpowers, it is absurd to think that the underlying mechanisms have much in common.

A number of ethological findings do indeed have analogies in group or international conflict—for instance, that effective threat requires efficient communication (cf. Stern et al., 1989*a*), and that rivals may try to conceal their true intentions or strengths. That animal territory owners are likely to win over intruders, whatever their relative strengths, finds parallels in the generalization that the winner in an international encounter often tends to be the side with more at stake, and in the finding that the attacker and defender are often guided by different criteria (Levy, 1989*b*; Goldstone, 1989). And the handicap theory of threat (and courtship), which holds that excessive displays, structures, and adornments are effective because they demonstrate that the individual can cope with "self-imposed" handicaps (Zahavi, 1975), is in harmony with the counterintuitive notion that the purpose of weaponry is not to build military capability but to display publicly that self-inflicted economic costs do not affect performance (O'Neill, 1989). But any similarity in causation that is implied—for instance, that the individual or side with more at stake is more strongly motivated—is seldom profound. A more profitable approach is to reflect that similar functional requirements have resulted in behavior shaped in animals by natural selection and in humans by interacting behavioral propensities affecting and affected by successive levels of social complexity and the sociocultural structure (see Figure 1.1).

Categorization of Individual Aggression

It is becoming increasingly apparent that even aggression between individuals is diverse, and it is necessary to come to terms with this diversity in order to understand its causal bases. To start with a relatively simple case, it is now generally recognized that the aggressive behavior of preschool children can be classified into several types (Blurton-Jones, 1972; Feshbach, 1970): (1) instrumental aggression, concerned with obtaining or maintaining objects, positions, or access to desirable activities; (2) hostile aggression, teasing aggression, or harassment, directed primarily toward annoying, teasing, or injuring another individual; (3) games aggression, which escalates from rough-and-tumble games to the deliberate infliction of injury; (4) defensive or reactive hostility, provoked by the actions of others.

As another example, Tinklenberg and Ochberg (1981) classified criminal violence into five types: (1) instrumental—planned; motivated by a conscious desire to eliminate the victim; not committed in anger; (2) emotive—hot-blooded; impulsive; often performed in extreme fear; (3) felonious—committed in the course of another crime; (4) bizarre—insane and severely psychopathic acts; (5) dyssocial—violent acts that are approved of by a reference group.

Such categories seem clear-cut but always turn out to be more difficult to use in practice than expected. For instance, hostile aggression may involve an attempt to bolster self-esteem or compensate for real or imagined slights, or self-assertiveness in the hope of gaining status in order to achieve long-term instrumental goals. Again, where defensive hostility concerns objects or space, it clearly links to instrumental aggression. And dyssocial violence may be planned and/or emotional; felonious violence may be emotional and instrumental.

Such difficulties arise because aggressive acts lack the motivational purity implied by the classificatory categories (Attili and Hinde, 1986). We may therefore ask whether the several types of aggression can be related to different combinations of hypothesized intervening variables. In the case of preschool children, three variables seem likely to have fairly general importance: (1) aggressiveness; in any given situation, individuals differ in their propensity to behave aggressively; (2) acquisitiveness, or motivation to acquire objects and situations; (3) self-assertiveness, or motivation to elevate one's position or status.

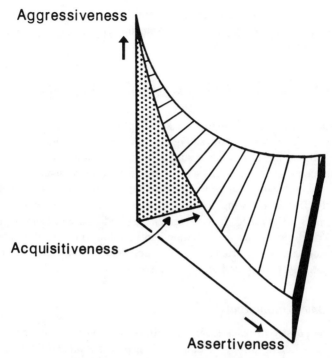

FIGURE 1.2. Simple model of relations between three behavioral propensities (aggressiveness, acquisitiveness, and assertiveness) and aggressive behavior. The latter would appear if the values of the three propensities produced a point above the striped plane. A more complex model would allow for three-way interactions.

The suggestion here is that aggressive acts have complex motivational bases and that several may operate simultaneously. (Motivation is, of course, used here in a broad sense to include all variables influencing the behavior in question.) Figure 1.2 illustrates the strengths of three motivations, each of which may contribute to an aggressive act. Aggression would occur if the child's motivational state were represented by a point above the striped plane; whether the act was labeled as instrumental or teasing would depend on the precise location of the point.

Of course, while heuristically useful, there is no suggestion that all aggressive acts can be understood in terms of these variables. The important issue is that, instead of trying to distinguish distinct, motivationally homogeneous categories of aggression, we should try to understand the relations between different instances of aggressive behavior, or the bases of individual aggressiveness, in terms of a spectrum of contributing variables. This is a more realistic approach than trying to constrain the diversity of aggression into artificial categories.

The Bases of Aggression Between Individuals

The complex nature of aggressive acts implies that, for instance, virtually all aspects of personality development may be relevant to the genesis of aggression. No attempt to cover such a broad spectrum is made here. However, although, as we shall see, war cannot be understood in terms of individual aggression, individual aggressiveness does contribute both directly and indirectly. In the following sections, therefore, the bases of individual aggressiveness are outlined. It is convenient to divide these into developmental factors, predisposing factors, eliciting and inhibitory factors, and the consequences of aggression through which natural selection has acted to maintain the potentiality for aggression in the human species (Figure 1.3).

Development in the Individual

The propensity to behave aggressively shows considerable stability. The stability coefficient for boys over a one-year period is around 0.80, and even over a 10-year period it is about 0.38 (Lefkowitz et al., 1977; McCord, 1983;

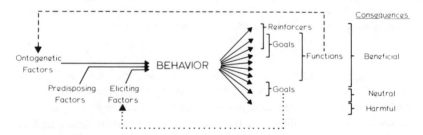

FIGURE 1.3. Relations between ontogenetic and causal factors and consequences. The distinctions between ontogenetic and predisposing and between predisposing and eliciting factors are often somewhat arbitrary. Among the consequences, the categories of reinforcers, goals, and functions only partly overlap. Although a goal is normally achieved as a consequence of behavior, an internal representation (anticipation) may contribute to causation (dotted line). Consequences may be beneficial yet may not provide material for the action of natural selection (i.e. not be functions in a strong sense). Exceptionally, harmful consequences can be goals. The discontinuous line indicates evolutionary consequences on the next generation (Hinde, 1990).

Olweus, 1979, 1984; Pulkkinen, 1988). Among girls it is often held to be considerably lower, but Olweus (cited in Parke and Slaby, 1983) found a high degree of stability over a 10-year period to age 19. Consistency varies with the type of aggression in question: offensive aggression in 8-year-olds is correlated with violence and criminality in adulthood, but defensive aggression is not (Pulkkinen, 1987). Consistency in environmental factors may, of course, contribute to consistency in aggression; cross-situational consistency in aggression at a given age may be low, at any rate in preschool children (Hinde, Tamplin, and Barrett, in press). Furthermore, a correlation of, say, 0.50 still leaves 75 percent of the variance unexplained. Nevertheless, the stability observed clearly poses a problem: what determines that some individuals develop a greater propensity to behave aggressively than others?

There is much evidence that differences in aggressiveness between animals have heritable bases (e.g., Scott and Fuller, 1965; Lagerspetz and Lagerspetz, 1971), and the same is likely to be true of humans (see, for example, the claims of Rushton et al., 1986). However, the formerly widespread belief that a doubling of the Y chromosome in males led to hyperaggressiveness has little foundation: rather, it seems that XYY males have a number of handicaps to overcome, as the result of which a small proportion becomes antisocial (e.g., Manning, 1989; Ratcliffe and Field, 1982).

Of greater interest, in part because they are more easily modifiable, are the environmental factors that contribute to the development of an aggressive propensity. Since, in our culture, most children grow up in families, research in this area has focused on the processes whereby family interaction patterns influence the development of aggressiveness, and especially the detailed processes whereby aggressive behavior is acquired. Classical conditioning, operant conditioning, and observational learning have all been implicated (e.g., Bandura 1973, 1977; Patterson, 1982). Children tend to repeat aggressive acts that have produced successful outcomes and to imitate the aggressive behavior of others if it has been seen to produce the required results. Indeed, the tendency to imitate admired others is retained throughout life.

Supplementing this approach, others have focused on how cognitive mediational processes, such as those involved in the decoding of cues, their interpretation, attribution of motives, and interpersonal perception, may affect the incidence of aggressive behavior (e.g., Dodge, 1982). Acquisition of the cognitive capacities involved here will clearly influence the incidence of aggression.

A third line of research focuses on the family concomitants of aggression. Studies have found particular aspects of potential child-rearing strategies to be related to aggression—for instance, parental coldness and permissiveness, inconsistent punishment, and power-assertive disciplinary practices (Hetherington, Stouwie, and Ridberg, 1971; Lefkowitz et al., 1977; McCord, 1988; McCord, McCord, and Howard, 1961; Martin, 1975). The effects of punishment are in fact complex: the child learns that aggressive behavior can have undesirable consequences but also suffers pain that induces aggression (vs. infra) and observes the parent behaving aggressively. From the latter he or she may deduce that, in some contexts at least, aggression is an acceptable type of behavior. It is perhaps partly for that reason that aggressive parents often have aggressive children (McCord, 1983; v. infra).

It is clear that the family concomitants of aggression are complex, and some studies indicate that the patterning of family variables is important. Thus Baumrind (1971) found that children of authoritarian (high parental control and low warmth) and permissive (low control) parents were more aggressive than those of authoritative (moderate control and moderate-high warmth). Following this lead, Hinde, Tamplin, and Barrett (in press) obtained comparable results, the aggression of preschoolers being least when parental strong control and warmth were more or less in balance. Of course, following the principles discussed in an earlier section, the child-rearing techniques used by parents depend in part on the child—and indeed also on other family members. The importance of recognizing that the family is a system of mutual influences has been emphasized, for instance, by S. Minuchin (1974; Minuchin and Fishman, 1981; see also P. Minuchin, 1985; Hinde and Stevenson-Hinde, 1988).

Family relationships are not the only factors affecting the development of aggressive propensities. Individuals outside the family may serve as role models, and the peer group may be an important source of influence (e.g., Hartup, 1983). However, since familial influences usually predate peer group influences, what the child gets out of the peer group depends in large measure on his or her previous experiences at home. Furthermore, evidence is accumulating that familial effects may be transmitted across successive generations (see below).

Whether we are concerned with intrafamilial or extrafamilial influences, the behavior of the socializing agent will be critically influenced by the values and norms of the society in which he or she lives. Some societies encourage aggressive behavior, whereas others place primary emphasis on harmonious relationships between individuals (Chagnon and Bugos, 1979; Eibl Eibesfeldt, 1979; Mead, 1950; Segall, 1989). Yet others encourage harmonious relationships between members of the in-group but hostility to outsiders (Goody, 1991; Stevenson, 1991; Triandis, 1991). Other norms may be specific to particular subgroups within a society. Furthermore, parents may have different norms for boys and girls, firstborns and later borns, in this social class and that (e.g., Hinde and Stevenson-Hinde, 1987; Radke-Yarrow, Richters, and Wilson, 1988).

In industrialized countries the mass media both reflect and create societal norms. Although the data are not entirely consistent, most studies show a consistent but not necessarily strong link between televised violence and the viewers' aggressive tendencies (Groebel, 1986; National Institute of Mental Health, 1982). It is important to remember here that a moderate effect demonstrated on a large sample is likely to mean a strong effect on some individuals. The effects are both short-term, aggressive actors serving as models and the aggressive material increasing the viewers' arousal; and long-term, including habituation and permissiveness toward aggression and a change in the accepted norms. Familiarity with violence on the screen can make violence attractive and salient.

Apart from the influence of the mass media, norms are likely to remain fairly consistent over time. This is in part because, for a variety of reasons (Hinde, 1979), individuals tend to seek out and associate with individuals whose values are similar to theirs (Byrne, 1971). Furthermore, individuals tend to seek out experiences that confirm their existing framework of beliefs, find contradictory experiences aversive, and integrate new information into the framework of beliefs and values that they already have (Festinger, 1957; Kelly, 1970; Newcomb, 1971).

This brief survey of developmental influences on aggression does scant justice to the vast literature on the subject. A more comprehensive review is provided by Parke and Slaby (1983).

Predisposing Situational Factors

The propensity to behave aggressively is influenced by a variety of social factors. There are, for instance, great differences in the incidence of violence between countries and even between parts of the same country (e.g., southern vs. northern Italy), and there are some cultures in which aggression is virtually absent (Montagu, 1978; Goody, 1991).

A variety of other situational factors may increase the probability that an aggressive act will be elicited. For instance, where individuals (or groups) see themselves as in danger of being exploited, they tend to cultivate an image of toughness and irritability. Such a setting was found in the nineteenth century in the frontier regions of the United States and is present in many modern cities (Pruitt, 1989; Archer and Gartner, 1984). Another issue here is the greater density of individuals in cities, which among other things increases the frequency of interpersonal contact, raises the emotional level (Freedman,

1975), and increases the feeling of being crowded (Zimbardo, 1969): the latter effect is likely to depend on the ability of individuals to comprehend and control or accept the situation (Chandler, 1985), and thus varies culturally.

Within cities, the design of buildings and the layout of streets may affect the incidence of violence: for example, high-rise buildings may diminish the feeling of community and be associated with alienation.

Another situational factor is the "long, hot summer." Increasing temperatures appear to be associated with an increase in crimes of violence (Anderson and Anderson, 1984). Many such issues can be embraced within the somewhat overflexible theory of frustration aggression, discussed below.

Another aspect of crucial importance concerns the relationship of the actor to authority figures who demand, authorize, or justify aggression (Milgram, 1974): this, of course, is an issue of special relevance in war.

Immediate Factors

Even given the presence of predisposing factors, individuals may or may not behave aggressively.

PERSONALITY

Males, especially adolescent males, are more likely to be aggressive than females (e.g., Segall, 1989). There are, however, also sex differences in the forms of aggression used. Eagly and Steffen (1986) found that males are more likely to inflict physical pain, but there is little difference between the sexes in the tendency to inflict psychological harm. Pulkkinen (1987) found defensive aggression to be more typical of females than offensive aggression (see also Frodi, Macaulay, and Thorne, 1977). Lagerspetz, Björkquist, and Peltonen (1988) found that 11- to 12-year-old girls tended to make more use of indirect aggression, such as spreading false rumors or manipulating friendships, whereas boys tended to use more direct aggression. Laboratory studies yield some evidence that individuals high on anxiety tend to be less aggressive than less anxious individuals (Dengerink, 1971). Impulsivity—the inability to wait for rewards—is also associated with aggression. Highly impulsive people are likely to use aggression and other socially unacceptable forms of behavior when they are frustrated (Graham, Doubleday, and Guarino, 1984). However, some individuals who commit violent crimes are normally overcontrolled and unable to express hostility but unnecessarily violent when they do (Megargee, 1966). Aggressive children are more likely to give an aggressive response under conditions of possible punishment, while less aggressive children are deterred (Patterson, 1976; Peterson, 1971). The same seems to be true of aggressive men (Berkowitz, 1978; Kelley and Schmidt, 1989). There is little satisfactory evidence to support the popular belief that many criminals are mentally ill (e.g., Moss, Johnson, and Hosford, 1984), though individuals who engage in hostile or teasing aggression seem insensitive to or to be reinforced by the pain of the victim (Olweus, 1984).

CURRENT MOTIVATIONAL STATE

Recent reviews on the physiological bases of aggression are given by Herbert (1989) and in van Praag, Plutchik, and Apter (1990): such issues will not be pursued here.

Research on the bases of aggression has been much influenced by the hypothesis that aggression is the result of frustration (Dollard et al., 1939). This postulates a link between the strength of aggressive motivation and the number and degree of frustrations recently experienced by the subject. The theory integrates many facts about aggression but is not perhaps so ubiquitously applicable as was first claimed. A major issue is the difficulty of defining frustration: given a broad enough definition, every aggressive act is easily accounted for and the theory is irrefutable. More recent modifications to the original theory include the need to specify what motivation is frustrated, some being more prone to lead to aggression than others, and the role of cognitive intermediaries, including perception and interpretation of the current situation, the perceived likelihood of a positive outcome, and the extent to which current frustrations are seen as aversive and unfair (e.g., Feshbach, 1989; Berkowitz 1989). It is easy to draw parallels between individual aggression induced by frustration and international aggression induced by perceived shortage of resources, but, as with animal/human parallels (see above), they concern primarily the functional consequences and not the causal mechanisms.

Aggression in response to frustration or harm is less likely if the frustration or harm is perceived to have been inflicted accidentally rather than intentionally. Among adults, much criminal aggression occurs in response to an insult or perceived wrong or injustice (Krebs and Miller, 1985). But what is perceived as insulting or unjust depends on both the personality of the individual and the norms of the culture: aggressive individuals are more likely to impute an aggressive motive than are less aggressive ones (Dodge, 1985), and norms vary between societies and between groups within a society.

Aversive stimulation and fear can also lead to aggression in both animals and humans: for instance, pain often induces an aggressive response (Ulrich, 1966). Pain appears to affect aggression specifically, though it also increases arousal (see below). Furthermore, generally unpleasant conditions, or stimuli that have been associated with such conditions, can also induce aggression. At this point, it will be apparent, predisposing and eliciting factors merge.

While much aggression can be accounted for in terms of frustration, pain, or fear, some cannot. Teasing aggression often seems to be motivated by a desire to witness the pain of the victim, dyssocial violence (see above) can be seen as an attempt to rise in status in the reference group, and some instances of psychopathic violence do not fit easily into any category.

Aggression is often associated with physiological arousal, and there is some evidence that physiological arousal facilitates aggression (e.g., Rule and Nesdale, 1976; Zillman, 1979), as indeed arousal within limits facilitates many other types of behavior (Berlyne, 1960). A high level of arousal may have an inhibitory effect, but the inhibition may affect either aggression itself or cognitive inhibition of aggression, resulting in more rather than less aggression (Zillman, 1979).

Where aggressive behavior is instigated by frustration or inflicted harm, it is likely to be associated with subjective feelings of anger or hostility, and everyday speech often implies that the behavior is caused by the emotion. This is often linked to a cathartic or energy model of emotion that supposes that an "internal energy" (often equated with the emotion) builds up until it is expressed in action. Such energy models of motivation formed an essential component in the theoretical schemes of Freud ([1923] 1947), McDougall (1923), and Lorenz (1966). They have, however, a number of problems and have now been discredited: in particular, contrary to the prediction of such a model, performance may be accompanied by either an increase or a decrease in aggressive motivation, the former being more likely if the aggressor is not emotionally involved (Feshbach, 1961). A decrease is usually consequent upon a change in the stimulus situation (e.g., Berkowitz, 1963; Hinde, 1960). In any case, anger does not always lead to aggression, and aggression is not always preceded by anger. Furthermore, emotions may be caused by behavior rather than (or as well as) vice versa. And emotions, far from being simple, have interrelated physiological, motivational, and cognitive components (e.g., Izard, 1982). Related to this, emotions are cognitively constructed and in some degree culture-specific, so that it is often difficult to identify a precise equivalent to Western anger in other cultures (e.g., Briggs, 1970; see also Sweet, 1973). None of these points, however, count against the view that physiological, motivational, and/or cognitive concomitants of subjective feelings of anger or hostility may play a part in the causation of aggression, and there is considerable evidence that aggression often comes from individuals who are emotionally aroused and act with little concern for the consequences (e.g., Berkowitz, 1978). An analysis of the relations between anger and aggression is given by Averill (1982).

THE VICTIM

Some individuals are more likely to elicit violence than others. Experimental evidence indicates that subjects are less likely to show violence to female as compared with male victims (Larsen et al., 1972). "Whipping boys" who are bullied in school tend to be either anxious, insecure, physically weak, and unpopular, or to be irritating, tension creating, and restless (Olweus, 1978). As noted earlier, however, the instigator of aggression is not necessarily the target: aggression may be redirected onto a more vulnerable or appropriate victim.

PRESENCE OF WEAPONS

Experimental evidence indicates that the presence of a weapon can augment aggressiveness (Berkowitz and Le Page, 1967); that the availability of a weapon may increase the intensity of other forms of violence (Berkowitz and Frodi, 1977); and that the use of weapons exacerbates the consequences of an aggressive incident (Morris and Hawkins, 1970). Here again there are analogies with intersocietal aggression, but the psychological mechanisms by which the presence of a weapon leads to individual aggression are not the same as from the national confidence accruing from superior armament.

Inhibitory Factors

The issues involved are to some extent the opposite to those operating in the induction of aggression. Thus individuals who have not been exposed to violence, have not had parents or other reference figures who condoned it, and have not been reinforced or seen others reinforced for violent behavior are less likely to show it themselves. Individuals who have learned to control aggressive tendencies and not to allow conflictful situations to escalate are less likely to be aggressive. Furthermore, most individuals acquire moral standards indicating that at least some acts of aggression, or acts against some people, are wrong (e.g., Hoffman, 1970; Kohlberg, 1976). For such standards to operate, certain cognitive skills, such as perspective taking, may be necessary (Goldstein, 1989; Staub, 1971). In many situations individuals are faced with a choice between aggressive and prosocial or cooperative behavior, and the developmental factors promoting choice of the latter alternative are not exactly the opposite to those promoting aggression (Hinde and Groebel, 1991; Radke-Yarrow, Zahn-Waxler, and Chapman, 1983).

In addition to these developmental factors, situational factors may operate to minimize aggression—such as the availability of alternative courses of action, or the presence of agents who would be likely to punish aggression (see above). Finally, in a confrontation humans use a variety of means to avoid actual aggression, such as placatory signals or gestures (e.g., giving food) or ritualizing aggression in a harmless display (see Eibl Eibesfeldt, 1979). Phenomenological parallels with war are obvious but not especially enlightening.

Ultimate Factors

Humans, given certain conditions, can behave aggressively. It is reasonable to suppose that the potential for aggression is a product of natural selection: earlier in our evolutionary history natural selection operated in favor of individuals with the capacity to behave aggressively in appropriate circumstances. This does not mean that humans are inevitably aggressive, but only that, given certain types of rearing environments and certain types of current circumstances, they have the potential for behaving aggressively. Thus humans have been shaped by natural selection to behave aggressively in circumstances in which it would pay them to do so. This does not, of course, imply that all aggression is appropriate or that individuals always behave aggressively when it would be best for them to do so: for a variety of reasons, some of which will be discussed later, behavior is often inappropriate.

Classical evolutionary theory held that natural selection operated through individual reproductive success. (Note, to counter two popular misconceptions, it does not operate for the good of the species, and it at most rarely operates in favor of one group or population of individuals as opposed to another.) To reproduce successfully, individuals must survive and be healthy and strong. Thus we may expect natural selection to have acted to promote aggression in circumstances and contexts in which it will promote an individual's health, survival, and reproductive success.

Recent evolutionary theory has also stressed that natural selection acts through the replication of genes. Thus an act that promotes the survival or reproduction of a relative, whose genetic endowment is largely identical with that of the actor, may be selected for, even though it involves costs to the actor (Hamilton, 1964; Trivers, 1972). Thus the critical issue is not how many descendants an individual leaves ("individual fitness"), but how successfully genes identical to those he or she carries are reproduced in subsequent generations ("inclusive fitness"). This theoretical approach ("kin selection") provides a biological explanation not only for a fact that we all take for granted— that parents defend and make sacrifices for their children—but also for the tendency to give help to, or behave aggressively in defense of, relatives as opposed to strangers (e.g., Essock-Vitale and McGuire, 1985). We shall see that this issue is relevant to a number of other issues raised later in this chapter—for instance, the extent to which aggression is directed toward relatives, and the nature of patriotism.

Conclusion

We have seen that full understanding of aggressive interactions between individuals requires us to tackle a number of distinct yet interrelated issues—the development of the capability or propensity to behave aggressively, involving interactions between aspects of genetic constitution, social experience, and cultural norms; the situational factors predisposing individuals to behave aggressively; the immediate factors leading to the elicitation of aggression; inhibitory factors; and the evolutionary processes that have provided humans with the ability to behave aggressively. This review does scant justice to our knowledge on these issues, incomplete as that knowledge still is. In what follows we shall see that many of the conclusions we have reached about individual aggression are relevant to, but need to be supplemented in, more complex social situations.

Aggression in Relationships

Intrafamily Violence

So far we have considered aspects of aggressive behavior relevant to short-term interactions—as might be the case for aggression between strangers. We now turn to violence between individuals who have a relationship with each other. Interestingly, comparisons between aggressive and peaceful prestate societies indicate that the latter are often characterized by rather loose bonds between individuals: individuals are expected to depend for emotional and material resources on the group rather than on other individuals. Such societies have an antiviolent value system, where quarreling, boasting, anger, and violence are stigmatized, so far as in-group members are concerned, but a belief in the evil nature of outsiders and in malevolent and violent spirits who prey on human beings and oppose the friendly spirits (McCauley (1990) and other contributions to Haas (1990)).

However, in Western countries, at least, a high proportion of aggressive acts occur between individuals known to each other, and many between individuals in close relationships (Daly and Wilson, 1988). For instance, the FBI report for 1982 indicated that, of cases where the relationship between murderer and victim was known, only 24 percent involved individuals who were strangers to each other, and a similar proportion involved family members. Furthermore, murders of one spouse by another were significantly more violent than those involving any other type of relationship (Goldstein, 1986). Aggression not leading to murder is probably relatively even more common inside families: the incidence of spouse and child abuse is not known for certain, for many cases go unreported—but it is certainly high (Engfer, 1986).

The high incidence of violence directed toward reproductive partners and children seems to contradict the preceding discussion of how natural selection has favored help to relatives. However, for one thing, stepparents are responsible for much child abuse, and spouses are not blood relatives. In addition, more proximate factors may be crucial. At the lowest level, perhaps, propinquity enters in. Individuals see relatives and friends more often than (by definition) they encounter individual strangers. And for that and other obvious reasons, conflicts of interest and frustrations perceived to be caused by a relative or acquaintance are especially likely to arise (see Daly and Wilson, 1988, for a comprehensive review).

Aggression directed toward familiar others is, of course, in marked contrast to international war. Yet studies of intrafamilial violence are of special interest in emphasizing the diversity of factors that lead to aggression. Personality factors certainly enter in, and these seem to stem in large measure from childhood experiences (see below). Predisposing factors, such as the economic situation of the family and poor relationships within the family, also play a role. Relationships within a family affect one another, and one tense dyad can produce widespread repercussions (Christensen and Margolin, 1988). In a study of child abuse in Germany, Engfer and Schneewind (1982; see also Engfer, 1986) found that the immediate antecedents of harsh punishment included characteristics of both child (problem behavior) and parent (anger-proneness and rigid power assertion), together with stress and conflict in the family (Figure 1.4). The mother's anger-proneness was related to her childhood experiences both through her personality characteristics (irritability) and through the incidence of family conflict. The latter was related also to socioeconomic factors and to maternal personality factors and educational goals. Such studies are of special importance in illustrating the complexity of the factors contributing to the use of harsh punishment, and the importance of considering present and past family relationships and socioeconomic factors. Indeed, a full understanding requires understanding of the dynamics of the relationships within the family, and of the manner in which each relationship within the family affects and is affected by others (e.g., Christensen and Margolin, 1988; Easterbrooks and Emde, 1988; Engfer, 1988; Meyer, 1988). Such intrafamily dynamics may differ between chaotic and harmonious families, according to socioeconomic factors, and so on (Radke-Yarrow, Richters, and Wilson, 1988).

Other studies have shown that such effects can be transmitted across successive generations. For example, Caspi and Elder (1988) provide data across four generations showing links between unstable parental personalities, mari-

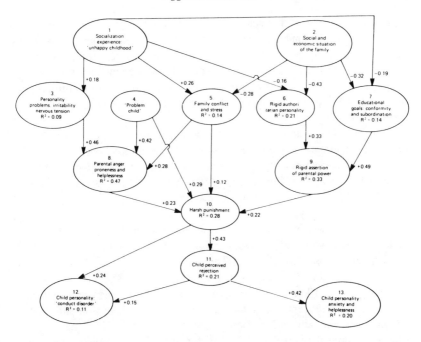

FIGURE 1.4. Empirical model of the causes of harsh maternal punishment of boys. The small figures indicate the path coefficients and R2 the variance accounted for. *Source:* Engfer and Schneewind (1982).

tal tension, ineffective parenting, problem behavior in the children, and their development of unstable personalities. Similarly Patterson and Dishion (1988) have shown that disruptions in parental discipline may lead to antisocial behavior in children and that this in turn may lead to problems in the next generation (see also Dodge, Bates, and Pettit, 1990; Engfer, 1988; Gelles, 1980; Meyer, 1988).

Cooperation, Trust, and Commitment

Finally, we may consider some interrelated factors whose presence is likely to reduce aggression within relationships. The maintenance of relationships involves cooperation between the partners and often also incurs costs in the expectation of long-term gains. For cooperation, commitment to the relationship, and trust that the partner is likewise committed, are usually essential. Aggression in close relationships is no doubt often due to perception by one partner that the other has reneged or is likely to renege.

A detailed review of the factors promoting cooperation, trust, and commitment would be beyond the scope of this chapter, but a brief discussion is necessary. Similar terms are applied to relations between groups or states, and, as discussed later, there are close parallels between the factors conducive to cooperation, trust, and commitment in interindividual and intergroup relations (see Axelrod, 1984; Feger, 1991; Gambetta, 1988; Hinde, 1987b; Hinde and Groebel, 1991).

There are some circumstances in which cooperation can occur without trust: (1) if there are no alternative courses of action, and both partners stand to benefit by cooperation; (2) if there are sanctions against defection: faith in the efficacy of the sanctions can replace trust; (3) if there is perception of a common goal of such importance that defection would be an inappropriate tactic for either party.

Usually, however, instead of or in addition to the presence of such circumstances, trust is involved. Certain conditions are conducive to this: (1) Trust implies certain shared values. (2) The development of trust should be self-reinforcing, in the sense that it is conducive to a relationship that maintains or enhances trust. (3) The extent to which trust develops depends on the information available: strangers tend not to be trusted because there is no information on which to build trust. Here there is a problem: the less information available, the more trust is needed. If all factors affecting all possible contingencies are known, trust is irrelevant. (4) In addition, in experimental data from games in which individuals have a choice between cooperating (and trusting the partner) or competing, cooperation is increased where long-term interests are stressed and where there is good communication. Machiavellian strategies become less likely the more structured the situation (Pruitt and Kimmel, 1976; Rabbie, 1991).

Trust (Boon and Holmes, 1991) may be specific to particular contexts or types of interaction within a relationship, or it may be general. In its absence, individuals are more prone to misinterpret ambiguous behavior as hostile, and less willing to attempt to solve problems constructively. Trust implies, and is necessary for, some degree of commitment to the relationship. Commitment may imply that each partner directs his or her behavior toward continuing the relationship, no matter what its nature (commitment for continuity), or that each strives to maintain or improve the quality of the relationship (commitment for quality). In interpersonal relationships these may exist either together or separately. Commitment may be imposed from the outside, as in an arranged marriage (exogenous commitment), or it may arise endogenously, in the course of the development of a relationship (Hinde, 1979). Commitment may be enhanced by familiarity: interaction with a partially predictable partner is preferable to interaction with a stranger. It is augmented also by the investment of resources in the relationship: investment made in the expectation of future gains requires continuation of the relationship for the reciprocation to be possible (e.g., Lund, 1985, 1991). In practice, of course, a developing relationship depends on continuing positive feedback in successive interactions—liking leads to prosocial behavior, prosocial behavior leads to liking, liking leads to reciprocation, reciprocation leads to trust, trust leads to further investment in the relationship, and so on.

Commitment usually requires belief in the partner's commitment. Expectation of continuity is essential if each partner is to incur costs now in the expectation of future rewards. Belief in the partner's commitment implies trust that the partner would not exploit opportunities for harm, because to do so would weaken the viability of a relationship that he or she also wishes to preserve. And belief in the partner's commitment brings a certain freedom of action—for instance, the possibility of personal growth and change without disruption of the relationship (Hinde, 1979).

It will be immediately apparent that nearly all the factors mentioned above as conducive to cooperation, trust, or commitment in interpersonal relationships apply also to intergroup relations: we shall return to this issue later.

Aggression Within Groups

In the last section we saw that much aggression occurs within close relationships and that, in the case of intrafamily aggression, full understanding requires us to come to terms with the dynamics of how one relationship may affect others within the family. Here we consider briefly some further factors affecting violence within larger groups. They are relevant to intergroup aggression only insofar as successful aggression against another group depends on minimizing intragroup conflict.

Not surprisingly, the issues here depend crucially on the nature of the group. At one extreme lies the unstructured, anonymous crowd, an aggregation rather than a group. Its very existence may depend on common short-term goals, but interpersonal issues can give rise to conflict. The proximity of others can augment physiological arousal and thus affect behavior, including the tendency to behave aggressively. In addition, anonymity can lead to a diminution in the effectiveness of social inhibitions and/or to the imitation of fellow members (Jaffe, Shapiro, and Yinon, 1981; Prentice-Dunn and Rogers, 1983).

Of more interest are the additional issues arising in structured groups—that is, in groups in which each individual has relationships with at least some others. These relationships often involve differences in status. The relationships may exist before group formation, or they may emerge as its consequence (see below). In either case, aggressive interactions within the group may be affected by coalitions or alliances. These have been well documented in nonhuman primates (e.g., Datta, 1983) and other mammals and can bring considerable advantages to the participants if resources are scarce. Comparative evidence indicates that individuals are more likely to ally themselves with a relative than with a nonrelative in taking aggressive action against a third party (Datta, 1983), and the same is probably true of humans (e.g., Chagnon and Bugos, 1979).

Competition for status can be seen as a link between the members of a group and the group itself, since status lies in the sociocultural structure of the group. The relationships that emerge often take the form of a dominance hierarchy—A bosses B, B bosses C, and so on. Insofar as the individuals low in the hierarchy accept their positions, this usually leads to a reduction in aggression. However, it may also be accompanied by the emergence of one or more leaders, and the consequences of this depend upon reciprocal relations between the norms and values of the group and the characteristics of the leader (see below).

The Nature of Groups

A whole series of new issues arises when we come to consider aggression between groups. Initially, we shall focus attention on aggression between relatively small groups, postponing discussion of international war. First, however, it is necessary to emphasize that for two or more groups to be in conflict, each must recognize itself as a group: it is thus appropriate to consider the nature of groups.

A psychological group has three crucial features: the members define themselves and are defined as a group; they are interdependent; and their social interactions are mediated, at least to some extent, by rules and norms characteristic of the group. There is no clear agreement among social psychologists as to which of these characteristics is of primary importance. One view has been that the perception of common characteristics is a first step toward group formation. The development of a child's social identity involves seeing him- or herself as a member of some social categories (e.g., girl vs. boy; black vs. white) and not others, and adults tend to see themselves as members of categories of similar individuals. Furthermore, experimental evidence suggests that individuals who perceive themselves to have common characteristics come to accept group membership, develop interdependence, and evaluate in-group members over out-group members. For instance, if individuals are brought together for a group discussion and given either green or blue labels and pens, they tend to identify with those with the same color labels as themselves and to esteem them more highly than those with differently colored labels (Rabbie and Horwitz, 1969). Thus Tajfel (1978; see also Sherif, 1958; Tajfel and Turner, 1986; Turner, 1982; Turner et al., 1987) suggested that identification was primary, interdependence and in-group bias following from it. More recently, however, Rabbie (1987, 1991) has distinguished between social categories, consisting of individuals who share at least one attribute in common, and social groups, whose members see themselves as interdependent. On this view, individuals who form a category because they share attributes such as skin color, gender, or occupation are likely to experience an "interdependence of fate," but only become a social group insofar as they do so. As individuals come to perceive themselves as interdependent, they cooperate more and develop an in-group bias.

It is not necessary to enter this controversy here. Everyday experience suggests that perceived identity, perceived interdependence, in-group bias, and in-group cooperation can be mutually facilitatory in at least some circumstances. Thus positive feedback processes can operate: belonging to a group contributes to an individual's social identity and helps to define his or her position in society. People therefore attempt to identify with groups that they esteem highly, and this requires that such groups should behave favorably in comparison with other groups. However, even if there is no objective evidence for the superiority of the in-group, individuals tend to perceive it more favorably (though see below). The more favorably the in-group is perceived, the more closely do its members identify with it, and the more they identify with it, the more they strive to enhance their own social image by enhancing its real or perceived characteristics (Tajfel, 1978).

In parallel, in-group similarities are accentuated, cohesiveness and in-group cooperation are facilitated, and group behavior becomes possible, permitting more effective social action than if the individuals acted independently. Group membership also provides a sense of security for individual members, and group formation facilitates acceptance of social judgments and explanations of complex events and provides justifications of social actions (Asch, 1952; Lott and Lott, 1961, 1965; Tajfel, 1981).

Looking at this issue from another point of view, the ubiquity of in-group preferences and stereotyping of outsiders is not really surprising. Groups that hold their own values to be true and those of outsiders to be false, and groups that believe their own members to be preferable to outsiders, are likely to succeed in competition with groups that do not have these characteristics. The instigation of group values for moral reasons is cheaper and more effective than coercion (McCauley, 1990; Shweder and Miller, 1985). This, of course, says nothing about the relative importance of natural or cultural selection in bringing about the propensity for group formation or differentiation.

Social categorization thus involves favorable evaluation of the in-group as opposed to the out-group. The only exceptions to this rule occur when under-privileged groups, such as ethnic minorities, accept the prejudices of the majority against themselves. Until the advent of feminism, women in many Western societies behaved in this way: such a situation tends, of course, to be self-perpetuating. But in general the extent of the differentiation between in-group and out-group, and the dimensions along which it is made, may depend upon the perceived stability and relations of the groups (Tajfel, 1981). Fur-thermore, contrary to some suggestions (Tajfel and Turner, 1979), it is not inevitably competitive: groups may be perceived as differentiated along di-mensions that are not necessarily conflictual, especially when cooperative relations between the groups are mutually beneficial (van Knippenberg, 1984; Rabbie and Horwitz, 1988).

Indeed, Brewer (1979) and Rabbie (1989) emphasize that in-group cohe-sion and out-group hostility may vary independently of each other. Positive attitudes about the in-group occur to the extent that individuals identify with it. This will occur the more if the individuals in the group perceive themselves to have a common fate, share space and are in physical proximity to one another, are positively interdependent, and have shared in group successes. Hostility to the out-group depends on a different set of factors, including especially the perception that the out-group is frustrating the goals of the in-group in an illegitimate way.

Groups inevitably acquire an internal structure, and one or more leaders are likely to emerge. In that the same individuals tend to emerge as leaders in different groups, leadership appears to depend on characteristics of the indi-vidual (Kenny and Zaccaro, 1983). However, experimental studies indicate that the precise characteristics conducive to leadership status vary with the situation (e.g., Vroom and Yetton, 1973; Chemas and Skrzpek, 1972; Strube and Garcia, 1981). In the real world, of course, leadership may depend on either subjugation of or consent by followers. In the latter case, consent will depend both upon interpersonal relationships, coalitions, and so on within the group, and upon dialectical relations between group norms and the leader's perceived characteristics. On the one hand, the values of the group, or those of the society of which the group forms a part, affect the characteristics conducive to high status—in some groups prosocial behavior may be what is looked for, in others competitiveness or aggression. The leader may in fact be chosen in part as a symbol of the goals of the group. But conversely, the leader may also determine or influence the goals of the group and may encourage or punish aggressiveness among the group members. This in turn may have a profound effect on the behavior of group members, who may discard social norms in order to conform to those of the current authority (e.g., Milgram, 1974). In Western societies, at any rate, the media play a critical role in determining group norms. As emphasized in an earlier section, newspaper, radio, and television both reflect the values and norms of the public and create them.

The issues sketched here—the mutual influences between group formation, perceived interdependence and similarity, and in-group bias, on the one hand, and the internal structuring of groups involving the emergence of a leadership role on the other—are of crucial importance in intergroup and intersocietal conflict, as discussed in the following sections.

Aggression Between Groups

Aggression between groups implies cooperation between individuals within each group. Thus, whereas in interpersonal relationships factors conducive to cooperation mitigate against violence, in intergroup disputes intragroup cooperation is almost a necessary prerequisite for intergroup aggression.

Many of the factors already discussed as contributing to the aggressiveness of individuals apply also to aggression between groups. For example, in most societies some groups have more power than others and may impose constraints or values on other individuals that run counter to their interests. If material and social resources are not distributed evenly within the society, some groups are likely to be frustrated, and intergroup strife becomes possible.

However, because of the special properties of groups, the aggressiveness of a group is not simply the sum of the aggressiveness of its members. Just because group membership is associated with a tendency to see the in-group as superior to the out-group, individuals see it as proper to behave aggressively to other groups in defense of the values of the in-group. Any perceived threat to the interests or values of the group can serve as an instigator to aggression. And dialectical relations between the aggressive propensities of the individuals within a group and the group norms (Figure 1.1) may exacerbate either.

In any confrontation situation, the internal dynamics of the group may escalate the tendencies toward violent action. The relative anonymity of individuals within groups, and arousal produced by the group situation, may augment the aggressiveness of group members. If aggressive behavior is valued by the group, individuals may seek out a target in order to show off their aggressive prowess to fellow group members and thereby increase their own status within the group: in this case, assertiveness enhances aggressiveness (Figure 1.2). Furthermore, a decrease in group cohesion can act as an internal elicitor: for instance, Groebel and Feger (1982) found that German terrorist groups were especially likely to show aggression if group cohesion faltered, and laboratory experiments are in harmony with this conclusion (Rabbie and Bekkers, 1976).

Of critical importance is the role of the leaders. Whether a confrontation or conflict of interests leads to aggression may depend absolutely on the leaders. A hierarchically structured group may be more likely to show aggression if led by an individual with strong aggressive propensities. Furthermore, personal relationships between the leaders of the opposing groups may play an important part. The complex issues that arise here have been most studied in the context of industrial wage negotiations, where intergroup divergence between management and unions may run contrary to the interpersonal considerations of the negotiators. If the intergroup issues predominate, the negotiations are likely to end in conflict, but if the interpersonal ones come to the fore, the result may lead to a cooperative settlement or to collusion (Walton and McKersie, 1965; Stephenson, 1984). Stephenson has shown that if intergroup disagreement is held constant, "increasing the opportunities for interpersonal exchange has the effect of making it harder for the party with the stronger case to exploit effectively the advantage it possesses." In general, the experimental data indicate that an emphasis on long-term interests, good communication, and structuring of the situation augment the probability of cooperation between groups (e.g., Pruitt and Kimmel 1976; Good, 1988). Mutual trust will be enhanced by the perception of a common goal, by an emphasis on shared values or respect for each other's values, and by openness (Gambetta, 1988). How far these factors operate in international disputes is an open issue.

Of course, nothing that has been said here implies that intergroup and interpersonal issues are absolutely distinct. For instance, leaders and negotiators must make plain their personal effectiveness as group representatives, and the interpersonal issue may involve the prospect of future intergroup ones. Furthermore, although the relations between groups involve processes quite different from those operating in the relationships between individuals, the issues affecting cooperation and trust in the latter have at least a heuristic value for understanding the former. Though in a slightly different form, the conditions conducive to cooperation and trust still apply. However, of special importance for the ameliorization of intergroup aggression is the recognition of a common goal or the feeling of intergroup interdependence (e.g., Sherif, 1966).

Thus to understand aggression between groups, we must come to terms both with the nature of social groups and with the special factors that operate in an intergroup situation. Intergroup aggression is related to interindividual aggression but has additional complexities. Full understanding, therefore, requires our analysis to cross and recross between the levels of social complexity.

The presence of leaders implies at least some degree of role differentiation and thus of institutionalization. The further this proceeds, the more the issues involved in intergroup conflict approximate those in international war.

War

The distinction between intergroup aggression and war is not absolute, but it is convenient to make such a distinction for two reasons.

First, war, or at least modern war, involves a much greater degree of role differentiation than does conflict between groups. War is an institution with a variety of prescribed roles, each with its rights and duties. Just as, in our society, the behavior of politicians and voters is in large part determined by the rights and duties associated with their roles in the institution of government, so is the behavior in wartime of generals, officers, and soldiers, doctors and nurses, munition and transport workers, politicians, and industrialists determined in large part by the several roles that they occupy. Although prestate groups that make war often have (by nurture, probably more than by nature) belligerent personalities (Chagnon, 1977), the relationship between aggressive personalities and war is certainly not a necessary one, and in modern war between industrialist countries the actual combatants are little influenced by their aggressive propensities. Nor are they affected by hope of personal gain. They may be influenced by a form of assertiveness, hoping to increase the status that the institution of war confers upon them by seeking promotion or decoration, though this is usually a minor issue. In actual combat, fear is certainly important. Fear can contribute to defensive aggression, though more usually the concomitant arousal augments the fear and reduces the efficiency of the combatant (Marshall, 1947). But the primary source of attempts to kill or injure the opponents is duty as determined by the combatant's role in the institution of war, which includes loyalty to and a tendency to cooperate with one's buddies (Stouffer et al., 1949) (Figure 1.5).

The second reason for distinguishing war from intergroup aggression is that war, at any rate modern war, involves conflict between societies each of which is complex and consists of many overlapping groups. In their discussion of international negotiations, Druckman and Hopmann (1989:99) emphasize that "international negotiations take place not between unified nation-states, but

Modern Warfare

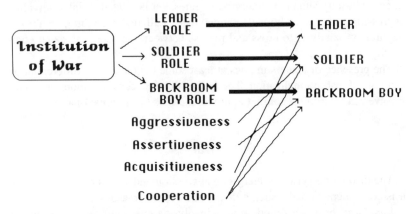

FIGURE 1.5. Modern war as an institution. The institution involves a number of roles, each with its constituent rights and duties. These play a major role in determining the behavior of the incumbents. Propensities for aggressiveness, assertiveness, acquisitiveness, cooperation, and other characteristics may also contribute. *Source:* Hinde (1989).

between large bureaucracies reflecting diverse and competing interests." Thus war embraces the issues of group aggression, but much else besides.

Although war differs from aggression at lower levels of social complexity, some of the issues discussed in previous sections apply also to war, and some of the issues salient in the case of war have some relevance at lower levels of social complexity. Animals do not make war (Huntingford, 1989), but we have seen that some matters arising from studies of animal aggression have analogues in international war (see p. 15). Individual aggression can be of direct importance in short-term interaction between combatants, though this is of little importance in modern war where the enemy is usually distant and unseen. When individual aggressiveness does play a direct role, the resulting behavior is often not condoned, as at My Lai. However, aggressive propensities can play an indirect role; for instance, they are utilized by propaganda (see below). And principles involved in the formation, integration, and internal dynamics of groups are of course highly relevant to the more complex organization of societies at war.

Of course, wars are heterogeneous. Tribal conflict, the Crusades, the two World Wars, and the nuclear era require different generalizations. Of particular importance are the increase in complexity and in the diversity of the roles of those involved, the greater destructiveness of weapons and the multitudinous processes required for their manufacture, and the related increased involvement of the civilian population (Pogge von Strandmann, 1991). To some extent, wars at different levels of social complexity and of technology require different generalizations. However, we have seen that attempts to classify individual aggression into causally homogeneous categories run into difficulties, and the same is even more true of war. Just because war involves more or less complex societies, the "causes" of any war are multiple and must be sought at many levels. Furthermore, as with individual aggression, it is important to take account of predisposing factors, of precipitating or eliciting factors, and also of factors that maintain the state of war or cycle of warlike activities (cf. Figure 1.3). For instance, in tribal societies food scarcity may lead to a raid on a neighboring group: if this results in death, the second group may seek revenge, and in due course a complex of myths, beliefs, and institutions with component roles may be built up around the pattern of warfare (Haas, 1990; McCauley, 1990). In war between states, changes in the sociocultural structure may involve changes in material needs or perceptions of material needs, changes in perceptions concerning the nature or perceptions of other groups, and the increased importance of a military elite or, in modern times, a military-industrial-scientific complex (see below), any of which may contribute to a continuation of the state of war.

Introducing the report of a conference on prestate warfare, Haas (1990) distinguished three models of causation used by the participants:

1. Materialist/ecological, where the causes of warfare are found largely in the material foundations of the cultural system. Thus Ferguson (1990) argued that the immediate causes of war almost always lie in conflicts over material goals—scarcity of resources, work situations, achieving security against threats, or (see Chagnon, 1990) women. Societal demographic, technological, and ecological/organizational factors determine how war is practiced. Structural factors (kinship, economics, and politics) explain the social patterning of war—how people are grouped to fight, how resource scarcity is translated into hostility, and how hostility is coordinated. Ideological characteristics of the society determine how war is perceived and how individuals act. Ferguson (1990) argues that infrastructural factors are primary, influencing structural ones and, with them, influencing ideology. My own emphasis would be on dialectical relations between them.

2. Biocultural, where the causes of war are ultimately to be found in a combination of ecological and biological elements. For instance, Chagnon (1977, 1990) argues that the traditional materialist approach is inadequate and must be supplemented by insights from sociobiology. Thus he contends that individuals behave as though they were attempting to maximize their reproductive success or inclusive fitness (vs. infra), though they may not always be aware that that is their ultimate goal. For example, the immediate motivation for

conflict may be status seeking, and, functionally, status provides better access to resources.

3. Historical context, where the causes of war are to be found in the historical context and individual motivations of those involved. The emphasis here is on the appraisal and interpretation of situations of resource depletion in terms of culturally given meanings influenced by the specific historical context (e.g., Robarchek, 1990).

These differences of emphasis in discussions of the causes of war in prestate society emphasize the need to come to terms with the dialectical relations between levels of social complexity if any understanding of modern war is to be achieved. That, of course, is an immense task (for a beginning, see Levy, 1989a & b; Tetlock, 1989). In what follows, a few issues of special relevance to modern war are discussed, and in a subsequent section we shall turn to the forces at diverse levels of social complexity that maintain war as an institution in the modern world.

Tribal war may depend on group decisions. In modern war the role of leaders, political and military, is paramount. Armies are almost invariably hierarchically organized, and leadership at every level from the local commander to the political head of state is a crucial issue. The importance of a charismatic leader was never more clearly demonstrated than by Winston Churchill, when he became prime minister of Great Britain at a moment when the United States, was hanging back and Britain was without allies and facing defeat. And, at the other end of the scale, every war brings thousands of examples of the importance of good leadership by platoon or crew commanders.

In wartime, leaders at every level must make decisions based on data that are incomplete and ambiguous. Inevitably, their response will be affected by their own experience in interpersonal conflict, and the preceding discussion of interpersonal and intergroup aggression is relevant here. However, the much greater complexity of the issues makes it impossible for leaders to consider all factors simultaneously. They may have to weigh international prestige, national gain, internal domestic issues, the probability of success, their own careers, and many other noncomparable factors against one another. They may have to assess the relative merits of alliances with other groups or states. They have to cope with differences of opinion between groups in their own country. The availability of weapons, which, as we have seen, can help to elicit aggression in individuals, may also have unconscious as well as supposedly conscious effects on the decisions of leaders. Their decisions may also be based on misperception or wishful thinking about the opponent's probable actions or on irrational assessments of probable gains and losses. In part because each side tries to conceal its true intentions, they may underestimate the opponent. Leaders may have to comprehend, or attempt to comprehend, an opponent with a very different cultural style. In addition, they may be very tired. For all these reasons their decisions may not be those of a "rational actor" (Britten, 1983; Druckman and Hopmann, 1989; Fischoff, 1991; Jervis, 1976; Lebow, 1989; Levy, 1989*a* & *b*; Quester, 1989; Stern et al., 1989*a,b*; Tetlock et al., 1989).

As mentioned under intergroup aggression, they may also be influenced by the extent to which action against an out-group may ameliorate internal political discord. Nixon's action in alerting his troops during the October war between Israel and Egypt in 1973, when he was under pressure at home because of his controversial role in the Watergate scandal, has been seen as an attempt to direct public attention to the international confrontation with the Soviet Union and thereby unite the nation behind him (Rabbie, 1989). In the same vein, public protest against the draconian economic measures of the Argentinian junta was defused (at least temporarily) by the Falklands/ Malvinas War (Hastings and Jenkins, 1983). Although such cases are convincing, it must be noted that correlational studies indicate little connection between domestic and foreign conflict (Levy, 1989*b*).

Leaders are also symbols, both for their own group and for others. Their qualities may therefore augment the extent to which individuals personify other groups, ascribing motives or planning actions as if the other group were an individual. Leaders themselves may personify the other group—both in their rhetoric and in their own decision making. Personification provides a way of thinking about complex issues, but it may also result in harmful simplification of real-life complexity.

Political leaders are usually guided by committees of specialist advisers, so issues of small-group dynamics may affect the course of international confrontations or war. A crucial issue here is the extent to which the consensus reached by a small-group discussion may not be a rational outcome of the integration of the different viewpoints of the participants. Rather, it is likely to be polarized according to the dominant group's norms, so that the members make recommendations more extreme than they would have done before the group discussion (Minnix, 1982). Furthermore, the decision-making processes are affected by the stresses induced by the importance of the issues, the ambiguity of the information at the participants' disposal, and the conflicting group and personal interests involved. A form of "groupthink" may occur, involving decreased mental efficiency, failure to test conclusions against reality, and neglect of moral judgment. Janis (1982) has ascribed a number of political decisions, seen in retrospect as erroneous and absurd, to the deleterious influence of group processes under stress on the decision-making process. Rabbie (1989) has demonstrated some of the processes involved experimentally. (A review of literature on decision making in groups is given by Tetlock et al., 1989.)

Moving up a further level, the existence of a supranational authority may be helpful in preventing war not only by enforcing but also by defining the criteria for justice between nations. In general, the rules that apply within groups (e.g., killing is wrong) may not apply between groups (Clayton and Lerner, 1991; Lerner, 1981; Tajfel, 1984), and the rules governing distribution among individuals may be perceived as unfair when applied across groups. For instance, selection of individuals for a particular type of training according to apparent merit may be seen as unfair to particular subgroups within the society, which are underrepresented among those selected (Brickman et al., 1981). A supranational authority is not essential for changing norms and rules but could facilitate the process by applying to its constituent groups principles of justice more closely allied to those usually applied to individuals within groups. And beyond that, the leaders of opposing groups may disagree as to the norms that apply in particular circumstances (Stern et al., 1989a): here again a supranational authority can help.

Attitudes toward the conduct of negotiations between groups or nations are changing from an emphasis on a confrontational style in which each side takes a position, making maximum bids from the start, to an emphasis on enlightened self-interest, where the interests of each party are explored. This can lead to an acknowledgment of interdependence and, insofar as the needs of the two parties are seen to be incompatible, diminishes the need for trust. Furthermore, negotiation is seen less as a short-term interaction between two parties that are otherwise independent, and more as involving an ongoing relationship in which both earlier events and the long-term consequences (and/or the expectations thereof) are crucial issues (Rubin, 1991).

Many of the principles concerning cooperation, trust, and commitment between individuals, discussed in an earlier section, apply also to intergroup and international relations in the absence of war and to relations between others during a war. The issues are, of course, much more complex at these higher levels of social complexity (see also Axelrod, 1984; Gambetta, 1988; Hinde and Groebel, 1991), but a little more than mere analogy is involved. One issue is that we tend to personify groups and apply to them concepts used in interpersonal relationships. But beyond that, the circumstances in which cooperation can occur without trust (absence of alternative courses of action; sanctions against defection; perception of a common goal or threat) are similar in the two cases. So also are the conditions conducive to trust (shared values; self-reinforcing properties; availability of information about the other; good communication, and perception of common long-term interests). The dependence of trust on shared values in part explains why confrontations between states with radically different ideologies and religions are peculiarly recalcitrant. Here there is another problem: individuals are usually strongly motivated to preserve the culture in which they have grown up and may even defend a culture they have adopted. No one wants to live in a uniform Coca-Cola culture. For that reason many conflicts arise in circumstances in which groups fear they will lose (or hope to reestablish) their identity and may lead to civil or international war (see Feger, 1991). This issue is of special prominence at the time of writing with the violence following the breakup of the Soviet Union and ethnic violence in Yugoslavia and elsewhere.

As in interpersonal relationships, given trust, ambiguous moves are less likely to be interpreted as hostile, and constructive solutions to disputes are more actively sought. And in international relations, also, trust implies commitment to the relationship, though that commitment may be formalized in a treaty. Commitment is likely to be enhanced by investment of resources in the partnership or alliance and by continuing positive feedback.

There is some hope that trust in and cooperation with societies with different cultures are becoming increasingly possible. At one time, improvements in communication primarily provided opportunities for the world's rich to exploit the world's poor. But they have also led to a greater appreciation of cultural diversity and to a greater feeling of responsibility for other human beings whether or not they have similar values. For example, in the United Kingdom at the beginning of the nineteenth century, the poor were the liability only of the parish in which they were born: poor living away from their birthplace could expect little assistance. In 1834 the parishes were grouped into districts, each of which supported a workhouse, and some attempt was made to improve uniformity of treatment. This was extended more widely in the 1860s when, with problems in the cotton industry, it became apparent that the resources of some parishes were inadequate for their own poor, and help from richer parishes was not forthcoming. The fate of the poor started to become a concern of the central government, and parishes unable to support their own poor were permitted to borrow. At the same time there was a tremendous increase in private charitable work—at first locally and later nationally organized. Nowadays the case of the unfortunate and the underprivileged is seen as a national concern. More than that, in times of great crisis or disaster help is extended, by both official and voluntary agencies, to distant populations of other races who are seen as suffering fellow members of humanity. This is especially remarkable if one remembers that only a few generations ago members of other races were seen as subhuman. The human sense of responsibility is expanding.

The Bases of the Institution of War

If international war can be seen as an institution with numerous constituent roles, each with its attendant rights and duties, we must seek to understand the forces that create and maintain that institution. The issues involved are intertwined but may be considered in the following categories.

Continuously Acting Everyday Factors

Although there has been little research on the matter, a number of mundane issues would seem to facilitate the acceptance of war. One is the use of war metaphors in everyday speech—"going over the top" and "getting dug in" are presumably derived from the First World War, "outflanking" from the days of more mobile battles. Such metaphors often appear in newspaper headlines connected with quite unmilitary matters and are a commonplace that we do not notice. Perhaps, as sexisms are being eliminated from everyday speech, warisms can also be reduced.

In writings about war, the horrors are often sanitized and the combatants ennobled. Fussell (1975), in his moving analysis of the myths and literary themes that surround war, has given a list of the "high diction" that, at any rate until 1914–18, concealed the true reality of war. Thus a "friend" became a "comrade," "danger" became "peril," "to be earnestly brave" became "to be gallant," the "dead" became "the fallen," "to win" became "to conquer," "actions" were "deeds," "not to complain" was "to be manly," and so on.

War toys, also almost ubiquitous in Western countries (but see Phillips, in press), introduce young children to the concept of war. The history that is taught in schools is too often primarily a history of wars. The UNESCO recommendation of 1974 that member states should foster education for peace is largely disregarded: Finland and to some extent the Soviet Union are among the few countries that have made some effort to implement it (e.g., Harris, 1986; Pulkkinen, 1989). Films about war usually sanitize its violence and emphasize its nobility (Winter, 1991).

Male chauvinism plays its role. Although, by nature and/or by nurture (see Adams, 1983), women in general value peace more highly than do men (Smith, 1984) and have played a major role in peace movements, they seldom participate in the decision-making processes that determine whether or not war shall occur (Langness, 1968; Pulkkinen, 1989; Ruddick, 1989). (We must be wary of generalization here: on these issues men and women differ only in degree, and Thatcher is an obvious exception.) And the current debate about the presence of women in the armed forces, instigated by the equal rights issue, is of great interest in this context. Rhode (1990) quotes a Marine commander, speaking against the recruitment of women to the U.S. armed forces, as saying, "When you get right down to it, you have to protect the manliness of war (p. 201)."

Although such issues may seem trivial, they no doubt contribute to the cheerful acceptance of war by so many recruits who are subsequently disillusioned by its reality (Brodie, 1990).

Pervasive Cultural Factors

As we have seen, societies differ in the status accorded to individual aggression, and the same is true of war. Some countries have a long record of belligerence; others, such as Switzerland, of neutrality. Some, such as Sweden, have changed their characteristics from aggression to peace loving. In some cases, specific factors enhancing the status of war can be identified: for instance, Nietzsche saw in the warrior human life at its best, and Social Darwinists saw war as a means to progress, armed struggle providing the test of which nation deserved international supremacy.

Of particular interest here is the relation between religion and warfare. In some societies, of course, there appears to be no contradiction, but in Christian countries the relation has been a complex one. The Old Testament is full of bloody battles, the Christian is often depicted as a soldier "fighting the good fight," and the imagery of the book of Revelation refers continually to war and death. Nevertheless, the early Christians accepted a form of pacifism, and it was not until the 4th century that the conversion of Constantine was instrumental in causing Christians to accommodate to militarism. Saint Augustine, attempting to justify the participation of Christians in wars, in effect became the founder of a "Just War" tradition that provided a moral justification for Christian participation in violence (e.g., Johnson, 1984; Teichman, 1986). On this view, wars were just if they were necessary to avenge injury or to maintain earthly justice. The history of the Just War concept has been sketched by Ramsey (1968) and by Santoni (1991). By legitimating at least some wars, the Just War tradition helped to maintain the institution of war across the centuries. Santoni emphasizes how Just War principles have been gradually adjusted to accommodate political aspirations and the increasingly indiscriminate nature of modern weapons.

A well-analyzed issue concerns the concept of sacrifice in Christian theology. The death of Christ is seen as a sacrifice, and the memorial feast of that death is spoken of as the eucharistic sacrifice. Sykes (1991) has demonstrated the close relations between the Christian language of sacrifice and the readiness of soldiers to die in battle in the First World War. His analysis of the way in which this came about draws to a considerable extent on the poetry of

Wilfred Owen. (Sykes, it must be added, does not underestimate the positive contribution that the Christian religion has to make in other ways, but he calls on Christians to face up to the betrayal of their own standards involved in its relation to warfare.) Again, Stern (1975) has documented the manner in which Hitler's ideology made use of the religious vocabulary of sacrifice in appeals to the German people to tolerate losses for the sake of the German *Volk*.

International Law

Modern international law, in its relations to war, owes much to the Just War tradition. It distinguishes between *jus ad bellum*, the right to resort to war, and *jus in bello*, concerning its conduct once it has started. With regard to the former, the Just War restriction became insignificant with the rise of modern states, so that between the 17th and early 20th centuries the right to go to war was almost unlimited. After the First World War, however, the League of Nations Covenant and subsequent treaties limited the right to go to war, though the implied recognition that there were some circumstances in which it was permissible to go to war can be interpreted as support for the institution of war. More recently the Charter of the United Nations ruled that the use of force for settling international disputes should be the monopoly of the United Nations. The only exception is that a state is permitted to use force to defend itself in certain circumstances if it is the victim of an armed attack. Although lack of Great Power unanimity in the decades after World War II undermined the functioning of this agreement, it can no longer be said that international law provides a legal basis for the institution of war (Collier, 1991). In its concern with *jus in bello*, however, international law maintains the Just War tradition in seeking to protect basic human rights if war does break out and to limit its extent and savagery (Greenwood, 1991).

Patriotism/Nationalism and Propaganda

The reality of war, especially modern war, is abhorrent. Nevertheless, many individuals have gone willingly to war, made sacrifices, shown outstanding courage, and even given up their lives for their country. Many have subsequently been disillusioned by their experiences (Brodie, 1990). Others have worked long hours and curtailed personal ambitions to support a war effort. For a threat of war to be plausible to outsiders, and even more for a war to be prosecuted, the motivation of the individuals involved must be maintained. What, we must ask, are the mechanisms involved? What is it that spurs individuals on? As we have seen, in most modern wars hope of individual material gain is not an issue, and individual aggressiveness is of at most indirect significance unless hand-to-hand fighting is involved. What prompts individuals to behave in ways that would appear to be against their own self-interest?

Experience suggests that one issue involves the ideals, religious or secular, relevant to the promotion of war and current in the culture. In what follows I shall argue that these ideals are a product of the basic propensities of individuals elaborated by group processes and by the social influences and propaganda induced by (and inducing) the institution of war. They motivate individuals to perform the duties associated with their particular role in the war machine.

Clearly important issues are devotion to country or religion, and belief in its superiority. Nationalism, according to Hinsley (1973), is a form of political loyalty that does not differ in any fundamental way from loyalty to clan, tribe, city-state, or empire, though the concept of "nation" is one that has evolved gradually and separately in different parts of the world. It is helpful here to distinguish between patriotism, involving love of one's own nation, and nationalism, involving attitudes of superiority or need for power over other national groups (Allport, 1927; Mead, 1929). Feshbach (1990; Kosterman and Feshbach, 1989), using an attitude questionnaire, identified two distinct factors, one involving love for one's own country (labeled patriotism), and the second involving feelings of superiority over other nations (nationalism). Although patriotism and nationalism were positively correlated in some samples, they had different functional properties. Individuals who scored highly on the nationalism scale tended rather strongly to have hawkish attitudes about nuclear weapons, while patriotism had only a weak relation to hawkish attitudes. Interestingly, with willingness to risk one's life in military action the difference was in the opposite direction: the correlation was stronger with patriotism than with nationalism. Thus the individuals high on nationalism were more willing to go to war but less willing to risk their lives than those high on patriotism.

Together, patriotism/nationalism constitute a powerful force for the maintenance of the institution of war. What are their sources? Unfortunately hard data are scarce, but circumstantial evidence is in harmony with the view that patriotism operates through basic propensities of individuals. Before pursuing this, it may be helpful to comment on the nature of the argument that is being used. To a biologist, who must measure costs and benefits in terms of reproductive success of self or relatives (see above), self-sacrifice involves incurring costs without benefits. It is thus an aspect of the more general problem of why individuals often behave in a biologically dysgenic manner. Several types of answers are possible. Some sociobiologists tend to argue that the behavior in question is adaptive, really: if only we could measure inclusive fitness adequately, we should find that it was augmented by the behavior in question. Such an approach strains credulity (Gould and Lewontin, 1979; Hinde, 1987a; Kitcher, 1985). A second possibility is that the behavior in question is due to inappropriate or excessive expressions of a propensity that is ordinarily adaptive. This could, for instance, account for gluttony, but it leaves open the question of why motivation should have been excessive or expression is inappropriate: it is not an adequate explanation to ascribe this to "pathology." It is also sometimes claimed that participation and/or bravery in war has been selected for, since they have more often brought access to resources, especially women, than death. This, of course, is speculative. A third answer is that the behavior in question was functional in our environment of evolutionary adaptedness but is so no longer: the so-called "irrational fears of childhood" (fears of darkness, being left alone, etc.) make little sense in most modern circumstances but were essential for survival in our environment of evolutionary adaptedness (Bowlby, 1969).

Related to these possibilities, Johnson (1986) has suggested that patriotism depends on an unconscious perception of fellow countrymen as kin. As we have seen, the principle of inclusive fitness provides an evolutionary explanation of the way in which individuals will incur costs in order to help others who are genetically related to them. Patriotism involves incurring costs to help individuals who are not related. Nevertheless, Johnson suggests, similar mechanisms may be involved. Kin selection requires mechanisms for distinguishing kin from nonkin. Johnson suggests that humans have been adapted to treat as kin those with whom they associate most intimately and most frequently (familiarity) and those who possess genetically based phenotypic traits that match those the individual has learned him- or herself to possess (similarity). (He later [1989] suggested that locational cues might also be important.) In support of the view that familiarity does affect attraction to others, considerable animal literature could be cited (Bateson, 1980), as well as the known attractiveness of familiarity to humans (Zajonc, 1968). The importance of similarity is amply demonstrated by the literature on its role in interpersonal attraction (Byrne, 1971).

Johnson further suggests that socialization processes manipulate cues based on these two principles so that individuals are willing to incur costs to help nonkin who possess features in common with kin or who are in some way associated with kin. In support of this view he notes, for example, that, in the United States at any rate, patriotic rituals are often associated with positive reinforcers experienced collectively, often with family or close friends under circumstances in which conditioning is especially likely. Furthermore, patriotism is often associated with the use of kin terms—motherland or fatherland, brothers-in-arms, our English-speaking cousins (and of course the term "patriotism" itself). Instrumental conditioning, observational learning affected by the presentation of medals at public ceremonies, and similar pressures augment the effects.

While in no way denying that a propensity to cooperate with kin against outsiders may play a role, it is important to bear in mind that other processes that do not depend on responsiveness to kin may also be important. Belonging to a group and promoting its interests may be important to individuals in a variety of ways, and natural selection may have acted to promote group behavior (Krebs and Davies, 1981) because of its immediate advantages to the individuals concerned, and not through kin selection. In favor of this view is the fact that the attractiveness of similarity extends to ideological beliefs even though individual differences in such characteristics have very limited genetic bases. Furthermore, data showing that similarity in nonverifiable beliefs is a more effective determinant of attractiveness than similarity in verifiable ones (Byrne, Nelson, and Reeves, 1966; Wheeler, 1974) are more in keeping with the view that similarity in beliefs is attractive because it confirms an individual's view of the world rather than because it is a cue for kinship. Individuals attempt to build up a coherent view of the world (Kelly, 1955, 1970), and it is reasonable to suppose that individuals who do so are more effective in competition with their peers.

For these and other reasons, it is reasonable to suppose that humans possess a propensity to associate with others similar to themselves that does not ultimately depend solely on kin selection.

Finally, a fourth approach to the sources of patriotism/nationalism, and the one most relevant here, is that the behavior in question is controlled primarily by the values, norms, or duties imposed by the sociocultural structure, which are themselves related, but only distantly related, to the basic propensities of individuals on which natural selection operated. The properties of the sociocultural structure are complex, influenced by many and diverse psychological propensities of individuals, by similarities and by conflicts of interests between individuals, and by historical, ecological, economic, and other factors. Aspects of the sociocultural structure, including national symbols, not only influence the behavior of individuals and of the relationships and groups that they form, but also are themselves the products of the social behavior of the members of the society. Although the sociocultural structure is thus indirectly but bidirectionally linked to the propensities of individuals, it does not reflect those propensities directly. Particular features of the sociocultural structure may reflect diverse and incompatible individual propensities and may be the result of the actions of individuals or groups exploiting others for their own ends. Individuals may thus be influenced to behave in ways not conducive to their own inclusive fitness. Human cognitive and linguistic capacities not only give flexibility to our behavioral propensities, but also enable us to reify them into principles, and these principles may become incentives for action even when that action is to the detriment of the actor (Kelley, 1979). In addition, the human tendency to seek social approval can impose heavy costs on the individual. Cultural values may demand sacrifices from individuals, and individuals willingly comply. The forces that drive humans to self-sacrifice are thus not solely a consequence of kin selection, nor are they solely simple exaggerations of basic propensities or expressions of such propensities in abnormal circumstances: rather, they are also products of the dialectics between those propensities and the sociocultural structure (see Hinde, 1987a, for fuller discussion).

What, then, are the basic propensities conducive to patriotism/nationalism? For the propaganda that augments patriotism/nationalism, three basic human propensities are of special importance. One is aggressiveness: this is indeed one place where individual aggressiveness does play a part, albeit an indirect part, in modern war. The propaganda often uses images that induce aggressiveness directly, or play upon fear and thus induce aggressiveness indirectly.

Propaganda also operates to maintain an image of the enemy as evil, dangerous, and even subhuman (Wahlström, 1987). The effectiveness of the enemy image depends on two other basic human propensities. One is the fear of strangers that appears in children toward the latter half of the first year and is maintained to some degree throughout life (Bronson, 1968). The second is the tendency, discussed above, for members of a group to exaggerate the differences between their own group and other groups and to emphasize the superiority of their own. The processes of in-group/out-group differentiation discussed earlier are clearly intrinsic to nationalism, and dependence on members of the in-group, especially in the face of external threat, will also contribute to patriotism. Compatible with this last point, Feshbach (1986, 1990), noting the frequent use of parental metaphors for one's country, suggested that a subject's patriotism might be related to her or his attachment to a parent. The data indicated that this was so for attachment to father, but not for attachment to mother. In addition, members of the out-group appear homogeneous, whereas in-group members are differentiated individually (see above). This applies at the societal as well as at the group level: for instance, before the changes in Europe symbolized by the demolition of the Berlin Wall, Westerners tended to see all the Eastern bloc countries as similar to one another—a view that subsequent events showed to be far from the truth.

The result of this process is that each side in a conflict can have similar denigratory views of the other. Both the German and the British propaganda during the two World Wars often carried the assumption that "God is on our side"; and during the Cold War period both Americans and Russians saw each other as aggressive, untrustworthy, and ruled by governments that exploited the people (Bronfenbrenner, 1961). Denigratory images of the enemy tend to have considerable resilience (Tetlock et al., 1989). They may also have ramifying correlates in other attitudes. Thus during the Cold War era, Thompson (1989) surveyed the perceptions of threat, attitudes to the Soviet Union, and feelings about various peace issues of more than 3,000 college students in various countries. Those subjects with strong anti-Soviet feelings scored high on militarism (i.e., wants order in life, respects uniforms, etc.), helplessness, general conservatism, denial of the risk of having nuclear weapons, and ethnocentricity. They also tended to be religious. They did not have moral objections to nuclear weapons and downplayed the risk of nuclear war and nuclear accident.

Propaganda can also be used to diminish the perceived horror of war. Winter (1991) has described the Images d'Épinal, which included a form of poster art circulated in France from private sources, and which during the First World War served to create a myth of war enthusiasm. The posters provided an inexpensive piece of patriotic art, for use on birthdays, and other occasions, representing the French soldier as part of a gallant historical tradition, sanitizing war, pointing to the special joys of military leave, emphasizing national unity, and so on.

Susceptibility to such propaganda is accentuated by a crisis situation. Self-awareness of anxiety increases with risk only up to a point: after that, defense mechanisms take over. Thus the anxiety of people living at differing distances from major hazards, such as power stations, is maximal at a distance of 2–4 kilometers, and then reduces sharply for people living nearer (Royal Society, 1983). As individuals become intensely fearful of impending war, or learn more about the horrors of nuclear war, they adopt defense mechanisms that keep the reality of that knowledge and fear at bay—apathy, dependence on authority, denial, cynicism, and so on. This is evident in the Thompson study cited above. Such tendencies are further exacerbated by the increasingly hierarchical social structure enforced in time of war, especially in military establishments. This, together with secrecy and other "security" measures, leads to a devaluation of individual initiative. Deindividuation is accentuated in the military by the wearing of a common uniform and the use of numbers instead of (or as well as) names. Such processes may facilitate the prosecution of a war, but they also make it more likely (Obholzer, 1989).

Finally, a caveat. The ideals of patriotism/nationalism are important motivating factors, but they are not the only ones that operate. Individuals who are disillusioned with the ideals that they are supposed to be fighting for may yet give up their lives for their comrades. Yet that patriotism/nationalism must surely play a major role in maintaining the institution of war is clear.

War as an Institutionalized Set of Institutions

So far we have considered war as an institution with constituent roles of politicians, soldiers, munition workers, and so on. In fact, of course, it is much more complicated than that, for in modern war (and preparations for war) we have to do with an institutionalized set of nested institutions. Eisenhower (1961) referred to the dangers of the military-industrial complex, which can perhaps more appropriately be described as the military-industrial-scientific complex. Each member of this trio is in fact to be seen as itself a nested set of institutions, with innumerable interrelations between them. Each institution is maintained by a particular set of forces, though a common factor, and perhaps the major one, is the career ambitions and inertia of the individuals concerned. The way in which these institutions help to precipitate war has been the subject of a number of studies (e.g., Levy, 1989a & b), but by their inertia they also help to maintain the institution of war.

As with other bureaucratic institutions, the military establishment has considerable resistance to change. Mackie (1989) has described a number of instances, including the way in which NATO responded to the recent change in Soviet thinking by seeing itself as essentially unchanged but with a global instead of a merely European role. More important in recent decades has been the manner in which military demands spurred on the arms race, with government policies subordinated to the weapons that became available. In the United States many issues were involved—for instance, inaccurate intelligence estimates of the strength of the Soviet Union and the governmental use of those estimates to justify defense spending; interservice rivalry to develop and display their own nuclear weapons (Prins, 1983); and worst-case assumptions about the supposed enemy's intentions.

Conscription can be regarded as another subinstitution of war, and the history of conscription in Finland illustrates another aspect of the conflict of interests between the military and the citizen, and the inertia of the former. In Finland there has been some provision for conscientious objection since 1922. However, there have been continuous discussions about the nature and extent of alternative service for objectors. This has not been merely a matter of the government against the objectors, for since 1966 the government has provided a substantial state subsidy to peace movement organizations. The Ministry of Education established and funded the Tampere Peace and Conflict Research

Institute in 1970, and the Ministry of Foreign Affairs created a special Disarmament Committee in 1971. Indeed, the Union of Conscientious Objectors, founded in 1974, has been funded by the state since 1976. Nevertheless, the Ministry of Defense has recently protested against the increase in the number of objectors and argued for extending the period of alternative service and integrating it into a "total defense system" For example, it is proposed that objectors serving in airport fire brigades should be informally affiliated with the Air Force. Strikes and hunger strikes against new legislation have involved a confrontation between the union and the government, and the concept of a "total defense system" seems now to have been dropped. The issue is of special interest because, although Finland places more emphasis on peace education than probably any other nation, 90 percent of young men go willingly into national service, and the memory of Finland's gallant resistance to invasion in the Second World War, and pride in the fact that it was never conquered, are potent forces (Phillips, 1991). The issue of conscription in Finland therefore embraces issues of individual and collective memories of the country's history, cultural ideals, and complex relations between defense and other institutions within and outside the government.

A comparable issue applies to the scientific member of the military-industrial-scientific complex. After the Second World War enormous sums were distributed by the U.S. government to defense contractors and to universities engaged in defense-oriented research (e.g., Burkholder, 1981; Rilling, 1989). Technology then spurred policy, and those who objected were labeled as Luddites who wanted to stop "progress." Scientists, pursuing their research, often produced more than requested—an issue well illustrated in the development of Multiple Independently-targetable Re-entry Vehicles (Prins, 1983).

The role of industry is even more important. Industrial firms became dependent on arms production, sought new markets for their current products, and developed new weapons to stimulate further demand. According to Prins (1983), official policies and competition between arms firms have led to the development of weapons vastly in excess of those required, the need for which has been rationalized, leading to new official policy, new demands by the military, even more powerful weapons, and so on. The inertia of the sequence is increased by the long lead time required to develop new weapons and by the competitiveness of scientists and industrialists to outdo each other in producing the most efficient and destructive weapons. Elworthy (1991) has documented the bureaucratic procedure involved in defense decision making in the United Kingdom, emphasizing how lack of accountability not only produces bad decisions and wastes money, but also perpetuates outmoded assumptions. The growth of the arms industry produces economic pressures against a reversal of the trend. And since a large part of the cost of the new weapons lies in their development, it is economically necessary for the arms-producing nations to sell arms to less industrialized countries. Thus a range of institutions, although themselves maintained largely by nonaggressive forces, help to maintain the institution of war. The military-industrial-scientific complex not only maintains the institution of war in the industrial nations, but also creates and exacerbates war elsewhere in the globe. Efforts to convert factories to peaceful purposes meet strong resistance (Cooley, 1977).

Lack of integration between the military and politicians results in further problems, so that either may pursue policies in ignorance of the real situation of the other (Levy, 1989b). Elworthy, Hamwee, and Miall (1989) have explored the assumptions made by a sample of politicians, civil servants, and scientists involved in nuclear decision making. They were able to pinpoint a whole range of unquestioned assumptions, some explicit and some implicit, that justified the view that nuclear weapons, originally designed as weapons of war, were now instruments of peace. Elworthy et al. emphasize that the individuals involved had thought about the issues but that their thinking involved a carryover from the aftermath of the Second World War, rather than a forward-looking vision. In a similar vein, Wertsch (1987) has argued that the language used in the nuclear debate was associated with unnecessary polarization of the issues.

Another factor here has been the belief that capitalism needs militarism to ensure continued growth. In the short term, there could be some substance to this view: the military alliance system of the 1950s, led by the United States, did support a global economic system and maintained the level of demand, stimulating economic growth. However, it has been argued that in the longer term, militarism leads to poorer economic performance. Those countries with small military budgets, such as Japan and Germany, have gained strong financial positions, while the United States is no longer strong enough to support an international capitalist system. The socialist system, also—but for different reasons—dependent on a wartime economy, has broken down. While the issues here are controversial, it seems that there could be hope that this prop of the institution of war could be severed if civilian, democratically accountable, state intervention in the system came to control arms production and took a global view of economic cooperation (Kaldor, 1991).

This is, of course, only a sketch of a few of the subinstitutions whose inertia contributes to the maintenance of the institution of war. They do, however, adequately illustrate the manner in which a variety of forces help to perpetuate the institution of war.

Conclusion

This chapter covers a wide spectrum, touching on aspects of aggression from the individual level, through aggression within relationships, to aggression within and between groups, and to international war. The nature of aggressive behavior differs between levels, and the explanatory principles necessary to understand it also differ. Nevertheless, individual aggression cannot be fully understood if the relationships and groups in which the individual is involved, and the cultural norms and values by which he or she lives, are ignored. Similarly, although individual aggression plays only a minor and mostly indirect part in war, the phenomena of international war, seen as an institution comprising roles that determine the behavior of individuals, cannot be fully understood unless the relations to lower levels of complexity are teased out. We have seen that individual aggressiveness contributes to the phenomena of war in a variety of ways including:

1. directly, through individual behavior in hand-to-hand combat.
2. indirectly, because the enemy is personified, so that individuals behave toward an enemy, or support war policies, as if the enemy were an individual.
3. indirectly, by contributing to the effectiveness of propaganda used to elicit public support for war.
4. indirectly, by contributing to nationalism.

Among the other individual propensities mentioned here are:

1. fear and frustration, leading to aggression.
2. the tendency to differentiate between in-group and out-group, contributing to patriotism and nationalism.
3. fear of strangers, contributing to nationalism.
4. assertiveness and/or acquisitiveness in leaders, politicians, or the population in setting the stage for and prosecuting the war.
5. the qualities of leaders and politicians and their abilities to cope with the special demands made on them.

Not only do these individual propensities affect processes at higher levels, but they are also affected by them. The intensity of individual aggression, the extent to which the enemy is personified, the qualities displayed by leaders, and so on all depend on the group situation in which they are placed and the sociocultural structure in which they participate. Indeed, the group processes themselves involve individual processes realized in the group situation. Among other consequences of these group processes, including in-group/out-group differentiation, are the following:

1. effects on combat between groups (e.g., loyalty to in-group members).

2. exaggeration of the difference between "us" and "them," facilitating denigration of the latter and the acceptance of a picture of the enemy as evil and subhuman.

3. distortion of discussion among, for instance, governing and advisory councils.

These group processes both affect the institution of war and the course of particular wars, and are also affected by the precise way in which war has been institutionalized and the current war situation.

The complexity and institutionalization of modern war, themselves consequences of individual propensities and group processes, also affect those propensities and processes. And in the longer term, the maintenance of war as an institution depends on dialectical relations between the levels of social complexity, on interactions between its subinstitutions (military-industrial-scientific complex), on other aspects of the sociocultural structure (traditions, religion, etc.), and on economic and political factors.

The causes of war are thus not to be found at any one of the traditional levels of explanation—individuals, the state, or the international system (cf. Choucri and North, 1987). Tetlock (1989) has compared the study of international conflict to looking through a microscope at successively lower levels of magnification—the individual decision maker, advisory groups, the lay agencies of government, the domestic and political environment, and the international system. Attempts to understand phenomena at any one level by an analysis confined to that level can achieve at most partial success because of the dialectical relations between levels. Attempts to "explain" phenomena at one level by analogy with phenomena at another are unlikely to lead to causal understanding because of the difference in complexity and because convergence between levels may be spurious. Furthermore, the values, beliefs, and institutions that constitute the sociocultural structure are a product of the propensities of individuals cooperating with and controlling one another, and at the same time influence the nature of those propensities. We must therefore tease apart the dialectical relations by which the sociocultural structure, including the institution of war, is related through group processes, relationships, and interactions to the propensities of individuals. It is necessary to alternate between analysis and synthesis, to cross and recross between the levels of social complexity, seeing each as a process in dynamic and dialectical relations with other levels. This is a necessary but hard enough task in studies of the behavior of individuals (Hinde, 1990), and infinitely more formidable here. However, a start has been made (Tetlock, 1989), and this is surely the road that must be followed. If we pinpoint specific prob   of dialectical relations between levels, and assess how the outcome is affected by the relevant situational factors, we shall slowly be led to a comprehension of the whole.

Returning, therefore, to the issue of whether war is to be studied in terms of actors adapting to the threats and opportunities presented by shifting balances of power in the international system, or whether it requires an understanding of basic human propensities, the answer must surely depend on the precise nature of the questions asked. If we seek generalizations about conditions conducive to the outbreak of war, we are assuming the institution of war and seeking an answer in terms of politics, economics, power balances, and other such factors. It is possible that characteristics of leaders might enter in. If we seek to understand particular wars, then basic human propensities, the idio-syncracies of individuals, and group processes in interaction with one another and with the institution of war must be taken into account. And if we seek to understand the longer-term question of the maintenance of the institution of war, we must seek to understand the dialectical relations between successive layers of social complexity in both diachronic and synchronic perspective.

Notes

I am grateful to the editors, referees, and to Professor L. Pulkkinen for helpful comments.

References

Adams, D.B. 1983. Why there are so few women warriors. *Behavior Science Research* 18:196–212.

Allport, F.H. 1927. The psychology of nationalism: The nationalistic fallacy as a cause of war. *Harpers Monthly* 2:91–301 (cited Feshbach, 1990).

Anderson, C.A., and D.C. Anderson. 1984. Ambient temperature and violent crime. *Journal of Personality and Social Psychology* 46:91–97.

Archer, D., and R. Gartner, 1984. *Violence and Crime in Cross-national Perspective.* New Haven: Yale University Press.

Asch, S. 1952. *Social Psychology.* New York: Prentice-Hall.

Attili, G., and R.A. Hinde. 1986. Categories of aggression and their motivational heterogeneity. *Ethology and Sociobiology* 7:17–27.

Averill, J.R. 1982. *Anger and Aggression: An Essay on Emotion.* New York: Springer Verlay.

Axelrod, R. 1984. *The Evolution of Cooperation.* New York: Basic Books.

Baerends, G.P. 1975. An evaluation of the conflict hypothesis. In G.P. Baerends, C. Beer, and A. Manning, eds., *Function and Evolution in Behaviour.* Oxford: Oxford University Press.

Bandura, A. 1973. *Aggression: A Social Learning Analysis*. Englewood Cliffs, N.J.: Prentice-Hall.

———. 1977. *Social Learning Theory*. Englewood Cliffs, N.J.: Prentice-Hall.

Bateson, P.P.G. 1980. Optimal outbreeding and the development of sexual preferences in the Japanese quail. *Zeitschrift für Tierpsychologie* 53:231–244.

Baumrind, D. 1971. Current patterns of parental authority. *Developmental Psychology Monographs* 4:1.

Berkowitz, L. 1963. *Aggression*. New York: McGraw Hill.

———. 1978. Is criminal violence normative behavior? *Journal of Research in Crime and Delinquency* 15:148–161.

———. 1989. Situational influences on aggression. In J. Groebel and R.A. Hinde, eds., *Aggression and War*. Cambridge: Cambridge University Press.

Berkowitz, L., and A. Frodi. 1977. Stimulus characteristics that can enhance or decrease aggression. *Aggressive Behavior* 3:1–15.

Berkowitz, L., and A. Le Page. 1967. Weapons as aggression—eliciting stimuli. *Journal of Personality and Social Psychology* 7:202–207.

Berlyne, D.E. 1960. *Conflict, Arousal and Curiosity*. New York: McGraw Hill.

Blurton-Jones, N. 1972. *Ethological Studies of Child Behaviour*. Cambridge: Cambridge University Press.

Boon, S.D., and J.G. Holmes. 1991. The dynamics of interpersonal trust: Resolving uncertainty in the face of risk. In R.A. Hinde and J. Groebel, eds., *Cooperation and Prosocial Behaviour*. Cambridge: Cambridge University Press.

Bossema, I., and R.R. Burgler. 1980. Communication during monocular and binocular looking in European jays. *Behaviour* 74:274–283.

Bowlby, J. [1969] 1982. *Attachment and Loss*. Vol. 1. Attachment. London: Hogarth.

Brewer, M.B. 1979. Ingroup bias in the minimal intergroup situation. *Psychological Bulletin* 186:307–324.

Brickman, P., R. Folger, E. Goode, and Y. Schul. 1981. Microjustice and macrojustice. In M.J. and S.C. Lerner, eds., *The Justice Motive in Social Behavior*. New York: Plenum.

Briggs, J.L. 1970. *Never in Anger: Portrait of an Eskimo Family*. Cambridge, Mass.: Harvard University Press.

Britten, S. 1983. *The Invisible Event*. London: Menard.

Brodie, M. 1990. *A World Worth Fighting For*. East Wittering, England: Goody.

Bronfenbrenner, U. 1961. The mirror image in Soviet-American relations. *Journal of Social Issues* 17:45–56.

Bronson, G. 1968. The fear of novelty. *Psychological Bulletin* 69:250–258.

Burkholder, S. 1981. The Pentagon in the ivory tower. *Progressive* (June 1981):25–31.

Byrne, D. 1971. *The Attraction Paradigm*. New York: Academic Press.

Byrne, D., D. Nelson, and K. Reeves. 1966. Effects of consensual validation on attraction as a function of verifiability. *Journal of Experimental Social Psychology* 2:98–107.

Caryl, P. 1979. Communication by agonistic displays: What can games theory contribute to ethology? *Behaviour* 68:136–169.

————. 1982. Animal signals: A reply to Hinde. *Animal Behaviour* 30:240–244.

Caspi, A., and G.H. Elder, Jr. 1988. Emergent family patterns: The intergenerational construction of problem behaviour and relationships. In R.A. Hinde and J. Stevenson-Hinde, eds., *Relationships Within Families*. Oxford: Clarendon Press.

Chagnon, N. 1977. *Yanamamö the Fierce People*. 2d ed. New York: Holt, Rinehart & Winston.

————. 1990. Reproductive and somatic conflicts of interest in the genesis of violence and warfare amongst tribesmen. In J. Haas, ed., *The Anthropology of War*. Cambridge: Cambridge University Press.

Chagnon, N., and P.E. Bugos. 1979. Kin selection and conflict: An analysis of a Yanamamö axfight. In N. Chagnon and W. Irons, eds., *Evolutionary Biology and Human Social Behavior*. N. Scituate, Mass.: Duxbury.

Chandler, M.J. 1985. Social structures and social cognitions. In R.A. Hinde, A.-N. Perret-Clermont, and J. Stevenson-Hinde, eds., *Social Relationships and Cognitive Development*. Oxford: Clarendon Press.

Chemas, M.M., and G.J. Skrzpek. 1972. An experimental test of the contingency model of leadership effectiveness. *Journal of Personality and Social Psychology* 24:172–177.

Choucri, N., and R.C. North. 1987. Roots of war: The master variables. In R. Vayrynen, ed., *The Quest for Peace*. London: Sage.

Christensen, A., and G. Margolin. 1988. Conflict and alliance in distressed and non-distressed families. In R.A. Hinde and J. Stevenson-Hinde, eds., *Relationships Within Families*. Oxford: Clarendon Press.

Clayton, S.D., and M.J. Lerner. 1991. Complications and complexity in the pursuit of justice. In R.A. Hinde and J. Groebel, eds., *Cooperation and Prosocial Behaviour*. Cambridge: Cambridge University Press.

Clutton-Brock, T., and S.D. Albon. 1979. The roaring of red deer and the evolution of honest advertisement. *Behaviour* 69:135–144.

Collier, J.G. 1991. Legal basis of the institution of war. In R.A. Hinde, ed., *The Institution of War*. London: Macmillan.

Cooley, M. 1977. Design, technology and production for social needs. *New Universities Quarterly* 32:37–49.

Daly, M., and M. Wilson. 1988. *Homicide*. New York: Aldine de Gruyter.

Darwin, C. 1872. *The Expression of the Emotions in Man and the Animals*. London: Murray.

Datta, S. 1983. Relative power and the acquisition of rank. In R.A. Hinde, ed., *Primate Social Relationships*. Oxford: Blackwell.

Dawkins, R., and J.R. Krebs. 1979. Animal signals: Information or manipulation? In J.R. Krebs and N. Davies, eds., *Behavioural Ecology*. Oxford: Blackwell.

Dengerink, H.A. 1971. Aggression, anxiety and physiological arousal. *Journal of Experimental Research in Personality* 5:223–232.

Dodge, K.A. 1982. Social information processing variables in the development of aggression and altruism in children. In C. Zahn-Waxler, M. Cummings, and

M. Radke-Yarrow, eds., *The Development of Altruism and Aggression*. New York: Cambridge University Press.

———. 1985. Attributional bias in children. In P.C. Kendall, ed., *Advances in Cognitive-Behavioral Research and Therapy*, 4. New York: Academic Press.

Dodge, K.A., J.R. Bates, and G.S. Pettit. 1990. Mechanisms in the cycle of violence. *Science* 250:1678–1683.

Dollard, J., L.W. Doob, N.E. Miller, O.H. Mowrer, and R.R. Sears. 1939. *Frustration and Aggression*. New Haven: Yale University Press.

Druckman, D., and P.T. Hopmann. 1989. Behavioral aspects of negotiations on mutual security. In P.E. Tetlock, J.L. Husbands, R. Jervis, P.C. Stern, and C. Tilly, eds., *Behavior, Society and Nuclear War*, Vol. 1. New York: Oxford University Press.

Eagly, A.H., and V.J. Steffen. 1986. Gender and aggressive behavior. *Psychological Bulletin* 100:309–330.

Easterbrooks, M.A., and R.N. Emde. 1988. Marital and parent-child relationships: The role of affect in the family system. In R.A. Hinde and J. Stevenson-Hinde, eds., *Relationships Within Families*. Oxford: Clarendon Press.

Eibl Eibesfeldt, I. 1975. *Ethology*. New York: Holt, Rinehart & Winston.

——— 1979. *The Biology of Peace and War*. London: Thames & Hudson.

Eisenhower, D. 1961. Public papers of the presidents of the United States, Dwight D. Eisenhower, 1960–61. Washington, D.C.

Elworthy, S. 1991. Defence decision-making and accountability. In R.A. Hinde, ed., *The Institution of War*. London: Macmillan.

Elworthy, S., J. Hamwee, and H. Miall. 1989. The assumptions of nuclear weapons decision makers. In L. Barnett and I. Lee, eds., *The Nuclear Mentality*. London: Pluto.

Engfer, A. 1986. *Kindesmisshandlung: Ursachen, Auswirkungen, Hilfen*. Stuttgart: Enke.

———. 1988. The interrelatedness of marriage and the mother-child relationship. In R.A. Hinde and J. Stevenson-Hinde, eds., *Relationships Within Families*. Oxford: Clarendon Press.

Engfer, A., and K.A. Schneewind. 1982. Causes and consequences of harsh parental treatment. *Child Abuse and Neglect* 6:129–139.

Essock-Vitale, S.M., and M.T. McGuire. 1985. Women's lives viewed from an evolutionary perspective. Part 2. Patterns of helping. *Ethology and Sociobiology* 6:155–173.

Feger, H. 1991. Cooperation between groups. In R.A. Hinde and J. Groebel, eds., *Cooperation and Prosocial Behaviour*. Cambridge: Cambridge University Press.

Ferguson, R.B. 1990. Explaining war. In J. Haas, ed., *The Anthropology of War*. Cambridge: Cambridge University Press.

Feshbach, S. 1961. The stimulating versus cathartic effects of vicarious aggressive activity. *Journal of Abnormal and Social Psychology* 68:381–385.

———. 1970. Aggression. In P.H. Mussen, ed., *Carmichael's Manual of Child Psychology*, Vol. 2. New York: Wiley.

―――. 1986. Individual aggression, national attachment and the search for peace. *Aggressive Behavior* 13:315–325.

―――. 1989. The bases and development of individual aggression. In J. Groebel and R. A. Hinde, eds., *Aggression and War*. Cambridge: Cambridge University Press.

―――. 1990. Psychology, human violence and the search for peace: Issues in science and social values. *Journal of Social Issues* 46:185–198.

Festinger, L. 1957. *A Theory of Cognitive Dissonance*. Evanston, Ill.: Row, Peterson.

Fischoff, B. 1991. Nuclear decisions: Cognitive limits to the unthinkable. In P.E. Tetlock, J.L. Husbands, R. Jervis, P.C. Stern, and C. Tilly, eds., *Behavior, Society and Nuclear War*, Vol. 2. New York: Oxford University Press.

Freedman, J.L. 1975. *Crowding and Behavior*. San Francisco: Freeman.

Freud, S. [1923] 1947. *The Ego and the Id*. London: Hogarth.

Frodi, A., J. Macaulay, and P.R. Thorne. 1977. Are women always less aggressive than men? *Psychological Bulletin* 84:634–660.

Fussell, P. 1975. *The Great War and Modern Memory*. London: Oxford University Press.

Gambetta, D. 1988. *Trust*. Oxford: Blackwell.

Gelles, R.J. 1980. A profile of violence towards children in the United States. In G. Gerbner, C.J. Ross, and E. Zigler, eds., *Child Abuse: An Agenda for Action*. New York: Oxford University Press.

Goldstein, A.P. 1989. Aggression reductions: Some vital steps. In J. Groebel and R.A. Hinde, eds., *Aggression and War*. Cambridge: Cambridge University Press.

Goldstein, J.H. 1986. *Aggression and Crimes of Violence*. New York: Oxford University Press.

Goldstone, J.A. 1989. Deterrence in rebellions and revolutions. In P.C. Stern, R. Axelrod, R. Jervis, and R. Radner, eds., *Perspectives on Deterrence*. New York: Oxford University Press.

Good, D.A. 1988. Individuals, interpersonal relations and trust. In D. Gambetta, ed., *Trust*. Oxford: Blackwell.

Goody, E. 1991. The learning of prosocial behaviour in small-scale egalitarian societies. In R.A. Hinde and J. Groebel, eds., *Cooperation and Prosocial Behaviour*. Cambridge: Cambridge University Press.

Gould, S.J., and R.C. Lewontin. 1979. The spandrels of San Marco and the Panglossian paradigm: A critique of the adaptationist programme. *Proceedings of the Royal Society B* 205:581–598.

Graham, S., C. Doubleday, and P.A. Guarino. 1984. The development of the relations between perceived controllability and the emotions of pity, anger and guilt. *Child Development* 55:561–565.

Greenwood, C. 1991. In defence of the laws of war. In R.A. Hinde, ed., *The Institution of War*. London: Macmillan.

Groebel, J. 1986. International research on television violence: Synopsis and critique. In L.R. Huesmann and L.D. Eron, eds., *Television and the Aggressive Child*. Hillsdale, N.J.: Erlbaum.

Groebel, J., and H. Feger. 1982. Analyse von Strukturen terroristischer Grupperingen. In *Analysen zum Terrorismus, Band 3: Gruppenprozesse*. Opladen: Westdeutsche Verlag.

Haas, J. 1990. *The Anthropology of War*. Cambridge: Cambridge University Press.

Halliday, T., and A. Houston. 1978. The newt as an honest salesman. *Animal Behaviour* 26:1273–1281.

Hamilton, W.D. 1964. The genetical theory of social behaviour. *Journal of Theoretical Biology* 7:1–52.

Harris, R. 1986. *The Teaching of Contemporary World Issues*. Paris: UNESCO.

Hartup, W.W. 1983. Peer relations. In E.M. Hetherington, ed., *Mussen Handbook of Child Psychology*. New York: Wiley.

Hastings, M., and J. Jenkins. 1983. *The Battle for the Falklands*. London: Pan Books.

Herbert, J. 1989. The physiology of aggression. In J. Groebel and R.A. Hinde, eds., *Aggression and War*. Cambridge: Cambridge University Press.

Hetherington, E.M., R.J. Stouwie, and E.H. Ridberg. 1971. Patterns of family interaction and child-rearing attitudes related to three dimensions of juvenile delinquency. *Journal of Abnormal Psychology* 78:160–176.

Hinde, R.A. 1960. Energy models of motivation. *Symposia of the Society for Experimental Biology* 14:199–213.

———. 1979. *Towards Understanding Relationships*. London: Academic Press.

———. 1981. Animal signals: Ethological and games theory approaches are not incompatible. *Animal Behaviour* 29:535–542.

———. 1987a. *Individuals, Relationships and Culture*. Cambridge: Cambridge University Press.

———. 1987b. Trust, cooperation, commitment and international relationships. *Current Research on Peace and Violence* 10:83–90.

———. 1990. The interdependence of the behavioural sciences. Croonian lecture. *Phil. Transactions of the Royal Society of London B* 329:217–227.

———. 1991. A biologist looks at anthropology. *Man*, 26:583–608.

Hinde, R.A., and J. Groebel, eds. 1991. *Cooperation and Prosocial Behaviour*. Cambridge: Cambridge University Press.

Hinde, R.A., and J. Stevenson-Hinde. 1987. Interpersonal relationships and child development. *Developmental Review* 7:1–21.

Hinde, R.A., and J. Stevenson-Hinde, eds. 1988. *Relationships Within Families*. Oxford: Clarendon Press.

Hinde, R.A., and J. Stevenson-Hinde. 1990. Attachment: Biological, cultural and individual desiderata. *Human Development* 33:62–72.

Hinde, R.A., A. Tamplin, and J. Barrett. In press. Home correlates of aggression in preschool. *Aggressive Behavior*.

Hinsley, F.H. 1973. *Nationalism and the International System*. London: Hodder & Stoughton.

Hoffman, M.L. 1970. Moral development. In P.H. Mussen, ed., *Carmichael's Manual of Child Psychology*, Vol. 2. New York: Wiley.

Holsti, O.R. 1989. Crisis decision making. In P.E. Tetlock, J.L. Husbands, R. Jervis,

P.C. Stern, and C. Tilly, eds., *Behavior, Society and Nuclear War*, Vol. 1. New York: Oxford University Press.

Huntingford, F.A. 1989. Animals fight, but do not make war. In J. Groebel and R.A. Hinde, eds., *Aggression and War*. Cambridge: Cambridge University Press.

Izard, C.E., ed. 1982. *Measuring Emotions in Infants and Children*. Cambridge: Cambridge University Press.

Jaffe, Y., N. Shapiro, and Y. Yinon. 1981. Aggression and its escalation. *Journal of Cross-cultural Psychology* 12:21–36.

Janis, I.L. 1982. *Victims of Groupthink: A Psychological Study of Foreign Policy Decisions and Fiascoes*. Boston: Houghton Mifflin.

Jervis, R. 1976. *Perception and Misperception in International Relations*. Princeton: Princeton University Press.

Johnson, G.R. 1986. Kin selection, socialization and patriotism: An integrating theory. *Politics and the Life Sciences* 4:127–154.

———. 1989. The role of kin recognition mechanisms in patriotic socialization: Further reflections. *Politics and the Life Sciences* 8:62–69.

Johnson, J.T. 1984. *Can Modern War Be Just?* New Haven: Yale University Press.

Kaldor, M. 1991. Do modern economies require our preparations for warfare. In R.A. Hinde, ed., *The Institution of War*. London: Macmillan.

Kelly, H.H. 1979. *Personal Relationships*. Hillsdale, N.J.: Erlbaum.

Kelly, H.H., and G. Schmidt. 1989. The "aggressive male" syndrome. In P.C. Stern, R. Axelrod, R. Jervis, and R. Radner, eds., *Perspectives on Deterrence*. New York: Oxford University Press.

Kelly, G.A. 1955. *The Psychology of Personal Constructs*. New York: Norton.

———. 1970. A brief introduction to personal construct theory. In D. Bannister, ed., *Perspectives in Personal Construct Theory*. London: Academic Press.

Kenny, D.A., and S.J. Zaccaro. 1983. An estimate of variance due to traits in leadership. *Journal of Applied Psychology* 68:678–685.

Kitcher, P. 1985. *Vaulting Ambition*. Cambridge, Mass.: MIT Press.

Kohlberg, L. 1976. Moral stages and moralization: The cognitive-developmental approach. In T. Lickona, ed., *Moral Development and Behavior*. New York: Holt, Rinehart & Winston.

Kosterman, R., and S. Feshbach. 1989. Toward a measure of patriotic and nationalistic attitudes. *Political Psychology* 10:257–274.

Krebs, D.L., N.B. Davies. 1981. *An Introduction to Behavioral Ecology*. Sunderland, Mass.: Sinauer.

Krebs, D.L., and D.T. Miller. 1985. Altruism and aggression. In G. Lindzey and E. Aronson, eds., *Handbook of Social Psychology*, Vol. 2. New York: Random House.

Lagerspetz, K.M., K. Björkquist, and T. Peltonen. 1988. Is indirect aggression typical of females? *Aggressive Behavior* 14:403–414.

Lagerspetz, K.M.J., and K.Y.H. Lagerspetz. 1971. Changes in the aggressiveness of mice resulting from selective breeding, learning and social isolation. *Scandinavian Journal of Psychology* 12:241–248.

Langness, L.L. 1968. Sexual antagonism in the New Guinea Highlands. A Bena Bena example. *Oceania* 3:161–177.

Larsen, K.S., D. Coleman, J. Forbes, and R. Johnson. 1972. Is the subject's personality or the experimental situation a better predictor of a subject's willingness to administer shock to a victim? *Journal of Personality and Social Psychology* 22:287–295.

Lebow, R.N. 1989. Deterrence: A political and psychological critique. In P.C. Stern, R. Axelrod, R. Jervis, and R. Radner, eds., *Perspectives on Deterrence*. New York: Oxford University Press.

Lefkowitz, M.M., L.D. Eron, L.O. Walder, and L.R. Huesmann. 1977. *Growing Up to Be Violent*. New York: Pergamon.

Lerner, M.J. 1981. The justice motive in human relations. In M.J. and S.C. Lerner, eds., *The Justice Motive in Social Behavior*. New York: Plenum.

Levy, J.S. 1989*a*. The causes of war: A review of theories and evidence. In P.E. Tetlock, J.L. Husbands, R. Jervis, P.C. Stern, and C. Tilly, eds., *Behavior, Society and Nuclear War*, Vol. I, 209–333. New York: Oxford University Press.

———. 1989*b*. Quantitative studies of deterrence success and failure. In P.C. Stern, R. Axelrod, R. Jervis, and R. Radner, eds., *Perspectives on Deterrence*. New York: Oxford University Press.

Lorenz, K. 1986. *On Aggression*. London: Methuen.

Lott, A.J., and B.E. Lott. 1961. Group cohesiveness, communication level and conformity. *Journal of Abnormal and Social Psychology* 62:408–412.

———. 1965. Group cohesiveness as interpersonal attraction. *Psychological Bulletin* 64:259–309.

Lund, M. 1985. The development of investment and commitment scales for predicting continuity of personal relationships. *Journal of Social and Personal Relationships* 2:3–23.

———. 1991. Commitment old and new: Social pressure and individual choice in making relationships last. In R.A. Hinde and J. Groebel, eds., *Cooperation and Prosocial Behaviour*. Cambridge: Cambridge University Press.

McCauley, C. 1990. Conference overview. In J. Haas, ed., *The Anthropology of War*. Cambridge: Cambridge University Press.

McCord, J. 1983. A longitudinal study of aggression and anti-social behavior. In K.T. van Dusen and S.A. Medrick, eds., *Prospective Studies of Crime and Delinquency*. Boston: Kluwer-Nijoff.

———. 1988. Parental behavior in the cycle of aggression. *Psychiatry* 51:14–23.

McCord, W., M. McCord, and A. Howard. 1961. Familial correlates of aggression in non-delinquent male children. *Journal of Abnormal and Social Psychology* 62, 79–93.

McDougall, W. 1923. *An Outline of Psychology*. London: Methuen.

Mackie, A. 1989. Military group and nuclear circumstance. In L. Barnett and I. Lee, eds., *The Nuclear Mentality*. London: Pluto.

Mackie. A. 1989. Military group and nuclear circumstance. In L. Barnett and I. Lee, eds., *The Nuclear Mentality*. London: Pluto.

Manning, A. 1989. The genetic bases of aggression. In J. Groebel and R.A. Hinde, eds., *Aggression and War*. Cambridge: Cambridge University Press.

Marshall, S.L.A. 1947. *Men Against Fire*. New York: Morrow.

Martin, B. 1975. Parent-child relations. In F.D. Horowitz, ed., *Review of Child Development Research*, Vol. 4. Chicago: University of Chicago Press.

Mead, G.H. 1929. National-mindedness and international mindedness. *International Journal of Ethics* 39:385–407.

Mead, M. 1950. *Male and Female*. Harmondsworth, U.K.: Penguin.

Megargee, E.I. 1966. Undercontrolled and overcontrolled personality types in extreme antisocial aggression. *Psychological Monographs* 80(3).

Meyer, H.-J. 1988. Marital and mother-child relationships. In R.A. Hinde and J. Stevenson-Hinde, eds., *Relationships Within Families*. Oxford: Clarendon Press.

Milgram, S. 1974. *Obedience to Authority*. New York: Harper & Row.

Minnix, D.A. 1982. *Small Groups and Foreign Policy Decision Making*. Washington, D.C.: University Press of America.

Minuchin, P. 1985. Families and individual development. *Child Development* 56:289–302.

Minuchin, S. 1974. *Families and Family Therapy*. Cambridge, Mass.: Harvard University Press.

Minuchin, S., and H.C. Fishman. 1981. *Family Therapy Techniques*. Cambridge, Mass.: Harvard University Press.

Montagu, A., ed. 1978. *Learning Non-aggression*. New York: Oxford University Press.

Morris, N., and G. Hawkins. 1970. *The Honest Politician's Guide to Crime Control*. Chicago: University of Chicago Press.

Moss, C.S., M.E. Johnson, and R.E. Hosford. 1984. An assessment of the Megargee typology in lifelong criminal violence. *Criminal Justice and Behavior* 11:225–234.

National Institute of Mental Health. 1982. *Television and Behavior*. Washington, D.C.: U.S. Government Printing Office.

Newcomb, T.M. 1971. Dyadic balance as a source of clues about interpersonal attraction. In B.I. Murstein, ed., *Theories of Attraction and Love*. New York: Springer.

Obholzer, A. 1989. The comfort of groups. In L. Barrett and I. Lee, eds., *The Nuclear Mentality*. London: Pluto.

Olweus, D. 1978. *Aggression in the Schools*. New York: Wiley.

———. 1979. Stability of aggressive reaction patterns in males: A review. *Psychological Bulletin* 86:852–875.

———. 1984. Development of stable aggressive reaction patterns in males. In R.J. Blanchard and D.C. Blanchard, eds., *Advances in the Study of Aggression* 1:103–137. New York: Academic Press.

O'Neill, B. 1989. Game theory and the study of the deterrence of war. In P.C. Stern, R. Axelrod, R. Jervis, and R. Radner, eds., *Perspectives on Deterrence*. New York: Oxford University Press.

Parke, R.D., and R.G. Slaby. 1983. The development of aggression. In E.M. Hetherington, ed., *Mussen Handbook of Child Psychology*, Vol. 4. New York: Wiley.

Patterson, G.R. 1976. The aggressive child. In E.J. Marsh, L.A. Hamerlynck, and L.C. Handy, eds., *Behavior Modification and Families*. New York: Brunner/Mazel.

———. 1982. *Coercive Family Process*. Vol. 3. Eugene, Oreg.: Castalia.

Patterson, G.R., and T.J. Dishion. 1988. Multilevel family process models: Traits, interaction and relationships. In R.A. Hinde and J. Stevenson-Hinde, eds., *Relationships Within Families*. Oxford: Clarendon Press.

Peterson, R.A. 1971. Aggression as a function of expected retaliation and aggression of target of aggressor. *Developmental Psychology* 5:161–166.

Phillips, B. 1991. The institution of conscription: The case of Finland. In R.A. Hinde, ed., *The Institution of War*, London: Macmillan.

Pogge von Strandmann, H. 1991. History and War. In R.A. Hinde, ed., *The Institution of War*. London: Macmillan.

Prentice-Dunn, S., and R.W. Rogers. 1983. Deindividuation in aggression. In R.G. Green and E. Donnerstein, eds., *Aggression: Theoretical and Empirical Review* 2:155–172. New York: Academic Press.

Prins, G., ed. 1983. *Defended to Death*. Harmondsworth, U.K.: Penguin.

Pruitt, D.G. 1989. Aggressive behavior in interpersonal and international relations. In P.C. Stern, R. Axelrod, R. Jervis, and R. Radner, eds., *Perspectives on Deterrence*, New York: Oxford University Press.

Pruitt, D.G., and M.J. Kimmel. 1976. Twenty years of experimental gaming. *Annual Review of Psychology* 28:363–392.

Pulkkinen, L. 1987. Offensive and defensive aggression in humans. *Aggressive Behavior* 13:197–212.

———. 1988. Delinquent development: Theoretical and practical considerations. In M. Rutter, ed., *Studies of Psychosocial Risk*. Cambridge: Cambridge University Press.

———. 1989. Progress in education for peace in Finland. In R.A. Hinde and D. Parry, eds., *Education for Peace*. Nottingham: Spokesman.

Quester, G.H. 1989. Some thoughts on "deterrence failures." In P.C. Stern, R. Axelrod, R. Jervis, and R. Radner, eds., *Perspectives on Deterrence*, New York: Oxford University Press.

Rabbie, J.M. 1987. Armed conflicts. In J. von Wright, K. Helkamay, and A.M. Pirtilla-Backman, eds., *European Psychologists for Peace*, Proceedings of Helsinki Congress, 1986.

———. 1989. Group processes as stimulants of aggression. In J. Groebel and R.A. Hinde, eds., *Aggression and War*. Cambridge: Cambridge University Press.

———. 1991. Determinants of instrumental intra-group cooperation. In R.A. Hinde and J. Groebel, eds., *Cooperation and Prosocial Behaviour*. Cambridge: Cambridge University Press.

Rabbie, J.M., and F. Bekkers. 1976. Threatened leadership and intergroup competition. *European Journal of Social Psychology* 31:269–283.

Rabbie, J., and M. Horwitz. 1969. The arousal of ingroup-outgroup bias by a chance win or loss. *Journal of Personality and Social Psychology* 69:223–228.

———. 1988. Categories versus groups as explanatory concepts in intergroup relations. *European Journal of Social Psychology* 18:117–123.

Radke-Yarrow, M., J. Richters, and W.E. Wilson. 1988. Child development in a network of relationships. In R.A. Hinde and J. Stevenson-Hinde, eds., *Relationships Within Families*. Oxford: Clarendon Press.

Radke-Yarrow, M., C. Zahn-Waxler, and M. Chapman. 1983. Children's prosocial dispositions and behavior. In E.M. Hetherington, ed., *Mussen Handbook of Child Psychology*, Vol. 4. New York: Wiley.

Ramsey, P. 1968. *The Just War*. New York: Scribner's.

Ratcliffe, S.G., and M.A.S. Field. 1982. Emotional disorders in XYY children. *Journal of Child Psychology and Psychiatry* 23:401–406.

Rhode, D.L. 1990. Definitions of difference. In D.L. Rhode, ed., *Theoretical Perspectives on Sennal Difference*. New Haven: Yale University Press.

Rilling, R. 1989. The militarization of science. In J. Hussard, T. Kibble, and P. Lewis, eds., *Ways out of the Arms Race*. Singapore: World Scientific.

Robarchek, C. 1990. Motivations and material causes: On the explanation of conflict and war. In J. Haas, ed., *The Anthropology of War*, 56–76. Cambridge: Cambridge University Press.

Royal Society. 1983. *Risk Assessment: A Study Group Report*. London: Royal Society.

Rubin, J.Z. 1991. Changing assumptions about conflict and negotiation. In R.A. Hinde and J. Groebel, eds., *Cooperation and Prosocial Behaviour*. Cambridge: Cambridge University Press.

Ruddick, S. 1989. *Maternal Thinking*. London: Women's Press.

Rule, B.C., and A.R. Nesdale. 1976. Emotional arousal and aggressive behavior. *Psychological Bulletin* 83:851–863.

Rushton, J.P., D.W. Fulker, M.C. Neale, D.K.B. Nias, and H.J. Eysenck. 1986. Altruism and aggression: The heritability of individual differences. *Journal of Personality and Social Psychology* 50:1192–1198.

Santoni, R.E. 1991. Nurturing the institution of war: Just War theory's justifications and accommodations. In R.A. Hinde, ed., *The Institution of War*. London: Macmillan.

Shweder, R.A., and J.G. Miller. 1985. The social construction of the person: how is it possible? In K. Gergen and K. Davis, eds., *The Social Construction of the Person*. New York: Springer Verlag.

Scott, J.P., E. and Fredericson. 1951. The causes of fighting in mice and rats. *Physiological Zoology* 25:273–309.

Scott, J.P., and J.L. Fuller. 1965. *Genetics and the Social Behavior of the Dog*. Chicago: University of Chicago Press.

Segall, M.H. 1989. Cultural factors, biology and human aggression. In J. Groebel and R.A. Hinde, eds., *Aggression and War*. Cambridge: Cambridge University Press.

Sherif, M. 1958. Supra ordinate goals in the reduction of intergroup conflict. *American Journal of Sociology* 63:349–358.

————. 1966. *Group Conflict and Cooperation: Their Social Psychology*. London: Routledge & Kegan Paul.

Simpson, M.J.A. 1968. The display of the Siamese fighting fish. *Animal Behaviour Monographs*, 1.

Smith, T.W. 1984. Gender and attitudes towards violence. *Public Opinion Quarterly* 48:384–396.

Staub, E. 1971. The learning and unlearning of aggression. In J.L. Singer, ed., *The Control of Aggression and Violence*. New York: Academic Press.

Stephenson, G.M. 1984. Intergroup and interpersonal dimensions of bargaining and negotiation. In H. Tajfel, ed., *The Social Dimension*, Vol. 2. Cambridge: Cambridge University Press.

Stern, J.P. 1975. *Hitler: The Führer and the People*. London: Fontana.

Stern, P.C., R. Axelrod, R. Jervis, and R. Radner. 1989*a*. Conclusions. In P.C. Stern, R. Axelrod, R. Jervis, and R. Radner, eds., *Perspectives on Deterrence*. New York: Oxford University Press.

————. 1989*b*. Deterrence in the nuclear age: The research for evidence. In P.C. Stern, R. Axelrod, R. Jervis, and R. Radner, eds., *Perspectives on Deterrence*. New York: Oxford University Press.

Stevenson, H.W. 1991. The development of prosocial behaviour in large-scale collective societies. In R.A. Hinde and J. Groebel, eds., *Cooperation and Prosocial Behaviour*. Cambridge: Cambridge University Press.

Stouffer, S.A. 1949. *The American Soldier*. Princeton: Princeton University Press.

Strube, M.J., and J.E. Garcia. 1981. A meta-analytic investigation of Fiedler's contingency model of leadership-effectiveness. *Psychological Bulletin* 90:307–321.

Sweet, L.E. 1973. Culture and aggressive action. In C.M. Otten, ed., *Aggression and Evolution*. Lexington, Mass.: Xerox College.

Sykes, S. 1991. Sacrifice and the ideology of war. In R.A. Hinde, ed., *The Institution of War*. London: Macmillan.

Tajfel, H. 1978. Contributions to H. Tajfel, ed., *Differentiation Between Social Groups*. London: Academic Press.

————. 1981. *Human Groups and Social Categories*. Cambridge: Cambridge University Press.

————. 1984. Intergroup relations, social myths and social justice in social psychology. In H. Tajfel, ed., *The Social Dimension: European Developments in Social Psychology*, Vol. 2. Cambridge: Cambridge University Press.

Tajfel, H., and J.C. Turner. 1979. An integrative theory of intergroup conflict. In W.G. Austin and S. Worchel, eds., *The Social Psychology of Intergroup Relations*. Monterey, Calif.: Brooks Cole.

————. 1986. The social identity theory of inter-group behavior. In S. Worchel and W.G. Austin, eds., *Psychology of Intergroup Relations*. Chicago: Nelson-Hall.

Teichman, J. 1986. *Pacifism and the Just War*. Oxford: Blackwell.

Tetlock, P.E. 1989. Methodological themes and variations. In P.E. Tetlock, J.L. Husbands, R. Jervis, P.C. Stern, and C. Tilly, eds., *Behavior, Society and Nuclear War*, Vol. 1. New York: Oxford University Press.

Tetlock, P.E., J.L. Husbands, R. Jervis, P.C. Stern, and C. Tilly, eds. 1989. *Behavior, Society and Nuclear War*, Vol. 1. New York: Oxford University Press.

Thompson, J. 1989. Perceptions of threat. In J. Hassard, T. Kibble, and P. Lewis, eds., *Ways out of the Arms Race*. Singapore: World Scientific.

Tinbergen, N. 1948. Social releasers and the experimental method required for their study. *Wilson Bulletin* 60:6–51.

———. 1952. Derived activities: Their causation, biological significance, origin and emancipation during evolution. *Quarterly Review of Biology* 27:1–32.

Tinklenberg, J.R., and F.M. Ochberg. 1981. Patterns of adolescent violence. In D.A. Hamburg and M.B. Trudeau, eds., *Biobehavioral Aspects of Aggression*. New York: Liss.

Triandis, H.C. 1991. Cross-cultural differences in assertiveness/competition vs. group loyalty/cooperation. In R.A. Hinde and J. Groebel, eds., *Cooperation and Prosocial Behaviour*. Cambridge: Cambridge University Press.

Trivers, R.L. 1972. Parental investment and sexual selection. In B. Campbell, ed., *Sexual Selection and the Descent of Man*. Chicago: Aldive.

Turner, J.C. 1982. Towards a cognitive redefinition of the social group. In H. Tajfel, ed., *Social Identity and Intergroup Relations*. Cambridge: Cambridge University Press.

Turner, J.C., M.A. Hogg, P.J. Oakes, S.D. Reicher, and M.S. Wetherell. 1987. *Rediscovering the Social Group: Social Categorisation Theory*. Oxford: Blackwell.

Ulrich, R.E. 1966. Pain as a cause of aggression. *American Zoologist* 6:643–662.

van Iersel, J.J.A., and A.C.A. Bol. 1958. Preening of two tern species. *Behaviour* 13:1–88.

van Knippenberg, A.F.M. 1984. Intergroup differences in group perceptions. In H. Tajfel, ed., *The Social Dimension*, Vol. 1. Cambridge: Cambridge University Press.

van Praag, H.M., R. Plutchik, and A. Apter, eds. 1990. *Violence and Suicidality*. New York: Brunner/Mazel.

Vroom, V.H., and P.M. Yetton. 1973. *Leadership and Decision-making*. Pittsburgh: University of Pittsburgh Press.

Wahlström, R. 1987. The image of enemy as a psychological antecedent of warfare. In J.M. Ramirez, R.A. Hinde, and J. Groebel, eds., *Essays on Violence*. Seville: Publicaciones de la Universidad de Sevilla.

Walton, R.E., and R.B. McKersie. 1965. *A Behavioral Theory of Labor Negotiations*. New York: McGraw Hill.

Wertsch, J.V. 1987. Modes of discourse in the nuclear arms debate. *Current Research on Peace and Violence* 10:102–112.

Wheeler, L. 1974. Social comparison and selective affiliation. In T.L. Huston, ed., *Foundations of Interpersonal Attraction*. New York: Academic Press.

Winter, J. 1991. Imaginings of war: Some cultural supports of the institution of war. In R.A. Hinde, ed., *The Institution of War*. London: Macmillan.

Zahavi, A. 1975. Mate selection: Selection for a handicap. *Journal of Theoretical Biology* 53:205–214.

Zajonc, R.B. 1968. Attitudinal effects of more exposure. *Journal of Personality and Social Psychology*, Monograph Supplement, 9:1–27.

Zillman, D. 1979. *Hostility and Aggression*. Hillsdale, N.J.: Erlbaum.

Zimbardo, P.G. 1969. The human choice. In W.J. Arnold and D. Levine, eds., *Nebraska Symposium on Motivation*. Lincoln: University of Nebraska Press.

2

Influence Techniques Among Nations

RUSSELL J. LENG

Introduction

Important foreign policy problems inevitably turn on questions of influence. The sovereignty principle encourages the assumption that each state in the global system enjoys the right to an unfettered pursuit of its interests, but the reality of interdependence in the global system means that no state can do so without affecting the interests of others. The web of relationships between nations is such that, particularly for large states, any foreign policy act, and not a small number of domestic acts, are likely to influence other states whether that is the intention or not. Moreover, the decentralized nature of the international system means that a state's ability to achieve and defend its interests, whether through cooperation or competition, is dependent on its capacity to influence the behavior of other international actors.

A survey of contemporary research on all internation influence relationships, inadvertent as well as deliberate, would be tantamount to a discussion of all international relations research. Therefore, to provide some focus to our discussion, and to avoid unnecessary overlap with other chapters in this series, this chapter focuses on the *techniques* of influence per se—the methods employed by governments that are *deliberately* engaged in the process of attempting to influence the behavior of others. Even with this restriction, we shall have to proceed at a fairly high level of generality within four broad categories of influence techniques: (1) diplomacy and negotiation, (2) coercive or contentious bargaining short of hostilities, (3) economic influence techniques, and (4) the use of force. Within each of these categories we will consider contemporary research describing how states have gone about the business of deliberately attempting to influence one another in the nuclear age, and offering prescriptions regarding which techniques are most likely to be effective in which situations. Before beginning the survey, however, it will be useful to define some of the concepts that we will be using in discussing influence, and to consider the major theoretical and methodological differences that exist among social scientists engaged in research on internation influence.

An Anatomy of Influence

Influence represents the relational component of a state's power. It is the means by which a state achieves its objectives through modifying or reinforcing the behavior of states or other international actors such as intergovernmental organizations. Governments may seek to attain influence for its own sake, but more often influence serves an instrumental purpose, either for the immediate attainment of some objective or as an investment to be used when needed.

An analytical framework describing the basic components of influence was presented in a seminal article by Singer in 1963. Singer began by distinguishing between an *influence attempt* and its *outcome*, or the target's reaction to the influence attempt. There are two components to an influence attempt: a *request* or demand that B behave in a manner preferred by A, and the influence techniques, or *inducements*, that A employs in an attempt to make B's predicted behavior coincide with A's preferred behavior. These influence techniques range from simple persuasion to promises, rewards, threats, punishments, and carrot-and-stick inducements of varying degrees and specificity. Inducements can be further categorized according to the type of instrument used—diplomatic, economic, or military—their intensity, and the credibility of A's commitment to take the threatened or promised action (see Leng, 1980).

The outcomes of influence attempts can be described according to the manner in which B responds to A's demands. Responses can range from outright compliance with the demand, to a placating response, to ignoring the influence attempt, to responding with a defiant counterthreat, or to some mix of accommodation and counterthreat. B's response to A's influence attempt can be influenced by a variety of factors, including: (1) B's perception of the comparative benefits, or costs and risks, of complying, or not complying, with A's demands, (2) B's estimate of the likelihood that A will carry out any inducements, (3) psychological factors, such as B's responsiveness to A, or B's resistance to threats, and (4) the effects of environmental factors, such as the actions of third parties.

A's choice of influence attempts and B's choice of responses also are presumed to be influenced by the relationship between the two parties—their comparative capabilities, the gravity of the issues at stake for each, the degree of friendliness/hostility in their relations, the presence and degree of a dependency relationship or of interdependence.

Viewed from a more macroscopic level, individual influence attempts can be seen as tactical moves that are the discrete components of an overall *influence strategy* designed to condition the target state to comply with the influencer's demands. Some of the most interesting recent work on interstate influence deals with the relative effectiveness of different types of influence strategies.

Two Theoretical Perspectives

The discussion in this chapter is confined largely to a survey of the findings from behavioral research on internation influence, with some reference to the methods employed. The researcher's selection of methods, hypotheses, and variables of interest, however, is inevitably tied to his or her theoretical perspective, or beliefs regarding the essential nature of the phenomena of interest. Before we turn to a survey of methods and findings, the reader should be alerted to two rather different ways in which researchers have viewed internation influence. The first, which I shall call the *strategic* perspective, grows out of the tradition of political realism. The second, which I shall call the *psychological* perspective, has its roots in the laboratory experiments and theorizing of social psychologists.

REALISM AND CONFLICT STRATEGISTS

The realist tradition has roots that extend back to Thucydides, but it became the dominant approach among American students of international politics after World War II, particularly after the publication in 1948 of the first edition of Morgenthau's (1973) *Politics Among Nations*. The book's unifying theme is that international politics can be understood as the pursuit of interests defined in terms of power. Power, of course, is intimately tied to influence. As Singer (1963:420) later put it, "The concept does not come to life except as it is observed in action, and that action can be found only when national power is brought into play by nations engaged in the process of influencing one another." Singer defined power simply as "the capacity to influence."

Given the insecurity of states in an anarchic international system, realism views international politics as a continuing struggle for power. In a "world where power counts," the supreme virtue is prudence, that is, a rational calculation of the advantages of alternative courses of action (Morgenthau, [1948] 1973:27). Thus deciding when and how to attempt to influence a target state must be based, inter alia, on the power that the would-be influencer can bring to bear. On the other side of the coin, the target state's decision as to whether or not it should comply with an influence attempt assumes a calculation of the cost in power that comes with compliance, as opposed to the costs and risks of resistance. Ideally, these judgments should be purely rational calculations, free of any contaminating emotional influences, and "motivated by a conscious calculation of advantages, a calculation that in turn is based on an explicit and internally consistent value system" (Schelling, 1960:4).

Working from these assumptions, internation influence relationships can be viewed as games of strategy, where the objective of each player is to maximize its own interests. This has encouraged a number of social scientists, whom I shall label *conflict strategists* (Burns, 1961; Schelling, 1960, 1966; Kissinger, 1957; Kahn, 1960, 1965), to turn their attention to describing and prescribing successful influence techniques in internation conflicts, that is, to manipulative bargaining. Although the conflict strategists do not assume that the most appropriate influence techniques are always coercive, their work has tended to focus on problems of deterrence and conflict, where the prescribed influence technique is some variant of what Schelling (1960:69) has called the "exploitation of potential force." Given this orientation, the purpose appears consistent with that stated by one of its proponents (Burns, 1961:26): the development of "a pure theory of power politics."

PSYCHOLOGICAL PERSPECTIVE

The deductive rationality of the conflict strategists' game-theoretic models and their emphasis on coercive bargaining can be contrasted with the bargaining experiments undertaken by researchers working from a social psychological perspective. These theorists (Rapoport, 1960; Deutsch, 1973; Bartos, 1974; Esser and Komorita, 1975; Pruitt and Rubin, 1986) have focused their attention on the psychological influences that produce deviations from the calculating rationality posited by the conflict strategists. There is a shift in focus from strategy choices to psychologically generated responses. The variables of interest include a tendency to respond to threats in a belligerent manner, the role of considerations of pride and prestige, and norms of equity and reciprocity.

Theorists adopting a psychological perspective also are likely to have a different attitude toward the purpose of studying influence techniques. The purpose is not to discover how to "win," but to learn how to avoid the dangers of conflict escalation and to find the path to mutually satisfactory settlements. Some of their work, in fact, has taken direct aim at what they consider the limitations and weaknesses of the approach taken by conflict strategists.

The contrast between the strategic and psychological perspectives will not always be obvious when we consider the research findings reported in this chapter. Some researchers combine the two. Nevertheless, it is useful to bear in mind that where one looks has a lot to do with what is found.

Methodology

Given the problem of access in international relations research, all of the findings cited below require some degree of inference from a different context. Some require an inferential leap from the mathematical calculations of formal models; others assume an analogy between interpersonal bargaining experiments and the behavior of the decision-making bodies of great nations; even those that deal directly with data from real-world situations require us to assume that the future will resemble the past. The reader will have to make his or her own judgments regarding the appropriateness of the analogous situation, or the length of the inferential leap required, but a degree of caution is appropriate in drawing conclusions in all cases. One useful rule of thumb is suggested by common sense. One can have more confidence in findings when they are reported in more than one study and, particularly, when they are reported in studies using different research methods.

LEVELS OF ANALYSIS

Most of the discussion that follows will be directed toward influence at the dyadic level of analysis: the government of one state attempting to influence the behavior of the government of another. This simplifies a more complex reality in which influence relationships may be reciprocal and multiple. While A is attempting to influence B, B may be attempting to influence A; C may be attempting to influence A *and* B, and so on. By staying at the dyadic level, with occasional digressions to consider special cases, such as mediation by third parties or extended deterrence, we will be able to maintain our focus on influence techniques per se. A second simplification is that of referring to nations as if they were unitary actors. My intention is neither to anthropomorphize states, nor to ignore the complexities of reaching foreign policy decisions within national decision making bodies (see Holsti, 1989). But, as our concern is with research dealing with the choices of influence techniques that these bodies make, as opposed to how they reach them, reference to the actions of states serves as a convenient form of verbal shorthand.

The research methods from which the findings discussed in this chapter have been drawn can be divided into four of the categories discussed by Tetlock (1989) in the first volume of this series: qualitative case studies, formal models, laboratory experiments and simulations, and empirical studies employing quantitative data. A brief overview of each, along with some comments on its utility in studying internation influence, follows.

QUALITATIVE CASE STUDIES

The case study, a close examination of the available written evidence, sometimes buttressed by interviews with surviving participants, and informed by the insights of scholars well versed in the politics, cultures, and histories of the states being studied, remains one of the mainstays of international relations research. The methods employed in these studies range from richly detailed narrative accounts of a single episode to highly structured conceptual frameworks applied to multiple cases of a particular class, such as Snyder and Diesing's (1977) study of 13 twentieth-century crises.

As we shall see in the discussion of findings below, case studies have played a major role in developing theory—and in presenting challenges to untested theories—particularly in deterrence relationships. Moreover, as

Tetlock (1989:670–671) notes, case studies can complement quantitative studies by providing richer and more contextually detailed accounts of influence relationships that go well beyond a simple description of who is doing what to whom, where, when, and how. In fact, there seems to be an interesting relationship between qualitative case studies and the data based studies that will be discussed below. Quantitative studies of influence often build their hypothesis testing on the foundation of insights gained from qualitative cases studies. Then, when those findings have been published, successive qualitative case studies are likely to point out the limitations inherent in the lose of detail and nuance that occurs in any quantitative study.

Missing from qualitative case studies are the scientific attributes of random selection, operational definitions, and objective testing, which are assumed to be necessary to produce cumulative findings. The number of cases considered is usually quite small, and the selection of the sample may be biased according to the particular interests of the researcher. The intuitive and idiosyncratic nature of the enterprise can lead to doubts regarding the objectivity and generalizability of the researcher's findings in studies in which the methods employed in generating and analyzing data are neither replicable nor corrigible (see Tetlock, 1989:672–673).

FORMAL MODELING: GAME THEORY

The spare, mathematical, rational choice models of game theory are methodologically at the opposite pole from qualitative case studies.[1] The strengths of game theory lie in its parsimony, its mathematical elegance, and its logical rigor. Game theory has been widely used in the study of influence as a means of developing prescriptive theory. Schelling (1960) employed a game-theoretic approach to *Strategy of Conflict*, the single most influential work on influence techniques by a conflict strategist, and his chief critic, Rapoport (1964), based much of his criticism on what he saw as a misuse of the method.

Game theory provides a means of exploring the logical consequences of alternative choices by goal-oriented, rational players in games of strategy, that is, situations in which each player's best choice of actions (or strategies) is dependent on the moves of the other player. The approach, therefore, takes into account the interdependence of the two (or more) players, while offering a parsimonious way to consider the consequences of their moves. In normal form, the game appears as a payoff matrix of outcomes based on the intersection of the strategy choices of the two players, with the payoffs based on at least an ordinal ranking of each player's outcome preferences.

Classic game theory posits that the moves of the two players be made simultaneously. Thus early attempts to employ game theory as an empirical tool were based on observing the evolution of behavior over many successive plays of the game, with the players reevaluating their strategy choices after each play. "Prisoners' Dilemma" games have provided far and away the most common structure for these experiments (see Rapoport and Chammah, 1965; Axelrod, 1984). Prisoners' Dilemma, which models a game in which a mutually beneficial compromise may be avoided because of a structure that encourages mutual distrust and defection from cooperation, has been seen as analogous to internation influence situations ranging from immediate deterrence to arms reduction.

Game theory more closely models internation influence, however, when the game is played in a sequential manner. Brams and Wittman's (1981) "theory of moves" offers a particularly useful model of the dynamics of a sequential game. The game begins with the players simultaneously choosing an opening strategy, which determines the initial outcome. Each player then has an opportunity to depart from that outcome. If one player does, then the other player has the option of staying at the next outcome—and ending the game—or departing by changing its strategy. The players continue to move sequentially in a strictly alternating fashion until the player who has the next move decides to stay at a particular outcome. The dynamics of the sequential game are not unlike the action-response process that I described above. A second innovation, which has grown out of this approach, is to assume that the players make their strategy choices in a nonmyopic manner, that is, they are assumed to make their choices among strategies by looking several moves ahead, rather than solely at the payoff associated with the next outcome. This brings game-theoretic models even closer to real world bargaining, where policymakers choose influence strategies based on the likely behavior of the two sides over several action-response sequences.[2] The exploration of non-myopic sequential games has produced a number of interesting insights particularly in internation influence in deterrence and crises (see Brams, 1985; Zagare, 1987).

The most often cited limitations of game theory are a function of two of its strengths: its elegant simplicity and rationality. First, the decisionmaking of a large governmental organization, with complex and often ambiguous networks of influence within the organization, is a far cry from the usually strictly binary choices presented in game-theoretic models. Moreover, students of international relations see influence situations fraught with problems of ambiguous information, with judgments clouded by a poor understanding of national priorities and confounded by emotional reactions. The elegant formulations of game theory, it is argued, neglect the psychological dimension of politics.

LABORATORY EXPERIMENTS

The empirical findings of social psychologists have been derived primarily from controlled experiments employing human subjects in a wide variety of influence situations. Some of this work has utilized game-theoretic models, most particularly prisoners' Dilemma (see, for example, Rapoport and Chammah, 1965), with human subjects playing the game against each other or against a "stooge" in the form of a computer. These techniques allow the researcher to isolate variables of interest and to measure their effects under controlled conditions.

Since internation influence is pursued between governments composed of human beings, it can be argued that the same psychological variables that affect humans in interpersonal experiments will be present in interactions between nations. It is argued (see Jervis, 1976) that those perceptual and psychological factors that can confound rational decision making at the interpersonal level are more potent at the international level, where the ambiguity of the available information, stressful situations, and political pressures to adopt belligerent postures are likely to intensify their effects. Thus, it is not surprising that social psychologists were among the first to point out the dark side to the prescriptions of the conflict strategists, in particular the tendency for coercive influence strategies to cause conflicts to spiral out of control.

Nonetheless, there is an enormous difference between a controlled experiment involving graduate students playing games where the stakes amount to a few dollars and the foreign policy decisions of experienced statesmen contending with problems that may affect the survival of their nations. Moreover, the very presence of laboratory controls over which variables come into play, which is one of the great advantages of controlled experiments, creates a situation in which it is hard to draw analogies to international politics. And, as Tetlock points out, "although it is easy to point out ways in which laboratory experiments differ from the 'real thing,' it is much more difficult to specify when the differences make a difference" (1989:663). It also is difficult to gauge the relative potency of psychological variables isolated in controlled experiments when the findings are applied to more "contaminated" real-world situations involving many players within the decision-making organization as well as without.

In sum, the findings from laboratory experiments allow for the testing of psychological variables that are often missing from the scenarios and game-theoretic formulations of the conflict strategists and formal modelers. As we shall see below, they have raised important questions about the validity of the descriptive and prescriptive propositions emerging from studies assuming goal-oriented rational decision making, while adding important new propositions emerging out of the psychological dimension of influence. On the other hand, the analogy between a laboratory experiment and the actions and interactions of nations requires a considerable inferential leap.

QUANTITATIVE STUDIES OF HISTORICAL DATA

After reviewing the extant research on the subject in his seminal article on internation influence, and noting some of the limitations associated with the methods mentioned above, Singer (1963:426) advocated employing "ex-post-facto experiments" using quantitative data generated from a sample of past internation influence situations in the real world. Such studies would provide a test of the extent to which the propositions and findings derived from the methods above can be confirmed by the behavior of real-world governments engaged in the process of influencing each other. To his credit, Singer took his own advice and began work on generating data for the Correlates of War Project, which has grown into the largest data-based study of the causes, conditions, and consequences of war in the modern state system. The theoretical orientation among political scientists applying these methods has, by and large, reflected Singer's view that it would be impossible to reach any closure on the relative validity of the competing propositions of the strategic and psychological views until operational means were developed to test the propositions against the behavior of nations engaged in influencing each other in the real world.

Data-based historical research on influence per se began in earnest in the 1960s with content analysis of the pre–World War I crisis. Robert North and his Stanford associates (North, Holsti, and Brody, 1964) applied a perception-mediated action-response model to the stream of intergovernmental communications between the Triple Entente and the Dual Alliance, which led to confirmation of the role of psychological and perceptual variables—particularly perceptions of hostility—in that crisis. Following on the heels of the North study, a number of new schemes were developed to code, classify, and analyze internation behavior.

The method, which has been labeled "events data research," consists of extracting descriptions of international events—the date, actor, target, location, and description of the action taken—from written records in the press and historical sources. These are then converted into chronologies and coded into machine-readable form for aggregate analyses along dimensions of interest, such as the escalation or deescalation of hostile actions by a particular pair of states over time. The most ambitious of the early events data projects was McClelland's (1968) World Event/Interaction Survey (WEIS), which began a day-to-day coding of all internation actions of sufficient salience to be reported by the *New York Times*. This writer's own research, the Behavioral Correlates of War project (BCOW), is a later-generation events data scheme designed to code events in historical internation crises, using a variety of sources, and in a manner that allows for a detailed examination of the internation influence process. Thus, besides offering the advantages of replicability and corrigibility that can be obtained only with operational research methods, by dealing with large samples of real-world action, events data are particularly useful in studying internation influence. The technique provides a means of mapping time series of patterns of escalation and deescalation in the level of hostility/cooperation in internation interactions, and, in the more detailed data sets, such as BCOW, of analyzing action-response models of internation influence.

The method, however, is not without its critics. First, there is the epistemological issue involved in drawing a connection between events as they are reported—and available to the researcher—and the interpretation of the events by the actual participants. One argument is that to extract actions from their historical-perceptual contexts deprives them of their substantive significance (Alker, 1987). A more common criticism is that generating data from the written record of verbal communications and forcing each "speech act" into a preset category misses the subtle nuances that are a critical component of influence attempts in internation communications.

By working with real-world events, events data researchers avoid the inferential leap between radically different environments required in applying the findings of game theory or the laboratory experiments of social psychologists, and the use of operational methods avoids the inherent subjectivity associated with qualitative case studies. Nevertheless, events data researchers cannot entirely escape the problem of establishing causality that bedevils the other approaches. Influence attempt–response models based solely on the actions of the participants, along with operationally measured contextual variables, raise the question of just which of the would-be influencer's actions, if any, has triggered a particular response from the influencee. As in any statistical research, the findings can tell us far more about central tendencies, that is, what patterns are likely to obtain over the long run, than about how a particular state will respond in a particular circumstance. In this respect, the problem is the opposite of that of qualitative case studies, where one can encounter questionable generalizations from a small set of cases. Interestingly, some convergence has been found (Leng and Walker, 1982) between the operational classification of influence strategies based on an action-response model using events data (Leng and Wheeler, 1979) and those obtained in Snyder and Diesing's (1977) qualitative comparative case study.

CONCLUDING COMMENTS

This review of the methods employed in generating the findings that are discussed in the remainder of this chapter has been intended to serve two purposes. The first has been to acquaint the reader with those aspects of the methods that make them applicable to the study of internation influence. The second has been to place them in perspective, both with regard to their relation to the strategic and psychological theoretical orientations described earlier, and with regard to the limitations inherent in the research method itself. As we consider the extant findings from contemporary research on internation influence, it is important to remember that their significance is always a function of how they were obtained.

Influence Techniques

Our survey of the substantive findings on internation influence begins with those influence techniques most frequently identified with integrative bargaining and then moves to progressively more contentious influence techniques.

Diplomacy

The traditional view of diplomacy is that of statesmen meeting to resolve their differences through negotiation, that is, through the presentation of proposals put forward ostensibly for the purpose of reaching agreement (Ikle, 1964:3). Internation negotiation frequently is more contentious than that characterization implies, but whatever the mix of conflict and cooperation, each party is attempting to influence the choices and actions of the other. Negotiation, like all internation relations, is ultimately a game of influence. But this does not mean that the techniques of influence are inherently coercive. In the many situations in which there is a convergence of interests, influence is more often a function of the classic diplomatic skills of ingratiation, compromise, and trustworthiness, as well as expertise in the question at hand. Bearing this in mind, we will begin our survey of findings on influence techniques with a look at preparatory techniques, techniques of persuasion, and positive inducements employed in negotiation.[3]

PREPARATORY TECHNIQUES

The influence process begins well before any formal negotiation, with much of it designed to structure the perceptions and attitudes of the other side. This may involve changing the structure of the situation, such as the dispatch of the battleship *Maine* for shore leave in Havana in January 1898, or the flurry of fighting just before a planned cease-fire in any war. But there are more subtle influence approaches as well. *Ingratiation* is a well-established practice preparatory to negotiation. Consider de Callieres' advice to the sixteenth-century diplomat: "an address always open, genial, civil, agreeable, with easy and ingratiating manners which assist largely in making a favorable impression upon those around him—these are the indispensable adjuncts to a negotiator's position" ([1716]1963:19). Of course, de Callieres also speaks of the overriding importance of those less contrived qualities that allow one to attain influence in any setting, such as a reputation for honesty, integrity, fairness, intelligence, and expertise. But, while these personal qualities can be viewed as capabilities that contribute to the diplomat's influence, they are not influence *techniques* that one may or may not employ in a given situation.

The techniques of ingratiation, which include the use of flattery, demonstrating opinion conformity, and granting favors (or bribes), continue to be considered a useful adjunct to efforts at persuasion. The little empirical research that has been done on the relative effectiveness of techniques of ingratiation has been undertaken by social psychologists (see Jones and Wortman, 1973), with the results suggesting, not surprisingly, that its effectiveness is dependent on avoiding the impression of having ulterior motives.

Ingratiation's opposite is *feather ruffling*, inducing a state of upset or discomfort that lowers the other party's resistance to yielding in the face of coercive influence tactics (see Pruitt and Rubin, 1986:47–49). The technique is most often employed in highly contentious bargaining, particularly in confrontations between radical revisionary and status quo powers, such as in Hitler's infamous 1938 bullying interview with Austria's Chancellor Schuschnigg at Berchtesgaden, or the tactics of the North Vietnamese in the early stages of the U.S.–Vietnam negotiations in Paris. Rather than to gain the confidence of the other side, the purpose is to confuse, distract, or even intimidate it. While there has been no systematic research on the relative effectiveness of the tactic,[4] it clearly runs the risk of causing the other party to break off the negotiations, particularly if it becomes aware of the intentions of the feather ruffler.

PERSUASION

Preparatory tactics are preludes to the main purpose of diplomacy: to persuade the other side through argument. The effectiveness of argument alone as an influence technique is dependent on achieving an atmosphere of mutual trust and understanding, so that it is understandably most appropriate for those negotiations in which there is a convergence of interests, or for that stage of negotiations when the parties are moving toward an integrative solution. Effective argument is frequently dependent on the other party's image of the quality of the party making the argument, particularly his or her expertise and trustworthiness. The first is particularly important in negotiations involving complex technical questions; the second becomes essential in negotiations involving security issues. Social psychologists have been particularly interested in investigating the latter, largely because of the difficulties associated with moving from an atmosphere of mutual distrust to an integrative settlement.

In describing the techniques for achieving the proper atmosphere in what he characterizes as a "debate," Rapoport (1960:285–288) borrows from Rogerian psychology to enumerate three steps in reducing distrust and the perception of threat: (1) effectively convey to the opponent that you understand his or her position, (2) communicate an understanding of those areas in which his or her position has some validity, and (3) demonstrate empathy. Kissinger's efforts in the Egyptian-Israeli disengagement accords of 1974 appear to be a good example of how a mediator can assist the parties in accomplishing the three steps suggested by Rapoport. Carter was less successful in that respect during the Camp David negotiations of 1978, but, as I shall point out below, he was able to employ other influence techniques to present a convincing argument that it was in the interests of each party to lower its aspirations to obtain an agreement.

PROPAGANDA AND INFORMAL TECHNIQUES OF PERSUASION

Outside of diplomacy per se, there are a large number of ways in which nations attempt to influence the attitudes of other governments and, more often, their citizens through persuasion. The most obvious of these is through propaganda: communication intended to influence the attitudes, opinions, and/or behavior of the population of another government. The specific purposes of propaganda can range from simply attempting to create a favorable atmosphere for diplomacy to inciting the population to revolt. The same wide range can been seen in the techniques, which range from "information services" providing news broadcasts with editorial opinion slanted to place the provider in a good light, such as the Voice of America, to virulent namecalling and the fabrication of stories designed to place the adversary in a bad light, as in the case of Hitler's campaign against Czechoslovakia in 1938. Research on the effects of propaganda efforts directed from one nation to the population of another has been inconclusive (see Davison, 1972:chap. 3); however, it is generally believed that it is most effective when directed at groups who share the same attitudes, such as a particular religious minority, and who already partially share the attitudes of the communicator (Holsti, 1983:196–200). This appears to be a subject that has been neglected by social scientists in recent years, with most of the extant research on the techniques and effects of propaganda published in the 1960s and early 1970s (Qualter, 1962; Martin, 1971; Davison, 1972).

The relative effectiveness of other forms of "public diplomacy," such as cultural and academic exchanges, the promotion of tourism, and conferences or seminars aimed at elites, is even harder to gauge, although the consensus view is that they encourage understanding and moderation. What is clear, however, is that, with the recent changes in the Soviet Union and Eastern Europe, there has been a virtual explosion in activities of this sort.

POSITIVE INFLUENCE TECHNIQUES

Of course, persuasion alone is rarely sufficient to influence diplomats with national interests at stake. The Middle East mediation efforts of neither Kissinger nor Carter were able to move the parties to agreement on the basis of argument alone. Both ultimately were forced to employ "heavier" bargaining tactics, in particular, American *promises* to monitor the agreements and provide material rewards to the negotiating parties.

Promises can be defined as actual or promised improvements in B's values relative to its expectations at the time of A's influence attempt (Baldwin, 1974:23). If A has led B to expect a strong negative sanction and then, in return for some desired behavior from B, offers to remove part of that sanction, the latter move qualifies as a positive inducement.

There are some significant advantages to the use of positive influence techniques (promises and rewards) over their negative counterparts (threats and punishments). For one thing, it is easier to back up an argument for the legitimacy of one's demands with promises than with threats. But perhaps the most important advantage of promises over threats lies in the positive effect that the inducement has on the attitude of the influencee toward the influencer. Experiments by social psychologists have shown that promises tend to beget promises, just as threats beget threats (Wall, 1977). And positive influence attempts are likely to produce positive—as opposed to negative—"spill-over" effects in other areas as well (Baldwin, 1974).

On the other hand, there are disadvantages to employing positive influence techniques. First, there is the nature of the technique itself. Success, in the form of compliance by the influencee, carries with it the cost of supplying the promised reward. As the United States has learned in the Middle East, and the Soviet Union has learned in Cuba, providing rewards can get expensive. Moreover, as promises are fulfilled, they may become less effective in the future. Although the credibility of the trustworthiness of the influencer increases, the influencee may become satiated. If he does not, he may be encouraged to demonstrate greater obstinacy in the future to obtain ever greater rewards for compliance.

As Pruitt and Rubin (1986:55) point out, determining how much to promise is a subtle and difficult undertaking. If too little is promised, it can be viewed as an insult; if too much is promised, it may be viewed as a bribe. There is also the danger of creating undesired dependency relationships. Galtung (1967), in fact, has suggested that the habitual use of positive inducements carries a greater risk of blackmail than the use of negative inducements. This is the situation that faced the United States in dealing with its South Vietnamese allies when the Americans decided that they were ready to sign a peace treaty with North Vietnam in the fall of 1972. South Vietnamese President Thieu threatened to complain publicly that the United States was "selling out" a government whose survival had become dependent on American military assistance.

Given the orientation of realists and conflict strategists mentioned above, it is not surprising that positive influence techniques have received far less attention from students of international politics than the use of negative influence techniques (see Baldwin, 1974:18–23). Consequently, suggestions regarding the effective use of positive influence techniques in internation relations must be based on inferences drawn from the interpersonal experiments of social psychologists. Interestingly, most of the findings suggest that *positive* inducements are most effective when the influencer has the requisites for the effective use of *negative* inducements as well: high threat capacity (Lindskold and Bennett, 1973), the backing of a tough constituency (Wall, 1977), and a reputation for being an unyielding bargainer in the past (Deutsch, 1973; Komorita and Esser, 1975; McGillicuddy, Pruitt, and Syna, 1984). Of course, it also helps to have a reputation for honoring one's commitments (Lindskold et al., 1972).

SELF-BINDING COMMITMENTS

An interesting variant of the promise is the positive self-binding commitment, that is, when the influencer commits him- or herself to carrying out a course of action beneficial to the target, regardless of what others do. When such commitments can be made credible, such as through a highly visible public announcement, they provide a means of engendering greater trust on the part of the target so that the two parties can move toward a mutually advantageous agreement.

A dramatic example of an effective self-binding commitment occurred when Egypt's Anwar Sadat announced his offer, in November 1977, to travel to Jerusalem to speak to the Israeli Knesset in order to remove the critical impediment (Egyptian nonrecognition) to beginning negotiations leading to the withdrawal of Israeli troops from the Sinai. Using that event as a prime example, Maoz and Felsenthal (1987) employ game theory to analyze the logic of situations in which self-binding commitments may represent the best bargaining strategy. The authors identify these as situations in which the status quo is harmful to both sides, but not the worst outcome for either, while mutual cooperation is the best outcome for the target (Israel) and the second best outcome for the influencer (Egypt). The worst outcome for either party occurs if it makes a cooperative move and the other side continues the non-cooperative status quo (Israeli troops withdraw, but Egypt withholds recognition, or vice versa). Since mutual cooperation gives the target (Israel) its most preferred outcome, the only reason, albeit a dominant one in the logic of game theory, for it to choose a noncooperative strategy is the fear of receiving its worst outcome. This is a very real fear for the target (Israel) because the influencer's (Egypt's) best outcome would obtain if it defected while the target cooperated. To get around this, the influencer makes a self-binding commitment to pursue a cooperative strategy by eliminating the noncooperative strategy as an option. This is what Sadat did when he unilaterally agreed to de facto recognition of Israel. Once this happens, the target (Israel) has no reason to choose a noncooperative strategy since mutual cooperation provides its best outcome. For such strategies to be effective, Maoz and Felsenthal (1987) argue that the influencer must have a good sense of the target's priorities, must convince the target that the commitment is a true change in strategy, and must make the self-binding commitment to the new strategy credible.

To sum up, the findings with regard to the use of positive inducements as influence techniques indicate that they offer important advantages in their effects on the attitude of the influencee. This is essential to any attempt to achieve an integrative solution to the problem at issue. The use of positive inducements can have disadvantages as well, however, most notably in the cost of carrying out promised rewards and the danger of creating undesired dependency relationships. This suggests that the most useful positive inducements are those cooperative initiatives that benefit both parties, as opposed to those that are carrots employed to induce the other side to accept an outcome favoring the inducer.

As to when positive inducements are most likely to be effective, findings from interpersonal bargaining experiments suggest that the reputation of the influencer, particularly with regard to firmness and reliability, is an important factor. We shall return to the question of the effectiveness of promises in comparison with threats after a consideration of threats and punishments per se.

Coercive Influence Techniques

Some degree of coercion is present in any social order in which there are sanctions prescribed for violations of group norms. Within states, the legal authority to carry out sanctions is vested in a central government and its executive organs. Thus threats are always present, even in open societies, where they may remain all but invisible for most citizens most of the time. In the international system, there is neither a central authority to maintain order nor a strong sense of citizenship that places concern for the order of the international community over the free pursuit of interests by its members. Thus individual states must resort to coercive means of self-help when the techniques of peaceful settlement fail. For these reasons, the overt use of threats and punishments is a common feature of internation influence.

The first part of this section begins by considering the character of threats and punishments and their advantages and disadvantages as influence techniques. Then it turns to a comparison of their relative effectiveness with that of positive and carrot-and-stick inducements. The second part focuses on the overall *influence strategies* employed in internation disputes, with particular reference to crisis bargaining and deterrence.

NEGATIVE INFLUENCE TECHNIQUES

Although the use of threats and punishments occurs in virtually all bargaining situations, coercive influence techniques are most prevalent in disputes in which the influencer sees little potential for peaceful settlement through integrative bargaining. Often, these are cases involving some degree of rivalry or antagonism between the parties, where the stakes and aspirations of both parties are high, and the influencer assumes that his resolve—his willingness to accept the risks of escalating conflict—is higher than that of the influencee.

The use of threats offers several advantages to the influencer. The most notable is that they require no tangible costs if the target complies. The use of threats also is consistent with the sense of aggrieved justice that often accompanies serious internation conflicts. Moreover, findings from recent research in social psychology indicate that threats are very effective in inducing compliance with influence attempts (see Pruitt and Rubin, 1986:55). Whether those conclusions can be extended to internation influence, however, is debatable, as we shall see in the discussion that follows.

There are two serious drawbacks to the use of threats. One is that they weaken the relationship between the threatener and the target actor by increasing the degree of distrust, suspicion, and hostility (Deutsch and Krauss, 1960). The other is that threats promote counterthreats and conflict escalation, particularly when the adversaries are both highly motivated (Rapoport, 1960) or relatively evenly matched in power (Leng, 1980). In fact, there is a tension between the potential immediate effectiveness of threats, particularly highly credible severe threats, such as the threat to use force, and their longer-term effects. It has been hypothesized that coercive tactics produce "residues" in the form of changes in the attitudes of the parties—and their constituencies—

that encourage the use of more coercive tactics at an equal or more escalated level of conflict and impair efforts at conflict resolution. Pruitt and Rubin (1986) refer to this as the *structural change* model of escalation. In fact, small-group bargaining studies by Deutsch and Krauss (1960) have found a negative association between the use of threats and conflict resolution.

The more common view of escalation among students of international politics is that of a *conflict spiral*. Escalation is seen as the consequence of spiraling sequences of action and reaction, or threats and counterthreats, by two determined adversaries. Whether the reactions are prompted by a desire to retaliate, or out of concern for security—to avoid the risk of appearing irresolute—the hypothesized consequences are the same.

The outbreak of World War I frequently is cited as the prototypical international example of a conflict spiral. Richardson's (1960) exponential model of the arms race preceding the war has been generalized by others (Rapoport, 1960; Pruitt, 1965) to the escalation of a prewar crisis. In their pioneering quantitative study of prewar diplomatic communications and military actions, North, Holsti, and Brody (1964) found a positive association between perceptions of hostility and the presence of a conflict spiral in the pre–World War I crisis. Using events data to analyze a sample of 30 militarized crises occurring between 1816 and 1970, Gochman and Leng (1983) found a positive association between the use of physical threats of force and crisis escalation. Leng (1980) also has found a positive association between the use of threats of force and defiant responses in internation crises when the influencer and influencee are evenly matched in military capability. That study also found a positive association between defiant responses to threats and the outbreak of war. The findings from the last two studies indicate, not surprisingly, that the effect of the type of threat is closely tied to its severity. More severe threats tend to yield more extreme responses—either outright compliance or defiance.

CREDIBILITY OF THREATS

Singer's (1963) model of internation influence posits that the influencee's decisional calculus has two dimensions: the utility or disutility of the inducement relative to the cost of compliance, and the probability that the threatened action will be carried out. Schelling's (1960, 1966) work has been particularly influential in placing considerations of *credibility* at the center of research on conflict bargaining. Schelling has argued that the credibility of inducements is a function of the influencer's reputation and its commitment to act.

Leng's (1980) quantitative study of influence tactics in 14 crises found, in fact, that there was a positive association between the specificity of the influencer's stated commitment to carry out a threat, and compliance by the influencee. These findings are consistent with Schelling's (1966) hypothesis, but another intriguing explanation is suggested from an interpersonal bargaining perspective. Lewicki and Rubin (1973) hypothesize that the greater the amount of information conveyed by a threat (or promise), the greater the probability that the target will view the influencer as powerful and in control of the situation. Viewed from this perspective, specificity becomes linked to perceptions of capability as well as credibility.

There are, however, some interesting exceptions to the general findings concerning the greater effectiveness of more credible inducements. Based on their case studies of disputes in which the United States was involved, George and Smoke (1974:chap. 17) note that even a highly specific threat may be circumvented, without a direct challenge, by a creative response. The Western airlift in response to the Berlin blockade of 1948–1949 is a good example of such a circumventing tactic.

Perhaps more important, there is evidence that, in crises between *evenly matched adversaries*, as threats become more specific, they are more likely to be associated with defiant responses. Leng (1984) found that in the three major postwar U.S.–Soviet crises, less specific threats, or warnings, were more likely to produce positive responses than their more specific, more severe counterparts. This is not surprising when one considers the domestic political costs and reputational costs—particularly with regard to one's reputation for resolve—that accrue when one complies with an explicit threat from a status equal.

IRREVOCABLE COMMITMENTS

If the credibility of a threat is dependent on the threatener's commitment to carry it out, the most credible threat occurs when the influencer creates a situation in which he no longer has the option of withdrawing the threatened punishment should the other party not comply. He is, to use Schelling's (1966:43) metaphor, burning his bridges before him. This can be done through a physical action, such as indicating a determination to defend certain ground by placing defending troops in a position where they cannot be evacuated under fire, as when Chiang Kai-shek stationed a large portion of his best troops on the island of Quemoy in the 1950s to discourage a mainland Chinese attack and encourage U.S. backing if they did attack (Schelling, 1966:44). A more common approach is to employ a strong, albeit not truly irrevocable, public commitment that creates disastrous political costs to the threatener should he retreat from it, such as President Kennedy's televised address at the outset of the Cuban missile crisis. Besides nailing down the credibility of the threat, the strong commitment offers the added advantage of shifting the initiative, including the responsibility for the consequences of the threatened action, to the other party.

In their comparative study of 13 interstate crises, Snyder and Diesing (1977:227–230) find only 4 clear examples of physical irrevocable commitments. Interestingly, all 4 were either by the Soviet Union or the United States.[5] The authors note that it is *difficult* to create a situation in which withdrawal is physically not possible. In their view, the key to the successful use of threats at least bordering on irrevocable commitments lies in engaging substantial additional political values that would be lost in any retreat, such as Kennedy's public commitment during the Cuban missile crisis.

NONVIOLENT ACTION

Nonviolent action, or nonviolent resistance, is a special case of the irrevocable commitment. The resister, in effect, tells the oppressive institution or group: "Under no circumstances will I deviate from what I am doing or have done." As an influence technique, it has been used primarily by out-groups against governments, not in relations between states. Nevertheless, given the increasing importance of subnational and transnational groups in the international community, and the successful recent uses of the technique in the Philippines and Poland, it would be a mistake to overlook the use of nonviolent action in any comparative consideration of influence techniques.

According to Sharp (1973:4), nonviolent action is based on the assumption that the exercise of power depends on the consent of the ruled, who, by withdrawing that consent, can control and even destroy the power of their opponent. The technique includes the refusal to perform certain acts as expected by custom, law, or authority (acts of omission), or the performance of acts *not* expected by custom or forbidden by law or regulation (acts of commission), or some combination of the two. Sharp (1973) has identified more than 200 techniques of nonviolent action, which he has divided into three major categories: nonviolent protest, noncooperation, and nonviolent intervention. Nonviolent protest consists of essentially symbolic acts—protest marches, public assemblies, or fasts—designed to produce an awareness of dissent. Noncooperation consists of actions designed to withhold support—strikes, consumer boycotts, withdrawal from all voluntary social activities—and thereby to cripple the operation and efficiency of the system. Nonviolent intervention offers the most direct challenge to authority, and the greatest risk to participants—outright defiance of government regulations, such as sit-ins, or activities to block military actions.

As in all influence attempts, the most appropriate technique depends on the situation, including the political and social culture, the degree of repression, the opponent's dependency on the cooperation of the general population, the resources available to the opponent, and, not the least, the opponent's ruthlessness (Sharp, 1973). With regard to the last point, it has been argued that nonviolent action could be an effective technique only when used against humane democratic regimes, that totalitarian regimes would resort to a level of terrorism that would crush any nonviolent resistance. With the recent events in the Philippines, Poland, and China, one would have to qualify any judgment on that issue. The Polish case, which met with an initial setback with the institution of martial law and then achieved a remarkable success in 1989, represents a very interesting approach to nonviolent action. In the words of Solidarity writer Adam Michnik, the Solidarity resisters decided to "live as if they were free," to ignore the "expected" restraints of totalitarianism—to build an open, free, and humane society from the grass roots (Schell, 1986). The tragedy of the Chinese students at Tiananmen Square, on the other hand, represents the dark possibilities of repression in a drama that has not yet been played out.

Unfortunately, although the applications and techniques of nonviolent action have been described and classified by a small number of scholars and activists (see Sharp, 1973, 1980; Boserup and Mack, 1975; Charney, 1978), nonviolent action has not received the attention it deserves from behavioral scientists. The technique, however, is likely to receive more attention in the future given the remarkable events of the past few years.

DETERRENT AND COMPELLENT THREATS

A useful distinction is made between *compellent* threats, which are intended to influence the other party to take some action (or to stop some action already under way), and *deterrent* threats, which are intended to keep the other party from starting (or stopping) some action (Schelling, 1966:59–60). The usual assumption is that it is easier to achieve compliance with the latter (Schelling, 1966:100). One argument in support of this view is that deterrent threats offer the advantage of passing the initiative—and responsibility—for conflict escalation to the other party; another is that the cost of compliance, in terms of one's reputation, is lower in the case of deterrent threats because there is no visible change in the influencee's behavior. Thus, it is argued, compliance is easier and defiance is riskier in the case of deterrent threats.

There is some empirical evidence to suggest, in fact, that compellent threats are more likely to be associated with crises escalating to war, although those findings should be tempered by recent evidence suggesting a connection between the *selection* of compellent threats and crises in which both parties expect the costs of war to be relatively low (Peterson, 1986). That is, states are more likely to issue compellent threats of force when they expect the costs of war to be relatively low. This is not surprising; however, Peterson (1986:282–286) also found that deterrent threats of force were more effective than compellent threats of force *only* when both parties expected the costs of war to be relatively low. That does not fit the conventional wisdom.

COMPARING THREATS AND PROMISES

While political scientists have focused most of their attention on the use of negative influence attempts, social psychologists have devoted considerable attention to the comparative effectiveness of threats and promises. This is a tricky question on which to reach any general findings for several reasons. First, the effectiveness of one type of influence technique or another is contextually dependent. One would have different expectations of the effects of threats between, say, a prison warden and an inmate as opposed to a normally congenial husband and wife. Second, there are confounding effects resulting from random behavior patterns and the choices of inducements. For example, when rewards and punishments are mixed, as they usually are, there is a tendency to use rewards following desirable behavior and a tendency to use threats when behavior is undesirable. If the influencee's behavior is fluctuating randomly over time, undesirable behavior is likely to improve somewhat and desirable behavior is likely to regress somewhat. Thus, the random fluctuation alone would encourage the observer to conclude that threats work more effectively than promises (see Kahneman and Tversky, 1973). In fact, one of the more suggestive findings from experiments by social psychologists is that while punishment is generally less effective than reward (Walters and Grusec, 1977), public beliefs tend to be the opposite, even following experiments in which the participants make the judgment (Kahneman and Tversky, 1973; Schaffner, 1985).

Baldwin (1974:30–31) notes a third confounding factor that can cause observers to overestimate the role of threats in internation conflict. Successful promises are visible because of the accompanying reward; unsuccessful threats are visible because of the accompanying punishment. But when threats succeed, or when promises fail, observers may be unaware that they have been used. As conflicts worsen, nations are less likely to comply with *any* influence attempts; hence, the casual observer will be most aware of unsuccessful threats because of their visibility. This may account for the widespread, but incorrect, view that when they are involved in serious conflicts, nations rely almost exclusively on coercive influence techniques. In fact, the mix of threats and promises is fairly even (see Leng, 1980). Findings such as this are particularly interesting in light of the enduring appeal of realpolitik assumptions about influence in relations among nations.

Bearing these points in mind, experimental research by social psychologists (Pruitt and Rubin, 1986:55) and events data studies of international crises (Leng, 1980) indicate that, on the whole, threats are more effective than promises in motivating the other party to comply—at least in the short run. On the other hand, threats are more likely to be associated with defiant responses and conflict escalation.

CARROT-AND-STICK INFLUENCE TECHNIQUES

It is not uncommon for governments to combine threats and promises in the same influence attempt. Leng's (1980) study of 14 internation crises found that carrot-and-stick influence techniques, which combine positive and negative inducements, were used with roughly the same frequency as either threats or promises. There is a commonsensical logic in this approach. As Snyder and Diesing put it: "a leavening of accommodative tactics in a primarily coercive strategy may minimize the risks of war, and some coercion in a dominantly accommodative strategy may reduce one's own sacrifices (or increase one's gains) in the search for a settlement" (1977:255). Adding an accommodative promise to a threat reduces the provocative nature of the threat while providing a face-saving concession for the other party. By the same token, accompanying a concession with a demonstration of firmness in the form of a threat may enable the conceding party to avoid appearing weak. Kissinger (1982:595) put it well when he described the U.S. approach to downplaying the significance of the Soviet retreat in the face of U.S. pressure in the "alert crisis" of 1973: "Many wars have started because no line of retreat was left open. Superpowers have a special obligation not to humiliate each other." Snyder and Diesing (1977:491) note that, in the sample of crises they examined, when one side yielded to the other, its adversary almost always offered a face-saving concession.

This logic has been borne out in Leng's (1980) study, as well as in a later study of three post–World War II Soviet-American crises (Leng, 1984). In both of these events data studies, carrot-and-stick inducements were found to be more effective than either threats or promises in eliciting accommodative responses, as well as less likely to incur the defiant responses associated with threats. Even in the highly charged atmosphere of the Cuban missile crisis, the U.S. ultimatum of October 27, 1962, was coupled with promises to refrain from any further invasion of Cuba and to remove its missiles from Turkey.

Influence Strategies

The particular types of inducements that accompany demands in the course of a dispute are components of a state's overall influence strategy, that is, its plan of action to condition the target to behave in the manner desired by the influencer. Leng and Wheeler (1979) distinguish among four basic types of influence strategies: *bullying, reciprocating, appeasing, and trial-and-error*. The most interesting findings have been associated with the first two influence strategy types: bullying and reciprocating. A bullying strategy is based on escalating negative inducements. Responses short of compliance are met with more severe threats or punishments on each successive influence attempt until the target has been induced to comply. A reciprocating, or "firm-but-fair" (Esser and Komorita, 1975), bargaining strategy combines tit-for-tat responses to both threats and promises, along with cooperative initiatives. Cooperative initiatives that are not reciprocated, however, are followed by immediate tit-for-tat responses.[6]

BULLYING INFLUENCE STRATEGIES

From the perspective of realists and conflict strategists, as well as some of the experimental findings related to the relative effectiveness of threats vis-à-vis promises, one would expect bullying strategies to be comparatively successful. A strong demonstration of resolve, coupled with inducements designed to raise the costs and risks of noncompliance, according to this perspective, is the best way to lower the opponent's level of aspiration. Some empirical support for this view has been found in interpersonal bargaining experiments (Bartos, 1970; Yukl, 1974). On the other hand, Brehm's (1960) "reactance theory" suggests that when an individual's, or group's, behavioral freedom is threatened, psychological reactance is aroused, creating a motivational state directed toward restoring the threatened freedom. Findings from experiments by Worchal and Brehm (1971) support the reactance hypothesis. Related to this is the observed tendency of conflicts to spiral out of control when relatively equally motivated adversaries are each intent on effectively employing bullying influence strategies.

The high stakes and risks associated with bargaining in internation disputes add another problematic dimension to the use of bullying tactics. While the stakes are often high enough to justify coercive tactics that might be deemed unacceptable in other situations, the risks of conflict escalation are also more serious. The risks are particularly acute in militarized crises where the threat of war—sometimes nuclear war—is present. Kahn (1965:3) refers to coercive bargaining in such cases as a "competition in risk-taking or . . . resolve." Each side attempts to influence the other by calculated increases in the level of conflict. To the extent that the escalation is controlled, it is through fear of the opponent's overreaction. Much of the literature of conflict strategists (Schelling, 1960, 1966; Kahn, 1965) deals with the "manipulation of risk" through controlled escalation.

In a comparative qualitative study of three conflicts involving the United States in the 1960s—Laos, Cuba, and Vietnam—George, Hall, and Simons

(1971) explored the tension between the effective use of an escalating coercive influence strategy and the avoidance of war. The authors suggested eight conditions for the successful use of coercive influence tactics: strong motivation on the part of the influencer, an asymmetry in motivation favoring the influencer, clarity of objectives, a sense of urgency, strong domestic support, usable military options, fear of escalation on the part of the opponent, and clarity concerning the terms of a settlement. Given these requirements, it is not surprising that, among the four basic influence types considered in the Leng-Wheeler (1979) study, bullying strategies were most often associated with crises escalating to war.

RECIPROCATING AND TIT-FOR-TAT STRATEGIES

The logic behind a reciprocating influence strategy, which combines tit-for-tat with occasional accommodative initiatives, is that the influencer demonstrates resolve and firmness in the face of attempts at coercion by the other party, while indicating a willingness to move to a cooperative settlement of the dispute. Tit-for-tat in its purest form requires an accommodative opening move, which is thereafter followed by strictly tit-for-tat responses to the other party's actions and reactions. Evidence of the effectiveness of tit-for-tat influence strategies began to appear in interpersonal bargaining experiments conducted by social psychologists in the 1960s and 1970s (Chertkoff and Conley, 1967; Esser and Komorita, 1975), but it received its greatest attention following a computer tournament conducted by Axelrod (1984) at the beginning of this decade.

Axelrod's (1984) tournament challenged the competitors to devise programs for the most effective overall play of Prisoners' Dilemma, a two-by-two (cooperate or defect) game[7] notorious for encouraging each player to adopt a strategy of defect, even though each would be better off if *both* choose to cooperate. Each contestant submitted a computer program containing his or her strategy, which competed for an extended series of plays of the simultaneous-move game against each of the other strategies submitted. The winning entry—a cooperative opening move followed by tit-for-tat—was submitted by Rapoport. The tit-for-tat strategy was particularly effective in eliciting cooperation from parties playing other strategies.

Axelrod (1984) suggested that the findings could be extended to a wide range of political bargaining situations, and he speculated that the relative effectiveness of tit-for-tat was based on four features: (1) it is "nice," that is, it opens with a cooperative move, and it is never the first to defect; (2) it cannot be exploited—there is instant retaliation for any defection by the opponent; (3) it is forgiving—despite any earlier defections, any cooperative move by the other side is rewarded on the next play, and, finally, (4) it is clear, that is, it is easily recognized by the other party.[8]

Computer games, of course, are far removed from internation bargaining, particularly when the game is based on simultaneous play, as it was in this case, as opposed to the alternating moves of a sequential game. Moreover, there is the question of whether the Prisoners' Dilemma model fits most internation conflicts (see Jervis, 1988*b*). And, even in Prisoners' Dilemma, a strict tit-for-tat strategy presents an obvious danger of the parties locking in to an escalatory pattern of reciprocated noncooperative strategies.[9] Some recent computer simulations, in fact, suggest that tit-for-tat strategies do not perform well in hostile environments (see Axelrod and Dion, 1988).

GRIT

A well-known variant of tit-for-tat, which offers a way out of conflicts deadlocked in reciprocated conflictual strategies, is Osgood's (1962) Graduated and Reciprocated Initiatives in Tension Reduction, or GRIT. GRIT is based on the assumption that a relationship based on mutual hostility and tension can be transformed by one party announcing its intention of initiating a change in the atmosphere through a sequence of accommodative actions, while maintaining a retaliatory capacity should the other party attempt to exploit the conciliatory moves. Even if it does, however, the party pursuing the GRIT strategy returns to the conciliatory strategy. Osgood (1962) based his rationale for GRIT on the assumption that conflict escalation was largely due to each party's distrust of the intentions of the other. What was needed was a clear demonstration of cooperative intentions to break out of the conflictive pattern. Lindskold, Betz, and Walters (1986) have found some support for the effectiveness of GRIT in interpersonal experiments in Prisoners' Dilemma games. Molander (1985) similarly found that in a "noisy" environment, in which there is a great deal of uncertainty regarding the actions and intentions of the other party, the introduction of a unilateral concession to a tit-for-tat strategy increases its effectiveness in inducing cooperation.

RECIPROCATING STRATEGIES AND REAL-WORLD CONFLICTS

Social scientists have long recognized that reciprocity assumes a prominent role as a norm for stable human relationships generally (Gouldner, 1960; Homans, 1961) and, in relations among nations, as the basis for international law and diplomacy. The prevalence of tit-for-tat patterns of behavior has been identified in a number of empirical studies of interstate bargaining (North, Holsti, and Brody 1964; Gamson and Modigliani, 1971; Leng and Wheeler, 1979). Leng and Wheeler's (1979) found that states employing *reciprocating* influence strategies in interstate crises had a higher rate of success—a diplomatic victory or compromise—than those employing any of the other three influence strategies. Reciprocating strategies, which represent something of a hybrid between tit-for-tat and GRIT, by modifying the tit-for-tat restriction by allowing occasional cooperative initiatives to break a deadlock in the dispute, were found to be particularly successful against states employing *bullying* influence strategies. Similar findings have been reported in a subsequent study of extended deterrence by Huth (1988), as well as Leng's (1984) study of post–World War II U.S.–Soviet crises.

The rationale for the effectiveness may be attributed partly to the ingredients for success that Axelrod (1984) associates with tit-for-tat, but a particularly important factor in internation conflict would appear to be the "firm-but-fair" character of the strategy noted by Esser and Komorita (1975). The party employing the reciprocating strategy does not initiate any belligerent moves that would threaten the freedom or prestige of the other party, but it demonstrates its resolve through consistent firmness in the face of any attempts at coercion, while indicating its willingness to move toward a cooperative settlement. Thus it avoids provoking escalation of the conflict without appearing weak or irresolute.

OPTIMAL THREAT

A variant of bullying, "optimal threat," has been suggested by the game theorists Brams and Kilgour (1988:chap. 6) as the optimal deterrence strategy in games of "chicken," that is, games in which mutual defection produces the worst outcome for both parties.[10] As in Prisoners' Dilemma, each gets its second best outcome if both cooperate. If one cooperates and the other defects, the cooperating party gets its second worst outcome and the defector gets its most preferred outcome. The authors argue that chicken represents the best approximation of a nuclear crisis, where mutual defection would mean nuclear war.

As a problem in rational choice, the authors begin with the assumption that the optimal threat is the minimum necessary to deter aggressive action by the other party. Their intriguing conclusion is that, in some situations, the best strategy is to respond to low-level aggressive acts at a level of coercion that exceeds tit-for-tat, and to respond to high levels of aggression at a less-than-proportionate level. James and Harvey (1989) have found some empirical support for the effectiveness of this approach over tit-for-tat in crises in which the United States and the Soviet Union have participated, either directly or indirectly, on opposite sides. The study, however, was limited to initial responses to particular acts, as opposed to considering the evolution of an influence strategy over the course of the crisis.

The continued exploration of variants of influence strategies makes it clear that the final word has not yet been heard on this subject; nevertheless, the findings to date suggest that reciprocity is a significant guiding principle in interstate interaction regardless of the mix of cooperation and conflict.

Economic Influence Techniques

There is no doubt that in a highly interdependent world, economic exchange is one of the dominant forms of internation influence, and certainly one of the most successful in terms of building international cooperation based on reciprocity. The international trade and monetary policies pursued not only by states, but also by intergovernmental organizations, such as the IMF and World Bank, can achieve political goals that go well beyond their immediate economic effects. Allies can be strengthened; adversaries can be weakened; international and regional integration can be promoted or blocked. Moreover, both trade and aid policies can be used to produce long-term dependency relationships. As one analyst (Baldwin, 1985:116) argues, the day-to-day operation of international trade is "one of the most spectacularly successful examples of international influence in history."

ECONOMIC COERCION

Given the success of reciprocal economic exchange as a mode of building cooperation among nations in a competitive environment, it is paradoxical that political scientists have devoted most of their studies of economic statecraft to the relative success and failure of negative economic sanctions. Perhaps that is because there is so little agreement in evaluating their performance. After analyzing 100 cases of economic sanctions in the modern era, Hufbauer and Schott (1985) conclude that, as a means of achieving political objectives, the technique is all but useless. Losman (1979) draws similar conclusions from a study of attempted boycotts directed at Rhodesia, Cuba, and Israel. A survey of the literature leads Strack to conclude that "there seems to be a consensus among scholars that sanctions are not only an ineffective means to secure policy objectives, but may well be dysfunctional or counterproductive, producing results opposite to those desired by the initiators of sanctions" (1978:xi–xii).

Nincic and Wallenstein (1983) reach the more moderate conclusion that while negative economic sanctions are rarely effective in producing major policy changes, they can play a successful deterrent role. But this view is rejected by Lindsay (1986), who surveyed 19 cases of trade sanctions employed between 1932 and 1982. After listing a string of major failures, such as the League of Nations sanctions against Italy in 1936, or the U.S. sanctions against Japan in 1941, Lindsay suggests that the poor performance record of the past may be an important factor in the failure of the threat of economic sanctions as a successful deterrent. He presents a similar catalog of failures to argue that economic sanctions have been no more effective in efforts to subvert regimes. The U.S. trade sanctions directed at Cuba failed to change the policies of that regime, and Rhodesia survived sanctions initiated by Great Britain for 14 years. Lindsay (1986:159) argues that trade sanctions are ineffective primarily because they fail to inflict serious economic pain on the target, usually because the influencer simply does not have the power to do so. A second crucial factor, however, is the relative value that the target places on the disputed behavior relative to the economic costs of the sanctions.

With this in mind, Baldwin (1985) notes that the stated political objectives of the most spectacular failures of political sanctions—stop the 1935 Italian invasion of Ethiopia, coerce white Rhodesians to accept majority rule, convince Castro to step down in Cuba, persuade the Soviet Union to change its political system—are unrealistic objectives for *any* influence technique short of a military invasion. To this list, one could add the U.N. Security Council demand in the fall of 1990 that Saddam Hussein withdraw his forces from Kuwait. On the other hand, it can be argued that the sanctions against Italy in 1935 would have succeeded had they been more comprehensive and universally applied, that the failure in Rhodesia has been balanced by success in South Africa, and that the sanctions against Saddam Hussein may have worked had they been given more time and had a way been found for Saddam Hussein to retain some face as he retreated. Whatever arguments one might make with regard to one case or another, however, Baldwin's basic point is irrefutable: One cannot expect any coercive influence technique to work if the costs and risks to the target of yielding are greater than the costs and risks of resisting.

Some analysts have argued that a more appropriate objective for economic sanctions is to signal the first step on a ladder of incremental escalation, which could lead to military sanctions (Nincic and Wallenstein, 1983:5). Economic sanctions are particularly useful in this regard because they represent a low level of escalation that can be leavened with positive influence techniques to demonstrate firmness to the target while reassuring others of one's sense of proportion and restraint (Baldwin, 1985:104–105). They offer the advantages of instruments of coercion and accommodation that can be finely calibrated and readjusted in ways that would be difficult, if not impossible, with military sanctions. They also, as the Persian Gulf War has illustrated, can lay the necessary groundwork to justify moving up the ladder of escalation to war.

Besides tailoring economic sanctions to realistic objectives, statesmen need to be aware of the contextual conditions most conducive to success. Keohane and Nye (1977:11–15) make a useful distinction between *sensitivity* and *vulnerability*. Sensitivity refers to how quickly the sanctions would be felt by the target state and how costly they would be. Vulnerability refers to the extent to which the target is able to adjust to the situation created by the sanctions. If it is an economic boycott, for example, does the target state have other markets to which it can turn? States that are dependent on particular commodities, either for consumption or export, can be highly sensitive to sanctions directed at those commodities. Oil is an outstanding example. States that are economically weak and isolated are generally considered to be the most vulnerable to economic coercion (Nincic and Wallenstein, 1983). They lack the means to either retaliate or to find alternative supply sources or outlets. It is necessary, of course, that the target state have some degree of dependency on trade with the influencer, but it also is important that the state employing the sanctions *not* be dependent on the target state for an outlet or source of supply.

The application of economic sanctions may affect different groups or classes within the target state to varying degrees, so that relative deprivation must be a consideration of the influencer. If the sanctions are being applied to produce internal changes, such as the United States' sanctions against the government of South Africa, the influencer does not want the very group that it is championing to be harmed the most by the sanctions. By the same token, for the sanctions to succeed, they must have a significant impact on groups or classes that have the power to influence the government (see Olson, 1979:471–494). Economic sanctions that have their only significant effects on the poor and powerless are unlikely to change the policies of an oligarchic or dictatorial regime.

Adjustments in trade or financial policies, ranging from various modes of preferential treatment, or the offer or denial of financial favors, to embargoes and boycotts, are the most common economic influence techniques. In recent years, covert or highly selective restrictions on the flow of capital, technology transfers, and intracorporate trade have been favored over more general, well-publicized trade sanctions. The prevailing view is that less public, more selective techniques yield a higher degree of compliance. As in all influence techniques, highly publicized sanctions challenge the target's reputation for resolve in a manner that can make compliance more difficult, while strengthening the unity of the target state in opposition to the influencer (Nincic and Wallenstein, 1983).

It could be that the allegedly high failure rate associated with economic sanctions is, in part, a result of researchers focusing most of their attention on highly publicized sanctions while neglecting more subtle forms of economic coercion (see Olson, 1979). The choice of more public forms of economic coercion, in fact, may be more related to the benefits that the government hopes to accrue to its domestic support, through an image of toughness, than to any expectations of coercing the target state to comply with its demands (see Olson, 1979; Baldwin, 1985:108–109). Highly visible economic sanctions can have important symbolic domestic benefits, particularly as a means of exhibiting forceful behavior without resorting to military action (Lindsay, 1986:170).

The economic sanctions against Iraq, which remained in place after the Persian Gulf War and continue as this is being written, richly illustrate many of the preceding questions surrounding economic coercion. The Iraqi economy is sensitive and vulnerable to the U.N. sanctions, particularly the oil embargo, but those suffering the greatest hardships do not have the power to fulfill the United Nations' demand that the dictatorial regime of Saddam Hussein be overthrown. Those who do have the power to comply with the demand, that is, those in power, consider the costs and risks of doing so greater than the costs and risks of resistance. Nevertheless, continuing the sanctions provides the sponsoring governments with a domestic image of resolve in the face of the Iraqi regime's resistance, and the flexibility of economic coercion as an influence technique allows the United Nations to loosen the sanctions to some degree in order to provide humanitarian relief to those who are suffering the most.

FOREIGN AID

Before leaving economic influence techniques, some mention should be made of the special case of foreign aid. Occasionally foreign aid is proffered for purely humanitarian reasons, such as in disaster relief, but more often it is coupled to a foreign policy objective designed to serve the interests of the donor. Frequently the primary objective is simply to strengthen an ally, but it also can involve an influence relationship, such as winning over a potential ally or creating a dependency relationship. In such instances there is an implicit or explicit quid pro quo; the giver expects something in return for the aid. As in trade relationships, the giver's influence comes from its ability to manipulate the flow of economic goods to the recipient. By the same token, the giver's capacity to influence the recipient through the flow of aid is positively associated with the value that the recipient places on the goods in question.

Following this logic, some analysts (Baldwin, 1985; Lindsay, 1986) believe that the manipulation of foreign aid can be a very effective tool of influence. Lindsay (1986:153–173) notes that the very need for economic aid suggests that the target state is economically weak and, therefore, vulnerable to economic pressure. Usually aid is sought in areas where there are no other substitutes, thus making it difficult for the target state to circumvent sanctions in the form of the cessation of aid. Moreover, the cessation of aid can have the effect of complicating the target government's relations with private financiers.

The last point touches on an aspect of foreign aid that poses a serious issue for the international community. Whether the donor is a state or an intergovernmental organization, such as the IMF or World Bank, most aid agreements require some quid pro quo on the part of the recipient. In recent years, the quid pro quo has increasingly come in the form of "restructuring," that is, changes in the recipient's economy, or even some aspects of its political system. In this respect, economic influence becomes a form of intervention that undermines the sovereignty of the recipient state. Although such agreements are reached voluntarily by both parties, the recipient is often in a financial position that allows no feasible alternative. When this occurs, foreign aid becomes a very potent form of influence indeed. Unfortunately, to date there have been virtually no aggregate or comparative empirical studies of the political consequences of such policies.

The Use of Force

Whether one views the use of military force in Clausewitzian terms, as a perfectly normal extension of foreign policy, or as a technique to be employed only in the most dire circumstances, there is no doubt of its continuing prevalence as an influence technique in the modern age. The effective application of military tactics and strategies per se lies outside the bounds of the essentially political subject matter of this chapter. It is the domain of the military strategist. Nevertheless, there have been some changes in military techniques since World War II that have had such profound implications for internation relations that they should be noted in any review of internation influence techniques.

Perhaps the most dramatic development is the increasing prominence of what Schelling (1966:chap. 1) has labeled the "diplomacy of violence." Schelling has made an interesting binary distinction between the use of "brute force" in conventional warfare and the diplomacy of violence. Brute force, whether employed in an invasion or defense, is designed to destroy resources, defeat and expel enemy military forces, and seize or hold territory. The pain and suffering that this action causes are seen as incidental to the military mission; they represent "collateral damage," in military parlance. With the application of the "diplomacy of violence," on the other hand, the pain and suffering are the immediate purpose of the use of force. Its ultimate purpose is to coerce the other side into giving the initiator what it wants in order to avoid further hurt and loss. Brute force is used to take what you want; the diplomacy of violence is used to coerce the other side into giving it to you. The former is effective when it is used; the latter is most effective when it is held in reserve, when the violence, or additional violence, is threatened. When the diplomacy of violence is employed, the use of force becomes a form of bargaining.

GUERRILLA WAR AND TERRORISM

Schelling (1966) notes that the use of the diplomacy of violence prior to World War II was generally the purview of the strong using its military advantage to coerce the weak into compliance, frequently after the enemy forces had been defeated. But with the resistance movements of the Second World War and the use of modern guerrilla tactics by weaker parties since then, the relationship has been reversed. Of course, guerrilla warfare and terrorism are not post–World War II phenomena. One of the earliest indications of the vulnerability of Napoleon's forces appeared in the guerrilla struggle conducted by the Spanish at the beginning of the nineteenth century, just as terrorism flourished later in that century. The difference lay largely in the targets of the attacks. Before World War II, guerrilla forces generally fought solely against the military forces of the other side, and terrorists launched their attacks at government officials, whereas, Schelling (1966:22–23) argues, the diplomacy of violence is launched against the entire nation— innocent civilians as well as troops and government officials.

Frequently guerrilla and terrorist tactics have been combined with the eventual use of conventional forces as well, such as in the Vietnam War, but even in these instances, victory has been dependent on inflicting sufficient pain and loss on the enemy to cause it to decide to abandon the struggle or reach a settlement.

The distinction between guerrilla warfare and terrorism has remained somewhat cloudy, perhaps partly because the two tactics are so often combined. In its purest form, guerrilla warfare is confined to the use of force against forces in the field, that is, legitimate military targets, whereas terrorism is directed deliberately, and often randomly, against noncombatants as well. Leaving aside the important moral distinction between the two,[11] the ultimate purpose is the same in both cases. Neither the modern guerrilla nor the terrorist expects to defeat the enemy forces militarily; the purpose is to coerce the enemy into submitting in order to avoid further pain and loss.

While international terrorism per se is a relatively minor form of the use of force in the total number of lives lost, which can be counted in the hundreds on an annual basis (see Kegley, 1990:15), the random and wanton nature of the violence has given it high visibility. On the other hand, there is little evidence that it has been an effective political instrument in its own right. There are no known instances of governments changing hands because of terrorist actions, although terrorism combined with guerrilla warfare led to successes in the Cuban revolution and Algerian independence movements of the 1950s (see Laqueur, 1976). While there is little reason to suspect that terrorism can be eradicated, the international cooperation necessary to reduce its occurrence and effectiveness may be more possible with the recent thaw in the East-West relations (see Schlagheck, 1988).

Academic research on terrorism appears to be very much in its infancy, with most writers concentrating on the question of how to deal successfully with the problem (see Livingstone and Arnold, 1986; Wardlaw, 1983; Stohl, 1988; Alexander, Carlton, and Wilkinson, 1978; Lacqueur, 1978).

During the first two decades after World War II, guerrilla warfare was used predominantly as a tactic by rebel groups within colonies seeking independence from Western powers. Once the decolonization was virtually completed, by the 1960s, the tactic continued within the Third World in civil struggles. These conflicts frequently have been internationalized by the participation of major powers, primarily the United States and the Soviet Union, as suppliers of weapons and military materiel. Recognizing the catastrophic consequences of a direct military confrontation, the superpowers have played the "game of influence," as Hoffmann (1978:172) has put it, by trying to influence the outcomes of internal conflicts in the less developed countries of the Third World. Although such tactics have added significantly to the level of violence and instability in the international system, this writer knows of no systematic empirical study indicating that such tactics have led to long term strategic benefits for either of the superpowers. On the other hand, the American experience in Vietnam and the Soviet experience in Afghanistan suggest that the balancing effect of the material support of the other superpower has been a significant factor in the success of a struggle by guerrilla forces against the conventional forces of an intervening superpower.[12] The recent thawing of relations between the two superpowers should have the effect of reducing this particularly ugly aspect of their competition. Whether it will result in a concomitant reduction in instability and violence in the less developed countries (LDCs) remains to be seen.

SHOWS-OF-FORCE AND GUNBOAT DIPLOMACY

Shows-of-force, which may include the limited use of force, are more traditional means of using one's military forces in coercive bargaining. The technique is intended to exploit the opponent's fear of a violent attack, and in that sense it would fit Schelling's (1966) notion of the diplomacy of violence. However, it is most often employed by parties enjoying an advantage in usable military capabilities, so that the threat is not just that of pain and suffering, but also that of being defeated militarily.

Blechman and Kaplan (1978:523–530), in an empirical study of American uses of shows-of-force, concluded that use of the technique was more likely to be successful: when there was a highly credible commitment to carry out the threatened military action (such as troops placed in the location to be defended); when the purpose was to deter, rather than compel, target action; and when force was displayed but not used against the target. The authors also concluded that land-based shows-of-force were more likely to be successful than gunboat diplomacy. This view, however, is not shared by all other analysts of military power (see Luttwak, 1974).

The most traditional and commonly used form of shows-of-force is gunboat diplomacy—the demonstration, threat, or use of limited naval force. Although the practice seems somewhat out of step with the modern age, it is still quite prevalent. Working with data from a more comprehensive study by Cable (1981), Mandel (1986) notes 113 instances of its use from 1946 to 1978. Of the 113 incidents, Mandel (1986:71) describes 53 percent as successes for the initiator, with only 20 percent as outright failures. According to Mandel's (1986:73) study, the technique is most successful when there is "a definitive, deterrent display of force by an assailant who has engaged in war in the victim's region" and who enjoys greater usable military capability and political stability than the victim.

NUCLEAR CRISES

It has been observed that "crises stand on a no-man's land between war and peace," where "diplomacy still dominates in the pursuit of national objectives, yet there are preparations for war" (Gottfried and Blair, 1988:308). It may not be an exaggeration to say that a nuclear crisis represents a no-man's land between peace and extinction.

The most widely researched question regarding nuclear crises concerns the choice of influence techniques for immediate nuclear deterrence, that is, when a dispute between two opposing states has evolved to a stage where at least one side is considering a nuclear attack and the other is attempting to deter it. Prescriptive academic research on immediate nuclear deterrence has been dominated by a strategic approach called "rational deterrence theory," which in its most developed form has resulted in deductive game-theoretic models, or by qualitative case studies. The findings from these two approaches are discussed in detail in the chapters by Shubik (1990) and by J. Stein (1990) in Volume Two of this series. To avoid rehashing those discussions, I shall confine this section to an overview of descriptive research dealing with the effects that the possession of nuclear weapons by one or both parties is presumed to have had on the internation influence process.

Let us begin with the case where both parties possess nuclear weapons. The enormous destructive power of the weapons can have a paradoxical effect on the influence process. On the one hand, the potentially catastrophic costs of nuclear war outweigh virtually all the other interests, thus placing new constraints on the range of coercive tactics available to contending nuclear powers. Some scholars have argued that the threat of nuclear war has had a sobering effect upon statesmen, which has enabled them to avoid the process of escalation that has led to war in other situations (Gaddis, 1986:99). Others have argued that each participant's awareness of the terrible costs of nuclear war—for both sides—raises the "provocation threshold," thus permitting more room for coercive tactics short of war (Osgood and Tucker, 1967:144–145). The nuclear crisis becomes, in the words of Snyder and Diesing (1977:455–456), a "surrogate for war." They argue that with war no longer viewed as a plausible option, success in nuclear crises becomes dependent upon demonstrating a greater willingness to take and to stand up to risks.

Organski and Kugler (1980:176–179) have found empirical evidence that post–World War II disputes involving nuclear powers *have* been characterized by a greater degree of risk taking than those involving non-nuclear states. On the other hand, there has been no empirical evidence to suggest that the relative balance in strategic capabilities has affected either the behavior or outcomes of nuclear crises (see Snyder and Diesing, 1977:458–459; Betts, 1987:213–214). If relative capability has made a difference in these crises, it appears to have been the local balance in conventional forces that has affected decision making, not the strategic balance (see Blechman and Kaplan, 1978, and, on the Cuban crisis, Blight and Welch, 1989). At least one analyst (Mueller, 1988:59) argues that the presence of nuclear weapons has had *no* effect on major power crisis behavior: "World war in the post-1945 era has been prevented not so much by visions of nuclear horror as by the generally accepted belief that conflict can easily escalate to a level, nuclear or not, that the essentially satisfied major powers would find intolerably costly." This is a virtually untestable proposition that is not widely shared by other researchers, who see an important difference in the potential for controlling the scope and costs of conventional as opposed to nuclear wars (see Jervis, 1988a:79–80). It also is inconsistent with the recollections of U.S. policymakers engaged in the Cuban missile crisis (see Blight and Welch, 1989).

Another interesting issue is that of the effect of nuclear weapons on state behavior in disputes between nuclear and non-nuclear powers. Classical deterrence theory suggests that states confronting nuclear adversaries will exhibit greater caution in the use of force than in other situations (Brodie, 1959; Howard, 1971). The empirical evidence, however, is quite mixed. Weede (1983), in a study of disputes occurring during the 1960s and 1970s, found some evidence to support the traditional view in cases of extended deterrence, that is, when a nuclear power is acting as protector of a non-nuclear ally. Huth and Russett (1984), on the other hand, offer contradictory findings indicating that the possession of nuclear weapons by the protector, or nuclear superiority in cases in which the protectors for both parties have nuclear weapons, is unrelated to success.[13] Similarly, an empirical study by Kugler (1984) of crises since 1945 indicates that (1) nuclear superiority does not affect the outcome of crises, and (2) nuclear weapons do not affect the behavior of states in the courses of the crises.

There are a number of plausible reasons why nuclear weapons may not be very effective deterrents against non-nuclear powers. Nuclear weapons have no military significance in the guerrilla wars that are most prevalent in third-world conflicts (Osgood and Tucker, 1967:158), and states are likely to be inhibited by domestic politics, international criticism, or moral considerations from using nuclear weapons against non-nuclear foes (Huth and Russett, 1984). There also is a more basic rational choice argument. The credibility of a deterrent threat is likely to be based less on the relative capability of the defender than on the *cost* of war relative to the value the defender has placed on succeeding. It is important to note, however, that these studies generally deal either with cases of extended deterrence—a nuclear power attempting to protect a nonnuclear ally—or immediate deterrence in instances when national survival is not at stake. If, in fact, a nuclear power finds its survival threatened directly by a non-nuclear power with conventional military superiority, the logic of the situation would be quite different.

Before leaving this section, it should be noted that much of the work on the potential effectiveness of the threat of nuclear war is necessarily speculative since there are so few instances to date of explicit threats to use nuclear weapons. The Soviets hinted at using nuclear weapons against China in 1969, and the United States considered the possibility of using nuclear weapons against China toward the end of the Korean War, but no explicit threats were issued. The only direct threats came during the two most recent superpower crises, in 1962 and 1973, when the United States placed its nuclear forces on alert (Gottfried and Blair, 1988:278–279). More recently, Israeli responses to threats from Iraq have implied the possible use of nuclear weapons.

Contextual Factors

The pursuit of influence, of course, does not occur in a vacuum. A large number of contextual factors can affect the choice of influence attempts and their relative success in achieving compliance with the influencer's demands. The research dealing with the effects of contextual variables on internation interaction can be conveniently ordered according to four levels of analysis: the individual decision maker, the decision-making body, the relationship between the states engaged in the influence process, and the state of the international system.[14]

INDIVIDUAL DECISION-MAKERS

At the individual level there are a number of cognitive and psychological constraints that are likely to affect the ways in which decision makers process information and make choices when dealing with other nations. There are a number of emotional variables that can confound rational choice in any decision-making situation—stress, fatigue, feelings of friendship or hostility, distrust, fear, and so on (see Holsti, 1989). Holsti (1976:29–30) notes that these psychological variables become more significant in nonroutine situations in which unanticipated events occur and information is ambiguous. And there are cognitive elements peculiar to internation relations that encourage misperception. The complexity and ambiguity of information (see Jervis, 1976) encourage decision makers to rely on preconceived beliefs, or "operational codes" (see George, 1969; Walker and Falkowski, 1984), in deciding how to deal with contending states. These factors become particularly important because of their effects on the decision maker's perception of the intentions and motivation of the other party, that is, how it is likely to respond to particular influence strategies. To mention just one salient example, Zinnes, North, and Koch (1961) found, in their study of perception and action in the pre–World War I crisis, that although German and Austro-Hungarian leaders considered their nations militarily overmatched, their perception of the hostile intentions of the Entente powers overrode the prudence that a decision based on capability would have dictated. Somewhat more generally, Suedfeld and Tetlock (1977) found an association between the level of stress and the analytic abilities of national leaders, and the likelihood of war in five 20th-century crises. For a useful summary of recent work on these questions, see Holsti's (1989) chapter on crisis decision making in the first volume of this series, or Oneal (1988).

DECISION-MAKING BODIES

There also are confounding forces that operate within national decision-making bodies, for example, "groupthink," the tendency of a desire for group solidarity to weaken cognitive and moral judgments (Janis, 1972), or bureaucratic politics (see Neustadt, 1970; Allison, 1971), or the pressures of domestic politics (see Lebow, 1981). Even within a small decision-making body, such as the Ex Comm group created by the Kennedy administration to deal with the Cuban missile crisis, deciding on a particular course of action can be more of an exercise in coalition building than a group judgment of the most reasonable course of action (see Allison, 1971). By the same token, some researchers have found, for example, that when their actions are closely watched by powerful constituents, decision-making bodies are more likely to adopt unyielding positions (see Bartunck, Benton, and Keys, 1975). Other findings relating to the dynamics of group decision making are described by Holsti (1989:19–22).

DYADIC RELATIONSHIPS

A third level of analysis of particular interest to students of influence is the relationship between the influencer and influencee, with most of the attention focusing on the comparative bargaining power of the two sides. Obviously, the enormous variations in capabilities that are a function of size, resources, and location are bound to affect the choice of influence techniques and their effectiveness. Stronger states possess a greater range of available rewards and punishments; weaker states may be forced to rely on persuasion when confronted by stronger powers. Moreover, for the weaker state there is a smaller margin of error; the risks of failure are greater.

This is not to say that the weaker state is without influence techniques appropriate to the situation. During the Vietnam conflict, the North Vietnamese effectively employed a negotiating strategy based on exploiting internal dissension within the United States. Habeeb and Zartman (1986) have shown how the Torrijo government of Panama effectively employed a variety of influence techniques appropriate for the weaker party in convincing the United States to renegotiate the Panama Canal Treaty. These tactics ranged from appealing to the higher principles of the United States' "good neighbor" policy toward Latin America, to seeking third-party intervention by a higher authority (U.N. Security Council), to exploiting their own weakness by threatening a governmental collapse if the United States would not cooperate. These, of course, are hardly tactics that were unique to this situation.

These studies suggest that bargaining power is not always just a question of which party is stronger according to the usual measures of military, economic, or political power. Habeeb (1988), in fact, makes a useful distinction in asymmetric negotiations between the participants' comparative structural power, which consists of the traditional measures of aggregate capabilities, and "issue-specific power," which is a function of the power that can feasibly be brought to bear on the issues at stake. Habeeb shows, in an analysis of three asymmetrical disputes—the Panama Canal negotiations, the U.S.–Spanish military bases negotiations, and the "Cod War" involving Britain and Iceland—that the latter can be quite different from the former.

Moreover, in settings outside of simple state-to-state bargaining, such as in international monetary organizations or in the specialized agencies of the United Nations, technical expertise often plays a large role, as does the more purely political process of coalition building with the membership. The latter may well be related to the ideological influence of certain members, as opposed to military or financial capabilities. Nye (1990) makes an interesting argument for a more subtle component of influence, which he calls "soft" or "co-optive" power: the ability of one nation to influence others to define their interests in ways consistent with its own. This sort of power is more a function of attraction than capabilities. In the case of the United States, it may be the attractiveness of its large markets, its democratic heritage, its pop culture, and the prevalence of English as a global second language. In Nye's (1990) view, this component of influence is becoming more important in a world where security issues appear to be assuming a less central role, an issue to which I shall return in the discussion of the global structure below.

Before doing so, however, we ought to consider the issue of bargaining power in those situations in which security interests are very much at stake— internation crises. Snyder and Diesing (1977:183–195) argue that in internation crises, bargaining power is a function of "perceived comparative resolve," which in turn is dependent on the parties' perceptions of relative capability and motivation. Considerable empirical research, in fact, has been devoted to the relationship between comparative military capability and internation dispute outcomes, with the surprising, but relatively consistent, conclusion that there is no systematic relationship between the two (Levy, 1988; Wayman, Singer, and Goertz, 1983; Maoz, 1983; Karsten, Howell, and Allen, 1984). These studies, however, have analyzed the connection between physical capabilities, as measured by the researcher, as opposed to the *perceived* relative capabilities of the two sides, which lies at the heart of the Snyder and Diesing proposition.

Other scholars have argued that the interests at stake are a more potent determinant of internation behavior (George and Smoke, 1974). Thucydides suggested this when he described how the woefully overmatched Melians refused to yield to an Athenian ultimatum in the Peloponnesian War. Betts presents an argument based on interest for the ultimate success of the militarily overmatched North Vietnamese against the United States: "The fundamental asymmetry of national interests was the critical factor, and overcame the salience of the greatly asymmetrical military burdens" (1980:523). In fact, there can be a paradoxical relationship between outward gains in capability and decreasing influence. This can occur if a state's appetite grows with its capabilities to such an extent that it threatens the interests for other states, thus encouraging them to collude against it. Maoz (1989) offers the hapless case of victorious Bulgaria at the end of the First Balkan War in 1913 to illustrate the phenomenon. Its military successes increased the Bulgarian appetite for additional territory to the point where its allies of just a few months earlier, in the First Balkan War, became its adversaries in the Second Balkan War.

Gochman and Leng (1983), in an events data study of a sample of 38 militarized crises occurring between 1816 and 1976, found that the crises were both more likely to escalate and to end in war when vital interests (political independence or territorial integrity) were at stake. The commonsensical notion, and that assumed by most traditional accounts of internation relations, is that there is an *interactive* relationship between capabilities and interests in determining state behavior. That relationship has not yet received extensive empirical testing.

RESPONSIVENESS AND RIVALRIES

In addition to these structural factors, psychological components of relationships between states can have a pronounced effect on their choices of influence strategies and the effectiveness of influence attempts. An important contextual variable originally introduced by Deutsch et al. (1957) and extended to conflict bargaining by Pruitt (1965) is a government's degree of *responsiveness*, that is, its sense of how cooperative and trusting it should be in dealing with another state. Responsiveness is generally viewed as a function of the government's image of the degree of friendliness or hostility in the other party's intentions, and of its past experience with the another state. Responsiveness is presumed to increase with cooperative experiences in the past and decrease with conflictive experiences. The greater the degree of responsiveness, the more likely a state is to employ an accommodative influence strategy and vice versa.

The role of responsiveness becomes particularly interesting in the case of states engaged in extended rivalries, such as Austria and Russia before World War I, the United States and the Soviet Union during the Cold War, or India and Pakistan and the Arabs and Israelis today. One important question concerns the effect that the outcome of a previous confrontation is likely to have on a state's behavior in a succeeding dispute with the same adversary. Working from a realpolitik perspective, Leng (1983) hypothesized that national decision makers whose states were unsuccessful in a preceding crisis would adopt more belligerent influence strategies in the next confrontation with the same adversary. The other party, no less determined to communicate its continuing resolve and willingness to accept the risks of escalation, would respond in kind, setting in motion a sequence of increasingly coercive threats and counterthreats. Thus, in the case of recurring crises, each new successive encounter would be more bellicose. The proposition was tested with events data describing the influence strategies of six pairs of states, each of which was engaged in three successive twentieth-century crises within a relatively short period,[15] and the findings supported the "coercion begets coercion" hypothesis. In a follow-up study, Leng (1984) explored the logical consequences of the realpolitik approach to learning from experience in a game-theoretic study. That study highlighted the importance of the opening move in determining the evolution of the crisis. A move to a coercive influence strategy by either party had the effect of reducing, or eliminating, accommodative options for the other party.

THE GLOBAL SYSTEM

Beyond the relationships between the parties involved directly, there is the potential influence exerted on their behavior by the way in which the global system is structured. There are many ways of looking at the structure of the system. One could begin with the norms established by the international legal regime, or consider the institutional arrangements devised by states to assist them in resolving issues, but by far the most common perspective has been to focus on the global power structure. Consequently, much of the empirical research on the relationship between the structure of the international system and influence relations among states has proceeded from a traditional realist perspective, with a strong emphasis on issues such as the balance of power and alliance linkages, particularly with regard to their association with war. The findings from a wide array of studies falling into this category, many of them associated with J. David Singer's Correlates of War project (see Singer, 1990), are reported by Levy (1989) in the first volume of this series. Singer's project deals directly with security issues, where a realist perspective would appear to be most appropriate. But the tendency of international relations researchers to extend the realist perspective to a far wider range of influence relationships has been challenged in recent years by theorists representing either interdependence or global economic system perspectives.

Interdependence theorists (see Keohane and Nye, 1977) challenge the realist assumptions of the state as a unitary and rational actor and note the increasing importance of nonstate actors, not only intergovernmental organizations, but also nongovernmental actors such as multinational corporations. Perhaps most important for our purposes, these theorists stress the relationship between the *issues* at stake on the one hand, and the influence techniques, most relevant arenas for decisions, and relative bargaining power of the participants on the other. The argument is that as the world becomes increasingly interdependent—economically, environmentally, socially—the attributes of influence change. National security does not dominate every agenda, and when it does not, military power cannot always be transformed into bargaining power.

Interdependence theorists also point out that the channels of global communication and influence are far more complex than the statecentric realist model suggests. In dealing with economic or environmental problems, for example, the most relevant communication networks may be through intergovernmental, or even nongovernmental, actors, and, when they are through governments, the key decision-making bodies may be rather different from those dealing with security issues. It also suggests that the factors that are likely to lead to more or less bargaining power may vary accordingly. When complex economic issues are being debated, for example, bargaining power may be partly a function of relative wealth and partly a function of technical expertise. In short, it is argued that in an increasingly complex and interdependent world, how much influence one or another party is able to bring to bear depends on the issues at stake, which representatives of which actors are participating in the decision making and bargaining, and the forum in which the bargaining takes place. To anyone who has witnessed the events of the past few years, the logic of many of the arguments presented by the interdependence theorists seems unassailable.

The second challenge to the traditional realist view comes from a variety of theorists who see the structure of the world capitalist system as dominating international influence relationships. This view has its origins in Marxist-Leninist theories of the dominating effects of world capitalism, although not all of the contemporary theorists focusing on the global economic structure as the key to understanding international influence are Marxists. What these theorists do share in common is the conviction that it is the capitalist global system that is at the heart of all international influence. A description of the variety of theories that have grown out of this tradition would be well beyond the scope of this chapter; however, one can get a sense of its impact by considering one of its most prominent variants, *dependency theory* (see Cardoso and Faletto, 1979; Dos Santos, 1970). In essence, dependency theorists argue that the global economic system is controlled by a core of wealthy industrialized capitalist states that have penetrated and exploited peripheral economies to create dependency relationships. Thus the less developed countries (LDC's) are dependent on the more developed industrial economies and on the global economic order fashioned by those economies. Dependency theorists argue that the perpetuation of this relationship not only relegates periphery states to a subordinate role in the global system, but it also limits their ability to conduct independent foreign policies. Consequently, all influence relationships between the core and periphery states are dominated by the reality of economic dependency, so that the techniques available to the periphery states are limited to protests and efforts at persuasion. Most of the earlier dependency studies were by Latin American theorists concerned primarily with problems of development among the LDCs (see Wallerstein, 1979, for a notable exception), and many have encountered sharp criticism from other scholars, with regard to both the empirical validity of their historical analyses and their global socialist objectives. Nevertheless, given the recent changes in eastern and central Europe, there can be little doubt regarding the importance of *issues* associated with the influence relationship between economically dependent states and the most powerful industrialized economies.

These issues become increasingly important as the world becomes more and more interdependent. Given a long-standing preoccupation with security issues, behavioral scientists have given very little attention to these questions. Moreover, there is an inevitable time lag that runs from the awareness of the salience of new issues, to the development of widely accepted new paradigms purported to deal with those issues, to the conduct of rigorous empirical research. At this point, the progress of behavioral research on this aspect of influence appears to be stalled in a debate over appropriate paradigms.

Conclusions

We began this survey of research on influence techniques by noting the strategic or psychological perspectives that are likely to affect how researchers approach questions of influence, and then moved to consider the strengths and weaknesses of the major methodological approaches to the study of influence. Considering the limitations inherent in each of the methods, I suggested that the reader exercise caution in judging the findings reported, particularly those that were not supported by more than one study.

There are, however, some interesting patterns that can be observed across a number of methodologically distinct studies. One of the most intriguing occurs in the convergence of findings from the experiments of social psychologists, qualitative case studies, and events data research regarding the relationship between promises and threats. Promises, which offer the important advantage of furthering a positive relationship with the influencee, are more likely to be effective when the influencer has the requisites for the effective use of negative inducements as well. Threats, while generally more effective than promises alone, are most effective when leavened by accompanying positive inducements. The presence of the latter reduces the degree of distrust, hostility, and potential conflict escalation associated with threats alone. Thus, carrot-and-stick inducements, which couple a firm demonstration of resolve with a willingness to make some concessions, appear to offer the most successful mix of influence tactics.

These conclusions are intriguing in light of the robust findings emerging from game theory, social psychology, and events data studies indicating the prevalence of reciprocity in internation conflict behavior, as well as the relative effectiveness of *reciprocating*, or "firm but fair," influence strategies. The two sets of findings suggest the point at which the strategic and psychological perspectives converge. In a world where power counts, states must demonstrate resolve if they wish to achieve their objectives, but in confrontations with other governments composed of human beings concerned with their prestige and independence, they must beware of backing the other side into a corner. The policy relevance of such findings is evident in light of complementary research on rivalries and dispute escalation suggesting the tendency of national leaders who are engaged in internation disputes to place their faith in predominantly coercive influence tactics. Findings such as these do not tell particular policymakers what they should do in a given situation, but they do offer insights on what to expect from particular classes of influence strategies over the long run.

Unfortunately, the convergence of research on internation influence is more the exception than the rule. Most of the findings reported in this chapter exist as solitary bits and pieces. In some areas, such as in studies of the use of economic sanctions, they are contradictory. In others, such as terrorism or nonviolent action, the research is in such a stage of infancy that there is little to report beyond the personal impressions of analysts. This is doubly unfortunate because as the presence of nuclear weapons has limited the use of conventional military force in major-power conflicts—although not necessarily in conflicts between minor powers—less conventional coercive influence techniques have become more prominent in the post–World War II era. The demise of the European colonial empires and the institutionalization of the principle of self-determination also have shifted the arena of international conflict to power struggles within states. The major powers have attempted to influence the outcomes of these struggles through the manipulation of economic and/or military aid, while subnational or transnational groups challenging existing regimes have come to rely on guerrilla warfare, terrorism, or nonviolent action. The recent demise of the superpower rivalry raises the question of whether the superpowers are capable of exerting their influence in a more stabilizing manner, or whether the absence of the threat of a superpower confrontation will unleash more internation violence in what used to be called the Third World.

A more optimistic scenario is one in which growing recognition of the economic and environmental interdependence of nations, along with the decline in superpower competition, creates a future in which greater importance will be attached to influence techniques designed to improve internation cooperation. Considerable research on the techniques of integrative diplomacy has emerged from the work of other social scientists, as well as a wealth of information from the accounts of practitioners, but a focus on cooperative, as opposed to coercive, influence techniques would represent a significant redirection of the research of international relations specialists. The problems of interdependence also suggest the increasing importance of other arenas of influence, particularly politics within intergovernmental organizations (IGOs), and between IGOs and states. These developments could make the statecentric and bilateral simplifying assumptions of the research reported in this chapter more problematic in the future.

In sum, while there has been some convergence of findings with regard to the more generic aspects of influence—threats and promises—the findings tend to be isolated, sparse, and even contradictory where more specific areas of influence are concerned. The latter is particularly true in the case of those influence techniques that have become more prevalent in the nuclear age. At the same time, the nature of the game of influence is continually changing with new developments in the international system, particularly the growing global interdependence and the demise of the Cold War. As these developments continue, students of internation influence will have to redirect their attention to the application of different influence techniques in different arenas. The silver lining in all of this is that the influence techniques likely to be of increasing importance as we approach the twenty-first century are those directed toward integrative, as opposed to coercive, bargaining.

Notes

1. That is not to say that one approach cannot be informed by, and even combined with, the other, as in Snyder and Diesing's (1977) study of crisis bargaining.

2. Just how far that horizon extends, that is, how many moves ahead policymakers calculate in making their choices, remains an open question.

3. A full discussion of diplomacy and negotiation per se appears in the Druckman and Hopmann (1989) chapter of Volume One of this series.

4. There is, of course, Stephen Potter's delightful tongue-in-cheek treatment, *The Theory and Practice of Gamesmanship: The Art of Winning Games Without Actually Cheating* (1948).

5. The Soviet blockade of Berlin in 1948–1949, the U.S. airlift that followed, the deployment of U.S. troops in Lebanon in 1958, and the raising of the Berlin Wall in 1961.

6. This is a departure from the original notion of tit-for-tat, which assumes that,

following the opening move, which must be cooperative, all succeeding moves are strictly tit-for-tat.

7. The payoffs, rank-ordered, with 4 equaling the best payoff, are: defect when other cooperates = 4, cooperate when other cooperates = 3, defect when other defects = 2, and cooperate when other defects = 1. In order to avoid the danger of receiving his or her worst payoff (1), each player chooses a strategy of defect, thus yielding a payoff of 2 for each.

8. A set of experiments by Komorita, Hilty, and Parks (1991) raises some questions regarding the actual ability of other players to recognize tit-for-tat strategies.

9. For a discussion of this drawback to tit-for-tat as a strategy in arms races, see Downs (1990:55).

10. The ordered payoffs for chicken are: defect when other cooperates = 4, cooperate when other cooperates = 3, cooperate when other defects = 2, defect when other defects = 1.

11. The difficult moral issues associated with both of these techniques are discussed in an excellent essay by Walzer (1977).

12. The Vietnam War ultimately was won with conventional forces from the North, although terrorism and guerrilla warfare played important roles in the earlier stages of the war.

13. To complicate matters further, Huth recently has completed an analysis (yet to be published) that is more consistent with Weede's (1983) findings.

14. Holsti (1989) offers a slightly different categorization in the first chapter of the first volume of this series, when he discusses decision making in crises. The distinction, however, is essentially one of emphasis, with Holsti devoting more space to organizational factors and this discussion placing greater emphasis on the relationship between the states engaged in bargaining.

15. The pairs were Austria-Hungary and Russia, France and Germany, Britain and Germany, India and Pakistan, Egypt and Israel, and the United States and the Soviet Union.

References

Alexander, Y., D. Carlton, and P. Wilkinson. 1978. *Terrorism*. Boulder, Colo.: Westview Press.

Alker, H.R., Jr. 1987. Against historical/disciplinary genocide as a prerequisite to history's scientific dissection: Putting historicity at the center of events data research. Paper presented at the meetings of the American Political Science Association, September, Chicago, Ill.

Allison, G.T. 1971. *Essence of Decision: Explaining the Cuban Missile Crisis*. Boston: Little, Brown.

Axelrod, R. 1984. *The Evolution of Cooperation*. New York: Basic Books.

Axelrod, R., and D. Dion. 1988. The further evolution of cooperation. *Science* 242:1385–1389.

Baldwin, D.A. 1974. The power of positive sanctions. *World Politics* 26:19–38.

———. 1985. *Economic Statecraft*. Princeton, N.J.: Princeton University Press.

Bartos, O.J. 1970. Determinants and consequences of toughness. In P. Swingle, ed., *The Structure of Conflict*. New York: Academic Press.

———. 1974. *Process and Outcome of Negotiations*. New York: Columbia University Press.

Bartunck, J.M., A.A. Benton, and C.B. Keys. 1975. Third party intervention and the bargaining of group representatives. *Journal of Conflict Resolution* 19:532–557.

Betts, R.K. 1980. Comment on Mueller: Interests, burdens, and persistence: Asymmetries between Washington and Hanoi. *International Studies Quarterly* 24:530–531.

———. 1987. *Nuclear Blackmail and Nuclear Balance*. Washington, D.C.: Brookings Institution.

Blechman, B.M., and S.S. Kaplan. 1978. *Force Without War: U.S. Armed Forces as a Political Instrument*. Washington, D.C.: Brookings Institution.

Blight, J.G., and D.A. Welch. 1989. *On the Brink*. New York: Hill and Wang.

Boserup, A., and A. Mack. 1975. *War Without Weapons: Non-Violence in National Defense*. New York: Schocken Books.

Brams, S.J. 1985. *Superpower Games: Applying Game Theory to Superpower Conflict*. New Haven, Conn.: Yale University Press.

Brams, S.J., and D.M. Kilgour. 1988. *Game Theory and National Security*. New York: Basil Blackwell.

Brams, S.J., and D. Wittman. 1981. Nonmyopic equilibria in 2 × 2 games. *Conflict Management and Peace Science* 6:39–62.

Brehm, J.W. 1960. *A Theory of Psychological Reactance*. New York: Academic Press.

Brodie, B. 1959. *Strategy in the Missile Age*. Princeton, N.J.: Princeton University Press.

Burns, A.L. 1961. Prospects for a general theory of international relations. In K. Knorr and S. Verba, ed., *The International System*. Princeton, N.J.: Princeton University Press.

Cable, J. 1981. *Gunboat Diplomacy 1919–1979: Political Applications of Limited Naval Force*, 2d ed. New York: St. Martin's.

Cardoso, F.H., and E. Faletto. 1979. *Dependency and Development in Latin America*. Berkeley, Calif.: University of California Press.

Charney, I.W. 1978. *Strategies Against Violence: Design for Non-Violent Change*. Boulder, Colo.: Westview Press.

Chertkoff, J.M., and M. Conley. 1967. Opening offer and frequency of concession as bargaining strategies. *Journal of Personality and Social Psychology* 31:864–872.

Dahl, R.A. 1957. The concept of power. *Behavioral Science* 2:203–214.

Davison, W.P. 1972. *International Political Communication*. New York: Praeger.

De Callieres, M. [1716] 1963. *On the Manner of Negotiating with Princes*. South Bend, Ind.: University of Notre Dame Press.

Deutsch, K.W., et al. 1957. *Political Community and the North Atlantic Area.* Princeton, N.J.: Princeton University Press.

Deutsch, M. 1973. *The Resolution of Conflict: Constructive and Destructive Processes.* New Haven, Conn.: Yale University Press.

Deutsch, M., and R.M. Krauss. 1960. The effect of threat upon interpersonal bargaining. *Journal of Abnormal and Social Psychology* 61:181–189.

Dos Santos, T. 1970. The structure of dependence. *American Economic Review* 60:231–236.

Downs, G.W. 1990. Arms race and war. In P.E. Tetlock, J.L. Husbands, R. Jervis, P.C. Stern, and C. Tilly, eds., *Behavior, Society, and Nuclear War.* Vol. 2. New York: Oxford University Press.

Druckman, D., and P.T. Hopmann. 1989. Behavioral aspects of negotiations on mutual security. In P.E. Tetlock, J.L. Husbands, R. Jervis, P.C. Stern, and C. Tilly, eds., *Behavior, Society, and Nuclear War*, Vol. 1. New York: Oxford University Press.

Esser, J.K., and S.S. Komorita. 1975. Reciprocity and concession making in bargaining. *Journal of Personality and Social Psychology* 31:864–872.

Gaddis, J.L. 1986. The long peace: Elements of stability in the postwar international system. *International Security* 10:99.

Galtung, J. 1967. On the effects of international economic sanctions: With examples from the case of Rhodesia. *World Politics* 19:378–385.

Gamson, W., and A. Modigliani. 1971. *Untangling the Cold War.* Boston: Little, Brown.

George, A. 1969. The operational code. *International Studies Quarterly* 13:190–222.

George, A., D. Hall, and W. Simons. 1971. *The Limits of Coercive Diplomacy.* Boston: Little, Brown.

George, A., and R. Smoke. 1974. *Deterrence in American Foreign Policy: Theory and Practice.* New York: Columbia University Press.

Gochman, C.S., and R.J. Leng. 1983. Realpolitik and the road to war: An analysis of attributes and behavior. *International Studies Quarterly* 27:97–120.

Gottfried, K., and B.G. Blair, eds. 1988. *Crisis Stability and Nuclear War.* New York: Oxford University Press.

Gouldner, A.W. 1960. The norm of reciprocity: A preliminary statement. *American Sociological Review* 25:161–178.

Habeeb, W.M. 1988. *Power and Tactics in International Negotiations: How Weak Nations Bargain with Strong Nations.* Baltimore, Md.: Johns Hopkins University Press.

Habeeb, W.M., and I.W. Zartman. 1986. *The Panama Canal Negotiations.* Washington, D.C.: Foreign Policy Institute, Johns Hopkins University.

Hoffmann, S. 1978. *Primacy or World Order: American Foreign Policy Since the Cold War.* New York: McGraw-Hill.

Holsti, K.J. 1983. *International Politics: A Framework for Analysis.* Englewood Cliffs, N.J.: Prentice-Hall.

Holsti, O.R. 1976. Foreign policy formation viewed cognitively. In R. Axelrod, ed., *Structure of Decision*. Princeton, N.J.: Princeton University Press.

———. 1989. Crisis decision making. In P.E. Tetlock, J.L. Husbands, R. Jervis, P.C. Stern, and C. Tilly, eds., *Behavior, Society, and Nuclear War*, Vol. 1. New York: Oxford University Press.

Homans, G.C. 1961. *Social Behavior: Its Elementary Forms*. New York: Harcourt, Brace.

Howard, M. 1971. *Studies in War and Peace*. New York: Viking Press.

Hufbauer, G.C., and J.J. Schott. 1985. *Economic Sanction Reconsidered: History and Current Policy*. Washington, D.C.: Institute for International Economics.

Huth, P.K. 1988. *Deterrence and War*. New Haven, Conn. Yale University Press.

Huth, P.K., and B. Russett. 1984. What makes deterrence work? Cases from 1900 to 1980. *World Politics* 36:496–526.

Ikle, F.C. 1964. *How Nations Negotiate*. New York: Harper and Row.

James, P., and F. Harvey. 1989. Optimal Threats: An Assessment of Superpower Rivalry in International Crises, 1948–1985. Paper presented at the annual meetings of the International Studies Association, Atlanta, Ga.

Janis, I.L. 1972. *Victims of Groupthink*. Boston: Houghton Mifflin.

Jervis, R. 1976. *Perception and Misperception in International Politics*. Princeton, N.J.: Princeton University Press.

———. 1984. *The Illogic of American Nuclear Strategy*. Ithaca, N.Y.: Cornell University Press.

———. 1988*a*. The political effects of nuclear weapons: A comment. *International Security* 13:79–80.

———. 1988*b*. Realism, game theory, and cooperation. *World Politics* 39:317–349.

———. 1989. Rational deterrence: Theory and evidence. *World Politics* XLI:183–207.

Jones, E.E., and C. Wortman. 1973. *Ingratiation: An Attributional Approach*. Morristown, N.J.: General Learning Press.

Kahn, H. 1960. *On Thermonuclear War*. Princeton, N.J.: Princeton University Press.

———. 1965. *On Escalation: Metaphors and Scenarios*, rev. ed. Baltimore, Md.: Penguin.

Kahneman, D., and A. Tversky. 1973. On the psychology of prediction. *Psychological Review* 80:237–251.

Karsten, P., P.D. Howell, and A.F. Allen. 1984. *Military Threats: A Systemic Historical Analysis of the Determinants of Success*. Westport, Conn.: Greenwood Press.

Kegley, C.W., Jr., ed. 1990. *International Terrorism: Characteristics, Causes, Controls*. New York: St. Martin's.

Keohane, R.O., and J.S. Nye, Jr. 1977. *Power and Interdependence: World Politics in Transition*. Boston: Little, Brown.

Kissinger, H.A. 1957. *Nuclear Weapons and Foreign Policy*. New York: Harper and Row.

————. 1982. *Years of Upheaval*. Boston: Little, Brown.

Komorita, S.S., and J.K. Esser. 1975. Frequency of reciprocated concessions in bargaining. *Journal of Personality and Social Psychology* 32:699–705.

Komorita, S.S., J.A. Hilty, and C.D. Parks. 1991. Reciprocity and cooperation in social dilemmas. *Journal of Conflict Resolution* 35:494–519.

Kugler, J. 1984. Terror without deterrence: Reassessing the role of nuclear weapons. *Journal of Conflict Resolution* 28:470–506.

Laqueur, W. 1976. The futility of terrorism. *Harper's* (March):99–105.

Laqueur, W., ed. 1978. *The Terrorism Reader*. Philadelphia: Temple University Press.

Lebow, R.N. 1981. *Between Peace and War: The Nature of International Crisis*. Baltimore, Md.: Johns Hopkins University Press.

Leng, R.J. 1980. Influence strategies and interstate conflict. In J.D. Singer, ed., *The Correlates of War: II*. New York: Free Press.

————. 1983. When will they ever learn? Coercive bargaining in recurrent crises. *Journal of Conflict Resolution* 27:379–420.

————. 1984. Reagan and the Russians: Crisis bargaining beliefs and the historical record. *American Political Science Review* 78:338–355.

Leng, R.J., and R.A. Goodsell. 1974. Behavioral indicators of war proneness in bilateral conflicts. In P. McGowan, ed., *Sage International Yearbook of Foreign Policy Studies*, Vol. 2. Beverly Hills, Calif.: Sage Publications.

Leng, R.J., and S.G. Walker. 1982. Comparing two studies of crisis bargaining: Confrontation, coercion, and reciprocity. *Journal of Conflict Resolution* 26:571–591.

Leng, R.J., and H. Wheeler. 1979. Influence strategies, success, and war. *Journal of Conflict Resolution* 23:655–684.

Levy, J. 1988. Review article: When do deterrent threats work? *British Journal of Political Science* 18:485–512.

————. 1989. The causes of war: a review of theories and evidence. In P.E. Tetlock, J.L. Husbands, R. Jervis, P.C. Stern, and C. Tilly, eds., *Behavior, Society, and Nuclear War*, Vol. 1. New York: Oxford University Press.

Lewicki, R.J., and J.Z. Rubin. 1973. Effects of variations in the informational clarity of promises and threats upon interpersonal bargaining. *Proceedings of the 81st Annual Convention of the American Psychological Association* 8: 137–238.

Lindsay, J.M. 1986. Trade sanctions as policy instruments: A re-examination. *International Studies Quarterly* 30:153–174.

Lindskold, S., Bonoma, T., Schenker, B., and Tedeschi, J. 1972. Some factors affecting the effectiveness of reward power. *Psychonomic Science* 26:68–70.

Lindskold, S., and R. Bennett. 1973. Attributing trust and conciliatory intent from coercive power capability. *Journal of Personality and Social Psychology* 28:180–186.

Lindskold, S., B. Betz, and P. Walters. 1986. Transforming competitive or cooperative climates. *Journal of Conflict Resolution* 30:99–114.

Livingstone, N.C., and T.E. Arnold. 1986. *Fighting Back: Winning the War Against Terrorism*. Lexington, Mass.: Lexington Books.

Losman, D.L. 1979. *International Economic Sanctions: The Cases of Cuba, Israel, and Rhodesia*. Albuquerque, N.M.: University of New Mexico Press.

Luttwak, E. 1974. *The Political Uses of Sea Power*. Baltimore, Md.: Johns Hopkins University Press.

McClelland, C.A. 1968. *International Interaction Analysis: Basic Research and Some Practical Applications*. Los Angeles, Calif.: University of Southern California Press.

McGillicuddy, N.B., D.G. Pruitt, and H. Syna. 1984. Perceptions of firmness and strength in negotiation. *Personality and Social Psychology Bulletin* 10:402–409.

Mandel, R. 1986. The effectiveness of gunboat diplomacy. *International Studies Quarterly* 30:59–76.

Maoz, Z. 1983. Resolve, capabilities, and the outcome of interstate disputes, 1816–1976. *Journal of Conflict Resolution* 27:195–229.

———. 1989. Power, capabilities, and paradoxical outcomes. *World Politics* 41:239–266.

Maoz, Z., and D.S. Felsenthal. 1987. Self-binding commitments, the inducement of trust, social choice, and the theory of international cooperation. *International Studies Quarterly* 31:177–200.

Martin, J.L., ed. 1971. *Propaganda in International Affairs*. Philadelphia: Annals of the American Academy of Political and Social Science, vol. 398.

Molander, P. 1985. The optimal level of generosity in a selfish, uncertain environment. *Journal of Conflict Resolution* 29:611–618.

Morgenthau, H.J. [1948] 1973. *Politics Among Nations*. New York: Knopf.

Mueller, J. 1988. The essential irrelevance of nuclear weapons: Stability in the postwar world. *International Security* 13:59–78.

Neustadt, R.E. 1970. *Alliance Politics*. New York: Columbia University Press.

Nincic, M., and P. Wallenstein. 1983. Economic coercion and foreign policy. In M. Nincic and P. Wallenstein, eds., *Dilemmas of Economic Coercion: Sanctions in World Politics*. New York: Praeger.

North, R., O. Holsti, and R. Brody. 1964. Some empirical data on the conflict spiral. *Peace Research Society Papers* 1:1–14.

Nye, J.S., Jr. 1990. *Bound to Lead*. New York: Basic Books.

Olson, R.S. 1979. Economic coercion in world politics, with a focus on north-south relationships. *World Politics* 31:471–494.

Oneal, J.R. 1988. The rationality of decision making during international crises. *Polity* 20:598–622.

Organski, A.F.K., and J. Kugler. 1980. *The War Ledger*. Chicago: University of Chicago Press.

Osgood, C.E. 1962. *An Alternative to War or Surrender*. Urbana, Ill.: University of Illinois Press.

Osgood, R.E., and R.W. Tucker. 1967. *Force, Order, and Justice*. Baltimore, Md.: Johns Hopkins University Press.

Peterson, W.J. 1986. Deterrence and compellence: A critical assessment of conventional wisdom. *International Studies Quarterly* 30:269–294.

124   BEHAVIOR, SOCIETY, AND INTERNATIONAL CONFLICT

Potter, S. 1948. *The Theory and Practice of Gamesmanship: The Art of Winning Games Without Actually Cheating*. New York: Holt.
Pruitt, D.G. 1965. Definition of the situation as a determinant of international action. In H.C. Kelman, ed., *International Behavior: A Social-Psychological Analysis*. New York: Holt.
Pruitt, D.G., and J.Z. Rubin. 1986. *Social Conflict*. New York: Random House.
Qualter, T.H. 1962. *Propaganda and Psychological Warfare*. New York: Random House.
Rapoport, A. 1960. *Fights, Games, and Debates*. Ann Arbor, Mich.: University of Michigan Press.
———. 1964. *Strategy and Conscience*. New York: Schoken Books.
Rapoport, A., and A. Chammah. 1965. *Prisoner's Dilemma*. Ann Arbor, Mich.: University of Michigan Press.
Richardson, L.F. 1960. *Arms and Insecurity*. Chicago: Quadrangle Books.
Schaffner, P.E. 1985. Specious learning about reward and punishment. *Journal of Personality and Social Psychology* 48:1377–1386.
Schell, J. 1986. Reflections (Poland). *New Yorker* (Feb. 3):47–67.
Schelling, T.C. 1960. *Strategy of Conflict*. Cambridge, Mass.: Harvard University Press.
———. 1966. *Arms and Influence*. New Haven, Conn.: Yale University Press.
Schlagheck, D.M. 1988. *International Terrorism: An Introduction to the Concepts and Actors*. Lexington, Mass.: Lexington Books.
Sharp, G. 1973. *The Politics of Nonviolent Action*. Boston: Porter Sargent.
———. 1980. *Social Power and Political Freedom*. Boston: Porter Sargent.
Shubik, M. 1990. Models of strategic behavior and nuclear deterrence. In P.E. Tetlock, J.L. Husbands, R. Jervis, P.C. Stern, and C. Tilly, eds., *Behavior, Society, and Nuclear War*, Vol. 2. New York: Oxford University Press.
Singer, J.D. 1963. Inter-nation influence: A formal model. *American Political Science Review* 57:420–430.
Singer, J.D., ed. 1990. *Models, Methods, and Progress: A Peace Research Odyssey*. Boulder, Colo.: Westview Press.
Snyder, G., and P. Diesing. 1977. *Conflict Among Nations*. Princeton, N.J.: Princeton University Press.
Stein, J.G. 1990. Deterrence and reassurance. In P.E. Tetlock, J.L. Husbands, R. Jervis, P.C. Stern, and C. Tilly, eds., *Behavior, Society, and Nuclear War*, Vol. 2. New York: Oxford University Press.
Stohl, M. 1988. *The Politics of Terrorism*, 3d. rev. ed. New York: Marcel Dekker.
Strack, H.R. 1978. *Sanctions: The Case of Rhodesia*. Syracuse, N.Y.: Syracuse University Press.
Suedfeld, P., and P. Tetlock. 1977. Integrative complexity of communications in international crisis. *Journal of Conflict Resolution* 21:169–184.
Tetlock, P.E. 1989. Methodological themes and variations. In P.E. Tetlock, J.L. Husbands, R. Jervis, P.C. Stern, and C. Tilly, eds., *Behavior, Society, and Nuclear War*, Vol. 1. New York: Oxford University Press.

Vasquez, J.A. 1983. *The Power of Power Politics: A Critique*. New Brunswick, N.J.: Rutgers University Press.

Walker, S.G., and L.S. Falkowski. 1984. The operational codes of U.S. presidents and secretaries of state: Motivational foundations and behavioral consequences. *Political Psychology* 5:237–266.

Wall, J.A., Jr. 1975. Effects of constituent trust and representative bargaining orientation on intergroup bargaining. *Journal of Personality and Social Psychology* 31:1004–1012.

————. 1977. Operantly conditioning a negotiator's concession making. *Journal of Experimental Social Psychology* 13:431–440.

Wallerstein, I. 1979. *The Capitalist World-Economy*. Cambridge, England: Cambridge University Press.

Walters, R.H., and J.F. Grusec. 1977. *Punishment*. San Francisco: W.H. Freeman.

Walton, R.E., and R.B. McKersie. 1965. *A Behavioral Theory of Labor Negotiations: An Analysis of a Social Interaction System*. New York: McGraw-Hill.

Walzer, M. 1977. *Just and Unjust Wars*. New York: Basic Books.

Wardlaw, G. 1983. *Political Terrorism: Theory, Tactics, and Counter Measures*. Cambridge, England: Cambridge University Press.

Wayman, F., J.D. Singer, and G. Goertz. 1983. Capability, military allocations, and success in militarized disputes. *International Studies Quarterly* 27:497–515.

Weede, E. 1983. Extended deterrence by superpower alliance. *Journal of Conflict Resolution* 27:231–253.

Worchal, S., and J. Brehm. 1971. Direct and implied social restoration of freedom. *Journal of Personality and Social Psychology* 18:294–304.

Yukl, G.A. 1974. Effects of the opponent's initial offer, concession magnitude, and concession frequency on bargaining behavior. *Journal of Personality and Social Psychology* 30:322–335.

Zagare, F. 1987. *Dynamics of Deterrence*. Chicago: University of Chicago Press.

Zinnes, D.A., R.C. North, and H.E. Koch, Jr. 1961. Capability, threat, and the outbreak of war. In J.N. Rosenau, ed., *International Politics and Foreign Policy*. New York: Free Press.

3

The Shadow of the Past: Learning from History in National Security Decision Making

WILLIAM W. JAROSZ WITH JOSEPH S. NYE, JR.

> What experience and history teach is this—that people and governments
> never have learned anything from history, or acted on principles deduced
> from it.
>
> —HEGEL

The broad continuity of human conflict, the cycles of wars and violence recorded in history, give powerful voice to Hegel's assertion that learning matters little in international politics. For the political scientist, the persistence of war in world politics rubs against the grain of scientific rationalism. Robert Gilpin has expressed this irony well: "A scholar of international relations has a responsibility to be true to this faith that the advance of knowledge will enable us to create a more just and more peaceful world. But, in honesty, one must inquire whether or not twentieth-century students of international relations know anything that Thucydides and his fifth-century compatriots did not know about the behavior of states" (1981:226–227).

Yet, as the century draws to a close, tremendous changes are refashioning international affairs, and the foreign policies of the states in the international system. The Cold War, which defined international politics for a generation, has ended, with the Soviet Union largely conceding the game. Across the former Soviet empire the states of Eastern Europe are struggling to build democratic governments and attempting to integrate into the international political economy. The future of the Soviet Union itself is uncertain. Its political institutions appear to have fallen as easily as its political monuments to past Communist leaders. What will take their place is still difficult to foresee, but the Communist past has firmly been interred.

It is tempting to account for these events by arguing in opposition to Hegel, that states are finally acting upon principles deduced from history—that states have learned. Thus, after 70 years of economic failure, the Soviet Union has come to see the folly of pursuing an expansionist foreign policy at the expense of internal economic development, and this has caused a revolution in Soviet foreign policy (Breslauer and Tetlock, 1991). Francis Fukuyama has argued (1989) in even broader terms and maintains that countries across the political spectrum have undergone an "ideological evolution" (p. 4) and become convinced of "the unabashed victory of economic and political liberalism" (p. 3). The startling changes that have occurred in the last decade of this century are indeed political events beyond the grasp of Thucydides.

While explanations of foreign policy that implicitly rely upon some notion of learning are commonplace, theoretical investigations of political learning have only recently emerged (Tetlock, 1991). Scholars have approached this issue armed with conflicting definitions, methodologies, and epistemologies, but it is still far from certain whether or not a new tool needs to be added to our analytical toolbox. The first purpose of this essay is to examine the need for theoretical investigation into the question of learning in international affairs. Second, we will survey contending approaches toward learning and international politics as they apply to the study of national security, noting common views and differences. We will offer a general definition of learning and a framework for examining the role of learning in explanations of foreign policy change. Then we will explore how scholars working within three general paradigms of learning analyze international political behavior: those who view international relations as "data driven" by rational nation-states; as "theory driven" by decision makers; or as "rule driven" by domestic and international institutions (Tetlock and McGuire, 1986:147–179). Finally, after assessing the progress of these approaches, we will briefly propose the adoption of a multistage model of learning as a prelude to more abstract theory building, and evaluate its utility by examining the role of learning in the aftermath of the Cuban missile crisis.

Why Bother with Learning?

The study of international relations is already cluttered up with concepts that are treated as variables in explanations of foreign policy but not tied to any integrative theory. The astute researcher can appeal to an ever expanding repertoire of variables in the course of explanation: a state's relative power; domestic regime type; political culture; elite politics; and so forth. Before adding to the confusion, we should be sure that new concepts strengthen our research, rather than just increase the size of our vocabularies.

Explanations of political events that evoke learning are especially attractive because they fit into a large gap in our knowledge: the process of social change. Despite years of speculation on why states pursue various foreign policies, we know relatively little about how and why policies change over time. All social scientists have had difficulty formulating general theories of change; political scientists have perhaps fared the worst. In the words of Samuel Huntington, sociologists "have regularly bemoaned their lack of knowledge concerning social change, but compared with past neglect of the theory of political change in political science, sociology is rich with works on the theory of social change" (cited in Genco, 1980:55). Alexander George echoed this observation regarding international relations theory: "empirical theory in international affairs so far has made little headway with the problems of understanding how the international system changes over time" (cited in Genco, 1980:55). In the 1990s, when so much of world politics is in flux, the silence of social science theory on the process of policy change is particularly frustrating.

The historical record also seems to show that despite the logic of an international system predicated on the use of force, nations have, at various times, formulated differing conceptions of national interest and posited different goals for state action. The Japan of the 1930s and the Japan of the 1980s both sought "security" at an abstract level, but how Japanese leaders define the content of that security has undergone a profound alteration. Changes of this sort have remained beyond our theoretical grasp.

Yet our need to understand political change runs ahead of theory formulation, and our analyses of events often incorporate causal explanations that seem plausible but are not part of any larger, more developed analytical framework. Learning is often used in this fashion. Many analyses of arms control, for example, rely upon rough notions of "learning" to give force to explanations of state behavior. Franklyn Griffiths (1989) argues that Soviet actions over time show clear evidence of "learning behavior" in dealing with the West regarding arms control since the Genoa conference of 1922. Thus, Moscow has learned via a process of "coming to terms with the principal adversary on means to reduce the risks and opportunity costs of an adversarial relationship." Griffiths is noting a change in Soviet behavior and attributing it to changes in Soviet calculations about the appropriate means to be used in diplomacy.

Similarly, Fen Hampson (1989) has suggested that learning brought new items onto the Soviet-American arms control agenda in the 1960s and 1970s. Evidence that atmospheric testing was environmentally harmful spurred the test ban treaty of 1963, and fears by scientists about the destabilizing consequences of ballistic missile defenses were important stimuli behind the first Strategic Arms Limitation Treaty.

While explanations that advocate learning as a cause for changed behavior are quite common, the exact nature of the causal connection is often vague, and scholars seem to use the term in a variety of different ways. This cacophony of usage is sometimes the result of applying a "fuzzy" concept and sometimes the result of deeper epistemological differences. As argued below, differing conceptions of the nature of international politics, and the appropriate actors to be considered, drive the diverging debate over the usefulness of learning as an analytical tool.

The Problem of Definition

The social sciences have traditionally advanced upon the backs of analogies drawn from the physical or biological sciences. A driving force behind the development of economics has been a series of analogies taken from the study of Newtonian physics,[1] and political science has freely in turn borrowed metaphors and analogies from economics. In the study of politics (as well as in the practice of politics), analogical reasoning is best used *heuristically*, to suggest causal links and relationships that are later put to empirical tests. Analogies are misused when cause and effect links are dogmatically transferred from one domain of knowledge to another and asserted to hold without further justification. Learning explanations of policy change have often fallen prey to these errors.

To sort through the confusion surrounding the use of learning in political explanation, we will start with a simple definition: learning is the acquisition of new knowledge or information that leads to a change in behavior.[2] At the very bottom, the term "learning" used in everyday language seems to suggest this much, and this definition serves as a sort of least common denominator. Different scholars argue for differing causal paths and other intervening variables, but it appears as though they all have at least this much in common: learning begins with the acquisition of information. If we start with a minimalist definition of learning, we can better see how this concept has been applied by scholars from very different epistemological perspectives.

Learning, as used in the scholarly literature, differs along three dimensions: *what* is learned; *who* is doing the learning; and *when* the learning takes place. First, scholars differ in their conceptions over *what* is learned. Joseph S. Nye, in a previous article, has captured these differences by noting that learning exists along a continuum from "simple learning," involving only the adoption of new tactics, to "complex learning," involving the pursuit of new goals (Nye, 1989; see also Argyris and Schon, 1978). Simple learning uses new information to adapt the means of policy, without altering any deeper goals in the ends-means chain. The actor merely uses a different instrument to attain the same goal. Complex learning, by contrast, involves recognition of conflicts among means and goals in causally complicated situations and leads to new priorities and trade-offs.

In the 1970s, when the United States altered its military strategy for defending Europe, emphasizing maneuver warfare over positional defense, it can be said to have engaged in simple learning. The goal of policy, the military defense of Europe, remained the same, but the means used to achieve that goal were altered. A state, such as Panama, that has disbanded its military forces has adopted a new definition of national security and consequently can be said to have experienced complex learning.

In practice, of course, means and ends, tactics and goals, may be difficult to cleanly differentiate. Is arms control a means for security, or a goal in and of itself? Useful distinctions for the purpose of analysis can, however, be made. Soviet acceptance of arms control in the 1970s lies more in the realm of simple learning, because the basic principle of armed struggle retained its place in Soviet ideology. By the end of the 1980s, the Soviet leadership had come to view arms control as a goal in itself, because of a reevaluation and deemphasis of the military basis for national security (Shenfield, 1987; Lynch, 1987).

Simple learning does not imply that the processes involved in developing new tactics or means of policy are by any means easy or uncomplicated; what is implied, however, is that new information will generally cause means to alter before goals are altered. Changing the goals of policy are more costly, and therefore more difficult, than changing the means.

Yet some analysts argue that only simple learning exists, because the nature of international politics constrains policy to an exclusive focus on military force, while others argue that nations can at times fundamentally redirect their foreign policies toward new goals. This difference drives policy debates as well. Throughout the 1980s, conservatives and liberals argued over whether the Soviet Union was pursuing arms control to acquire a tactical "breathing space" before embarking upon the usual course of military competition, or whether a new set of interests and priorities, primarily the health of the domestic economy, had emerged in the minds of the Soviet leadership.

Second, scholars differ as to which level of analysis learning explanations best apply. Since the publication of Kenneth Waltz's *Man, the State, and War* (1959), the application of levels of analysis has been a valuable organizing device. We shall not break with that tradition. When a learning explanation is invoked, it is important to ask *who* is doing the learning. As with most concepts in international relations, learning can be employed as a causal factor operating at the level of the state, of individual decision makers, or of the organizations and bureaucracies that constitute the state, and the choice of level of analysis has important consequences for explanations of behavior that use learning as a causal variable. Those arguing from the perspective of the individual or the organization posit additional intervening variables upon which learning operates. Cognitive theorists, working at the level of the individual, argue that for learning to change either goals or tactics there must first be a change in individual cognitive beliefs about the nature of the world or cognitive structures for processing information. Organizational theorists, by contrast, argue that new information affects the choice of tactics or goals through organizational structures and bureaucratic routines.[3]

Third, students of international relations disagree about the appropriate time frame to use when discussing the possibility of learning. Most writers who examine international politics from the perspective of the state argue that learning occurs in "real time"; that is, that the learning that is most relevant to explaining policies occurs as states respond to changes in the international environment. The historical past, in this view, does not intrude upon the present. Scholars from the cognitive and organizational schools argue that the time frame for learning must be extended back further into the past. Decision makers or organizations are influenced by events that occurred in their past and shaped beliefs, or cognitive or organizational structures, and impinge upon judgments about the present.

Schematically, learning analyses break down as follows:

Who Learns?	What Is Learned?	When Do They Learn?
The state	Primarily tactics	As the system changes
Decision makers	Cognitive beliefs/ structures	During crises
Organizations	Routines and patterns	During formation or reorganization

This conceptualization of learning explanations will serve as a guide for the subsequent discussion, but several caveats need to be kept in mind. Even within this spare definition of learning, it is important to note what is included and what is not. Learning explanations are a subset of other explanations that focus upon policy change, and policies may change for a large variety of reasons.[4] Leaders may die or be removed from power; factions within the leadership shift or change; political generations may change, bringing new leaders with new values to the fore. Learning is only one possible explanation of change, and it must be kept analytically separate from other explanations of change if it is to have any value. The focus of learning explanations is upon information, and how information acts to either alter perceptions of constraints or generate goals and interests.

Second, a common cause of confusion is that learning implies progress toward "better" decisions or more reasonable goals. Yet, just as individuals learn to take up jogging or dieting, they also learn to smoke or overeat. The proper focus of a learning explanation is upon how new information changes either existing decision rules or the goals of action themselves, and makes no judgment about the normative content of action. States or statesmen can learn patterns of behavior that provoke wars, prolong conflict, or hinder peaceful negotiation. There need be no assumption that all learning is for the better.

Explanations of Foreign Policy

Additional order can be brought into the survey of learning explanations by first noting the common elements of most explanations of foreign policy (and indeed, most of the social sciences) and how learning explanations fit in.

While scholars may disagree upon the relevant actors in international politics, some preferring to focus upon international institutions, some upon the state, some upon organizations within the state, and some upon individuals, most adopt a broadly similar view of how action comes about. Borrowing from Jon Elster (1989), the actions taken by states, organizations, or individuals can be seen as the by-product of two "filtering operations." First, the actor faces environmental constraints that place limits upon possible courses of action. In explaining the defense policy of a developing nation, for example, the combination of level of industrial development, domestic scientific knowledge, and the international nuclear nonproliferation regime may effectively rule out nuclear deterrence as a viable policy choice. The actions that are not ruled out by existing constraints make up the "opportunity set" from which the actor chooses.

Once options are limited, the explanation passes through a second filter that actually selects an option from the opportunity set based upon some notion of the actor's goals, mediated by a process of (more or less) rational choice. Thus, an actor's behavior is effectively explained when we account for the opportunities the environment presents and the goals toward which decisions are made.

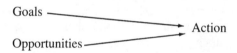

Obviously, this explanatory framework does not hold for those scholars who argue that much state action is stochastic or random. But the majority of work in the field implicitly uses this framework, even though there are deep disagreements about the actors in international politics, the definition of what counts as environment, and the extent of rationality appropriate to the actors. As developed below, different scholars see learning entering into this explanatory pattern in very different ways.

Learning I: Rational, Data-Driven States

Neorealism: Learning as Rational Adaptation

A strong current in contemporary thinking on sources of foreign policy is based upon rational choice theories adapted from neoclassical economics. Blending older realist concepts about the nature of international politics and a new methodological awareness, the resulting "neorealist" framework employs the tools of game theory and concepts borrowed from microeconomics and has brought a welcome precision to discussions of power, influence, and bargaining in interstate relations.[5]

Neorealism is founded upon a set of core behavioral assumptions that modify and extend the older realist tradition.[6] Three assumptions guide and shape the research of scholars working within this paradigm (Keohane, 1983:508):

1. States are the fundamental actors in world politics.
2. States can be conceptualized as unitary rational actors, which calculate the costs of alternative policies in order to maximize their utility.
3. States seek power, and they define their interests in terms of power.

Neorealism asserts that states are the most significant unit of analysis in which to comprehend international politics. The need for examining the internal structures of states or the deliberation of national leaders disappears in neorealist writings. They assert that the logic of the international system poses such a hard constraint upon state action that the states become functionally equivalent and act the same regardless of internal structure or regime type.

Further, neorealists argue that states can be treated as unitary, rational decision makers. States have well-defined sets of preferences that are logically coherent and stable, and logical sets of decision rules for selecting alternate policies. Internal characteristics of the decision process—leadership personalities, bureaucratic structure, political factions—are held to be of minor importance in neorealist analysis.

For neorealist scholars, in a world populated by rational states seeking power, the international environment becomes the most important constraint upon the direction of foreign policy. Neorealism emphasizes the way in which the anarchic international system causes all states to seek security through the use or threat of military force. Fear of domination by a single state will cause the formation of balances of power.

The rationality assumption in neorealist theory provides the means to link the behavior of the states to changes in the system. As states perceive changes in the environment, they act to alter their behavior. This conception of international politics is rather mechanistic, with states acting as "cybernetic" devices that easily respond to changes in external conditions (Steinbruner, 1974). Should one state attempt to acquire hegemony, the others perceive this and will cooperate long enough to restore the balance of power. The logic that dictates policy is: "the enemy of my enemy is my friend." Thus, during World War II, the American and British governments easily pushed aside their scruples about dealing with the Bolshevik regime in the Soviet Union when they were faced with the threat of Hitler.

But the balancing behavior predicted by the theory is always tactical; each state's fundamental interest, to preserve its independence by preventing another state from accumulating preponderant power, remains unchanged. This is because the structural characteristics of the system—anarchy and a lack of hierarchical order—completely dominate the behavior of the states. In terms of the previous diagram:

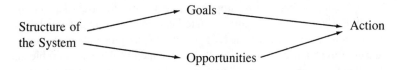

The goals of the states are given by assumption: the maximization of power in order to survive as sovereign states in an anarchic world. Similarly, the absence of any coercive power or government above the states limits cooperation and ensures that force will be the ultima ratio of international politics.

The role of learning in this system of explanation is limited to two forms. First, it is assumed that states will have the facility to learn about the environment they face and adjust their foreign policy accordingly. Like rational choice economics, neorealist theory assumes that information is free and its provision is not problematic, and that states will be able to process and analyze information on their environment, formulate alternate paths, and choose the one that maximizes power, or in some formulations, security.[7] The end result of power maximization by like-minded states is that the states in the international system will engage in balancing behavior. For this to occur, at least some of the states, some of the time, must be able to discriminate emerging threats and act accordingly. As Waltz argues, they will adjust the means of policy, choosing to balance by internal efforts during periods of bipolarity and through alliances during periods of multipolarity, but their basic goal, interest defined in terms of power, remains immutable. Only simple learning will be in evidence.

However, the ideal standards of frictionless learning in neorealist theory are rarely borne out in the practice of states. Judging the international environment, assessing threats and their relative proximity, formulating alternate courses of action, and then choosing the "best" policy is rarely a description of the actual behavior of states. They often perceive their environment only with great difficulty and formulate responses amid confusion and uncertainty.

As William C. Wohlforth (1987) has shown, perceptions of the balance of power are subject to a great deal of confusion and error. Wohlforth examines the perceptions of Russian power on the eve of World War I and discovers systematic errors on the part of the combatants in estimating Russian strength. France, England, and Italy all showed the tendency to overestimate the efficacy of the Russian military, while Germany and Austria repeatedly underestimated the Russians.

This issue remains beyond the scope of neorealist theory. As long as the internal structure of the states is fixed by assumption, the theory cannot grapple with questions involving differing perceptions of reality on the part of states, or differing decision-making and information-processing capabilities.[8]

Second, and perhaps most important, neorealist theories depend upon learning to assure the uniformity of state behavior that supplies much of the force of the logic of the neorealist argument. Having relied upon assumptions of learning to shape state behavior, the theory then declares it unproblematic and excludes learning from further analysis. To see this point in more detail, it is important to examine the analogous arguments in neoclassical economics.[9]

The assumption in economics that firms maximize profits is not picked at random out of thin air, but is part and parcel of the deeper logic of economic argument. The maximization of profits is a decision rule whose evolution standard neoclassical theory takes to be relatively unproblematic as firms adapt in an extremely competitive environment. Neoclassical economics does not necessarily assume that all firms maximize profits, only that those that do will survive and those that don't will be pushed into bankruptcy. The result, after several iterations, is that the only firms left in a competitive market are those that maximize profits. This process of adaptation is left unanalyzed because it is assumed to be unproblematic. In the words of Robert E. Lucas, Jr.: "Technically, I think of economics as studying decision rules that are steady states of some adaptive process, decision rules that are found to work over a range of situations and hence are no longer revised appreciably as more experience accumulates" (1986:218).

This notion of the evolution of efficient decision rules is explicitly carried over to neorealist analysis, but the justification for it is much weaker. While the competition of the market ensures that firms that don't maximize fail, there is no corresponding mechanism for states in the international system. As Waltz acknowledges, "The death rate among states is remarkably low" (1979:95). Yet neorealism depends upon a certain degree of homogeneity in the actions of the states that compose the system. If competition in the international system is not so severe as to ensure similar behavior, why do states act similarly in Waltz's analysis?

Waltz argues for two separate learning processes that lead to the adoption of relatively similar decision rules by the states in the international system. First, Waltz holds that states are in a competitive system, and "competition produces a tendency toward the sameness of the competitors" (1979:127). The logic behind this, Waltz argues, is that states that maximize will "do better," and others will emulate their success (1979:77). In support he notes the adoption

by the Continental powers of the general staff system in the wake of the
Prussian victories over Austria in 1866 and France in 1870.

Second, Waltz maintains that a process of socialization operates within the
system that promotes common norms and patterns of behavior (1979:74–76).
Here Waltz notes that the level of tension between the United States and the
Soviet Union has slowly diminished over time. The "worries" and "tensions"
that marked U.S.–Soviet relations have not continued into the present, and
Waltz sees this as evidence that the two countries "are learning gradually how
to cope with each other" (1979:175).

These two modes of learning are presented with very little discussion,
although they are far from obvious. The international system is indeed competitive, yet states do not operate so close to the margin that this competition
causes them to immediately imitate the policies and structure of the current
leader. States differ in what "doing well" means and accordingly have differing notions of success. Even if success were obvious, and the criteria for
success are relatively easy to perceive, Waltz assumes that states can easily
and costlessly change policies. This assumption is difficult to support.

The introduction of socialization is especially puzzling in a theory built
upon rational choice. Ikenberry and Kupchan note that socialization is the
internalizing of norms and value orientations, and that norms and values
"occupy the analytic dimension that lies between deep philosophical beliefs
about human nature and more narrow beliefs about what set of politics will
maximize short-term interests, and they therefore serve to guide state behavior
and shape the agenda from which elites choose specific policies. [In] general
terms, we conceptualize socialization as a process of learning in which norms
and ideals are transmitted from one party to another" (1990:285, 289). The
question of the transmission of norms and values among the states in the
system is a large theoretical and empirical puzzle. To assume that it exists and
then to build further theory in such a way as to prevent the examination of this
assumption is not likely to yield progress in our understanding of international
politics.

This brief discussion of learning and neorealism leads to several observations. First, it helps to answer the question of why we should be bothering
with learning at all. Like the theories of neoclassical economics from which it
borrows, neorealism receives much of the force of its argument not from
rational choice alone, but from the assertion that all actors hold similar decision rules (Arrow, 1987:205). It is this similarity that allows the theory to
make general predictions about how states will act in an anarchic environment. While this assumption can be justified in certain areas of economics,
where the penalties for suboptimization are severe and where information is
unambiguous, it does not seem to apply to international politics.

In addition, the procedures by which the actors come to formulate these decision rules (emulation, and especially socialization) are not open to investigation within the context of the theory. Neorealism enters in only after these basic decision rules have been "learned" by the states in the system, and neorealism declares this learning process to be unproblematic and exogenous to the theory. Acknowledging that decision rules are the product of an adaptive process beyond the grasp of strict rational choice assumptions, neorealist theorists implicitly open the door for explanations cast in terms of how states choose their decision rules, yet the analytical framework they employ prohibits the investigation of these important questions.

Second, the emphasis that neorealism places upon efficient adaptation to the international environment leads to an important logical anomaly within the theory: it becomes difficult to understand why certain wars erupt. No state entered World War I with the expectation that it would lose. Many wars exhibit this pattern and are, in Geoffrey Blainey's words, "dispute[s] about the measurement of power" (1973:114).[10] That is, for war to result from the actions of rational, calculating agents, there must be an asymmetry of information, or differential calculating ability on the part of the actors, and this is prohibited by the assumptions of the theory.

Analogously, it is difficult to see how rational economic actors possessing the same information and the same calculating ability would ever agree to trade securities on the stock exchange. Clearly the notion of trade implies that one party buys in the belief that the stock will rise, while the second party sells in the belief that it will fall; but both expect to profit by the exchange (Arrow, 1987:205). The same holds true for war: both sides believe they will win, yet neorealism has no explanation for this pattern of behavior.

Third, more generally, aside from the question of the evolution of decision rules by the state, neorealism simply brackets too many problematic questions that are evident in the conduct of foreign policy. Neorealism is a structural theory that focuses upon the situational constraints created by the presence of anarchy in the international system. It argues that the constraints of the system are so strong that there is little need to peer into the "black box" of domestic decision making. Anarchy compels the nations in the system to seek power and engage in balancing to forestall hegemonic domination by any single state. But supplying content to the empty notion of "national security" is much more difficult than the assumptions of rational choice imply. Many of the interesting questions of international politics involve the formation of the interests and preferences of the states in the system.[11] Certain states have chosen definitions of national interest that effectively remove them from the realm of neorealist theory, with its emphasis upon issues of force and war. Richard Rosecrance (1986) argues that Japan, for example, has chosen the role of a "trading state," rather than spend resources on military security. John Mueller (1989) would add the Netherlands and Sweden to the list of one-time participants in the power struggle who have chosen to "opt out" of the game. Treating the definition of national interest as an unproblematic assumption given by theory is intellectually unsatisfying.

The same can be said for the treatment of the structure of the state in neorealist theory. The existence of competing bureaucracies within the state often makes even the assessment of threat a source of internal conflict. A prime example is the battle that raged throughout the 1970s between the Department of Defense and the Central Intelligence Agency over estimates of Soviet military strength (Prados, 1982). Bureaus and organizations within the state can cause a "unitary" government to pursue differing, and even contradictory, policies. Does the U.S. government follow a consistent policy toward Japan? The U.S. State Department prefers to adopt a conciliatory tone toward Japan, focusing on the importance of the U.S.–Japanese security arrangement. The Commerce Department, with a differing view of the content of U.S. security, often exacerbates U.S.–Japanese relations with charges of unfair trade practices. Which is the U.S. "preference," conciliation or antagonism?

Finally, all theoretical constructs are abstractions from reality, simplifying certain features of the real world and holding other features constant. But, by focusing on structural constraints, neorealist theory chooses to disregard the fact that nations are historically situated and that history affects their interpretation of the constraints, and therefore their choices as well.

This neglect of historical context has recently been criticized by Robert Jervis, who noted:

> Perhaps the most important limitation of the work on anarchy is that it looks at individual actors, their preferences, and their choices, and thus blinds us to the broader setting in which behavior occurs. Problems arise in a context and out of a history, and not all patterns are the product of careful or even conscious choice. . . . Issues arise in particular historical contexts that shape preferences and behavior. (1988:319–320)[12]

It is easy to redescribe events in terms of neorealist theory. The propositions are so loosely structured ("states seek to maximize power") as to incorporate a wide range of behaviors. However, to recast events in the language of theory is not to explain them. Problems and puzzles can be stated at any given level of analysis, but at which level is a solution best sought? Political science has other theoretical tools in its tool kit that may do a better job of explaining how history influences the course of interstate relations—tools that can usefully begin to set boundary conditions for when learning will matter and when it will not; tools that will illuminate how and when new goals arise, rather than merely describe how unitary state actors adapt to changing environmental conditions.

Neorealism at once illustrates the need to examine learning as a cause of foreign policy change, and the need for moving beyond the narrow strictures of neorealist assumptions. Much of the explanatory force in neorealism comes by way of an assumption regarding learning—that states will adapt over time and will learn through either experience or emulation the optimal decision rules for survival in the international system. But the core assumptions of neorealism—rationality and a unitary state—prohibit a deeper investigation of learning behavior.

Criticizing neoclassical economics, John Maynard Keynes wrote: "The classical theorists resemble Euclidean geometers in a non-Euclidean world, who, discovering that in experience straight lines apparently parallel often meet, rebuke the lines for not keeping straight—as the only remedy for the unfortunate collisions which are occurring. Yet, in truth, there is no remedy except to throw over the axiom of parallels and to work out a non-Euclidean geometry" (cited in Davidson, 1991:142). In a similar fashion, scholars of international politics recognize that learning does occur, and it often finds a way into our explanations of political phenomena. Yet it cannot be easily fit into our existing theoretical frameworks. Rather than declare learning to be out of bounds for theoretical analyses, perhaps we need to reexamine the assumptions upon which we construct our theories.

Since learning seems to deal with how information is perceived, analyzed, and acted upon, it is useful to consider examinations of decision making to see how historians, cognitive psychologists, and political scientists have viewed the decision-making arena and the role that learning plays.

Learning II: Theory-Driven Elites

Rather than focus upon the actions of states in the international system, other groups of scholars have chosen to work from the bottom up by studying individual decision makers in an effort to grasp the most basic ways in which the past influences the present. One strand of research has sought to provide empirical evidence in the form of ideographic studies of decision makers' use of history to guide current behavior. A second strand of research has sought to delve deeper into individual problems of perception and information processing regarding past events by incorporating the findings of cognitive psychology into their work.

Ideographic Studies

Studies of elite decision making differ radically from studies based upon assumptions drawn from models of rational, utility maximization. In place of a world of complete and perfect information, decision makers are faced with either uncertain or ambiguous information, or with too much information, overloading the decision process. Options are not selected after reviewing the entire range of possibilities, and decision rules do not emerge in an evolutionary process of trial and error leading to the "best" decisions. Rather, precedents from the past often act to limit the range of opportunities perceived by decision makers, and guide their choices. The resulting decision rules are quite likely far from optimal.

The problem stems, it is argued, from the structure of the human mind itself and the unavoidable tendency to use the past to form and guide interpretations of the present. As David Hume noted long ago, the mind is constructed so that "those instances of which we have no experience, resemble those, of which we have had experience" (1969:bk. 1, pt. 3, sec. 6).[13] This trait of human inference, to interpret the present through the lens of the past, has been a rich vein of research that has yielded many insights into how decision makers learn from history. The past offers up principles for action, templates for threat assessment and decision, lessons of what can go wrong, and countless other aids to decision making. In two important works, one written singly and one written with Richard Neustadt, historian Ernest May has amply illustrated the pervasiveness of reasoning via historical analogy in government decision making (May, 1973; Neustadt and May, 1986; see also Jervis, 1976).

May and Neustadt show the widespread use of analogical reasoning in a variety of detailed cases spanning American foreign (and domestic) policy of the postwar years that runs counter to the assumptions of neorealist theory. Learning of the invasion of South Korea in June 1950, President Truman did not sit back and dispassionately weigh the consequences for U.S. power. Instead, he interpreted the event and the threat it posed by referring to the "lessons" of the 1930s. To Truman, the issue was less about Korea itself and its impact upon the world balance of power than about what consequences could follow if the United States did not forcefully react.

May's and Neustadt's work prompted other efforts to investigate the role of historical analogies in elite decision making. Dwain Mefford (1987:221–244) discovered that analogical decision making is not limited to the United States. For the Soviet Union as well, decision makers tend to use the past as a guide for present choices. Mefford examines references in the Soviet press and memoir literature to the Polish and Hungarian crises of the 1950s and argues that Soviet actions in Czechoslovakia in 1968 turned upon Soviet decision makers' estimates of whether they were facing another Poland, or another Hungary. Analogy, it appears, is the basis of human cognitive abilities. Other scholars agree that analogical reasoning may be not simply one of the many cognitive processes at work in the activity of defining a situation, but the most fundamental and pervasive (Mefford, 1987; Johnson-Laird, 1980; Keane, 1988; Ortony, 1979).

These empirical studies are important. They show us the limits of abstract conceptions of substantive rationality, and the utility of looking at individual decision makers instead of unitary states. Decision makers do not use complete and perfect information even when it is available in the outside environment. Instead they use lessons and principles drawn from past events to interpret ambiguous information, fill in the gaps in incomplete information, and categorize and sort overabundant information.

This type of research, however, must be undertaken with a great deal of care. Decision makers use history for a variety of purposes, and not all of them are examples of learning with causal force upon policy change. Presidents, prime ministers, and general secretaries are political leaders as well as the ultimate decision makers in their governments. Part of their role is to persuade and justify as well as analyze and decide. A president who refers to "Munich" may be learning from the past but may also be attempting to belittle an opponent with an image of weakness from the past, or trying to win public support via an appeal to emotion. Not every use of the past is a use that provides evidence of learning. Care must be taken to prove that learning from the past played a causal role in the decision process.

Ideally, political scientists would like to begin to set the boundary conditions for the ways in which history shapes decision making. It would be useful, for example, to be able to explain why certain analogies crop up more than others; to predict which analogies would have the greatest impact; to mark off situations in which analogical reasoning plays a more limited role.

The initial work on the use of analogies was largely empirical. When it did have a theoretical focus, that focus was toward prescriptive theory, designed to instruct decision makers on how to avoid the pitfalls of faulty analogical reasoning.[14] Given the central role of analogy as one of several cognitive strategies for handling information, other scholars have attempted to construct bridges between the realms of cognitive psychology and decision-making studies.

Learning and Cognitive Psychology

Philip Tetlock and Charles McGuire (1986) have identified a "cognitive research program" on foreign policy within the larger international relations literature. According to Tetlock and McGuire, there is enough coherence in this research program to identify two core assumptions that guide its investigations. First, the international environment imposes heavy information processing demands upon policymakers. Policymakers must continually cope with fragmented, incomplete information. Policymakers must choose among options whose consequences may not be fully known and that represent value trade-offs. Second, as a consequence, policymakers resort to a variety of simplifying strategies to aid the decision process (1986"149–150).

The cognitive research program argues for an alternate conception of action in social science.

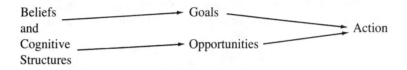

Scholars following this path of research hold that beliefs and cognitive structures are causally prior to the formulation of goals and the perception of the opportunities available. Beliefs about the nature of the world, the other actors in the system, principles of causality, and so on constitute an actor's belief system. Cognitive structures are devices the actor uses to decode and interpret information. Together, they condition the actor's perception of objective reality, influencing which opportunities are perceived and which goals are sought.

Thus, in this paradigm learning is defined as a change in either fundamental beliefs or cognitive structures. Changes in beliefs or structures will in turn lead to changes in tactics (simple learning) or changes in goals (complex learning).

Following these assumptions Yuen Foong Khong (forthcoming) has written an important work that is a first step toward setting the study of analogical reasoning in foreign policy formation within the larger context of a cognitive research program. Khong shows how four analogies drawn from history (Malaya, Korea, Dien Bien Phu, and Munich) served as evaluative tools for decision makers debating the U.S. intervention in Vietnam.

Khong's innovation is to disaggregate the cognitive functions these analogies possessed. Rather than just argue that analogies matter, he shows *how* decision makers used analogies to diagnose the nature of the Vietnam conflict; define the political and moral stakes; predict the likelihood of success; and constrain their choice of strategy. By charting policy debates in great detail Khong shows that analogies were crucial in the change of American policy to escalate the war. Khong carefully separates out the rhetorical use of analogies to persuade opponents and justify decisions and demonstrates how analogies had causal effect on the decisions taken by President Johnson and his cabinet.

Khong's research indicates that although a cognitive approach to the problem of learning from history is information intensive, especially when contrasted with parsimonious theories such as neorealism, the result is a deeper level of explanation. If states engage in balancing behavior, it is difficult to explain why the United States did not intervene at moments when the international balance of power could be seen as tipping in favor of the communists: China (1949); Vietnam (1954); Indonesia (1965); Angola (1975). Khong replies that to argue in these cases "that assessments indicated that the U.S. was unlikely to succeed or that the stakes were not considered as vital . . . is to beg the question how one arrives at these assessments. . . . In the case of Vietnam, historical analogies played a major role in such assessments" (chap. 8, p. 6).

Toward a Cognitive Theory of Learning?

Is it possible to move beyond the study of analogies toward other types of learning and nonlearning within the cognitive research program? Other authors have begun to work in this direction, offering an additional definition of learning as "change in cognitive structures" (Larson, 1988; Tetlock, 1991). Cognitive structures are those heuristics and simplifying mental constructs that individuals use to help them structure reality. Because these structures lie at the bedrock of perception, any change in them is likely to lead to either a change in the tactics individuals use to reach their goals, or a change in the goals themselves. It is this aspect of cognitive change that therefore qualifies as learning.

Researchers working in this area have greatly expanded our descriptive knowledge of common cognitive structures and the strategies used to ease the burdens of information processing. Much work has been done on cognitive maps (Axelrod, 1976; Bonham, Shapiro, and Trumble, 1979), schema theory (Larson, 1985:50–55), operational codes (George, 1979), and the whole range of decision making tools that individuals use to sort and analyze information and to deal with a changing environment.

A significant portion of this research is directed at the study of biases in cognition that deviate from the assumptions of rationality (Kahneman, Slovic, and Tversky, 1982; Kahneman and Tversky, 1972; Tversky and Kahneman, 1983; Tversky and Kahneman, 1981). Interpretations of past events, existing in memory as shorthand schemata, are evoked by surface similarity to present events and overwhelm a fresh reading of the evidence. But aside from cataloging the kinds of things that can go wrong in the decision making process via inappropriate analogies and incorrectly attributed schemata, it is difficult to generalize to a larger theory.

For example, in any given situation, the number of analogical events that can be brought to mind is quite large. Yet not all are salient to the same degree. Some are easier to apply because they are more "available" to our minds. Tversky and Kahneman (1973) argue that this process of availability can apply to the tendency to reason by analogy to the past. According to their research, the more salient an event, the more memorable or recent it is, the more likely it is to serve as a pattern for the future.

Availability does indeed seem to be important in the problem of analogy selection for foreign policy decision makers. Glenn Snyder and Paul Diesing (1977:321) note the powerful impact that the 1912–1913 Balkan Wars had upon the calculations of British statesmen prior to the outbreak of World War I. In the earlier crises, Germany had played the role of the balancer, and British officials believed that in 1914 Germany would once again act as a stabilizing factor. The Balkan War analogy, however, blinded them to those features of the 1914 situation that differed from the earlier crises, especially the changes in the passivity of Germany's alliance partners.

In this example, a historical analogy was used as a cognitive structure—a means of making sense of information. What the British "learned" at one point in time, when the earlier Balkan Wars became a template for future conflict in the Balkans, acted as a brake upon learning as the situation changed. Confronted with a new environment in 1914, the British did not analyze what had changed, but interpreted the present in light of the lessons of the past.

But cognitive structures interact with other mental constructs. There is ample evidence that individual belief systems themselves strongly influence the availability of analogical heuristics. Even individuals of the same age cohort who have lived through the same events often select different historical episodes as "available" to guide their thinking. They may also interpret the same event quite differently and draw divergent lessons for the future. This will limit the quest to create a general learning theory applicable to the study of foreign policy.

The research of Ole Holsti and James Rosenau (1979) illustrates these tendencies. They found that "hawks" and "doves" in the United States tended to extract different lessons from the Vietnam War. Hawks saw the war as the confirmation of their beliefs in an expansionist Soviet Union, the importance of alliance commitments, the validity of the domino theory, and the problems of graduated escalation. Doves, however, saw the war as evidence of the dangers of involvement in wars of national liberation; the problems with military advice; the validity of the notion that third-world revolutions are nationalistic; and that the United States should decrease its role in the world. What surprised both Holsti and Rosenau was the complete lack of overlap and consensus in the lessons the hawks and doves drew from their exposure to the same historical event.

Similarly, William Zimmerman and Robert Axelrod (1981) have investigated the range of Soviet opinion on lessons of the Vietnam conflict and also found a wide divergence of views. Soviet opinion, gleaned from a close reading of the Soviet press, reflected differences over whether military force or economic support was responsible for the outcome of the war; whether the North Vietnamese benefited the most from the efforts of the Communist party or from broad public support; whether the United States became more or less aggressive as it became weaker; and whether the North Vietnamese victory signaled good prospects for other national liberation movements or good prospects for peace.

Not surprisingly, Zimmerman and Axelrod also found that the Soviets as a group drew different conclusions about the Vietnam conflict than did the Americans in the Holsti and Rosenau study. They noted, "Soviet commentators learned substantially different lessons than American elites and attentive publics—partly because Moscow was on the winning side, and partly because the war was filtered through the internal and external experiences of the Soviet Union. Different perspectives result in different lessons" (1981:19).

The variability of lessons learned creates difficulties for a general theory of cognition-based learning. Although there is a plethora of evidence that indicates that decision makers do indeed build cognitive structures based upon past experiences, there is as yet no way of specifying what types of individuals select what types of lessons. Attempts by cognitive scientists to create general models of analogy selection have not been very successful even for extremely simple systems (Tamashiro, 1984; Schank, 1982; Holyoak, 1985; Keane, 1985).

But more important, although we know that decision makers use schemata and other heuristics, we do not know how these decision guides themselves are formed, and more critical for a cognitive learning theory, we do not know how or when they change. As Robert Jervis has remarked, "Previously, change in beliefs could be seen as an almost self-explanatory result of new information, but a stress on the power of schemata makes such changes puzzling" (1986:328). The empirical research that establishes the existence of cognitive frameworks also tends to argue for their durability.

This is not surprising when the logic behind the existence of cognitive structures is recalled. Cognitive "shortcuts" exist because decision makers are overwhelmed by the information that confronts them. That same information cannot be used continually to monitor and correct the decision heuristics themselves. Even in the face of information that contradicts a principle or guide to decision making, individuals cannot constantly reconsider and alter their principles and beliefs. To force the reevaluation of a cognitive framework, contradictory evidence must pass a certain threshold. Unfortunately, we cannot at present say how high that threshold must be.

One study compared the cognitive maps of American officials before and after the 1973 Yom Kippur war. While the decision makers did interpret new information in light of existing cognitive structures, they did not tend to make major adjustments in their thinking. There was no evidence of changes in their thinking although the war came as a major surprise to the decision makers involved (Bonham, Shapiro, and Trumble, 1979). Glenn Snyder and Paul Diesing, in their study of crisis behavior, echo this finding. Background beliefs tend not to vary. "Change in background image for a government usually results from a change of regime, or a shift in the balance of power within a regime, not from individuals changing their minds" (1977:329).

Therefore, while cognitive theories of learning are an important beginning, they ultimately cannot stand on their own. Research has uncovered evidence of both change and consistency in beliefs. Often, however, out of a multitude of lessons drawn by individuals, one interpretation of the past emerges as dominant and shapes the judgments of government officials. The influence of "Munich," for example, was felt by a generation of statesmen. What causes one lesson to predominate? Individuals learn a variety of lessons from the same experience, but over time certain common belief structures may form. The resulting cognitive structures are "sticky"; they persist in the face of contradictory information and contradiction by events. But, it is obvious that *policies* do change. The challenge for social scientists is to place the study of change within a larger theoretical framework.

Individuals, even decision making elites, exist in governments as members of other groups. Individuals act in the context of organizations, institutions, and bureaucracies. Organizations empower individuals and the ideas they carry. Perhaps organizational theories of learning are needed as adjuncts to the insights of cognitive psychology.

Learning III: Rule-Driven Organizations

As the research based on the cognitive paradigm illustrates, decision makers do not confront the data of experience cold: they possess a variety of cognitive structures, often constructed upon their selective knowledge of the past, that categorize, select and screen information about the present. Yet in complex, modern society, organizations often stand between the individual and his or her perception of reality. Herbert Simon notes,

> the elaborate organizations that human beings have constructed in the modern world to carry out the work of production and government can only be understood as machinery for coping with the limits of man's abilities to comprehend and compute in the face of complexity and uncertainty. (1979:501)

Organizations shape the knowledge structures of decision makers either by "preprocessing" the information given to them or by acting in more subtle ways in the process of legitimizing and codifying a certain set of preferences. Organizational theorists argue that organizations act as important intervening variables shaping both goals and opportunities:

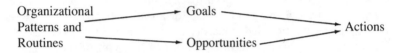

Thus, it is useful to speak of a third locus for discussions of learning: rule-based learning by organizations (March and Olsen, 1984:734–737). Hugh Heclo argues that

> To speak of learning by society or groups should not imply reifying society into a discrete organic mind responding to holistic stimuli. Social learning is created only by individuals, but alone and in interaction these individuals acquire and produce changed patterns of collective action. (1974:306)

Organizational learning that affects foreign policy can be divided into three forms. First, the organization can act as an *input* that shapes elite learning at a higher level in the government structure. The most apparent influence of this type of learning is in the collection and presentation of information by organizations for later use by decision makers. Second, organizations themselves can be conceived of as learning in the sense that events cause changes to be made in the *structure* of an organization that modify its response the next time a similar event is encountered (March and Olsen, 1984:745–746). Third, organizations can "leverage" individual beliefs, giving them *power* in the policy process that they might not have had without organizational backing.

Organizations as an Input to Individual Learning

Many organizations, or subunits of organizations, not only gather information, but also actively seek out "lessons" from past behavior for use in the future.[15] Thus, when looking at foreign policy behavior, one sees organizations existing as mediating structures between the raw data of the rational actor interpretation, and the cognitive biases and knowledge structures of the cognitive model. There is an intermediate step between the reality "out there" and its perception (through various cognitive lenses) by decision makers. Organizations often must convert the "data" into information; in the process it is compressed and weeded, often changing its content (Wildavsky, 1979:235). This occurs because there is an intrinsic tension between individual learning, defined as a change in individual behavior in response to new information, and organizations, which seek stability and work to promote their organizational mission. While the individual seeks information, the organization may not be structured in such a way as to provide it (Wildavsky, 1979:30–31).

Examples of the effects of organizations upon foreign policy learning are not difficult to find. One of the enduring puzzles of World War II is to explain the Japanese initiation of the war. For statecentric, rational actor models, it is a problematic case because a weaker power attacked a stronger power, thus difficult to describe as straightforward "utility maximization." The usual explanation is that the alternatives to attacking the United States were judged to be less acceptable than war, thus justifying a policy that Japanese officials knew was fraught with risk.

The cognitive research program alerts us to the difficulty of weighing courses of action and ranking alternatives. However, it is not necessary to look immediately for cognitive biases to explain this action by Japanese decision makers. One can instead examine the distortions caused by organizations in the production and dissemination of information about American power before the war.

The Japanese intelligence service did not make any systematic attempt to estimate the potential economic power of Japan's adversaries, choosing instead to focus solely upon operational intelligence needed to prosecute war operations. Historically, this was not its organizational role and mission. An organizational reform attempted in the mid-1930s to infuse Japanese strategic thought with broader concepts of power and the role of economic potential in future conflicts was strenuously resisted (Peattie, 1975). When a section of the intelligence apparatus finally did produce a study of comparative American-Japanese potential, showing the United States had a tremendous advantage, it was shelved by the army chief of staff. A second analysis, showing that the United States could outproduce Japan in strategic goods by a factor of 10 to 1 resulted in its author being removed from intelligence duties and given command of an infantry regiment (Barnhart, 1984; Miwa, 1975:126–127). Thus, in this case, a focus upon the organizational collection, interpretation, and dissemination of information is more useful for an explanation of an anomaly from strict rationality than a cognitive perspective focusing upon the biases of specific individuals.

Organizations shape not only the information available to individuals, but also the menu of alternatives from which individuals choose. In distinction to rational actor models that view the individual as choosing from all alternatives, organizations and bureaucracies may restrict and "preselect" a set of options placed before decision makers. As March and Olsen comment,

> Alternatives are not automatically provided to a decision maker; they have to be found. Search for alternatives occurs in an organized context in which problems are not only looking for solutions, but solutions are looking for problems. Information about the consequences of alternatives is generated and communicated through organized institutions, so expectations depend on the structure of linkages within the system, as well as the ways in which biases and counterbiases cumulate. (1984:740)

Of course the impact of organizational selection is not automatically transmitted into policy. Cognitive variables at the level of the individual decision maker can override an organization's recommendations. John Erickson (1984) notes that in opposition to the military and political reports that were placed before him, Stalin relied upon an analogy to the civil war period when assessing the purposes and chances for success in the winter war with Finland in 1939.

Organizational Learning

Organizations themselves can usefully be conceived as learning in response to changes in their environment and the receipt of new information. Personnel changes are made, hiring policies altered, departments shuffled and reorganized, and budget priorities realigned. But the processes at work are highly politicized. Organizational "lessons," contrasted with individual lessons, are often the product of a process of negotiation and bargaining within the organization, and not the result of applying reason and logic to a study of the past. The U.S. Army's evaluation of the Vietnam War is an example of this difference (Lovell, 1984).

Organizational structure is often an important factor in the learning process. The existence of subunits that monitor policies and provide feedback is crucial if an organization is to relate performance and goal achievement (March and Olsen, 1984:746).[16] Within a state, lessons learned by various organizations will tend to differ as the mission of the organizations differs. Thus, in distinction to the state-dominated models of learning, once the "black box" is opened and the component bureaucracies of the state are revealed, differential learning is also revealed. Francis Fukuyama (1986) notes that different institutions within the Soviet state tend to draw different lessons from the Soviet's third-world interventions and offer differing assessments of why the Soviet policies in the Third World failed.

Organizations and Power

Institutions are important because they can bring power to bear upon particular ideas. Learning is not simply a matter of information and analysis. This is often taken for granted when studying elites—they already have power, so their ideas matter; this may not always be the case (Heclo, 1974:311). First, policymakers at the top level of government do not always agree. Whose policy preferences win out in the course of bureaucratic pulling and hauling often turns on the question of who can bring the most organizational assets to bear.

Second, cognitive research seems to indicate a fair amount of stability in cognitive structures. It would appear that, short of dramatic events that lead to wholesale changes in beliefs and assumptions, the sources for change are to be found outside the established political elite. But which ideas and lessons have impact is often a function of the institutional power behind them.

Arthur Stinchcombe (1968) comments that institutions can convey a number of advantages upon the beliefs of individuals within those institutions. First, institutions can provide access to the media and to the public for ideas. Second, the function of many institutions is to provide input directly to policymakers. As Stinchcombe notes, "Institutionalized values get full-time attention and thought while uninstitutionalized values depend on amateurs" (1968:112–113; see also Van Evera, 1988). Organizations may also extend individual learning by anchoring it in institutional structures, giving individual lessons a durability and longevity they might not otherwise have had. Organizations may institutionalize knowledge and the lessons learned by individuals. Over time, they may change other actors' interests as they gather and channel information. These institutions can be transnational as well as national, thus providing new sources of ideas as well as potential coalition partners (P. Haas, 1989; see also E. Haas, 1983; Keohane and Nye, 1974).

The study of organizational learning offers important insights into how the past affects the formation of government policy. Like the cognitive paradigm, it offers an important corrective to rational actor models of adaptation, but, also like the cognitive model, many of its findings are scattered without the coherence of a larger theory in which to ground them. The selection of lessons by organizations remains problematic. For example, in studying the intelligence organizations before World War II, May (1984:508) remarks that analysts did learn the lessons of World War I and did pay attention to the changing nature of military technology. But the debate was split, with some analysts arguing that technology had shifted the balance in favor of offensive strategies and some arguing that defensive strategies would prevail. No causal pattern for these differences emerged (1984:508). This illustrates the difficulties and indeterminacies of organizational learning.

Unfortunately, at present, only sporadic attempts have been made to integrate the concepts of organizational learning into the international relations literature (Etheredge, 1985; Long, 1981).[17]

This review of the literature has shown that there exist important differences and important trade-offs in each of the approaches discussed. The three approaches remain separate from one another, and although it is doubtful whether they can be integrated into a "grand theory" of learning, more work can be done on how the theoretical fragments we possess may be pieced together into useful mid-level theories of change.

Structural notions should not be neglected, although it appears that the image of easy adaptation to environmental change given by neorealist theories needs to be revised. It is likely, however, that structural constraints shape the process of idea selection in subtle ways. In earlier historical periods, the range of internal debates was much wider than it was in the postwar period. Snyder and Diesing note,

Empirically, in none of the bipolar crises do we find anything like the range of internal variation that we find say, in 1905, between Holstein and the Kaiser, or between Rouvier and Delcasse, or between Izvolsky and the rest of the Russian government in 1908, or between Chamberlain and Churchill in 1938. In the crises of the post-1945 period for the United States there were few significant differences within the government about what the national interest was, or what it was worth (with the possible exception of Quemoy, 1958), although there were differences about tactics to be employed in the bargaining process. (1977:529)

One possible hypothesis is that environmental constraints, most important the balance of power and the degree of bipolarity in the system, were a limit upon the range of "acceptable" debate. Structural factors—the broad notion of the balance of power—may act upon domestic-level learning by narrowing the range of options considered.

The work of cognitive and organizational theorists has greatly refined our notions of learning and its importance in explaining foreign policy change. Thanks to their efforts we have a rich set of concepts at hand with which to explore the impact of information on beliefs, cognitive structures, and organizational processes. Rather than close down an investigation of learning via restrictive assumptions, these works open up new areas for scholarly investigation.

In the cognitive and organizational frameworks, much of the work on learning has tended to proceed in an inductive fashion, piling up examples of successful learning but lacking an integrative framework. Thus, general learning explanations of foreign policy change have not progressed. While researchers agree that learning can be an important causal variable, they have little idea of the boundary conditions and limits that circumscribe generalizable learning-based theories of change.

It may be useful to conceive of learning as a series of concentric rings of analysis. At the center, individuals learn via changes in beliefs or the cognitive structures that guide and form their thinking. This is perhaps the most fundamental level of analysis. Without identifying change at this level, it is difficult to determine whether or not a learning explanation of policy change is called for.

However, analysis cannot stop at this level. Cognitive research shows that different individuals often draw different lessons from the same experience. Having ascertained that cognitive change did occur, the researcher must then ascertain whether or not this change in ideas was selected and became rooted in a large institutional context. As argued above, it is this selection process that gives changes in the beliefs and cognitions of individuals their permanence and larger influence in the process of policy change.

We need to account for both how new ideas arise, and the role cognitive structures play in either fostering or suppressing their rise, and how ideas are selected and become part of the decision-making agenda (Adler, 1989).

This conception of learning holds promise as one path toward addressing the weak spot of policy change in the study of international politics. Much work, however, remains to be done. Empirical analyses can often be quite difficult to conduct. However, the rewards of such research can be substantial. In the final section of this essay we shall examine the limited learning evident in the Cuban missile crisis in order to pursue generalizations on the stimuli and limits of government learning.

Learning in Crisis: The Kennedy Administration

Crises and Policy Change

Research on foreign policy has long noted a link between foreign policy crises and policy change. Learning is often used as a cause of change, but the exact causal process is unspecified.

Much of the work on crises and change in the international system is conducted under a modified neorealist framework that treats change as unproblematic. It is assumed that rational, unitary states will be certain about their own goals and preferences and hold uncertain subjective beliefs about the preferences of other states in the system. Reliable information is hard to obtain. States use crises as an important source of information on the preferences of the other actors in the system. States "update" their subjective beliefs in a Bayesian fashion, discounting information in accordance with the strength of their beliefs (Huth, 1988; Ward, 1989). The basic logic of the argument is that strongly held expectations of an adversary's behavior will require strong evidence for their modification. Many authors working within this framework have focused upon crises as times when states are most apt to test and update their assumptions about their adversary's preferences. Explorations using this type of subjective utility model leave the source of decision makers' beliefs unspecified, but they do address the question of learning as response to new information in a much more direct fashion than do the strict neorealist arguments.

Although it is often maintained that biases in cognition invalidate the simple process of Bayesian learning, Paul Huth (1988) notes that a potential attacker may cope with uncertainty not by employing a cognitive strategy of imposing preexisting beliefs and expectations on the interpretations of new information, but by comparing initial beliefs with the immediate bargaining behavior of the defender to test the validity of those ideas and expectations. These observations have been upheld in empirical work on crisis behavior in the Middle East. Alan Dowty (1984), in a work analyzing the behavior of American decision makers during the Middle East crises of 1959, 1970, and 1973, discovered that the decision makers did not display any signs of cognitive rigidity. According to Dowty, decision makers did accept evidence that altered their perceptions about the goals of the opposition, the costs of U.S. action, and the state of the military balance (1984:340).

R. Harrison Wagner (1988) has examined the Cuban missile crisis as an instance of this type of interactive learning. He argues that the pattern of reciprocal probing that occurred during the crisis was the result of each side attempting to learn the true preferences of the other side. Wagner notes that the structure of these types of interactions can have an important limiting effect upon learning. Each side has a strong incentive to bluff and conceal its true preferences. In order for threats to be credible and not be perceived as bluffs, they must be costly to the side that issues them. Wagner is seeking to establish a model of interaction and learning that relies upon rational decision making in the face of uncertain knowledge of the opponent's preferences. He explicitly sets his model against psychological explanations of the missile crisis that criticize the existence of rational behavior.

Yet the data on learning and crises at this level of analysis are not uniform. If states do update their assessments of other states, change via this type of learning should be greatest after repeated interaction with the same adversary. Russell Leng (1986, 1983) has sought to find empirical evidence for this dynamic by analyzing repeated conflicts by adversary pairs. He examined six adversarial pairs: Russia–Austria-Hungary, 1908–1914; France-Germany, 1905–1914; Britain-Germany, 1936–1939; India-Pakistan, 1947–1971; Egypt-Israel, 1947–1962; United States–Soviet Union, 1948–1962.

According to Leng's analysis, each side exhibited more aggressive coercive bargaining after each successive round of the conflict. One of Leng's principle findings is that the diplomatic loser in the preceding dispute was the first to threaten the use of force in the next encounter (Leng, 1983). Thus, as the cycle of interaction continued, the probability of conflict increased. Leng interprets this pattern as learning: each state "learns" to repeat by the strategy that prevailed in the previous encounter. This appears to indicate that something is occurring during crises that extends beyond probing behavior. Unless this pattern is broken by the successful resolution of a dispute, the conflict between the two states is increasingly militarized, and armed conflict results.

The importance of iteration and repetition has also been stressed by other scholars working within different traditions. Richard Ned Lebow, whose own work relies heavily upon psychological factors, nonetheless adds support to Leng's findings (Lebow, 1981:301–333). Lebow examined three crises that preceded the outbreak of World War I: Morocco (1905–1906), Agadir (1908–1909), and Bosnia (1911). Although Lebow is much more inclined to see psychological factors standing behind the increasing probability of war as the periods of crisis repeat, he does accept the general point that crises are periods of learning about one's adversary: "Crises can accordingly put interstate conflicts into sharper focus by providing insights into the state of mind and the objectives of the protagonists" (1981:309).

The historian Charles Maier also agrees that this process of iteration often appears to alter the preferences of states. Maier (1988:fn. 19) speculates that had the tempo of crises after 1945 paralleled that of 1905–1914, an escalation of threat and counterthreat might well have overwhelmed even atomic deterrence.[18]

These observations point to an interesting puzzle: the relationship between crisis interaction and policy change. The pattern of crises between the United States and the Soviet Union is an anomaly for Leng's hypothesis, because after repeated crises after World War II, they were somehow able to step off the path of direct, face-to-face confrontation. A common explanation is that the Cuban missile crisis forced a reevaluation of fundamental beliefs about the dangers of nuclear war and a consequent lessening of American-Soviet Cold War tensions. Kenneth Waltz (1979:175), arguing from the strict confines of neorealism, also sees the early 1960s as a turning point in the "socialization" of the United States and the Soviet Union, but he gives little insight into the inner workings of this mysterious process. Yet without stepping inside the "black box" of the state, and examining in detail changes at both the cognitive and organizational level that affected future policy, the attribution of learning remains a post hoc rationalization of policy change.

The Missile Crisis and Policy Change

McGeorge Bundy, Kennedy's national security adviser, has recently underscored the notion of the Cuban missile crisis as a turning point in postwar U.S.–Soviet relations. Bundy writes,

> The risk of nuclear war in the thirteen days was real and the most important single consequence of the missile crisis may be that neither side wants to run such risks again. . . . The preeminent meaning of the Cuban missile crisis, for participants and observers alike, and for the quarter century of history that has followed, is that having come so close to the edge, the leaders of the two governments have since taken care to keep away from the cliff. (1988:461–462).

This interpretation of events, which seems to stress learning that occurred during the crisis and the subsequent institutionalization of these lessons, appears in a variety of accounts of the nuclear era. Alexander George and Gordon Craig, for example, argue that "it is not an exaggeration to say that the horror of the missile crisis was a kind of shock therapy for both leaders. It brought to a head long-standing dissatisfactions with the Cold War on both sides and strengthened their determination to move away from its worst aspects toward a better alternative" (1983:127). Richard Ned Lebow echoes this view, noting, "If Moscow and Washington learn to coexist, future historians may well see the Cuban missile crisis as a significant positive turning point in their relations" (1981:332).

Other scholars, while agreeing that learning occurred in the wake of the crisis, disagree about the lessons learned. James Nathan has argued that "as a result of the crisis, force and toughness became enshrined as instruments of policy" (1975:269). In Nathan's view, the ethic of bargaining from strength led to an eclipse of diplomacy and negotiation that characterized American foreign policy throughout the 1970s.

These disagreements over the lessons of Cuba persist because there is no clear definition of learning and because the process of learning is not explicitly formulated. The path from individual cognitive change, through the institutionalization of lessons and beliefs, to a change in foreign policy is complex and can be exceedingly difficult to trace.

The Cuban crisis is important to examine in detail not only because questions still linger about its larger relevance for U.S. foreign policy, but also because documentation and evidence that have been released in the last several years make these questions somewhat easier to answer. Transcripts of several discussions between Kennedy and his advisers have been released, along with extensive interviews of all the major American participants.[19] With these new materials and a supporting conceptual framework, we can begin to answer some of the questions that remain concerning the role of learning in the crisis.

Changing Beliefs: The Danger of Miscalculation

One of the obstacles encountered in traversing the ground from a change in individual cognition to a convincing explanation of a foreign policy change is to show exactly how learning "mattered." Care must be taken to demonstrate *who* learned *what* lessons, and how these lessons *persisted* over time, coming to affect the formation of foreign policy.

The court historian of the Kennedy administration, Arthur Schlessinger, argued that "at its most elementary level, Cuba was a primer that taught Kennedy misjudgments could easily lead to nuclear war" (1965:832–833). This is a commonly accepted version of the "lesson" of the Cuban missile crisis. The notion that the missile crisis taught the dangers of "misjudgments" is a good place to start, but it is not specific enough to capture the dimensions of both cognitive change and cognitive rigidity in President Kennedy and the other members of his administration.

The theoretical literature cautions against assuming that any simple, single lesson immediately flows from a historical event to the minds of government leaders. There must first be a change in either fundamental beliefs or cognitive structures. Further, following the work of Holsti and Rosenau, it is plausible to hypothesize that the "hawks" and "doves" of the missile crisis would have learned different lessons.

Analyses of the decision making during the Cuban missile crisis have traditionally used the terms "hawks" and "doves," coined during the crisis, to categorize the positions of the top officials. These categories, however, are not sufficiently precise for a discussion of learning. But they can be differentiated on the basis of subordinate beliefs about the likely paths toward nuclear war, and postcrisis beliefs can be compared with precrisis beliefs.

No one within the administration was complacent about the dangers of nuclear war. All recognized the risk of miscalculations, but they differed greatly over *whose* miscalculations mattered (those of the Americans or of the Soviets) and *how* those misjudgments would come about (without warning or step-by-step). Beliefs about the peril of miscalculation were derived from two subordinate beliefs: a view of the rationality of decision making in the Soviet Union and a conception of the dynamics of escalation.

From the beginning of the Kennedy administration, a leitmotif of strategic thinking was to find a middle path between the idiocy of massive retaliation and the utopia of disarmament. Recognizing that nuclear weapons presented problems for traditional conceptions of military strategy, the administration had to discover how nuclear weapons might be used *politically*, to secure political goals. The most obvious manifestation of this theme was the development of the strategy of flexible response, but the basic question of the utility of nuclear weapons was a recurring topic in all discussions of the use of force (Stromseth, 1988).

While all in the administration agreed that nuclear war was to be avoided, they disagreed over how this might best be accomplished. The divergence in viewpoints resulted from the conjunction of beliefs about the clarity of the "nuclear frontier" and the rationality of the opposing side. The nuclear frontier refers to a conceptualization of the escalation process. The hawks or hardliners within the administration generally believed that escalation proceeds in discrete, clearly defined steps that decision makers can control. The process of escalation becomes what Thomas Schelling calls a "brinksmanship" (1960:199–201).

Because they believe that there is a gap separating the initiation of conventional force from the launch of nuclear attack, the hardliners argue that forceful actions directed against the Soviet missiles in Cuba, even a substantial surprise air strike, would not automatically result in a larger war. Thus their advocacy of the use of force stems from an underlying belief that threats of force are not overly risk laden. Because escalation takes place a step at a time, and the boundary separating the conventional from the nuclear frontier is sharp, there is little danger that one could "stumble over the brink" and begin a nuclear war by accident. The march toward the frontier of nuclear use is a ladder of escalation, on which opponents would not skip rungs in a rush to get toward the top. Once an opponent saw that you were prepared to ascend that staircase and prevail, the opponent would back down. The chance of actually reaching the point of nuclear war was very small.

Hardliners also tended to hold a supporting belief in the rationality of the other side and the availability of information on the military balance. If the decision maker believes that the opponent he or she faces is rational, and that the opponent also knows he or she is outgunned, then there is little chance of a war starting. If the vagaries of misperception are ruled out, then the political utility of nuclear weapons becomes a relatively simple matter: strive for numerical superiority and clearly communicate your interests. The opponent will do what is rational in this case: back down. Miscalculation can only occur because one side has not made the effort to achieve superior forces and communicate its will clearly. These beliefs underlie the common image of the hawk or hardliner, who believes that superiority of power translates easily into efficacious threats.

The doves within the administration held the opposite views. They believed that both the boundary that separates the nuclear world and the rationality of the opposing side are unclear. For doves, the advent of the nuclear era forced military policy into the realm of accident, in which the decision maker recognizes that miscalculation can be driven by two powerful, but independent, logics. Uncertain where the boundary of nuclear war lies, and aware of the possibility of irrational decisions or irrational decision-making processes, the decision maker will avoid the use of low-level force or threats of force. States do skip steps on the ladder of escalation. If the assumption of the rationality of the other side is taken away, then the certainty of the workings of threats based upon superiority becomes clouded. The other side may be pushed by "irrational" domestic forces that prevent the capitulation required by rational calculation. Misperception may intervene. The credibility of the threat may be called into question. Miscalculation arises in this view because of limits on the opponent's rationality. Whereas in the first case misjudgments could be decreased by superiority or clear commitments, the possibility of irrationality allows for factors to intrude that are beyond the control of decision makers, and wars that neither side wants can erupt accidentally. These policy positions and their underlying beliefs can be diagrammed as follows:

Can the Nuclear Frontier Be Known?

		Yes	No
	Yes	I. Rational Deterrence "Hawks"	III. Escalation Spirals
Are Decision Makers Rational?			
	No	II. Escalation Spirals	IV. Accidents "Doves"

Quadrants I. and IV. are occupied by the ideal-type hawks and doves discussed above. There are also two other policy positions. Quadrant II is the world of escalation spirals, in which threat brings forth counterthreat and uncontrolled escalation is an ever-present possibility. It is a world midway between those of the hawks and doves. However, in this world, uncontrolled escalation is not the paramount danger. Decision makers still perceive the nuclear frontier and will presumably take great pains to avoid it. Thus force can be judiciously used in international bargaining, because even if the opponent turns out to be less than completely rational, the path toward war remains a set of clear steps and there is still the possibility of defusing the conflict before the threshold of nuclear war is crossed.

The third quadrant in the diagram is also a realm of escalation spirals and also a midway position between hard and soft policies. In this case, decision makers do not believe that escalation will proceed in a series of even, easily controlled steps. In this characterization, the consequences of decisions to employ force are not easy to predict. There is a substantial danger of miscalculation because the level of threat cannot be precisely calibrated. The "edge of the brink" is fuzzy. However, the belief in the rationality of the opponent mitigates the danger of war by miscalculation. Miscalculation is unlikely to arise through misperception or accident. The rationality of the opponent constrains his or her responses. Thus, in realm III, the use or threat of use of force is seen as efficacious for low levels of conflict.

While this characterization of beliefs above is no doubt crude, it does illuminate the distinctions between the central beliefs of the decision makers on the Ex Comm and the policies they advocated. Officials whose cognitive frameworks resemble those of quadrant I, believing a clear superiority of forces and well-articulated commitments would minimize risks, were the "hawks" of the crisis who advocated either an air strike against the Cuban missiles or an air strike plus an invasion. In the missile crisis, Secretary of the Treasury Douglas Dillon; John McCone, director of the Central Intelligence Agency; Dean Acheson, former secretary of state; Assistant Secretary of Defense Paul Nitze; and the Joint Chiefs of Staff argued for firm policies and the use of high levels of military force.

The "doves" were those in quadrant IV, who felt that any use of force entailed high risks of escalation and consequently advocated a purely negotiated settlement to the crisis. The trade of American Jupiter missiles in Turkey for the Soviet missiles in Cuba was a possible option. Contrary to other analyses of the crisis, according to the characterization used here, only U.N. ambassador Adlai Stevenson initially fits this description.

Those in the Ex Comm who argued for the imposition of a naval quarantine occupied the middle positions of quadrants II and III. Secretary of Defense

McNamara; Ted Sorensen, special counsel; McGeorge Bundy, national security adviser; Under Secretary of State George Ball, and President John Kennedy, concerned about either a loss of control or a breakdown of rationality, desired a relatively mild application of force, followed by subsequent negotiation.

Estimating the Threat

Keeping in mind this crude framework, we can now look at several questions involving learning. First, the neorealist argument holds that the perception of shifts of power and threat in the international system is fairly straightforward. States engage in a form of simple learning, modifying their policies in response to changes in the overall balance of power.

However, the transcripts of the meetings that took place on the first day of the crisis, October 16, 1962, show that the assessment of the balance of power can be quite convoluted, and the cognitive framework sketched above can help sort out the confusion.

Members of the Ex Comm disagreed at the start about how installation of Soviet missiles in Cuba would alter the balance of power.[20] The hawk Maxwell Taylor, believing that nuclear weapons could indeed be used to manipulate the risk of war and coerce an opponent, saw the addition of 40 launchers to the Soviet ability to strike the United States as a significant threat. Addressing the president, he argued, "You're quite right in saying that these, these are just a few more missiles, uh, targeted on the United States. Uh, however, they can become a, a very, a rather important adjunct and reinforcement to the, to the strike capability of the Soviet Union. . . . To our nation it means a great deal more" (White House Tapes, 1985:185).

McNamara, viewing escalation as extremely problematic and very likely to escape control, was much more sanguine about the missiles. When Bundy asked, "How gravely does this change the strategic balance?" McNamara replied, "Mac, I asked the Chiefs that this afternoon, in effect. And they said, substantially. My own personal view is, not at all" (White House Tapes, 1985:184). McNamara agreed with the Chiefs that the missiles could not remain in Cuba, but he viewed the threat in political terms, not military terms. For McNamara, the Soviets had placed the missiles in a clear area of U.S. interest, despite American warnings. To let them stay was a threat to the reputation of the United States, but not necessarily its military strength. George Ball would underscore this point in discussions years later: "The President and all the others agreed that the balance of power hadn't changed significantly. But the point was that the Soviets had done this thing deceitfully and surreptitiously. *This* was what we couldn't accept" (Blight and Welch,

1989:25). Without understanding the underlying cognitive structures used by the decision makers in the Kennedy administration, it becomes difficult to understand the reasons for these differing assessments of what type of threat the Soviet missiles in Cuba presented to the United States.

Assessing the Options

The cognitive framework employed by the members of the Ex Comm also aids in understanding the initial position the decision makers took in response to the missiles in Cuba. In the first "unofficial" Ex Comm meeting, four possibilities for U.S. action were discussed: (1) do nothing, (2) initiate diplomatic action, (3) bomb or invade Cuba, and (4) implement a naval blockade. The "dove" position—do nothing—was most forcefully argued by Adlai Stevenson, Kennedy's ambassador to the United Nations. Stevenson went on record during the initial meetings as opposing the use of force as too dangerous, and arguing instead for a trade of American missiles in Turkey for the Soviet missile in Cuba (Martin, 1977). In a memo to the president written on October 17, Stevenson counseled, "I feel you should make it clear that the existence of nuclear missile bases anywhere is negotiable before we start" (cited in Bernstein, 1980:105). Stevenson's ideas were quickly, and somewhat rudely, dismissed. The group diverged over whether an air strike to destroy the missiles and their supporting air bases or a gradual squeeze involving a blockade was the best strategy.

On the morning of October 16, Dillon repeatedly pushed for a quick air strike to remove the missiles. His thinking appears to be consistent with the framework above. He believed that the process of escalation could be controlled, and that the Soviets were rational and not likely to respond without thinking or to fall prey to accident. He remarked, "I think that the chance of getting through this thing without a Russian reaction is greater under a quick, uh strike than, uh building the whole thing up to a, a climax then going through" (White House Tapes, 1985:179). Taylor appears to be arguing that presented with a fait accompli the Soviets would do the rational thing and back down.

George Ball doubted that the events set in motion by a U.S. air strike could be so easily contained. Ball argued, "You go in there with a surprise attack. You put out all the missiles. This isn't the end. This is the beginning, I think . . ." (White House Tapes, 1985; 194). Ball's thinking emphasizes the uncontrollability of the chain of events set in motion by a resort to force. This in turn causes him to question the option of an air strike and to question Taylor's certainty that the nuclear frontier will not be broached. Ball later recalled that his concerns over the dynamics of the process of escalation were reinforced by his concerns about the Soviet leadership. He commented, "We thought Khrushchev was unpredictable, that he was a loose cannon, and that he was clearly demonstrating his audacity" (Blight and Welch, 1989:34). In the transcripts of the initial meetings, remarks by Robert McNamara also show understanding of the difficulty of controlling the escalation process once military solutions were adopted (White House Tapes, 1985:183).

Experiencing the Crisis

The dimensions of this cognitive framework not only shaped the response of the Ex Comm members to the Soviet action, but also appear to have shaped the perception of the crisis itself. Sorensen, McNamara, and Bundy, the advocates of the softer graduated squeeze of the quarantine, all have written of the fear of escalation they experienced during the crisis. Robert McNamara has described his thoughts on the final days of the crisis:

> I cannot recall leaving the White House after it had been decided which message to reply to and after the reply had been drafted and approved by the President. . . . It was a Saturday evening [October 26, 1962]. I can remember the sunset. . . . I, at least, was so uncertain as to whether the Soviets would accept [our offer] . . . that I wondered if I'd ever see another Saturday sunset like that . . . that may sound over-dramatic, but that was the way I was feeling at the time. It was that serious a problem. [I was worried] about the possible effect on our country of even one of those warheads—nuclear warheads—being launched against us. (1989*a*:11; 1989*b*:101–102)[21]

Remarkably, other members of the Ex Comm recall feeling little or none of this sort of fear. Paul Nitze, for example, argues the danger was wildly overestimated by McNamara and many others (Blight and Welch, 1989:148–149).[22] Moreover, neither Douglas Dillon nor Maxwell Taylor has recalled feeling any fear of nuclear war, inadvertent or otherwise, during the final days of the missile crisis. Both remained convinced that because of the U.S. strategic superiority, the Soviets didn't dare act in any way that might invite a U.S. nuclear response (Welch and Blight, 1987:12–18). Taylor later commented, "I never heard an expression of fear of nuclear escalation on the part of any of my colleagues. If at any time we were sitting on the edge of Armageddon as nonparticipants have sometimes alleged, we were too unobservant to notice it" (*Washington Post*, 5 October 1982).

The preceding discussion shows that the cognitive frameworks held by the members of Kennedy's Ex Comm did play an important part in shaping their views of the nature of the threat posed by the missiles and the appropriate U.S. response to Khrushchev, and they even affected the way the members experienced the crisis. In contrast to the assumptions of neorealist theory, the processing and use of information by decision makers is extremely problematic. The assumption that leaders react in a simple fashion to changes in the environment obscures more than it reveals about international politics. Our understanding of the decision process can be greatly enhanced by taking a cognitive approach.

The Evolution of Beliefs

Knowing what to look for, we can now ask whether the thinking of Ex Comm members about the clarity of the nuclear frontier or the rationality of the opponent changed as the result of the crisis. Did attitudes and beliefs held in the beginning days of the crisis alter by its end?

There do not appear to have been any major changes of beliefs by any of the major participants as a result of the crisis. There was nothing comparable to Jimmy Carter's revelation in the wake of the Soviet invasion of Afghanistan: "My opinion of the Russians has changed most drastically in the last week" (1980). The crisis seems to have *hardened* the perceptions of those involved. The hawks came away from the crisis more convinced than ever that the boundary line of nuclear war was clear and could best be avoided by confronting a rational adversary with superior forces backed up by the will to use them.

Acheson, Nitze, Rostow, Taylor, Dillon, and others continued to maintain their earlier views that threats of force were politically efficacious. In their evaluations of the missile crisis, the hardliners maintained that the strategic nuclear superiority of the United States ultimately carried the day. In testimony before the House Committee on Armed Services, Air Force chief of staff Curtis LeMay stated early in 1963: "I am convinced that superior U.S. strategic power, coupled with the obvious will and ability to apply the power, was the major factor that forced the Soviets to back down in Cuba." This sentiment was echoed in stronger terms by Admiral George Anderson, chief of naval operations, who stated: "It was not the danger of nuclear war that really make [*sic*] Khrushchev back off. . . . I think he recognized . . . if we had invaded or used conventional air power, he would have been licked and he could not stand that type of licking." The conclusion of the hardliners was emphatic: military superiority yielded distinct payoffs.[23]

Their thinking is perhaps best captured in an interview with General Taylor (Blight and Welch, 1989), several years after the crisis. Taylor's remarks illustrate how both a belief in the possibility of controlled escalation and a belief in the rationality of Soviet decision makers were important factors in his advocacy of military action to remove the missiles.

Q: [S]ome of the civilians do recall worries . . . that really run to
          two or three steps up the ladder of escalation. The Soviets don't
          accept our demand; there follows an air strike; the Soviets then
          feel impelled to strike the missiles in Turkey; the Turks call on
          NATO for support; we feel we have to do something in Europe;
          the Soviets then launch a nuclear exchange . . . In your mind,
          there was no legitimacy in this worry?

TAYLOR: Not the slightest.

Q: Because Khrushchev could look up that ladder—

TAYLOR: If he was rational. If he was irrational, I still expected his col-
          leagues to look after him.

Q: And at the top of the ladder, if I understand what you saw cor-
          rectly, the imbalance between the damage we could do to the
          Soviets and they could do to us in a nuclear exchange was so—

TAYLOR: Oh, of course.

Q: —so enormous—

TAYLOR: Of course.

Q: —that that would restrain them.

TAYLOR: Yeah.

In Taylor's mind, the ability to control the application of force combined
with the assumed rationality of Soviet leadership meant that the risks of using
force to remove the missiles were negligible at best.

McNamara steadily hewed to his view that the high risk of war made
military actions too dangerous. He has noted: "By the time of the Cuban
missile crisis my views were pretty well fixed and they haven't changed a lot
from that day to this. . . . This is an extremely important point and it relates
to whatever lessons are to be drawn from the missile crisis. The lesson is this:
The risk of inadvertent nuclear war should lead to extreme caution in determining actions that affect that risk or may increase it" (Blight and Welch,
1989:196, 189).

The views of the president, however, are the most difficult to disentangle.
Critics have argued that it is difficult to find deep, coherent principles in much
of Kennedy's foreign policy (Paterson, 1989). Kennedy's inaugural address
set the tone with such statements as "we should never negotiate out of fear,
but never fear to negotiate." His administration saw the creation of both the
Peace Corps and the Green Berets; the formation of the Arms Control and
Disarmament Agency and a dramatic expansion of U.S. strategic forces.

Kennedy seems to have had two views on the dynamics of escalation during a militarized crisis. At times, Kennedy seemed to apply the view of the hawks that military strength produced a "clarity of thought" in the mind of the opponent. Military superiority, combined with evidence of a willingness to use it, was the most effective instrument of diplomacy.[24] An opponent faced with overwhelming forces will of necessity back down. Thus, time and again Kennedy emphasized the importance of military strength.

Yet Kennedy also had an appreciation for the uncontrollable aspects of escalation. During the 1954–1955 Quemoy-Matsu crisis, Kennedy called for a negotiated settlement to the crisis, despite Republican arguments that negotiation was tantamount to appeasement (Cuervo, 1988:137). At a press conference on June 2, 1961, Kennedy noted that he had experienced "three world wars, and it [was] impossible to study the origins of each of these struggles without realizing the serious miscalculations which were made by the leaders on both sides" (Johnson, 1978:105).

During the course of the missile crisis, Kennedy's worries about miscalculation—because of the uncertainty of both the boundary of the nuclear frontier and the rationality of the Soviet leadership—became more pronounced. Roughly midway through the crisis, in a meeting with Sorensen, Kenny O'Donnell, and his brother Robert, the president remarked, "The great danger and risk in all of this is a miscalculation—a mistake in judgment." He seemed to apply this analysis to both the initiating and defending sides in the crisis, for he discussed both the British miscalculations of German intentions in World War II and Hitler's own irrationality (Kennedy, 1971:40).

In a conversation with the British ambassador David Ormsby-Gore during the crisis, Kennedy underscored the point that the dangers of miscalculation are beyond the scope of stronger threats and deterrence. He noted, "This world really is impossible to manage so long as we have nuclear weapons" (Horne, 1989:504). As Richard Neustadt (1971) argues, by the end of the crisis, a crucial component of Kennedy's thinking on the dangers of miscalculation was the conviction that Khrushchev was subject to a host of pressures that might degrade the rationality of the Soviets envisioned by hawks such as Maxwell Taylor. Neustadt writes,

> What Kennedy appears to have believed is that Khrushchev might be a ruler somewhat like himself, beset by uncertainties in seeking evidence and weighing it, likely to misjudge its meaning in another country's context, susceptible to human imperfections of emotion and fatigue, plagued also by the bureaucratic imperfection of communication and control. Khrushchev's long message on Friday night, October 26, seems powerfully to have reinforced this presidential point of view. (1971:117–118)

After the crisis, during a radio and television interview on December 17, Kennedy reiterated the problem of control and rationality:

> There is nothing—one mistake can make this whole thing blow up. So that—one major mistake either by Mr. Khrushchev or by us here—so that is why it is much easier to make speeches about some of the things which we ought to be doing, but I think that anybody who looks at the fatality lists on atomic weapons, and realizes that the Communists have a completely twisted view of the United States, and that we don't comprehend them, that is what makes life in the sixties hazardous. (U.S. Government, 1963:898–899)

These views on miscalculation receive support from Kennedy's decisions during the crisis. Although the idea of trading the missiles out was broached by Stevenson and summarily rejected in the earliest meeting of Kennedy's advisers, Kennedy continued to mull this idea over as an alternative to what he saw as escalation and a likely loss of control. Dean Rusk (early 1987) provided new information indicating that the president had not abandoned the option of a public trade of American missiles in Turkey for Soviets missiles in Cuba. Rusk recounted,

> [By the evening of October 27,] it was clear to me that President Kennedy would not let the Jupiters in Turkey become an obstacle to the removal of the missile sites in Cuba because the Jupiters were coming out in any event. He instructed me to telephone the late Andrew Cordier, then at Columbia University, and dictate to him a statement which would be made by U Thant, the Secretary General of the United Nations, proposing the removal of both Jupiters and the missiles in Cuba. Mr. Cordier was to put that statement in the hands of U Thant only after further signal from us. That step was never taken and the statement I furnished to Mr. Cordier had never seen the light of day. So far as I know, President Kennedy, Andrew Cordier and I were the only ones who knew of this particular step. (Blight, Nye, and Welch, 1987:179; Rusk, 1990:240–241).

McGeorge Bundy argues that this step does not by itself necessarily mean that a policy of trading missiles would have resulted (Blight and Welch, 1989:84). But it does show that the president was sufficiently fearful of inadvertent nuclear war that he would eventually have been willing, in the phrase of former State Department counsel Abram Chayes, to "buy the missiles out"—to trade publicly, even at the risk of having to pay a heavy political price, both domestically and within NATO.

What actually would have happened if the Soviets had rejected the American offer of October 27 is considerably less hypothetical than was formerly the case, due to the release of information from American and Soviet sources subsequent to Rusk's revelation in early 1987. In December 1987 the transcription of tape recordings was released of the Ex Comm discussions on the penultimate day of the crisis, October 27. They reveal a president evidently at odds with his advisers over the Khrushchev proposal to trade missiles. It is possible to see, in this document, that Kennedy believes the trade is far preferable to a war he clearly believes is increasingly likely. His advisers worry about the effects of the trade on NATO unity. Kennedy worries about war. In January 1989 at conference in Moscow on the missile crisis, former ambassador Anatoli Dobrynin argued that Kennedy himself was the source of the idea to trade missiles, the president himself having suggested it through his brother Robert, who was meeting secretly with Dobrynin the evening of October 26. This may explain Kennedy's evident enthusiasm for the missile trade in the transcript of the October 27 Ex Comm meetings. It was he, Kennedy, who suggested it to Khrushchev, as a way to exit the crisis before his fear of inadvertent nuclear war became a fact.

Is this sufficient evidence for a claim of complex learning on Kennedy's part? Does his willingness to trade the missiles at the end of the crisis indicate a shift in his thinking from the earlier part of the crisis? Had he come to finally accept the proposition that because of the possibility of miscalculation, a military settlement to the crisis was out of the question? Even given the unique access to recordings, documents, and interviews that exist for the missile crisis, these questions are very difficult to answer. We don't have a definitive statement by Kennedy that clearly indicates his thinking before the crisis and his thinking at its conclusion. At best we have glimpses into a complex and often contradictory mind. It does seem likely that the crisis highlighted the script of inadvertent war that had previously formed part of Kennedy's cognitive framework, and can be seen in his earlier statements about the Quemoy-Matsu crisis. But, as argued in the next section, Kennedy's learning was only partial and never achieved permanence because it never became institutionalized.

Preserving the Lessons: The Problem of Institutionalization

In the wake of the crisis, it appears as though accounts of the event that speak of great lessons are overstated. There were a variety of lessons *reinforced* by the crisis, but many of them were lessons learned in other contexts. The hardliners in the Kennedy administration were for the most part individuals with long records of government service who had experienced the most intense period of the Cold War. Nitze, Acheson, the Joint Chiefs, and the others seemed to have learned their lessons about the use of force in bargaining in an earlier period, and Cuba did not change those views.

McNamara, Bundy, and Sorensen had no previous foreign policy experience and appear to have brought in a different set of attitudes. Yet the crisis also appears to have had little effect on the attitudes of these individuals. What is more important is the fact that they were not in government during the earlier period of the Cold War. McNamara asserts that his views were "pretty well set" by the time of the crisis and didn't change as a result. If this is correct, it supports the contention that little *individual* learning resulted from the crisis.

This does not necessarily end the story, however. Although individuals may not have changed a great deal as the result of the crisis, learning at the organizational level may have occurred as various lessons were selected and institutionalized.

It can be argued that evidence of an increase in Kennedy's appreciation of the danger of accidental or inadvertent war can be seen in his advocacy of both the teletype Hotline agreement and the Limited Test Ban Treaty. The passage of these agreements, therefore, also institutionalized Kennedy's thinking in the government. In this sense, the moderate ideas "won" the process of selection. In a sense, the degree of change in Kennedy's beliefs may not be as important as the fact that they did lead to a series of new agreements with the Soviet Union.

There does appear to be some justification for this view. The Hotline was originally advocated by Gerard Smith, head of policy planning at the State Department in January 1960 (Weintal and Bartlett, 1967:196). The idea received a cold reception by then Secretary of State Christian Herter and was shelved. The usefulness of timely communication, however, began to circulate in the press during the first year of the Kennedy administration. Kennedy himself initially disapproved of the idea. Evidence for the effect of the missile crisis is more a matter of correlation than hard evidence. Kennedy did change his mind on the issue of the Hotline in the wake of the crisis, but it cannot be proven that this was the result of a lesson learned by the president.

The long and arduous test ban negotiations also provide slight evidence of a change in Kennedy's thinking and the consequent institutionalization of this change in the form of an international treaty. Kennedy initially favored the ban, but he was unwilling to commit himself politically to its success. After the missile crisis, Kennedy was much more willing to use his power as the president to secure the test ban agreement. Ronald Terchek (1970:19–20) argues that the decision to pursue the LTBT was a "personal decision" borne of the conviction that the spread of nuclear weapons would increase the likelihood of inadvertent nuclear war.

Holding aside examples such as the Hotline and the test ban, modifications to the cognitive frameworks of decision makers do not translate effortlessly into changes in policy or organization. A variety of political and institutional impediments stand between cognitive change and the formation of foreign policy. Presidents may be able to alter policy directly on the basis of changes in their beliefs. Jimmy Carter's reevaluation of the Soviet Union in the wake of the 1979 invasion of Afghanistan, and the subsequent grain embargo, is perhaps a good example. Often, however, presidents or members of their administration must seek an indirect means of influencing the "lessons" learned by the government.

In the case of the Cuban missile crisis, a variety of political constraints hindered the direct transmission of changed beliefs into changes in policy. The lessons that appear to have resulted from direct influence are fairly minor. First, not all members of the administration drew the same lessons from the crisis; not all experienced the same degree of fear; few altered their views about the dynamics of crisis escalation or the likelihood of rational opponents.

Yet the members of the administration did not all carry their views forward in the public debate that ensued in the aftermath of the missile crisis. Congress held hearings and journalists speculated over the ultimate lessons learned, but those most concerned with the dangers of escalation or miscalculation were notably silent.

Kennedy showed in the test ban negotiations the powerful ability of the president to mobilize opinion, disseminate information, and legitimize new policy concepts.[25] Yet in the wake of the crisis, the themes of inadvertence that had seemed so powerful in October largely disappeared from view. Part of the reason was political. Kennedy faced potentially damaging political consequences in the aftermath of the Cuban missile crisis (Patterson and Brophy, 1987). Contrary to the charges by some critics, considerations of domestic politics were remarkably absent from decisions made during the course of the crisis. The president did not, for example, shift to dramatic, decisive military action to boost the Democrats' ratings in the polls. As Thomas G. Patterson and William J. Brophy note, "The politics of the Cuban issue in the fall of 1962 was spirited and acrimonious but had limited impact on the president's momentous decisions" (1987:325).

But domestic politics were much more intrusive in the aftermath of the crisis and the approach of the November congressional elections. Prior to the missile crisis, in August 1962, Senator Charles Keating had been claiming that the Soviets were installing offensive weapons in Cuba. Kennedy was therefore vulnerable to charges that no matter how successful he had been in getting the missiles out of Cuba, he failed in preventing their initial deployment. Indeed, on the day after the resolution of the crisis, the conservative

San Francisco Examiner expressed the hope that Kennedy would now "repudiate those among his advisers who have sold their 'soft' line until it brought the United States to the brink of nuclear disaster" (cited in Kern, Levering, and Levering, 1983:136). Eisenhower, campaigning for the Republicans, noted that Kennedy's success in the crisis would not have been possible without the level of preparedness ensured by the spending priorities of the Eisenhower administration (Weaver, 1962:1).

The Kennedy administration was especially sensitive to its vulnerabilities regarding attacks from the conservative right. Concern for how a particular policy would play against criticism from the right had become instinctive. Carl Kaysen, in a memo to Bundy, during the summer of 1961 when the United States was looking for a peaceful solution to the Berlin crisis, warned, "As the crisis grows tenser, the ability of the Administration to espouse a policy that involves concessions to the Soviets diminishes, for the opposition will attack it" (1961:8).

This same logic appears to have been operating in the aftermath of the crisis. Attacked by the right for "softness" toward Cuba, the administration could not concede what had in fact been an important part of its strategy for removing the missiles: a willingness to quietly offer concessions. Thus, neither Kennedy nor other members of the Ex Comm could publicly acknowledge the role of the implicit trade of the Jupiter missiles in Cuba, and in fact they tried to distance themselves from the suggestion that a trade had occurred.

The first of the detailed retrospectives of the crisis, by Stewart Alsop and Charles Bartlett, sought to place the burden of any "softness" toward the Soviets firmly upon Adlai Stevenson. The article, based on interviews with unidentified officials, charged that Stevenson, in advocating the trade of Turkish missiles, had "wanted a Munich. He wanted to trade the Turkish, Italian and British missile bases for the Cuban bases" (1962:16–20). The Republicans attacked, with Senator Goldwater calling for Stevenson's resignation, arguing that both Stevenson and aide Arthur Schlessinger had "consistently urged a soft policy on communism," but the criticisms were deflected away from Kennedy (Ingalls, 1962:1).

Although Kennedy sought publicly to assure Stevenson that he was not behind the story, doubts remained because of Kennedy's close personal ties to Alsop and Bartlett.[26] Kennedy did nothing to dispel the view that Stevenson was the only member of the Ex Comm who favored negotiation, thus distancing himself from Republican accusations of conciliation toward the Soviets.

Nonetheless, the coincidence of the removal of the Jupiters with the resolution of the missile crisis proved to create powerful suspicions by Republicans. During congressional testimony in February 1963, McNamara was repeatedly pressed by Congressmen Jamie L. Whitten and Harold Oster on the existence of a "deal" between Khrushchev and Kennedy. McNamara's reply to Whitten: "There was absolutely no deal" (U.S. House of Representatives, Hearings before the Subcommittee of the Committee on Appropriations, 1963:31, 57). While agreeing with Congressman Charles Bennet that it was time to "clear the air on the trade," McNamara declined further comment (U.S. House of Representatives, Hearings on Military Posture and H.R. 2440, 1963:276). In response to a question of why the Soviet Union removed the missiles, McNamara replied, "I believe it was by the controlled application of force and the clear recognition by Khrushchev that we were prepared to exert whatever force was necessary to force them out."[27] To have acknowledged that the administration struck a deal, however subtle, with the Soviet Union would have invited a form of "massive retaliation" from the Republican right.

The role of the missiles in Turkey was to remain hidden until recently. The memoir accounts of the Kennedy administration by Sorensen, Schlessinger, and Robert Kennedy all deny that Kennedy was interested in using the Turkish missiles to end the crisis. Robert Kennedy's account of the meeting with Dobrynin stresses that "there could be no quid pro quo" on the matter of the missiles in Turkey (Kennedy, 1971:108). However, years later, Ted Sorensen, the ghostwriter of Kennedy's account, has acknowledged that discussion of the "deal" was expunged from the book, even though it was in Robert Kennedy's diary, on which the book was based (Bundy, 1988:434). In these ways, political pressures to avoid the partisan charges of "weakness" prevented the selection and the transmission of important lessons of the crisis.

In addition, the extent to which the president appears to have been prepared to find a peaceful solution to the crisis was hidden even from some members of the Ex Comm. The recent disclosure by Dean Rusk of the existence of a plan to negotiate through the offices of the U.N. is another example of a lesson that got sidetracked. As Bundy has written,

> Secrecy of this sort has its costs. By keeping to ourselves the assurance on the Jupiters, we misled our colleagues, our countrymen, our successors, and our allies. We allowed them all to believe that nothing responsive had been offered in reply to Khrushchev's second message. We thus encouraged the conclusion that it had been enough to stand firm on that Saturday. (1988:434)

Advocates of learning-based policy change would disagree and point to Kennedy's June 10, 1963, speech at American University. In the speech, Kennedy's old, Cold War rhetoric gave way to new formulations of the U.S.– Soviet relationship. Kennedy declared, "We must re-examine our own national attitude . . . toward the possibilities of peace, toward the Soviet Union, toward the course of the Cold War and toward freedom and peace here at home." Kennedy also cautioned his audience "not to see only a distorted and desperate view of the other side, not to see a conflict as inevitable, accommodation as impossible, and communication as nothing more than an exchange of threats" (U.S. Government, 1963:460, 461). Indeed, the speech is a dramatic departure from earlier statements and signaled a change in the public debate.

But Kennedy's political caution seems to have caused him to always temper his remarks. There are other instances of public speeches that provide evidence of little willingness to depart from the mold of Cold War speechmaking. A speech he intended to give in Waco, Texas, on November 22, 1963, contained the message that he wanted to make America number one again, "not number one but, but number one period" (Patterson, 1989:20). Kennedy's speech then continues in this vein by discussing the strategic buildup.

Bundy has captured this ambiguity in the president's thinking that prevented him from personally initiating a dramatic, new course in the nation's foreign policy:

> Kennedy never addressed in any final way the very grave problem of "enough is enough." He never abandoned the belief that superiority was a requirement of political leadership in the United States. . . . Kennedy was a man of great intrinsic wisdom about nuclear weapons, but not yet ready, anymore than his predecessor who understood the matter has he did, to take the lead in bringing it across to the country that a sufficient level of nuclear strength had long since been reached by the United States and also by the Soviet Union. (1985:214)

Kennedy was, after all, a politician, not an arms control theorist or an international relations scholar. His concern for maintaining his administration hindered any deep change in his personal beliefs and blocked what change there was from a more fundamental institutionalization.

Additional constraints on learning beyond the administration also existed. Contrary to Kennedy's announced desire that the Cuban crisis would herald a more cooperative phase of U.S.–Soviet relations, other voices began to argue that the missile crisis proved the folly of negotiating with the duplicitous Soviets (Marder, 1962:A27; Alsop, 1962:A13).

Public opinion polls show an initial receptivity to the calls for negotiations between the Soviet Union and the United States (Gallup, 1972). In response to the question "Do you believe it is possible or impossible to achieve a peaceful settlement of differences with Russia?" the polls showed:

Survey Date:	12/15/59	1/16/62	12/18/62	6/26/63	11/11/64
Possible:	66	53	63	49	58
Impossible:	23	34	31	37	24
Don't Know:	11	13	06	14	18

While there was an increase in the level of optimism shortly after the resolution of the missile crisis, the gain appears to have come from the "don't know" category. Further, the number of those who felt that peaceful cooperation was possible was not as great as in the 1959 survey. Kennedy had only a small "window of opportunity" in which to institutionalize his selected lessons of the crisis. Would public opinion have supported a wider negotiating agenda with the Soviet Union?

Survey questions on specific areas of policy reflect a continuing skepticism toward dealing with the Soviets. For example, when asked if the United States should reduce its armed forces if the Soviet Union agreed to equal cuts, the public responded as follows:

Survey Date:	9/14/60	8/20/63
Yes, should:	46	46
No, should not:	41	40
No opinion:	13	14

There does not appear to have been a widespread public "lesson" about the benefits of cooperation via arms control in the wake of the missile crisis. But could the president, via an active policy of presidential "persuasion," have altered patterns of support for negotiations? The question is provocative. Kennedy was able to turn the tide of public opinion in favor of the test ban, but whether he could have secured public support for wider arms control negotiations in the wake of the crisis remains a matter of speculation.

In refusing to acknowledge the search for a diplomatic solution to the Cuban missile crisis, however, the Kennedy administration passed up the opportunity to legitimate diplomacy as a means for dealing with its adversaries. Instead, a protracted process of public debate over the "lessons" of the missile crisis ensued.

Concerns about the dangers of miscalculation, aside from the few public statements of Kennedy, were largely expressed by the "opinion leaders" in the press. An editorial in the *New York Times* argued, for example, that both sides in the crisis displayed caution when faced by the destructive potential of nuclear weapons. "Nor could either guarantee that once a show down was forced in Cuba—even an armed encounter between two ships at sea—it would be able to reverse the process of escalation that might begin" ("US Challenges and Soviets Recoil," *New York Times*, 28 October 1962:sec. 4, p. 2). Similarly, James Reston wrote that the conduct of the administration members in the missile crisis shows they are "rejecting the conclusion of the traditional 'hardliners' that the way to deal with Moscow everywhere in the world is to be 'tough' as in Cuba" (1962:1).

Yet the hardliners' position, stressing the importance of nuclear superiority, seems to have been more prevalent. Joseph Alsop, writing in the *Washington Post*, argued that the missile crisis may have been started by Soviet perceptions of U.S. "softness," and he counseled that cooperation in the future was possible only if "we can avoid implanting new doubts about our stoutheartedness" (1962:A13). The *New York Times* was less circumspect about the relevant lessons:

> We can profit enormously from the lessons learned in the week of grave crisis. It must be clear by now that "negotiation at any price" members of Mr. Kennedy's Advisory group have been false prophets. Our willingness to negotiate and to dilute our minimum demands to reach an accord on Berlin and disarmament and nuclear testing encouraged the Soviet Union in her rash adventure in Cuba. ("Editorial Comment on Cuba Accord," 30 October 1962:17)

Between the extremes of conclusions on the dangers of inadvertence and the hardliners' belief that force could be threatened and applied with little risk stood a host of ambiguous and often contradictory beliefs. As Arthur Krock observed at the time, "A great American debate on these matters will be held" (1962:sec. 4, p. 11).

Thus, it appears that from the initial postmortems of the Cuban missile crisis, a variety of divergent lessons emerged, mirroring the views of the members of the Ex Comm but without any consensus.

Institutional and Organizational Learning

The political climate, and the concern within the Kennedy administration about appearing "soft" during the crisis, meant that the lessons that *were* reinforced during the crisis in the minds of the moderates were *not* placed directly before the public. An impression of the thinking of the Kennedy administration gained from just reading congressional testimony and statements to the press would present a very different picture than that revealed by the transcripts of the Ex Comm discussions.

For this reason, before any conclusive remarks about learning by the administration can be made, it is important to assess the evidence that exists for organizational learning. Were the lessons that were stated in public the same lessons that the bureaus of the government received?

In many respects, the government over which Kennedy presided was not structured so as to easily absorb the conclusions drawn by the higher leadership. The previous Eisenhower administration was one in which the government literally floated on a sea of paper. Policy deliberations were codified in a flood of memoranda and studies that streamed from the National Security

Council. The National Security Council planning board produced a yearly planning document entitled "Basic National Security Policy" that was "a set of written general policies approved by the President which would serve as a set of guidelines for the overall government" (Destler, 1977:152). In this way, the thinking of the top officials in the government was automatically institutionalized and set down in a written record. According to Dean Rusk, the system of transmission from the leadership to the bureaucracy under Eisenhower went so far that any time the secretary of state spoke to the president over the telephone, someone would listen in on a third phone, transcribe the conversation, and circulate it to anyone within the State Department who should be involved on the question (Rusk, 1985:192).

When Kennedy entered the White House, one of the first changes was to dismantle what he perceived to be a large and cumbersome national security bureaucracy. According to Douglas Dillon, on the advice of Harvard political scientist Richard Neustadt, Kennedy "abolished effectively the National Security Council as it had worked under President Eisenhower. That destroyed the various channels of communication and put them on a somewhat more personal and informal arrangement" (1985:142).[28]

Kennedy further loosened the bureaucratic fabric of the national security apparatus by routinely circumventing established chains of command and lines of communication. One of his important innovations was the creation of the White House "situation room" that permitted the White House to receive State, Department of Defense, and Central Intelligence Agency cable traffic without prior screening by those agencies (Destler, 1977:157). Frustrated with what he perceived as the slow pace of policy under Eisenhower, Kennedy pursued a distinctive hands-on style of management that got results but often left the bureaucracy in the dark about established policy (Halberstam, 1977: 312–313).

This meant that no longer was the institutionalization of lessons automatic, as it had been under Eisenhower. Because Kennedy pursued so many of his policies shielded from the bureaucracy, he did not leave the stamp of his ideas upon the larger bureaucratic organization. While he did change how the bureaucracies did their job, they did not become infused with the principles and beliefs that motivated his own action. According to Dillon, in the area of economic policy, Kennedy's dismantling of some of the bureaucratic machinery meant that his own "pragmatism" regarding economic policy was never institutionalized as a bureaucratic value (1985:29).

 Much the same appears to have happened in the wake of the missile crisis. On the one hand, the president and his advisers were intent on avoiding charges that they had not shown sufficient toughness on the Soviets, and the president appears to have gone to great lengths to conceal from his advisers his own thinking about the trading of missiles in Turkey. Given these constraints, the lessons that the moderates drew from the crisis do not appear to have sunk very far down into the bureaucracy.

The same cannot be said of those who took a harder line during the crisis. Not feeling politically vulnerable, they appear to have had a much easier time disseminating their views in the government. This can be seen in the histories and reviews of the crisis produced within the bureaucracy.

The main analysis of the lessons of the crisis was produced under the direction of Walt Rostow, head of policy planning at State, and Paul Nitze at the International Security Agency of the Department of Defense.[29] Among the lessons drawn by the study were the following: Kennedy and some of his advisers had feared nuclear war too much; the Soviets would not have escalated military action during the crisis because they recognized U.S. superiority, and to escalate in the face of that superiority would be suicidal; the Soviet withdrawal was not the result of U.S. words, but only U.S. actions—only after the United States took all steps necessary for an invasion. The portion of the text that is unclassified begins with the following statement: "the Cuban crisis in October 1962 showed the effectiveness of the controlled and graduated application of integrated political, military, and diplomatic power. I would like the U.S. to be prepared to use its power in similar and integrated graduated fashion wherever that is possible in other crisis situations" (Chang, 1962:fiche 2194).

This memo recapitulates the thinking of the hawks on the missile crisis and appears to have been widely circulated within the government, an earlier version by Rostow even serving as the basis for a talk by Ball to the Europeans in November 1962 (Chang, 1962:fiche 3237). Similar thoughts surface in memoranda and studies prepared by other departments (Chang, 1962:fiche 2296).

The themes that are familiar in the transcripts and the recollections of the moderates—the emphasis on loss of control, miscalculation, and rationality—do not appear to have made it into the histories or memoranda circulated further down in the bureaucracy. Even the operational histories of the crisis, which often contain abundant detail of the blockade, are silent on some of the well-known accidents that occurred during the crisis.[30]

On balance, it appears as though the lessons of the crisis that received the most attention of the bureaucrats were those drawn by the hardliners. The importance of superiority and the bargaining advantages it could convey are replicated in the studies carried out at lower levels of the bureaucracy. Not surprisingly, the silence at the top of the administration on the dangers of inadvertence, and the willingness to negotiate, begot silence on these issues across the bureaucracy.

Lessons and counterlessons of the crisis have followed one another in subsequent years. In response to Robert Kennedy's *Thirteen Days*, which emphasized some (though not all) of the "softer" lessons on loss of control and irrationality, Dean Acheson (1962:44–77) issued an attack on Kennedy's interpretation in *Esquire* magazine that stressed that luck played more a role in the outcome than a wise administration policy. Several years later, Acheson was again to excoriate Robert Kennedy, claiming that both he and the president were "guilty of high school thought" and that the president was "out of his depth" in the missile crisis (Raymont, 1971:11; "Acheson Terms Kennedy 'Out of Depth' as President," *New York Times*, 7 July 1971:12.).

This sort of intramural sniping over the penultimate "lessons" of the crisis has continued (Rodman, 1982).[31] Yet now, 20 years later, more is known of the actual course of the crisis, and the remaining officials from the Kennedy administration have spoken more openly of their decisions. Mark Falcoff (1989:63–73), while critical of the risk-averse behavior of former officials Robert McNamara and McGeorge Bundy, decries the "Establishment Consensus" that has formed around their more recent interpretations of events. Falcoff argues that Cuba "rendered the notion of a ladder of escalation very nearly irrelevant for the purposes of policy" (1989:69). Given the diversity of views at the end of the missile crisis, this seems to overstate the point, but it is an indication that the views of the more moderate members of the Ex Comm have gained ground in the latest stages of the debate.

Bundy, McNamara, Sorensen, Rusk, and others in the administration have been able to serve important roles as "transmission belts" carrying their lessons into the present, despite their relative silence in the initial years after the crisis. Having left active government service but remaining influential in shaping public debate on superpower relations, they have been uniquely positioned to convey their personal understandings of the missile crisis to a large audience. They have acted to reinforce their version of the lessons by publishing widely in the years since the missile crisis (Bundy, McNamara, Rusk, and Taylor, 1982:85–86). The far-ranging debate on the crisis conducted in the press and in academic journals has continued to keep the issue of the ultimate lessons of the crisis very much an open question.

Conclusions

Foreign policy change is an extremely complex phenomenon. Intuitively, analysts are drawn to emphasize the emergence of new ideas in the policy process, and this has led in turn to discussions of learning. Learning has a role in explanations of change, but it is an analytical concept that must be used with a great deal of care.

First, learning *is* a problematic process, and if the Cuban missile crisis shows nothing else, it does show that learning cannot automatically be assumed to take place as nations adjust to their external environment. That the balance of military power weighed most heavily in favor of the United States at the time of the crisis is beyond dispute. Yet there is no straight-line conclusion about U.S. behavior that can be drawn from the military balance. The leadership in the government had differing interpretations of the significance of the balance itself. The evolution of new ideas, new definitions of national security or national power, is an important phenomenon in international politics and thus is a fit subject for theoretical speculation.

Second, a full explanation of change that invokes learning must be sought at a variety of different levels of analysis. Unfortunately, our theoretical constructs at this stage are not well developed. Learning appears to transcend the levels of analysis that have long guided theories of foreign policy. In our analysis of the Cuban missile crisis, it is important to see how the levels of analysis interact and constrain one another, so that a complete explanation cannot be sought at a single level.

Individuals matter. The simple notions of government learning that stress frictionless adaptation to new information do not appear to be relevant in the case of the Cuban missile crisis. The officials involved in the crisis did not exhibit the same response to the crisis. They drew very different lessons from the past, which profoundly influenced their perceptions of what was at stake in the crisis and how the United States should respond. Scholars need to be aware of the importance of delving inside the "black box" of the state, instead of assuming common outlooks and belief structures.

Institutions also matter. Because of conflicting interpretations of the past, the ability to get ideas institutionalized is crucial. However, the missile crisis points out how difficult this task is to decipher. The flow of information within the government appears to be a key component in the institutionalization of a particular idea. In the case of the missile crisis, important lessons dropped out of the picture. The willingness of the Kennedy administration to negotiate the trade of missiles was obfuscated in the aftermath of the crisis. This affected the dominant conception of the strategy the administration actually pursued in the crisis and the subsequent lessons drawn from that strategy.

Finally, we are clearly far from a general theory of foreign policy change that relies upon learning as a central independent variable. The boundary conditions for when learning may apply and when it is epiphenomenal are not known. The important questions of analogy or heuristic selection and institutionalization are similarly obscure. Theory construction in international relations has often been overly ambitious. We have jumped to formulate general theory before we have had a clear understanding of the basic causal mechanisms at work. At this early stage of theory building, the ratio of empirical work to theory construction is likely to be quite high. International relations theorists would do well to take the advice Gabriel Almond once proffered to theorists of comparative politics: we need to "take the cure of history." Solid empirical research into the *process* of learning, based upon carefully defined and delineated concepts, will ultimately yield a theoretical payoff and increase our understanding of policy change.

Notes

This chapter was written by William W. Jarosz under the supervision of Joseph S. Nye, Jr.

1. Philip Mirowski (1989) argues that more often than not, mechanistic analogies drawn from physics have been counterproductive in the development of economic thought. This is an appropriate caution for other social scientists as well.

2. Cognitive theorists may argue that by emphasizing changed behavior we have focused upon an inappropriate dependent variable. After all, wouldn't we say that someone who used to exercise because it was fashionable but now exercises because it is good for her health has "learned" despite the lack of any change in behavior? The distinction between behavior change and cognitive change is correct, but we hold that at this stage of theory development learning that does not affect behavior is not useful for developing a more general theory of foreign policy. However, we do argue that cognitive change is a necessary condition for learning, though in and of itself it is not sufficient to establish causality for changed behavior. See discussion below.

3. Our approach differs slightly from that used by Tetlock (1991). Rather than list five typologies, we emphasize three, essentially collapsing belief systems and cognitive structures into a single category. In addition, our definition eliminates the fifth category used by Tetlock, efficiency arguments, because we note that learning may either lead to more efficient pursuit of state interests or cause the state to compromise important goals.

4. Policy change can either be a return to previously tried policies, or a new, untried innovation. On political innovation see Polsby (1984).

5. The most complete discussion of neorealism is Keohane (1986). For a critical view see Nye (1988). Kenneth Waltz is very careful to differentiate his work as a theory of international politics rather than a theory of foreign policy. The distinction is similar to that between a theory of the market in economics and a theory of the firm. The former studies what happens when a group of like-minded entities interact; the latter is concerned with the actors themselves. Yet Waltz also claims that his theory will shed light on foreign policy decisions (Waltz, 1979:121–122).

6. On the concept of "hard core assumptions" serving as a base for research programs, see Lakatos (1970:91–196).

7. As discussed below, other scholars strongly doubt whether these assumptions are valid or useful.

8. Waltz would reply that "a theory at one level of generality cannot answer questions about matters at a different level of generality" and that his theory is about outcomes at the level of the international system, not the foreign policy of individual nations (1979:121). Nonetheless, he offers "tests" of his theory by examining foreign policy decisions, and so presumably the international system is reflected in foreign policy decisions.

9. Through his work, Waltz repeatedly compares the international system to an economic market (1979:91). The analogy is useful for some purposes, but there is not necessarily a one-to-one correspondence.

10. Not all wars, of course, exhibit this characteristic. Wars arising from unilateral attack, such as the Soviet war with Finland or Iraq's attack of Kuwait, lack this feature.

11. For an excellent discussion on the theoretical anomalies posed by efforts to limit nuclear proliferation see Smith (1987).

12. For additional comments on neorealism's disregard for history see Cox (1986:204–254).

13. For a modern treatment on the problems of reasoning from the known to the unknown see Goodman (1979).

14. To be fair to May and Neustadt, it should be pointed out that some effort is devoted in *Thinking in Time* to the problems of salience and analogy selection. See especially chapter 9, "Placing Strangers," pp. 157–180.

15. One of the more striking examples is the United States Army's Center for Army Lessons Learned at Fort Leavenworth, Kansas. The center tries to extract and centralize lessons learned in the course of combat and field training. See Halloran (1988:2E).

16. However, organizational differences across countries should not automatically be assumed to lead to differing inputs for decision makers. Ernest May notes that in both world wars, the variation in intelligence organizations appears to have had little effect upon the quality of the assessments they provided national leaders. (See May, 1984:532).

17. We would like to thank Alexander George for these citations. Institutional perspectives in general remain, as March and Olsen comment, "an empirically based prejudice, an assertion that what we observe in the world is inconsistent with the ways in which contemporary theories ask us to talk" (1984:747).

18. On the importance of escalation and repetition, see also Bell (1971).

19. Among the published sources are "White House Tapes and Minutes of the Cuban Missile Crisis," *International Security* 10, no. 1 (1985:164–203; "October 27, 1962: Transcripts of the Meetings of the ExComm," *International Security* 12, no. 3 (1987/88):30–92; Blight and Welch (1989:77–82).

20. As Tractenberg (1985:147) notes, in the documents there is no discussion of real numbers of warheads or launchers, or of relative megatonnage, or a host of technical issues. The decision makers during the Cuban missile crisis simply didn't

conceptualize of the balance of power in the terms that would later become commonplace in discussions of military strategy.

21. McNamara's original remarks can be found in a videotaped discussion between former Ex Comm members and Richard E. Neustadt, June 1983. The videotape is available at the Alfred P. Sloan Foundation, New York City.

22. Ray Cline, the deputy director of the CIA, recently estimated that in his own view the risk of nuclear war in October 1962 must have been less than 1 in 1,000. (Cline, 1989:191).

23. Thus, James Nathan (1975) argues that one of the enduring lessons of the crisis was in fact negative—the hubris of power.

24. Thus, in the book that grew from his senior honors thesis at Harvard, *Why England Slept*, Kennedy argued that the failure of England before the war was not in Chamberlain's diplomacy, but in the unwillingness to spend on arms earlier in the 1930s. (Cuervo, 1988:131–141).

25. On the ability of presidents to use information see George (1980). Kennedy was both interested in and adept at managing the media. For a detailed analysis of Kennedy's use of the press, see Kern, Levering, and Levering (1983).

26. Stevenson's biographer doubts Kennedy's veracity. See Martin (1977). For press accounts, see "Men and Policy: The Stevenson Affair," *New York Times*, 10 December 1962:11.

27. McGeorge Bundy, in his recent book, has admitted that the "secret assurance" did cause "difficulties" that often caused administration officials to overemphasize the importance of military strength, in order to deflect questions about a secret deal. (See Bundy, 1988:447).

28. Dillon (1985) argues that it was this disruption of communications that was partially to blame for the abortive Bay of Pigs plan.

29. Unfortunately, this study has not been declassified in its full form. Sanitized extracts are available that show the main directions of its thinking (see Chang, 1990, fische 2941, "IASA Draft NASM," 18 February 1963; further insight can also be gained from the discussion in Weintal and Bartlett, 1967:54–56; and Nitze, 1989:237–238).

30. The best example is the detailed study prepared under the direction of Frank Sieverts, special assistant to the assistant secretary of state for public affairs. Sievert's work, based upon State, Defense, and CIA documents, augmented with interviews, was finished on August 8, 1963, and received a top secret–eyes only classification.

31. For a good overview of the literature spawned by the debate see Medland (1988).

References

Acheson, D. 1969. Dean Acheson's version of Robert Kennedy's version of the Cuban missile affair: Homage to plain dumb luck. *Esquire* (February):76–77.
Adler, E. 1989. Cognitive evolution: A dynamic approach for the study of international

relations and their progress. CSIA Working Paper No. 89-4. Cambridge, Mass.: Center for Science and International Affairs.

Alsop, J. 1962. Matter of fact. *Washington Post*, 29 October:1.

Alsop, S., and C. Bartlett. 1962. In time of crisis. *Saturday Evening Post*, 8 December:16–20.

Argyris, C., and D. Schon. 1978. *Organizational Learning: A Theory of Action Perspective*. Reading, Mass.: Addison-Wesley.

Arrow, K. 1987. Rationality of self and others in an economic system. In R.M. Hogarth and M.W. Reder, eds., *Rational Choice: The Contrast Between Economics and Psychology*, pp. 201–215. Chicago: University of Chicago Press.

Axelrod, R., ed. 1976. *Structure of Decision: The Cognitive Maps of Political Elites*. Princeton, N.J.: Princeton University Press.

Barnhart, M.A. 1984. Japanese intelligence before the Second World War: "Best case" analysis. In E.R. May, ed., *Knowing One's Enemies: Intelligence Assessment Before the Two World Wars*, pp. 424–455. Princeton, N.J.: Princeton University Press.

Bell, C. 1971. *The Conventions of Crisis: A Study in Diplomatic Management*. New York: Oxford University Press.

Bernstein, B.J. 1980. The Cuban missile crisis: Trading the Jupiters in Turkey? *Political Science Quarterly* 95(1):97–125.

Blainey, G. 1973. *The Causes of Wars*. New York: Free Press.

Blight, J.G., J.S. Nye, and D.A. Welch. 1987. The Cuban missile crisis revisited. *Foreign Affairs* 66:170–189.

Blight, J.G., and D.A. Welch. 1989. *On the Brink*. New York: Hill and Wang.

Bonham, G.M., M.J. Shapiro, and T.L. Trumble. 1979. The October war: Changes in cognitive orientation toward the Middle East. *International Studies Quarterly* 23(1):3–44.

Breslauer, G., and P. Tetlock. 1991. *Learning in U.S. and Soviet Foreign Policy*. Boulder, Colo.: Westview Press.

Bundy, M. 1985. Kennedy and the nuclear question. In K.W. Thompson, ed., *The Kennedy Presidency: Seventeen Intimate Perspectives of John F. Kennedy*. Lanham, Md.: University Press of America.

————. M. 1988. *Danger and Survival: Choices about the Bomb in the First Fifty Years*. New York: Random House.

Bundy, M., and J.G. Blight. 1987. October 27, 1962: Transcripts of the meetings of the ExComm. *International Security* 12(3):30–92.

Bundy, M., R.S. McNamara, D. Rusk, and M. Taylor. 1982. The lessons of the Cuban missile crisis: Twentieth anniversary of the crisis. *Time*, 27 September.

Carter, J. 1980. Interview on ABC Television, 1 January.

Chang, L., ed. 1990. The Cuban missile crisis, (1962, microform), Washington, D.C.: National Security Archive.

Cline, R. 1989. Cuban missile crisis. *Foreign Affairs* 68(4):190–196.

Cox, R.W. 1986. Social forces, states, and world orders: Postscript. In R.O. Keohane, ed., *Neorealism and Its Critics*. New York: Columbia University Press.

Craig, G.A., and A.L. George. 1983. *Force and Statecraft*. New York: Oxford University Press.

Cuervo, R.F. 1988. John F. Kennedy and the Munich myth. In P. Harper and J.P. Krieg, eds., *John F. Kennedy: The Promise Revisited*. New York: Greenwood Press.

Davidson, P. 1991. Is probability theory relevant for uncertainty? A post Keynesian perspective. *Journal of Economic Perspectives* 5(1):129–143.

Destler, I.M. 1977. National security advisers to U.S. presidents: Some lessons from thirty years. *World Politics* 29(2):143–176.

Dillon, D.C. 1985. The Kennedy presidency: The economic dimension. In K.W. Thompson, ed., *The Kennedy Presidency: Seventeen Intimate Perspectives of John F. Kennedy*. Lanham, Md.: University Press of America.

Dowty, A. 1984. *Middle East Crisis: U.S. Decision-Making in 1959, 1970, and 1973*. Berkeley: University of California Press.

Elster, J. 1989. *Nuts and Bolts for the Social Sciences*. New York: Cambridge University Press.

Erickson, J. 1984. Threat identification and strategic appraisal by the Soviet Union, 1930–1941. In E.R. May, ed., *Knowing One's Enemies: Intelligence Assessment Before the Two World Wars*. Princeton, N.J.: Princeton University Press.

Etheredge, L. 1985. *Can Governments Learn?: American Foreign Policy and Central American Revolutions*. New York: Pergamon Press.

Falcoff, M. 1989. Learning to love the missile crisis. *National Interest* 16:63–73.

Fukuyama, F. 1986. *Moscow's Post-Brezhnev Reassessment of the Third World R-3337*. Santa Monica, Calif.: Rand Corporation.

———. 1989. The end of history? *National Interest* 16:3–18.

Gallup, G.H. 1972. *The Gallup Poll: Public Opinion, 1935–1971*. New York: Random House.

Genco, S.J. 1980. Integration theory and system change in Western Europe: The neglected role of systems transformation episodes. In O.R. Holsti, R.M. Siverson, and A.L. George, eds., *Change in the International System*. Boulder, Colo.: Westview Press.

George, A. 1979. The causal nexus between cognitive beliefs and decision-making behavior: The "operational code" belief system. In L.S. Falkowski, ed., *Psychological Models in International Politics*. Boulder, Colo.: Westview Press.

———. 1980. *Presidential Decisionmaking in Foreign Policy: The Effective Use of Information and Advice*. Boulder, Colo.: Westview Press.

Gilpin, R. 1981. *War and Change in World Politics*. Cambridge, England: Cambridge University Press.

Goodman, N. 1979. *Fact, Fiction, and Forecast*, 3d. ed. Indianapolis: Hackett.

Griffiths, F. 1989. The Soviet experience of arms control. *International Journal* 19(2):304–364.

Haas, E.B. 1983. Words can hurt you; or who said what to whom about regimes. In S.D. Krasner, ed., *International Regimes*. Ithaca, N.Y.: Cornell University Press.

Haas, P.M. 1989. Regimes and epistemic communities. *International Organization* 43(3):377–403.

Halberstam, D. 1977. *The Best and the Brightest*. Greenwich, Conn.: Fawcett Publications.

Halloran, R. 1988. Lessons the military learns, with a sense of urgency. *New York Times*, 2E, 18 September.

Hampson, F.O. 1989. Headed for the table: United States approaches to arms control prenegotiation. *International Journal* 19(2):365–409.

Heclo, H. 1974. *Modern Social Politics in Britain and Sweden: From Relief to Income Maintenance*. New Haven: Yale University Press.

Holsti, O.R., and J. Rosenau. 1979. Vietnam, consensus and the belief systems of American leaders. *World Politics* 32(1):1–56.

Holyoak, K.J. 1985. The pragmatics of analogical transfer. *Psychology of Learning and Motivation* 19:59–87.

Horne, A. 1989. *Macmillan, 1957–1986*, Vol. 2. London: Macmillan.

Hume, D. 1969. *Treatise of Human Nature*. Baltimore, Md.: Penguin.

Huth, P.K. 1988. *Extended Deterrence and the Prevention of War*. New Haven, Conn.: Yale University Press.

Ikenberry, G.J., and C.A. Kupchan. 1990. Socialization and hegemonic power. *International Organization* 44(3):283–315.

Ingalls, L. 1962. Goldwater demands Stevenson ouster. *New York Times*, 1, 13 November.

Jervis, R. 1976. *Perception and Misperception: International Politics*. Princeton, N.J.: Princeton University Press.

———. 1986. Cognition and political behavior. In R.R. Lau and D.O. Sears, eds., *Political Cognition*. Hillsdale, N.J. Lawrence Erlbaum.

———. 1988. Realism, game theory, and cooperation. *World Politics* 40(3):317–350.

Johnson, G.W. 1978. *The Kennedy Press Conferences*. New York: Earl M. Coleman Enterprises, Inc.

Johnson-Laird, P.N. 1980. Mental models in cognitive science. *Cognitive Science* 4:71–115.

Kahneman, D., P. Slovic, and A. Tversky, eds. 1982. *Judgment under Uncertainty: Heuristics and Biases*. Cambridge, England: Cambridge University Press.

Kahneman, D., and A. Tversky. 1972. Subjective probability: A judgment of representativeness. *Cognitive Psychology* 3:430–454.

Kaysen, C. 1961. Thoughts on Berlin. Memo to the President. National Security File, No. 82, Berlin, Germany, 22 August. Boston: John F. Kennedy Library.

Keane, M.T. 1985. On drawing analogies when solving problems: A theory and test of solution generation in an analogical problem-solving task. *British Journal of Psychology* 76:449–458.

———. 1988. *Analogical Problem Solving*. Chichester, England: Ellis Horwood Limited.

Kennedy, R.F. 1971. *Thirteen Days: A Memoir of the Cuban Missile Crisis*. New York: Norton.

Keohane, R.O. 1983. Theory of world politics: Structural realism and beyond. In A. Finifter, ed., *Political Science: The State of the Discipline*. Washington, D.C.: American Political Science Association.

Keohane, R.O., ed. 1986. *Neorealism and Its Critics*. New York: Columbia University Press.

Keohane, R., and J.S. Nye, Jr. 1974. Transgovernmental relations and international organizations. *World Politics* 27(1):39–62.

Kern, M., P.W. Levering, and R.B. Levering. 1983. *The Kennedy Crises: The Press, the Presidency, and Foreign Policy*. Chapel Hill, N.C.: University of North Carolina Press.

Khong, Y.F. Forthcoming. *War and Analogical Thinking*. Princeton, N.J.: Princeton University Press.

Krock, A. 1962. After the crisis. *New York Times*, 28 October, S.4:11.

Lakatos, I. 1970. Falsification and the methodology of scientific research programs. In I. Lakatos and A. Musgrave, eds., *Criticism and the Growth of Knowledge*. Cambridge, England: Cambridge University Press.

Larson, D.W. 1985. *Origins of Containment: A Psychological Explanation*. Princeton, N.J.: Princeton University Press.

———. 1988. Learning in U.S.–Soviet relations: The Nixon-Kissinger structure of peace. Paper delivered at the annual meeting of the American Political Science Association, Washington, D.C.

Lebow, R.N. 1981. *Between Peace and War*. Baltimore, Md.: The Johns Hopkins University Press.

Leng, R.J. 1983. When will they ever learn? Coercive bargaining in recurrent crises. *Journal of Conflict Resolution* 27(3):379–419.

———. 1986. Realism and crisis bargaining: A report of five empirical studies. In J.A. Vasquez, ed., *Evaluating U.S. Foreign Policy*. New York: Praeger.

Long, S.L., ed. 1981. *Handbook of Political Behavior*, Vol. 2. New York: Plenum Books.

Lovell, J.P. 1984. "Lessons" of U.S. military involvement: Preliminary conceptualization. In D.A. Sylvan and S. Chan, eds., *Foreign Policy Decision Making*. New York: Praeger.

Lucas, R.E., Jr. 1986. Adaptive behavior and economic theory. In R.M. Hogarth and M.W. Reder, eds., *Rational Choice: The Contrast Between Economics and Psychology*, pp. 217–242. Chicago: University of Chicago Press.

Lynch, A. 1987. *The Soviet Study of International Relations*. New York: Cambridge University Press.

McNamara, R.S. 1989a. *Blundering into Disaster: Surviving the First Century of the Nuclear Age*. New York: Simon and Schuster.

———. 1989b. *Out of the Cold: New Thinking for American Foreign and Defense Policy in the 21st Century*. New York: Simon and Schuster.

Maier, C.S. 1988. Wargames: 1914–1918. *Journal of Interdisciplinary History* 18(4):819–850.

March, J.G., and J.P. Olsen. 1984. The new institutionalism: Organizational factors in political life. *American Political Science Review* 78:734–737.

Marder, M. 1962. Showdown changes whole tenor of Cold War. *Washington Post*, 25 October:A27.

Martin, J.B. 1977. *Adlai Stevenson and the World: The Life of Adlai Stevenson*, 2 vols. Garden City, N.Y.: Doubleday.

May, E.R. 1973. *"Lessons" of the Past*. London: Oxford University Press.

————. 1984. Conclusion: Capabilities and proclivities. In E.R. May, ed., *Knowing One's Enemies: Intelligence Assessment Before the Two World Wars*. Princeton, N.J.: Princeton University Press.

Medland, W.J. 1988. *The Cuban Missile Crisis of 1962*. New York: Praeger.

Mefford, D. 1987. Analogical reasoning and the definition of the situation: Back to Snyder for concepts and forward to artificial intelligence for method. In C.F. Hermann, C.W. Kegley, Jr., and J.N. Rosenau, eds., *New Directions in the Study of Foreign Policy*. Boston: Allen and Unwin.

Mirowski, P. 1989. *More Heat than Light: Economics as Social Physics, Physics as Nature's Economics*. New York: Cambridge University Press.

Miwa, K. 1975. Japanese images of war with the United States. In A. Iriye, ed., *Mutual Images: Essays in American Japanese Diplomacy*. Cambridge, Mass.: Harvard University Press.

Mueller, J.E. 1989. *Retreat from Doomsday: The Obsolescence of Major War*. New York: Basic Books.

Nathan, J. 1975. The missile crisis: His finest hour now. *World Politics* 27(2):256–281.

Neustadt, R. 1971. Afterword. In R.F. Kennedy, *Thirteen Days: A Memoir of the Cuban Missile Crisis*. New York: Norton.

Neustadt, R.E., and E.R. May. 1986. *Thinking in Time: The Uses of History for Decisionmakers*. New York: Free Press.

Nitze, P.H. 1989. *From Hiroshima to Glasnost: At the Center of Decision*. New York: Grove Weidenfeld.

Nye, J.S., Jr. 1988. Neorealism and its critics (book review), *World Politics* 40(2):235–251.

————. 1989. Nuclear learning and U.S.–Soviet security regimes. *International Organization* 41(3):371–402.

Ortony, A., ed. 1979. *Metaphor and Thought*. New York: Cambridge University Press.

Patterson, T.G. 1989. Introduction: John F. Kennedy's quest for victory and global crisis. In T.G. Paterson, ed., *Kennedy's Quest for Victory: American Foreign Policy, 1961–1963*. New York: Oxford University Press.

Patterson, T.G., and W.J. Brophy. 1987. The political dimension. In R.A. Divine, ed., *The Cuban Missile Crisis*, pp. 278–325. New York: Markus Wiener.

Peattie, M. 1975. *Ishiwara Kanji and Japan's Confrontation with the West*. Princeton, N.J.: Princeton University Press.

Polsby, N.W. 1984. *Political Innovation in America: The Politics of Policy Initiation*. New Haven, Conn.: Yale University Press.

Prados, J. 1982. *The Soviet Estimate: U.S. Intelligence Analysis and the Soviet Military Threat*. New York: Dial Press.

Raymont, H. 1971. Acheson, in '62, lauded Kennedy action of Cuba. *New York Times*, 20 July, p. 11.

Reston, J. 1962. The president's view. *New York Times*, 29 October.

Rodman, P.W. 1982. The missiles of October: Twenty years later. *Commentary* 74:45–53.

Rosecrance, R. 1986. *The Rise of the Trading State: Commerce and Conquest in the Modern World*. New York: Basic Books.

Rusk, D. 1985. Reflections on foreign policy. In K.W. Thompson, ed., *The Kennedy Presidency: Seventeen Intimate Perspectives of John F. Kennedy*. Lanham, Md.: University Press of America.

———. 1990. *As I Saw It*. Edited by D.S. Papp. New York: Norton.

Schank, R.C. 1982. *Dynamic Memory: A Theory of Reminding and Learning in Computers and People*. Cambridge, England: Cambridge University Press.

Schelling, T.C. 1960. *The Strategy of Conflict*. Cambridge, Mass.: Harvard University Press.

Schlessinger, A. 1965. *A Thousand Days*. Boston: Houghton Mifflin.

Shenfield, S. 1987. *The Nuclear Revolution: Explorations in Soviet Ideology*. New York: Routledge and Kegan Paul.

Simon, H.A. 1979. Rational decision making in business organizations. *American Economic Review* 69(4):501.

Smith, R.K. 1987. Explaining the non-proliferation regime: Anomalies for contemporary international relations theory. *International Organization* 41(2):253–281.

Snyder, G.H., and P. Diesing. 1977. *Conflict Among Nations*. Princeton, N.J.: Princeton University Press.

Steinbruner, J.D. 1974. *The Cybernetic Theory of Decisionmaking*. Princeton, N.J.: Princeton University Press.

Stinchcombe, A.L. 1968. *Constructing Social Theories*. New York: Harcourt, Brace and World.

Stromseth, J.E. 1988. *The Origins of Flexible Response: NATO's Debate over Strategy in the 1960s*. New York: St. Martin's.

Tamashiro, H. 1984. Algorithms, heuristics and the artificial intelligence modelling of strategic statecraft. In D.A. Sylvan and S. Chan, eds., *Foreign Policy Decision Making*. New York: Praeger.

Terchek, R.J. 1970. *The Making of the Test Ban Treaty*. The Hague: Martinus Nijhoff.

Tetlock, P. 1991. Learning in U.S. and Soviet foreign policy: In search of an elusive concept. In G. Breslauer and P. Tetlock, eds., *Learning in U.S. and Soviet Foreign Policy*, pp. 20–61. Boulder, Colo.: Westview Press.

Tetlock, P., and C. McGuire, Jr. 1986. Cognitive perspectives on foreign policy. In R.K. White, ed., *Psychology and the Prevention of Nuclear War*, pp. 147–179. New York: New York University Press.

Tractenberg, M. 1985. The influence of nuclear weapons in the Cuban missile crisis. *International Security* 10(1):137–163.

Tversky, A., and D. Kahneman. 1973. Availability: A heuristic for judging frequency and probability. *Cognitive Psychology* 5:207–232.

————. 1981. The framing of decisions and the psychology of choice. *Science* 211:453–458.

————. 1983. Extensional versus intuitive reasoning: The conjunction fallacy in probability judgment. *Psychological Review* 90(4):293–315.

U.S. Government. 1963. Public Papers of the Presidents: John F. Kennedy, 1 January 1962–31 December 1962. Washington, D.C.: U.S. Government Printing Office.

U.S. House of Representatives. Hearings before the Subcommittee of the Committee on Appropriations, 88th Congress, 1st session. 1963. 6 February:31, 57.

U.S. House of Representatives. Hearings on Military Posture and H.R. 2440, Committee on Armed Services. 1963. 30 January–25 February:276.

Van Evera, S. 1988. Why states believe foolish ideas: Non-self-evaluation by government and society. Paper presented at the annual meeting of the American Political Science Association, Washington, D.C.

Wagner, R.H. 1988. Uncertainty, rational learning and bargaining in the Cuban missile crisis. Unpublished mss., University of Texas, Austin.

Waltz, K. 1959. *Man, the State, and War: A Theoretical Analysis.* New York: Columbia University Press.

————. 1979. *Theory of International Politics.* New York: Random House.

Ward, H. 1989. Taking risks to gain reassurance. *Journal of Conflict Resolution* 33(2):274–308.

Weaver, W. 1962. Eisenhower says GOP furnished impetus on Cuba. *New York Times*, 1, 30 October.

Weintal, E., and C. Bartlett. 1967. *Facing the Brink.* New York: Scribner's.

————. 1989. *Facing the Brink: An Intimate Study of Crisis Diplomacy.* New York: Scribner's.

Welch, D.A., and J.G. Blight, eds. 1987. The eleventh hour of the Cuban missile crisis. *International Security* 12:5–92.

White House Tapes. 1985. White House tapes and minutes of the Cuban missile crisis. *International Security* 10(1):164–203.

Wildavsky, A. 1979. *Speaking Truth to Power: The Art and Craft of Policy Analysis.* Boston: Little, Brown.

Wohlforth, W.C. 1987. The perception of power: Russia in the pre-1914 balance. *World Politics* 39(3):353–381.

Zimmerman, W., and R. Axelrod. 1981. The lessons of Vietnam and Soviet foreign policy. *World Politics* 34(1):1–24.

4

Models of Strategic Behavior and Nuclear Deterrence

MARTIN SHUBIK

Game Theory Models, Games, and Simulations

The prime purpose of this chapter is to provide an overview of the worth of game theory modeling, and to a lesser extent the activities of gaming and simulation in the study of war in general and nuclear deterrence in particular.

In everyday usage the verb *to deter* means "to discourage or restrain from acting or proceeding through fear, doubt, etc." It also means "to prevent, check, arrest" (Random House Dictionary of the English Language).[1]

The concept of deterrence is intuitively obvious to most, yet extremely hard to define rigorously in a useful operational manner. In essence it is a threat or negative sanction that is sufficient to discourage another from pursuing a course that might otherwise be taken. The concept of threat is intimately related to the formal announcement of a strategy in game theory. A key problem in the link between a formal game-theoretic strategy and actual deterrence is in making explicit the plausibility of adhering to the announced strategy.

Before one can place game theory models in context, it behooves us to appreciate what the theory is and purports to do without concerns for context.

In this section a brief overview is presented. An attempt has been made to make it reasonably nontechnical and self-contained. Those familiar with the basics of game theory may wish to proceed directly to the section entitled "Modeling and the Application of Game Theory." That section raises questions concerning the relevance and realism of the modeling assumptions made implicitly in the description of players, payoffs, and solutions.

A Brief Tour of Game Theory

The title of game theory is a misnomer that exemplifies the clash between mathematical and nonmathematical cultures. It is basically the mathematical theory of strategy. Von Neumann may be credited with the title derived from the use of chess and poker as a source for many of the basic concepts. But to the nonmathematician the term "game theory" has unfortunate connotations such as "it is only a game," implying that it is not serious. By using the word *game* for the study of military or other strategic exercises, the social problem of communication may have been made more difficult. This appears to have been the case in the original introduction of war gaming to the Prussian staff. It was when the chief of staff observed that "it's not a game at all, it's training for war" that the future of war gaming was assured.

The language of game theory is the language of strategy. It provides a precise way to describe the key elements in situations in which there are many actors with different goals, resources, and information, each with only partial control over the factors determining the outcome.

The Structure of the Game

Three different levels of description of a multiperson strategic game were offered by von Neumann and Morgenstern (1944). They are: (1) the extensive form of a game, (2) the normal or strategic form, and (3) the coalitional, cooperative, or characteristic function form. These three different representations provide sequentially decreasing amounts of detailed information about the situation being modeled.

The extensive form is the most detailed; it provides a complete description of process, concentrating on the structure of moves and information. The strategic form suppresses details concerning moves and is designed for the analysis of strategic alternatives and their outcomes. The coalitional form is provided to aid in evaluating the benefits and powers of coalition formation.

In almost all situations of interest there is both a community and divergence of interests. Pure opposition arises for the most part in tactical situations such as duels. Opposition is a binary relationship. Whenever there are three or more parties, it is impossible to have opposition among all of them. There is always room for cooperation, even if the only form of the cooperation is for one group to gang up against the rest.

THE EXTENSIVE FORM

Only the simplest of examples are provided here. A detailed and reasonably precise but not highly mathematical exposition can be found elsewhere (Shubik, 1982).

Consider a game where there are two players, each of which must choose from a set of two moves. Suppose that Player A makes his selection first, and Player B selects his move after A but before he is informed of the selection made by A. In a second instance we may assume that Player B is informed of A's move prior to selecting his own. The distinction between these two models shows up in the difference in the information sets illustrated in the "game tree" diagrams shown in Figures 4.1a and 4.1b.

In Figure 4.1a the game begins at the top node, which is labeled with both a 0, indicating that this is the start, and a name P_A, indicating that the name of the player called upon to select a move at that choice point is Player A. The two branches leading out of the choice point are indexed so that we have a name for each move. Here they are 1 and 2. They each lead to a new choice point for Player B, each labeled P_B. Player B can choose between two moves labeled 1 and 2 at each choice or decision point. The two choice points (or

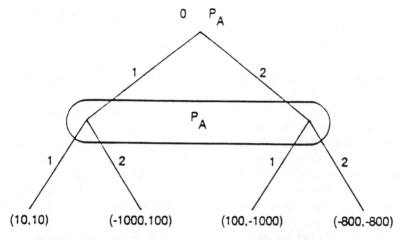

FIGURE 4.1A. A model of a 2-player game, presented in extensive form.

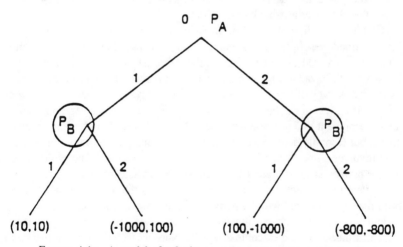

FIGURE 4.1B. A model of a 2-player game, presented in extensive form.

positions) belonging to B are encircled by a closed curve indicating that they belong to the same information set. This means that as far as B is concerned he cannot distinguish between being at either position as the move selected by Player A is unknown to him at that time. It is of interest to note that time does not enter into this diagram cardinally, but only ordinally. It tells us the order of moves, not how long has elapsed between them. In many situations, as the

length of time increases between moves, so does the possibility for information leaks. This requires further modeling.

The only difference between Figure 4.1a and 4.1b is that in the first there is
one information set drawn around B's two choice points, while in the second
there are two separate information sets. These indicate that B is informed of
A's move prior to having to move himself.

At the bottom of each terminal branch of each tree there is a pair of
numbers. These numbers indicate the payoff to Player A and B, respectively.
The end of each terminal branch leads to an outcome from a play of the game
described (a play can be formally defined as a path from the initial choice
point—or root of the game—to the end of a terminal branch).

It is important to distinguish between an outcome and the value of an
outcome. An outcome in a game that has a finite termination—tic-tac-toe or
naughts and crosses, for instance—is a well-defined objective fact. The value
of the outcome to each player depends upon the preference system of each
player. Thus, except for explaining where the preference evaluation comes
from, the game tree description is an objective or physical description of
every possible way a game can be played.

Although the logic of the notation enables the mathematician to produce a
fully defined description of a game such as chess, the size of the combinatorics involved in general makes the game tree description impractical.
Even with the availability of high-speed computers, the possibilities for an
exhaustive survey of alternative strategies are highly constrained. At this point
an important lesson can be learned in modeling. Logical considerations permit
the development of a notation for the exhaustive description of a game such as
chess, but technological considerations indicate that the way individuals must
play involves some form of aggregation or simplification as the proliferation
of alternatives is far too great to be considered exhaustively.

Although in Figures 4.1a and 4.1b the branches that represent moves have
been merely numbered with no particular contextual connotations, in an actual game meaning must be attached to the moves. Experimental evidence
indicates that a change in context in what appears to be otherwise the same
game may influence play (see Simon, 1967).

THE STRATEGIC FORM

The transition from the extensive form, or game tree description, of the
game to the strategic form is achieved by the reduction of detail so that each
player considers only the set of strategies at her command. In theory this
reduction is logically straightforward. In practice it is replete with difficulties.
But it has the virtue that the starkness and extreme simplicity of the mathematics help to illustrate the distinction between a strategy as it is carefully defined

in game theory and the meaning of the word *strategy* as it is used in military and corporate planning. In particular, formal game theory makes no distinction between strategy and tactics. Such a distinction appears to require context. One of the difficulties in considering the viewpoint of a Vegetius, Clausewitz, Jomini, or other writers on the art and science of war is that as technology and the context of society change, so do the definitions of the boundary between strategy and tactics. For many purposes in human affairs it is a good idea to keep definitions relatively vague until there is an operational need for precision. In formal mathematical modeling vagueness is not easy to deal with. The game theory concept of a strategy is logically simple and straightforward. It is a complete contingent plan that provides an operating rule for all agents under all circumstances that might arise. The two simple games illustrated in Figures 4.1a and 4.1b can be used to make the concept clear. In order to plan for contingencies one needs to be able to recognize that they have occurred. Thus in the game shown in Figure 4.1a there will be no contingent planning on the behalf of either Player A or B. A is required to move first, so her choice is constrained to selecting either move 1 or move 2. B moves next, but if she is not informed of A's choice, she cannot select an action based upon A's move; thus B's strategy is no more than choosing between her move 1 or move 2. In the game illustrated in Figure 4.1b, matters have become more complicated. The choice problem for A is as it was before, but that for B has changed.

An easy way to understand the nature of the strategic opportunity that faces B is to imagine that Player B is represented by an organization consisting of a commander and two agents. Each agent is located at one of the information sets of B. In order to achieve full flexibility in planning, there are four books of instructions that Commander B could issue to her agents. They are as follows;

If A uses Move 1, B uses 1; if A uses Move 2, B uses 1
If A uses Move 1, B uses 1; if A uses Move 2, B uses 2
If A uses Move 1, B uses 2; if A uses Move 2, B uses 1
If A uses Move 1, B uses 2; if A uses Move 2, B uses 2.

The strategic form can be represented as a matrix where the left-hand border of the matrix is a list of the strategies available to Player A and the top border of the matrix is a list of strategies available to Player B. Thus in the two examples illustrated, the game shown in Figure 4.1a gives rise to a 2×2 matrix, and the game shown in Figure 4.1b gives rise to a 2×4 matrix. These are shown in Tables 4.1a and 4.1b.

Although the definition of strategy carries over to games of any size, the number of strategies for a game even as constrained as tic-tac-toe is astronom-

TABLE 4.1A

Player A	Player B	
	1	2
1	10,10	−1000,100
2	100,−1000	−800,−800

TABLE 4.1B

Player A	Player B			
	1,1;2,1	1,1;2,2	1,2;2,1	1,2;2,2
1	10,10	10,10	−1000,100	−1000,100
2	100,−1000	−800,−800	100,−1000	−800,−800

ical.[2] A major battle engagement has far more factors and variables than a chess game. It is evident that a general does not work out all contingencies and think in terms of a complete game in strategic form. In general, in strategic planning five or six alternatives are already a large number (see Miller, 1956). Thus we suspect that in contrast with the profusion of microscopic details in moves and information that give rise to myriads of formal strategies in a game of any complexity, in military, corporate, and other societal planning, strategic planning involves both a high level of aggregation and, in most instances, delegation. At some point the plan calls for decentralization of decision making to the local commander.

At this point a warning must be made. For purposes of exposition the simplest of game trees have been used, and these give rise to games in strategic form that can be represented in one instance by a 2 × 2 matrix and in the other by a 2 × 4 matrix. Much has been made of the 2 × 2 matrix. Beyond doubt it is an excellent expository device; but it is highly limited, and there is a danger that in strategic analysis the oversimplification can be misleading.

THE COALITION OR COOPERATIVE FORM

If we were interested only in negotiations and measuring the possibilities for successful accommodation and cooperation between the players, we could achieve a simplification beyond that of the strategic form by representing the two-player game illustrated above by three numbers. They are the amount that Player A can guarantee for himself without cooperation, the amount that

TABLE 4.2   The Characteristic Function

$$v(A) = -800, \quad v(B) = -800$$
$$v(A,B) = 20$$

Player B can guarantee without cooperation, and the amount that the two of them could achieve jointly. We can read these amounts directly from the matrices in Table 4.1a or 4.1b. They can be displayed as indicated below:

The function $v(s)$ is known as the characteristic function of a game, where S is a set of players. The calculation of its values involves both conceptual and computational problems. Confining our remarks to the two-person example here, the values attached to what the individuals can achieve alone have been based upon worst-case scenarios. What can A absolutely guarantee? This implicitly assumes a military attitude of evaluating capabilities rather than being concerned with intentions, asking why should B minimize A's payoff. We may wish to use a different evaluation that takes into account the cost of threat.

A different problem is encountered in defining the value for $v(A,B)$. The way the value of this was obtained was by looking over the matrix in Table 4.1a (or Table 4.1b), finding the cell with the joint maximum, and adding the two numbers together. But this slips in the implicit assumption that the payoffs are measured in units similar to both sides and that adding payoffs has meaning. This is a highly context-specific assumption (see Table 4.2) and often not reasonable.

Further comments on the cooperative form are made below. We recapitulate the observations on the different formal representations of a game. The extensive form is the most detailed and process oriented. The strategic form lays stress on the concept of strategy and the direct link of all strategies to payoffs. The coalitional form stresses the combinatorics needed to consider the divergence and community of interests that various parties and groupings of parties have in negotiating outcomes that are mutually satisfactory.

The Nature of Players

A critically important simplification in formal game theory is the concept of what constitutes a player. In formal game theory the player is a bloodless, institution-free abstraction. It is important for the political scientist to appreciate both the parsimony of this abstraction and the price paid for it.

The player is an entity or decision-making atom endowed with a set of preferences. The great variety that the structure of these preferences may take is indicated in the section entitled "Preferences and Utility Theory." Each player is assumed to be endowed with perfect comprehension of the structure of the game, no passion or personality, and the ability to carry out all computations without error.

The key modeling convention is that of *external symmetry*. Unless it is made specific in the modeling of the game, all properties of all players are assumed to be the same. If one wishes, for example, to say that the perceptions of Player A are twice as fine as those of Player B, or her reaction time is twice as fast as that of Player B, then this must be modeled specifically and be reflected in the mathematical formulation.

Instead of being a human being, Player A could be an organization or even a nation-state. But if this is so, then the mathematical formulation that is meant to reflect this feature must be present explicitly in the model.

National defense and war are complicated phenomena, and it is easy to leave out critical variables when attempting to present an abstract representation of the phenomena for analysis. Items such as morale, bravery, national will to resist, and a host of other factors are difficult to characterize abstractly.

Possibly one of the greatest difficulties in communication between the mathematically inclined modeler, the political analyst, and those concerned with operations involves the level of detail selected. There is a constant tug-of-war between adding irrelevant detail and leaving out critical factors.

Preferences and Utility Theory

More or less in keeping with much of economic and political theory based on models of the rational utilitarian individual, it is frequently assumed that the player in a formal game has a well-defined set of completely ordered preferences over all outcomes encountered in the game. In many instances not only are the preferences for the individual assumed to be completely ordered, but they may also be assumed to be representable by a utility or other numerical payoff function.

The strategic problems analyzed by game theory are completely apart from questions concerning the representation of individual preferences. The strategic aspects of interlocked decision making can be studied with any assumptions about individual preferences.

If aggregates such as a bureaucracy or a nation state are treated as a single player, then it may be desirable to deal with a complex representation of the preferences or the choice criterion employed by the aggregate entity regarded as a player. Instead of well-ordered preferences obeying conditions such as transitivity, other structures may provide for better representations. A survey of some of the alternative assumptions is provided in some detail elsewhere (see Shubik, 1982:chaps. 4 and 5). There is a considerable technical literature on the representation of preferences, and further references are supplied in the chapters noted above.

In contrast with individualistic economic analysis where the assumption of well-known preferences appears to provide an adequate first-order approximation to much of economic reality, such is not the situation in studying most problems involving defense policy.

Two-Person Constant-Sum Games and Solutions

The first formal game model to be analyzed was the two-person zero-sum game.[3] It is a game with only two players where whatever is won by one side is lost by the other. The sum of net winnings and losses is always zero. There is a slightly broader class of games referred to as games of pure opposition, or in the Soviet literature as "antagonistic games." They play a particularly important role in the concepts of game theory inasmuch as there is a solution concept associated with zero-sum games that may be regarded as a sophisticated extension of the concept of individual rationality to a situation involving two players. This is the well-known maximin solution in which *because* the situation is one of pure opposition, it makes sense for each player to assume that the other is out to do him as much damage as possible. The reason for the validity of this assumption is that the attempt by B to damage A is operationally the same as B trying to maximize his own payoff.

The zero-sum game has direct application in the study of weapons evaluation, force allocation, dueling, and other tactical situations in which as a good first-order approximation the situation can be described as one involving pure opposition. A simple example known as a Colonel Blotto game serves to illustrate the zero-sum game. It is named after a mythical colonel who has two divisions at his disposal and must use them to defend two forts. The enemy has two divisions to use in his attack. If the attacking force is less than or equal to the defending force in size, the defenders win. If the attacking force is larger, it wins the fort. Suppose the value of capturing or keeping a fort is 100. We can represent the allocation of the attacking and defending forces to the two forts by a pair of numbers, where the first indicates the divisions assigned to the first fort and the second, to the second (see Table 4.3).

The meaning of the entry in the upper left-hand corner of the matrix is as follows. Colonel Blotto defends the first fort with his two divisions and leaves the second fort undefended. The attacker attacks the first fort with both divisions and does not attack the second fort. In this instance the payoff is 200

TABLE 4.3   The Colonel Blotto Game

Colonel Blotto	Enemy		
	(2,0)	(1,1)	(0,2)
(2,0)	200	0	0
(1,1)	0	200	0
(0,2)	0	0	200

to Colonel Blotto as he keeps both forts. The payoff to the opponent is −200, but we do not need to note it as it is implicit if we know that the game is zero sum. The other entries can be interpreted in a like manner.

An emphasis on the zero-sum game comes about naturally for three reasons. It provides a fair approximation to the nature of tactical combat. There is a large body of mathematical methods that enable the analyst to actually calculate what the optimal or Maximin strategy should be. Furthermore, the solution is congenial with the pessimistic viewpoint that calls for the consideration of the enemy's capabilities rather than intentions. The "planning for the worst" or maximin bias may have considerable justification when the situation being studied can be adequately represented by a zero-sum game. However, virtually all strategic problems (and for that matter almost every international dealing between nations) require representation by nonconstant-sum games, that is, situations that involve a mixture of interests where there is neither pure opposition nor pure coincidence of interests. The application of a maximin principle to such a game may verge on paranoia, as is indicated in the section "Two-Person Nonconstant-Sum Games."

Two-Person Nonconstant-Sum Games

Most two-person games involve an intermix of interests. The simplest illustration of a situation in which both sides have strategic freedom is given by the 2 × 2 matrix game. There are two players, each has two strategies, and the payoffs are indicated in Table 4.4. If both players use their first strategy, each obtains 16. If Player A plays 1 and Player B plays 2, then A obtains −20 and B obtains 30. If A plays 2 and B plays 1, A obtains 30 and B gets 0. If both play 2, then A gets 0 and B obtains −20. It is plain from the structure of the matrix that the employment of strategy 2 dominates the employment of strategy 1 for Player A as an optimal reply against whatever the other player chooses. This is not true for Player B. What constitutes a solution to this game? Should it be the strategy pair (1,1) that gives equal payoffs of (16,16),

TABLE 4.4   A 2 × 2 Mixed Motive Game

	Player B	
Player A	*1*	*2*
1	(16,16)	(−20,30)
2	(30, 0)	(0,−20)

which are both symmetric and jointly optimal, or do we expect it to be (2,1), with nearly all of the gain going to Player A? This is illustrative of the debate in the development of the theory of games concerning what constitutes a solution to a nonconstant-sum game.

A critical distinction in the selection of solutions is between normative and behavioral approaches. Considerations of joint optimality suggest that an adviser might tell both players involved in the game in Table 4.4 to select their first strategy because it is jointly optimal and symmetric (but is symmetric "fair"?). Yet when this game played without face-to-face communication under a variety of briefings player A tends to select his second strategy.

The pair of strategies (2,1) is referred to as an equilibrium pair of strategies; it defines an equilibrium point. This is referred to as a *noncooperative equilibrium* in the sense that it exhibits a circular stability based upon independent reasoning concerning best responses.

A pair of strategies constitutes an equilibrium pair if each strategy is a best response to the other. The only noncooperative equilibrium point in the game in Table 4.4 is given by the strategy pair (2,1). In this instance these strategies could also result from a considerably different set of intentions, that is, the maximin bias. If A expects B to try to damage him as much as possible, he will use his second strategy.

Table 4.5 shows a different game where the joint maximum and a noncooperative equilibrium coincide but the maximin mode of behavior is differ-

TABLE 4.5   A Game with Two Noncooperative Equilibria

	Player B	
Player A	*1*	*2*
1	(10,10)	(−3,−2)
2	(−2,−3)	(0,0)

ent.[4] There is a second noncooperative equilibrium strategy pair using the strategies (2,2) with payoffs of (0,0).

Several important lessons may be learned from this example. It is easy to find situations in which the behavior manifested may be consistent with several highly different sets of intentions; thus observation of actions alone often are not sufficient to enable one to infer intentions.

The joint maximum solution is often too optimistic an assessment. The maximin solution is closely allied to the military bias of pessimism calling for evaluation of the other side's potential. The noncooperative equilibrium has been used heavily in both conversational and analytical applications of game theory to defense. But the fact that there may be many equilibria that differ considerably in terms of the outcomes and that the same manifested behavior can arise from highly different intentions implies that noncooperative equilibrium analysis must be used with extreme caution.

The n-Person Problem

The cooperative or coalitional form of the two-person game has been given. This can be directly generalized to the n-person game for an arbitrary number of individuals. The *characteristic function* v(s) is a function defined for every set of players. It is usually assumed to be superadditive, implying that any two sets of players can jointly obtain at least as much in coalition as they could by independent action. This can be expressed formally as follows: Consider S and T to be two coalitions of players that do not have members in common (S $\cap$ T = 0) Then:

$$v(S) + v(T) \Leftarrow v(S \cap T).$$

The number of coalitions increases as 2^n for a game involving n players. Thus for a 20-player game there are over a million coalitions. Fortunately, when considering models of situations such as alliances or cartels, five or six players are often enough. Furthermore, special structure often cuts down the number of coalitions that turn out to be critical to any analysis. The calculation of the structure of the characteristic function can be regarded as a presolution in and of itself. These numbers alone provide a guide to the estimation of the degree of community or opposition of interests among groups.

The apparatus of formal game theory is designed to consider the implications of the general structure of games of any size, including games with masses of small and individually strategically insignificant players (such as a single voter in a presidential election). A class of games called *simple games* where the value of any coalition is either 0 or 1 appears to be of particular significance in command and control network problems. There is a close relationship between these games and the work done on the reliability of electrical networks (See Dubey and Shapley, 1979) where the concern is to characterize the failure conditions under which the network will no longer function.

Many Cooperative Solutions

Although three descriptions of an n-person game have been provided, no general prescription has been offered concerning what constitutes a solution to a game. Indeed, there is no universally accepted solution concept. For games in strategic form the most utilized solution has been the noncooperative equilibrium. But it is not the only solution, does not give unique predictions, and in some instances does not even appear to be particularly reasonable.[5] These difficulties become even more apparent when one studies games with more than two players.

The coalitional form representation clearly lays emphasis upon the possibilities for bargaining and collaboration. The two best-known solution concepts for games in coalitional form are the *core* and the *value*.[6]

The basic idea behind the core is to use the information about the power of all coalitions to locate ways of dividing the joint proceeds in such a manner that no subgroup has the power to overthrow the suggested division by independent action. A simple example illustrate this. Table 4.6 shows a three-person game where all players together can obtain a payoff of 4, but in coalitions of two their payoffs vary as is indicated.

An imputation is a set of numbers, one for each player, that add up to the amount that all of the players can obtain by cooperation. Thus, for example, the triad of numbers (.5, 1.5, 2) is an imputation in this three-person game. It adds up to 4. Not only is it an imputation in the game, but it is also in the core of the game because there is no coalition that can do better by going out alone. Players 1 and 2 obtain 2 in the suggested imputation. Alone they could obtain 1. Players 1 and 3 together obtain 2.5; alone they could obtain 2. Players 2 and 3 together obtain 3.5; alone they could obtain 3. There are many other divisions in the core, and there are well-developed mathematical techniques

TABLE 4.6 A Three-Person Game
in Coalitional Form

$v(1) = 0$, $v(2) = 0$, $v(3) = 0$
$v(1,2) = 1$, $v(1,3) = 2$, $v(2,3) = 3$
$v(1,2,3) = 4$

TABLE 4.7   A Game Without a Core

$v(1) = 0$, $v(2) = 0$, $v(3) = 0$
$v(1,2) = 3$, $v(1,3) = 3$, $v(2,3) = 3$
$v(1,2,3) = 4$

---

for finding them. Unfortunately, not all games have nonempty cores. The completely symmetric game shown in Table 4.7 provides an example.

It is easy to check that no matter how the players divide the 4 units among themselves, it is impossible to do so in a way that each individual obtains at least 1.5. But if they do not obtain this amount, there will always be some pair that gets less than 3 and hence would be better off without cooperation. In essence, when a core exists, all parties are in a position to find a mutual accommodation where they know that going it alone does not pay. When a core does not exist, this is an indication that the clash of all parties over the division of joint gain cannot be resolved without modifying claims justified by "we can do better alone."

When a core exists, a political solution can be obtained by an appeal to economic reasoning that all enforceable claims can be simultaneously fulfilled. When the core is empty, there is a need for diplomacy to avoid conflict.

The other widely accepted cooperative solution concept, the value, can be viewed as a combinatoric version of the idea of marginal value of the individual. Suppose we had a society in which a coalition structure leading up to the coalition of the whole were formed randomly and incrementally. For example, we might begin with Player 2, then add 1, then add 3. Suppose that we were to consider every way of doing this and credit each player with the increment in value that he adds by joining the coalition at that time. If we multiply all of these increments by the probability that he enters a coalition by a random drawing at any particular instance, we obtain an expected value of the worth of a player to the group as a whole. The value is that set of rewards that add to the full product (4 in the example in Table 4.6) and is divided in proportion to the expected contributions of each player. In this example it happens to be $(5/6, 8/6, 11/6)$. As the game in Table 4.7 is completely symmetric in the role of all three players, the value is $(4/3, 4/3, 4/3)$. But this point is not in the core. There is no core in this game.

Both the core and the value have been utilized and applied at some length to economic analysis. The value has led to considerable work in voting.[7] These are static, relatively parsimonious models that have proved highly valuable in the development of economic theory, but they offer little insight into two-person games of any sort. If nuclear deterrence is considered as involving more than two countries, then the exploratory worth of these solutions is high in the investigation of the worth of alliance structures.

Dynamics and Incomplete Information

In the section on game structure, the extensive form of the game was noted. Comment was made to the effect that the extensive form deals with a full description of process and spells out the nature of moves and information. Thus it would seem that it is the appropriate form to apply to the analysis of bargaining, threats, deterrence, and situations involving essentially historical processes. It is here that the formal analogy between parlor games and many human activities wears thin. The game tree begins at a specific choice point (formally referred to as the root of the tree). Furthermore, the tree has a finite end. The analogy for chess or checkers is clear. But the analogy to Russian-Polish relations is not so clear. In many human affairs there is always a yesterday and a probability that there will be a tomorrow. Not only do history and hope raise fundamental difficulties with the use of the finite game tree, but other problems of considerable concern also exist with the representation. In processes such as bargaining or random search there is no nice, clean sequential structure such as that which exists in chess. Moves tend to be to a great extent in random sequence. A may talk first, but there is a chance that B talks first. In many board and other parlor games the sequence of moves is given more or less rigidly by the rules. In much of bargaining and negotiation not only is the sequence fluid, but even the rules are not cut and dried. New ideas and unthought-of possibilities may be of importance. The formal language of the game tree can, in theory, handle the randomness of moves, but not without complication. Furthermore, in fluid situations it is not clear that the strategic analyst is benefited by trying to catch the type of detail stressed by the extensive form.

There now exists a substantial literature dealing with games that have no finite ending. A certain amount of thought has also been given to trying to portray the presence of history rather than selecting some arbitrary starting point.[8]

Another important limitation in the structure of formal game theory has been that in the original formulation uncertainty enters only in the form of jointly known probability distributions. In other words, all players are meant to share (possibly different refinements of) the same sets of information. There are no subjective differences of opinion concerning the same event. The work of John Harsanyi (1967, 1968*a* & *b*) on games with Bayesian players has offered a way of introducing lack of information. But the cost in mathematical complexity is high. However, the literature is growing, both in formal game theory and in application to specific problems such as problems in inspection (See Aumann and Maschler, 1967) and the economics of agency (Arrow, 1985).

The study of agency theory involves the consideration of relationships between a principal and one or more agents where uncertainty and differences in information are present. The twin problems of moral hazard and adverse selection appear. An example of moral hazard is when an agent may claim to have performed a service that has not been performed, but the principal has no clear way of knowing. An example of adverse selection is when an offer is made to insure risk to a group, but only those who know that their proclivity to accidents is greater than the norm take the policy. The principal cannot distinguish between the low-risk and high-risk individuals before issuing the guarantees.

Agency theory is concerned with the design of contracts and incentive systems that will ensure best-efforts performance from all agents. Unfortunately the gap between agency theory and actual institutional design complete with considerations of morale, sense of responsibility, and cultural norms and codes of behavior is hardly reflected in the relatively parsimonious consideration of individualistic economic motivation.

Leaving aside the complexities of analysis with incomplete information, a reasonable question to ask is, is there a consensus among game theorists concerning the appropriate solution concept for a game in extensive form, even when there is perfect information? Figures 4.2a and 4.2b show two games. In the first instance, by simple backward induction the solution is clear. Without precommitment they both employ their second strategy. In the game in Figure 4.2b, if Player A has selected his second move, Player B is confronted with a choice of moves yielding either 10 or 9. As a straightforward utilitarian he should select his first move and obtain 10. This rules out his threat to play his second move thereby obtaining 9 but leaving Player A with -100. The idea behind the concept of a *perfect equilibrium* (Selten, 1975) is that after the fact it may be "irrational" to carry out a threat, hence no rational player will do so. In this game if Player A were to use his first strategy, he would end up with 9 regardless of the action of Player B. B on the other hand can select move 1 and obtain 12. If A selects 2, B could have threatened to punish him at little cost by selecting 2. But the strict application of nonhistorical local maximization rules out B punishing A once deterrence has failed because at that time reprisal is not "plausible."

A basic misunderstanding of many political scientists (for example, George and Smoke, 1974:73) is that this type of solution is somehow *the* game theory solution to such a problem and that the work of Schelling (1960) showed what

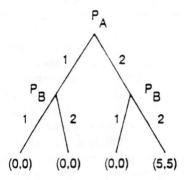

FIGURE 4.2A. A model of a 2-player game, in extensive form.

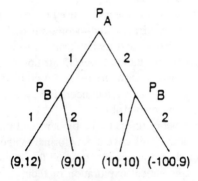

FIGURE 4.2B. A model of a 2-player game, in extensive form.

was wrong with the formal game theorists. It was and still is recognized that there is no universally accepted normative or behavioral theory among game theorists that covers threat, deterrence, and precommitment. There are examples, counterexamples, and stories. But the pure extension of the model of the individual rational person into a context-free multistage game does not appear to provide enough structure to suggest a unique satisfactory theory.[9]

Modeling and the Application of Game Theory

Three Levels of Game-Theoretic Application

In discussing the applications of game theory it is desirable to recognize at least three distinct levels of activity. I suggest they are (a) conversational, (b) low church, and (c) high church game theory. These somewhat casual terms are not meant to be pejorative but are suggested to provide intuitive distinctions among the highly different uses of a relatively broad body of knowledge.

Conversational game theory could also be described as senior political adviser, essayist, and strategic consultant game theory. Its concerns are with models, concepts, ideas, examples, counterexamples, insights, suggestions, new views, paradoxes, highlighting of pitfalls, and intuitive appreciation of context.[10] It is true that once some preliminary insights are grasped, such as the concept of a 2×2 matrix game as the representation of a strategic confrontation, one needs little formal training to generate many insightful analogies and discover many paradoxical situations. But this can be done in two modes. One is where the expositor knows little more formal theory than the elementary examples utilized. The other is where the overall formal theory serves as a basis for editing the advice given. A senior adviser should be in a position to employ the second mode.

The term "low church game theory" is used to cover mathematical modeling applications based on formal game-theoretic models where the emphasis is upon the use of the model and its applications to a specific discipline or problem. Thus weapons evaluation models, attrition studies, and arms races where a formal mathematical structure may be used to calculate solutions fall into this province that lies between the theorist and the quantitatively inclined individual with operating responsibility.

High church game theory refers to the fundamental mathematical development of the methodology. This covers new formal mathematical structures to represent conflict and bargaining situations and the invention of new solution concepts and the mathematical exploration of their properties. Such an activity may be pursued by individuals with little concern for context or application. However, it is necessary for the growth of application provided that there is a sufficient flow of ideas and understanding among the practitioners at all three levels. Although such is probably the case in the development of economics, it is not true to as great an extent in the overall study of political science and in the study of defense and deterrence in particular.

The Strategic Audit

The basic theme of this chapter is that game-theoretic methods have a considerable contribution to make the study of defense. But at the highest levels of advice giving it is modeling and the insights of conversational game theory that must come to the fore. The value of high-level advice needs to be based not only on an understanding of and feeling for context, but also on an in-depth appreciation of what calculation and formal theory have to offer.

In the section "Game Theory Models," a sketch was given of the formal assumptions that go to make up the basic elements of game-theoretic analysis.

Many of the modeling restrictions assumed in order to produce a well-defined mathematical structure do not match our assumptions about the facts of the problems faced in the fog of battle or the miasma of international negotiation. This section provides a checklist for the adviser and strategic modeler that connects and contrasts with the checklist for the formal mathematical models.[11]

In strategic modeling in general and in the study of deterrence in particular there are seven broad headings for the basic checklist of key features of the model. They are:

1. scope;
2. time frame;
3. players or strategic actors;
4. rules of the game and strategy sets;
5. outcomes, payoffs, and goals;
6. uncertainty and perception; and
7. behavioral assumptions.

A finer breakdown of these elements is suggested in Table 4.8.

Rigid rational utilitarian analysis may on the surface appear to fit many models in economic theory and finance. But in the world of strategic planning of any sort the realities are far from this. Table 4.9 contrasts the difference in stress between the mathematical modeler and game-theorist methodologist and the viewpoint of the strategic consultant or conversational game theorist. The attitude of the latter must be more congenial to those of sociologists, psychologists, and historians than that of mathematicians. Both views are needed, but for different purposes.

A few comments on the application of this modeling scheme to defense studies are noted.

SCOPE

The broader the scope, the more difficult it becomes to select relevant variables and specify payoffs. Herman Kahn's (1962) catch phrase "thinking the unthinkable" highlights our inability to conceptualize the unexperienced. The suggestion that generals and countries prepare to fight the last war may contain a high element of truth, but it contains no prescription as to how we go about displaying the appropriate imagination to plan for the next one (or its avoidance).

TIME FRAME

Most of formal game theory analysis is devoted to event rather than clock time. The length of time between moves is hardly studied. Virtually all of the analysis is devoted to the implications of the sequence or ordering of action

TABLE 4.8   A Strategic Modeling Checklist

1. *Scope*
   a. Top strategic: survival at stake,
   b. Strategic, but below survival,
   c. Tactical.

2. *Time Frame*
   a. Date of analysis,
   b. Length of period covered,
   c. Event oriented, fixed clock, or an intermix,
   d. Nature of initial condition assumptions,
   e. Nature of terminal condition assumptions.

3. *Players or Strategic Actors*
   a. Level of aggregation of individuals and institutions,
   b. The number of strategic players,
   c. External symmetry assumptions,
   d. The verification of "strategic dummies."

4. *Rules of the Game and Strategy Sets*
   a. Relevant political detail: own and other,
   b. Relevant bureaucratic detail: own and other,
   c. Relevant technological knowledge: own and other,
   d. Information and communication conditions,
   e. Scope and feasible actions.

5. *Outcomes, Payoffs, and Goals*
   a. The clear distinction between physical outcomes and their
      evaluation,
   b. Short- and long-term payoffs,
   c. Payoffs defined on a finite or indefinite horizon,
   d. The description and measurement of preference,
   e. Risk measures,
   f. Team, group, or individual goals,
   g. Zero-sum or nonconstant-sum environment.

6. *Uncertainty and Perception*
   a. The assessment of the nature of outside uncertainty,
   b. The belief in and knowability of the payoffs,
   c. General faith in the model.

7. *Behavioral Assumptions*
   a. Rationality or constrained rationality,
   b. Risk behavior under time pressure and/or stress,
   c. Instinctive or programmed behavior,
   d. Problems in perception and comprehension.

TABLE 4.9   Formalism and Application[a]

Mathematical Game Theory	Strategic Advice
Rules of the game;	Laws and customs of society;
Impersonal undifferentiated individuals;	Personal detail may count;
No aspects of socialization;	
Fixed well-defined payoffs;	Socialization is implicit;
	Payoffs are difficult to define and may change;
Perfect intelligence;	Limited intelligence;
No learning;	Learning often relevant;
No coding problems.	Perception and coding problems important.

[a]Despite several attempts no generally accepted successful theory of learning in the context of a game has been developed. Recently some progress has been made in studying finite automata as a way of considering limitations on players (see Rubinstein, 1986).

rather than elapsed time. The game tree lays out sequence, not elapsed time. The game tree representation, although it fully describes the process, does not indicate how long the game lasts, thus it does not reflect an important aspect of the rules of play. The timing of an attack in nuclear warfare involves a matter of minutes (see Bracken, 1983; Blair, 1985). Thus the whole concept of studied reply to action has to be reconsidered as the time scale is reduced to decisions that must be made by trained reflex, by instinct, or by adherence to preformulated contingency planning. In some sense it would appear that at this point formal game theory might come into its own as an essential part of contingent planning. But the proliferation of "what-if" scenarios is exponential, and in actuality only a handful of alternative scenarios can be generated in advance, even given high-speed digital computers.

In planning and in gaming the description of initial and terminal conditions may have great influence on the analysis. One of the key problems in our historical understanding even to this day is determining when the point of no return was crossed in the start of many wars. It may be relatively easy to date the first shot, but that could have even taken place before the point of no return had been reached. Terminal as well as initial conditions are noted, because (as was perceptively observed by Ikle, 1971) the possibilities of war termination, though frequently covered in the rhetoric of total victory, are rarely considered in the more sober analysis of how to enable all parties to extricate themselves from bloodbaths. World War I and the Iran-Iraq war of the 1980s provide examples.

PLAYERS OR STRATEGIC ACTORS

As has been noted, formal game-theoretic analysis can be carried out with virtually any assumptions concerning preferences or goals. When the players

are assumed to be units such as a nation-state or a set of institutions compos-
ing a nation-state, our ability to even describe the goals of these entities is
limited. If complex preference structures are postulated, the ability to carry
analysis to any depth becomes constrained by the complexity of the model.

Two valuable contributions of methodology to avoiding basic traps in strategic analysis are the explicit consideration of external symmetry and the
verification of strategic dummies. It is highly desirable that differences in the
assumptions about the players be made explicit. In weapons evaluation, for
example, it is usually assumed that the tank crews on each side are in essence
identical. In assessing the war potential in the Middle East, one obtains a view
that is hardly consistent with the existence of Israel if one weights the Israeli
Army, for example, on a one-to-one basis with the Egyptian Army. What
should these weightings be and how do we calculate them?

United States and Soviet military thinking frequently tends to concentrate
on bipolar situations in which the actors are primarily if not only the Soviet
Union and the United States. Strategic analysts frequently make a modeling
decision to exclude a nation from consideration as an active player because it
does not appear to be sufficiently important. Yet one of the prime lessons to be
learned from formal game theory involving three or more players is that it is
extremely hard to judge a priori the strategic strength of a player as long as he
has some freedom of action. A safer procedure is to include doubtful players
into the analysis and then let the analysis establish that they manifest little, if
any, influence in any of the outcomes.

RULES OF THE GAME AND STRATEGY SETS

Institutions and complex operating systems take on a life of their own. This
is well recognized in the political process where there are rarely, if ever,
complete rules written to explain, for example, all the relationships between
the House of Lords and the House of Commons. Despite catch-22 phrases
such as "ignorance of the law is no excuse," it is well known that it is
impossible for any single individual to know all of the protocol governing
even a reasonably well defined complex system. In discussions of command
and control systems concern has been voiced over the provincialization of a
system under attack. But this possibility exists in day-to-day operations where
no single individual is in a position to maintain an overview that is much
deeper than dangerously superficial.

OUTCOMES, PAYOFFS, AND GOALS

The catch phrase "is that a threat or a promise?" serves to illustrate the
importance of being able to distinguish an outcome and the value of that
outcome to a player. Even in football or horse races, winning the game is not

necessarily the same as winning for some players if the game is fixed. A key proposition in effective deterrence is to make sure that each player fully comprehends the value placed by the others on various outcomes. The dangers of misperception have been stressed by Jervis (1988).

Conversational Game Theory

Ellsberg (1961*a* & *b*), Rapoport (1960, 1964), Schelling (1960, 1966), Shubik (1964, 1968, 1971), and to some extent Raiffa (1982) among others provide examples of conversational game theory. There is an occasional calculation and numerical example, interspersed in a discussion that recognizes the qualitative difficulties in obtaining the appropriate model of human affairs.

Ellsberg (1961*a*) uses a not fully defined 2 × 2 payoff matrix to discuss and illustrate problems in sensitivity analysis to consider when changes in weaponry and outcome evaluation are stabilizing or destabilizing. In his paper on risk and ambiguity a key problem in modeling and context is posed strikingly. Suppose that you are told that you must draw a ball from one of two jars. If you select a red ball, you win a prize. You are informed that in jar 1 there are precisely 50 red and 50 black balls. For jar 2 you are informed that you are to be told nothing whatsoever about how its contents were selected. Are you indifferent between the two choices?

The work of Schelling (1960) paradoxically simultaneously set forward the uses of conversational game theory, raised fundamental questions that illustrated problems in precommitment, not easily treated in basic game theory, but somewhat misinterpreted the role of the extensive form (Schelling, 1960:chap. 5). Many of Schelling's perceptive examples were based on 2 × 2 matrix game illustrations, as was much of the work of Rapoport and associates. Rapoport's early book (1960) contains an intermix of simple mathematical models, 2 × 2 game examples, a comparison between real and theoretical arms races, and many questions and observations on the ethics of debate. For those interested in the problems of contrasting formal game theory with the problems of modeling actual negotiations and bargaining, Rapoport's book is a valuable preliminary to reading Raiffa's (1982) work on the art and science of negotiation. This book provides a perceptive blend of case histories, gaming, and elementary theory that asks in an operational way, just how useful is professional strategic analysis to those faced with bargains and negotiations?

Two further works are noted as good examples of the mixture of insight, simple mathematical models, and illustrators of the paradoxes and pitfalls in the study of conflict and cooperation. They are the collected essays of Schelling (1984) on choice and consequence and essays in honor of Anatol Rapoport

(Diekmann and Mitter, 1986). In both of these the richness of the examples to be gleaned from the 2 × 2 game is displayed, and a mixture of discussion and experimental results concerning paradoxical effects of social behavior is noted.

At a more formal level, but important to appreciating the uses and limits of 2 × 2 games, the study by Rapoport, Guyer, and Gordon (1976) provides an exhaustive investigation of the 78 strategically different strongly ordinal 2 × 2 matrix games that can be constructed. This count is accompanied by a taxonomic discussion of all of the games and experimentation with sensitivity analysis on many specific games.[12] In the taxonomy the Prisoners' Dilemma game[13] (see Table 4.10) is in a class of its own, where an apparently reasonable definition of individual rational choice conflicts with joint rationality. Both players have a strongly dominating strategy, that is, a strategy that is better than the other in each contingency. If Player B plays 1, then a payoff of 10 is better than 5. If B plays 2, a payoff of 0 is better than −12.

Several thousand papers have been written on the Prisoners' Dilemma and on experiments with this game in various forms. Axelrod (1984) has suggested a whole theory of the evolution of cooperation based heavily on this one 2 × 2 matrix game. Despite its attraction to experimental social psychologists and to conversational game theorists, we should be somewhat cautious about the level of generalization that can be fruitfully obtained from results with a single matrix game.

The development of military operations research and of formal game theory does not supply directly the needs of strategic analysts to understand the logical complexities of threat and deterrence. Conversational or essay-oriented game-theoretic thinking that is highly sensitive to context fulfills this vital role. But on the whole the gap between the methodology of game theory and the general understanding in the political science profession and at the war colleges as to what it can contribute has been and is too large.

It would probably be unwise and uneconomic to expect that the political science graduate courses and the staff and war colleges should absorb much in the way of mathematical formalism. Variations on five or six well-known and

TABLE 4.10   Prisoners' Dilemma

| Player A | Player B | |
	1	2
1	(5,5)	(−12,10)
2	(10,−12)	(0,0)

specially studied games such as the Prisoner's Dilemma, the Dilemma of the Commons, the Battle of the Sexes, and the game of Chicken all are richly suggestive and offer valuable analogies and insights, but a deeper understanding of the methodology might increase the value of these examples as both their strengths and limitations are better understood.

Low Church Game Theory

The phrase "low church game theory" is coined to cover the broad area of application where the stress is on obtaining and interpreting the solution to a problem that has been more or less completely formulated mathematically. No attempt is made here to suggest that the classification offered is watertight. For example, much of the work of Brams (1984) falls somewhere between what has been termed conversational and low church, as does Rapoport's discussion of arms races intermixed with simple mathematical models for which solutions are obtained. There is a large body of heavily mathematical military operations research where the work crosses the boundary in the other direction, that is, between low church or applied goal-oriented analysis and high church or mathematics- and methodology-oriented game theory where the interest is in theorem building, tool construction, and the extension of the methodology itself.[14]

The Mathematics of Conflict (Shubik, 1983*a*) is an edited volume that presents a reasonably exhaustive coverage of many applied tactical game-theoretic models encompassing dueling, Lanchester attrition processes, and differential game pursuit and evasion models. Even at the tactical level modeling problems are considerable, and a classical operations research paper on the requirement for the theory of combat by Weiss (1983) provides considerable insight into how to proceed. Institutions such as RAND, Institute for Defense Analysis (IDA), and Center for Naval Analysis (CNA) have been the locus of much of the direct military applications of game theory. The overlap of this literature and the literature in political science is, unfortunately, limited.

High Church Game Theory

Game theory as a form of mathematics with its own justification can be studied without concern for context or administrative usefulness. Debate may be held over the relevance of various representations and whether various solutions should be regarded as normative or behaviorally inspired.[15] But these debates can be set aside by the practitioner in his or her work. However, the sponsor of research may wish to channel funding in the direction that is perceived to have the greatest applied payoff (unfortunately, it is frequently extremely difficult to make such a judgment with any accuracy).

Some solution concepts pose many mathematical problems.[16] A taste for them is essentially individual and motivated by the aesthetics of doing mathematics rather than solving world problems.

Problems in Modeling Deterrence

The Theory of Threats and Bargaining

The theory of threats and bargaining has been approached from every level of game theory. Perhaps the most valuable for the immediate use of those who consider policy has been the analogies and paradoxes generated in conversational game theory.

These include the Doomsday machine of Herman Kahn (1961) as the ultimate example of a precommitted threat and Schelling's (1960, 1976) discussion of many examples. Related to both conversational game theory and the large legal, labor, and business literature on bargaining are Raiffa's (1982) experiments and insights on negotiations. Beyond that there is a large formal literature on fair division and a fast-growing literature in game theory applied to economics.

Essentially the work can be broken down into five sections: (1) conversational game theory; (2) formal fair division models; (3) basic solution theory for games in extensive form; (4) models involving automata or constrained rationality; and (5) specific dynamic models set in context.

1. The use of game-theoretic analogy and examples in essay form is probably here to stay and is part of a process making the consideration of strategic consequences more explicit. Both its production and the validity of its use depend upon the art, care, and sophistication of the producers and consumers.

The adoption of new modes of thought is measured in generations. Basic concepts such as the difference between zero-sum and nonconstant-sum games and the difficulties in reconciling naively defined individual and joint rationality are gradually making their way into general discourse.

Mainly in the domain of formal game theory there is a large literature dealing with normative models of fair division (see Roth, 1979, for a survey of many of the axiom systems, and Shubik, 1982, for a less technical coverage). The basic models have been those of Nash (1950, 1953) on the two-person bargaining problem with fixed and variable threats and the extensions of Harsanyi (1959) and Shapley (1953) to n-person problems with various conditions on both threats and the description of preferences. The details are not of direct concern here, but several aspects of the implicit and explicit assumptions and deductions from this work are of importance to the political scientist.

2. In order to produce an explicit model it becomes necessary to clearly define the concept of threat. This immediately raises basic conceptual problems concerning capabilities and intentions, as well as specification of preferences and damage exchange rate considerations. In evaluating the plausibility of a threat, does one assume a worst-case analysis, or should the cost of carrying out the threat be considered? If it should be considered, how do we measure costs and relative costs? The critical lesson that is learned is that it is impossible to separate out fair division considerations from measures of power. The fair division axioms invariably involve considerations built up from optimality and symmetry. But before these can be applied, either explicitly or implicitly, assumptions are made about initial entitlement, claims, ownership, and strategic alternatives available to all individuals and groups. The characteristic function (noted above in the section entitled "Many Cooperative Solutions") has within it a host of implicit assumptions concerning the power of groups. Virtually all of this theory is in vitro. It is cut out of time, yet one of the most perplexing problems in the "rightful and just claims" of nations is determining where history begins. What are traditional borders and claims, when does the clock start?

Fair division theory is normative, and for the most part the individual actors are without personality and are assumed to have well-defined preferences.

Both in application to models of economic and other bargaining and in raising basic questions concerning theory development, game theorists have been concerned with the difficulties in defining rational behavior in a world without strictly enforceable precommitment. Bargains and negotiations take place in real time with a haze of uncertainty. The abstract normative cooperative solutions do not fit our needs to understand the processes of negotiation. Other solutions are needed. The noncooperative equilibrium appears to be a candidate.

3. The noncooperative equilibrium solution seems to have some behavioristic merit in a game in strategic form. It has the property of circular stability, or phrasing it differently, if all parties are at an equilibrium point, the system is self-policing. It is in no one's self-interest to deviate. Unfortunately, both modeling and solution difficulties appear with attempts to apply noncooperative solutions to bargaining problems. Considerable modeling difficulties are encountered in merely trying to describe bargaining in extensive form. The works of Cross (1969) and Stahl (1972) both provide good coverage and discussion of the problems of modeling.[17] They offer formal bargaining structures and suggest solutions. It is important to stress that it is both difficult and

probably undesirable to try to completely separate normative from behavioral considerations. A key problem in virtually all negotiations is to design procedures and institutions that will facilitate the bargaining process.

In dealing with games in extensive form, it is difficult to carry out an analysis that is institution free. The rules of the game provide a description of the carriers of process and are thus in essence elemental institutions. The discussions noted are biased toward economic bargaining and negotiation. In asking how this literature fits with the problems of international arms negotiations, one has to explore both the divergences in essential modeling and the relevance of the solution concept adopted.

Van Damme (1983) provides a handy summary of many of the variations on the theme of noncooperative equilibrium, including perfect, strictly perfect, strong, proper, and so forth. The message should be clear. When there is a proliferation of modifications to a solution concept and when the solution is far from unique, it usually means that the concepts or the models or both do not provide a satisfactory way to analyze the problem at hand.

Binmore (1986) in a publication entitled "Modeling Rational Players" provides a rogues' gallery of many of the paradoxical examples that challenge the formal game theorist attempting to find a satisfactory theory for dynamic games. The splendidly simple paradox posed by Rosenthal is noted as an example to illustrate one among the many difficulties encountered. The game shown in Figure 4.3 is interpreted as follows: Player A moves first. If he selects his first move, the payoff to him is 10 and to B the payoff is 3. If he selects move 2, B gets the move. If B selects his first move, A obtains 4 and B obtains 5. If B selects move 2, the choice goes back to A, who can select move 1 with payoffs of (6,6) or select 2 with payoffs of (5,2).

The perfect equilibrium has Player A select his first move and Player B use the strategy that if he is called on to select a move, he selects his second move.

A solution concept suggested by Kreps and Wilson (1982A) called the

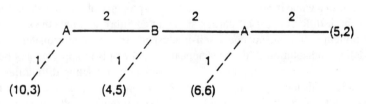

FIGURE 4.3. A game illustrating a paradox of sequential play.

sequential equilibrium is closely related to the perfect equilibrium of Selten. The equilibrium they describe is given by a set of moves accompanied by an appropriately updated expectation at the moves.

Suppose that you are Player B and you are told that A has selected his second move and that you are called on to move, what do you do? The solution concepts rule out the possibility that A gives B the move. If A had been rational, you should have never been called upon to move. Thus you must have some form of theory of A's error generation or irrationality if you are required to move.

4. A different approach to studying sequential play has been suggested by Rubinstein (1986) and applied to the Prisoners' Dilemma. He considers the game as being played by two finite automata where there are maintenance costs that must be paid for every state of the machine that is to be available. Implicit in Rubinstein's model is a "use them or lose them" view of armament. If it costs you to maintain an arsenal that is never actually physically utilized but has maintenance costs, you will eventually get rid of it.

Smale in earlier work has considered limits on memory, and Radner has investigated near (or epsilon) equilibria. But despite these promising starts, the formulation and analysis of bounded rationality models is only in its early stages.

The reason for these brief comments on limited rationality models at this point is to indicate that to a great extent behavioral approaches, gaming, and simulations are complementary to the mathematical approaches. The complexity of formal models of *homo ludens* in games in extensive form is enough to signal that the interface between game theory models and behavioral models is probably one of the most important areas for future research in deterrence theory. The future development of adequate models is a two-way process; the game theory methodology provides a building kit, but considerable hand-tailoring is required to construct reasonable models of deterrence that are tractable, plausible, and sufficiently relevant.

When we turn to the type of problems actually faced in negotiations and threats, we see that although all of the concerns dealt with by formal game theory are usually present, there are also many others that are either not touched upon at all or only present in a formal manner. For example, the assumption of symmetry is often used in some form in the mathematical axioms concerning bargaining theories, yet a paper such as that of Foster (1978) points out the considerable technical and conceptual difficulties in even being able to perceive what parity is between two differently structured forces.

The value of a threefold approach involving behavioral understanding and gaming; institutional understanding and context relevancy; and appreciation of the methodology of game theory is basically present in Raiffa's (1982) work on bargaining.

5. In the recent literature on games in extensive form, consideration has been given to the development of reputation and to the understanding of conditions for renegotiation. Selten (1978) formulated "the chain store paradox" in which he examined the problem faced by a chain store trying to build a reputation for toughness in order to discourage potential entrants from actually going into competition. Kreps and Wilson (1982b) and others have extended this work considering reputation where there may be noise or random elements present. Benoit and Krishna (1988) and others have considered games with the possibility of renegotiation, where they try to make rigorous the general idea that after A has violated his agreement with B, it still may pay both sides to renegotiate rather than have B carry out his threat or do nothing. Political scientists concerned with deterrence should be aware of these developments. However the game-theoretic work on deterrence is for the most part not merely at a high level of abstraction, but the formal description may lack features deemed to be essential to analysis. The vocabulary of game theory is not yet rich enough to deal with concepts such as resolution, probity, stamina, conviction, stubbornness, and a host of other concepts that are part of the gestalt that defines reputation for individuals and institutions.

Related to the study of threats and deterrence has been the concern for the evolution of cooperation. In political science the work of Axelrod (1984) has received considerable attention in part due to some apparently striking results with the success of a "tit-for-tat" strategy in repeated plays of the Prisoners' Dilemma game. Unfortunately, the robustness of this elementally simple threat strategy does not seem to generalize much beyond the somewhat special context of this special matrix game, and no adequate general theory has emerged.

The 2×2 game has played a central role in providing ideas concerning threats and counterthreats. The Rapoport, Guyer, and Gordon (1976) taxonomy of all strictly ordinal games is based in part on dynamic considerations. They describe certain outcomes as being force and threat vulnerable.

Brams and Wittman (1981) use a categorization that is even more explicitly dynamic. They consider the following sequence of actions: (1) The players select a move simultaneously thereby picking an initial outcome; (2) Either player can unilaterally select a different move; (3) The other player may then react and the alternation can continue until neither wishes to change further. They define nonmyopic rationality and consider nonmyopic equilibria.

For nonmyopic rationality it is assumed that no player will move from an outcome that will not lead to improvement at the final equilibrium and that the

TABLE 4.11   The Game of Chicken

Player A	Player B	
	1	*2*
1	(3,3)	(2,4)
2	(4,2)	(1,1)

players anticipate only a single play of their supergame. They show that 37 out of the 78 games have nonmyopic equilibria; 36 have a cycle, and 5 have neither a cycle nor a nonmyopic equilibrium. The Prisoners' Dilemma is the only game with two nonmyopic equilibria.

The idea of Brams and Wittman that a taxonomy should be based on dynamic consideration is highly suggestive, as is their argument that an equilibrium should be nonmyopic. Table 4.11 shows the game of Chicken with the payoffs (3,3) being the outcome of the only nonmyopic equilibrium—Brams and Hessel (1984) extend the original analysis to games that can be played more than once and suggest a measure of threat power in a sequential game. Unfortunately, their new game is not well defined. Neither the payoffs nor the influence of length of play are made clear.

Zagare (1981) applies the concept of a nonmyopic equilibrium to the situation in the Middle East.

Arms Races and Escalation

The study of arms races and escalation provides a reasonably wide and well-defined domain for both conversational and low church or plain operations research type of game theory to produce and solve specific models, which even though possibly oversimplified nevertheless illustrate problems of some operational concern. Richardson (1960) was an English meteorologist and physicist dedicated to the promotion of peace studies and the preservation of peace. He engaged in a large statistical study in an attempt to identify the causes of war and in the 1940s and 1950s produced a large data base on the outbreak of war and several formal mathematical models of arms races escalating to full hostilities. Since his work many formal mathematical models of arms races and other resource battles have been built. They also relate closely to two large bodies of literature on attrition in fire exchange and to many models in the study of duopolistic competition in economics. The early work of Lanchester (1916) provided much of the impetus for the first, and Cournot (1838) provided the earliest formal duopoly model.

The models in general are described as simultaneous difference equations with time treated in finite hunks (see, for example, Rapoport, 1960); as simultaneous differential equation models with time treated as continuous (Richardson, 1960; Intriligator, 1967; Intriligator and Brito, 1984; Mayer, 1986); or as differential games, stochastic games, or parallel dynamic programs.

Despite the considerable array of mathematical apparatus, the political scientist or defense analyst must be concerned with determining the relevance of these models. Several valuable lessons can be learned.

The mathematics provides useful insights and parables that illustrate that relatively simple processes may contain feedbacks within them that can explode apparently stable systems.

The limitations of our knowledge of mathematics more or less guarantee that the models must be relatively simple when compared with the actual phenomena to be studied. Thus, unless the problem involves a reasonably well defined and constrained physical process, the results can only be usefully interpreted as indicating the direction of motion in an extremely small domain. In many human affairs as the domain changes, so does the importance of various driving factors. Thus the elements that launch a crisis may be replaced by factors that were not operative at the start.

The mixture of formal analytical models, together with games and simulations, has an important conceptual lesson to teach to the social sciences as a whole. The distinction between "game theory" solutions, mechanistic solutions, and behavioral solutions for the study of human behavior in situations involving conflict and cooperation is at best vague. There is no airtight trichotomy. There is no unified party line among high church game theorists as to what constitutes the correct solution to an n-person dynamic game. At best (even with all the assumptions about individual goal-oriented conscious rational behavior) there is some agreement concerning solution concepts that seem to fit reasonably well for problems in specific contexts. The context of global nuclear brinkmanship is not one for which there is a unified view.

The formal concept of strategy shows that it is clear that in a process of any complication humans at best employ only a highly limited set of the strategies theoretically available. They cut down by aggregation, delegation, procrastination, lack of perception, and many other devices for simplifying action. Rules such as "damn the torpedoes, full speed ahead," "always draw to a Jack," "do not shoot until you see the whites of their eyes," and "shoot first, ask questions later" are well-defined but relatively simple formal game-theoretic strategies.

Simple escalation processes that can be captured by low-dimensional fixed differential equations will be called "mechanistic" because the strategies em-

ployed exhibit great rigidity and small scope and often give the appearance of
wrong-headed learning.

Simulations where simple learning conditions have been introduced and
where the dynamics of interaction of many rules of behavior can be traced by
computer are referred to as "behavioral" because they appear to portray great
flexibility (often to the extent that it is extremely difficult to interpret what can
be learned from the output). These two can be interpreted formally as game-
theoretic strategies. The difference between them and the science fiction view
of what is meant by a "game theory strategy" is that the justification given for
a behavioral strategy comes from the ad hoc construction of decision rules,
defended by observations from social psychology, political science, or for
other reasons, whereas the phrase "game theory strategy" is often used to
imply optimal strategy. This in turn implies that there exists some well-
defined superrational way for an individual to play in a dynamic multiperson
nonconstant-sum game. Although some individuals with a purely philosophical bent (see Harsanyi, 1982) feel that there may be some unifying solution
theory that leads to a unique outcome supported by the set of optimal game
strategies, this view is not widely shared.

A simple game has been proposed to illustrate some of the paradoxes of
escalation known as the dollar auction (Shubik, 1971). A dollar is auctioned
with the rule that the highest bidder obtains the dollar, but both the highest
bidder and the second highest bidder pay. Thus, for example, if A has bid 95
cents and B has bid a dollar, there is an incentive for A to bid over a dollar for
a dollar in order to cut losses. Many simple experiments with this game have
been conducted (See Teger, 1980), and it is relatively easy to see individuals
paying more than a dollar for the dollar.

O'Neill (1986), however, offers a solution that is obtained by enlarging the
model. He observed that in the original formulation of the game no limits
were given on the resources of the players. He introduces explicitly the size of
the resources available. With this extra specification he is able (by means of a
backward induction} to argue that for any specification of resources there is a
specific finite amount that a player should bid. He then goes on to discuss the
relevance of the dollar auction to the escalation of international conflict and
presents a comparison of the differences between the simple model and the
"real thing." This discussion brings to focus the points made by Beer (1986)
on the highly different uses of paradigms, models, and metaphors in the
production and consumption of the social sciences.

Those developing basic theory and new tools often wish to be more "relevant" than they appear to be in their ability to utilize what they know in
examining the pressing real problems of society currently at hand. It is suggested here that it is desirable that paradoxes be examined, examples sug-

gested, and metaphors offered. But the caveat should be *cum grano salus*. Metaphor has much to recommend it (see, for example, Brams, 1984), but the interweave among metaphor, model, and policy conclusion must be approached with extreme care.

Crisis Stability

Crisis stability is far too important a problem to be left primarily to mathematical modeling in general and game theory in particular. But there are many special questions and conceptual problems that can be posed where the attempt to specify models of extreme simplicity offers valuable insight. What are some of the key questions? These may well precede the models. For example:

1. Could disarmament be as or more destabilizing than increasing armament (in part this is one of the questions investigated by Intriligator and Brito, 1984)?

2. Does the reliability and accuracy of nuclear weapons increase or decrease potential stability?

3. What does Murphy's law as applied to command and control systems do for international security? Is more or less dependence on error safer? (See Bracken, 1983; Blair, 1985).

4. Can we devise structural measures of the degree of potential for cooperation or conflict in any situation?

5. Can we develop behavioral measures of stability?

6. How good, mutually understood, and credible are our first- and second-strike measures of effectiveness?

7. What is the sensitivity of the system to IFF (identification, friend or foe) errors?

8. How are nuclear damage payoff functions to be characterized and how do they influence the stability of the game?

9. Does "potlatch" behavior fit into a rational analysis of defense expenditures?

10. Does revenge have a rational game-theoretic meaning?

All of the questions noted above undoubtedly depend upon the context of the crisis and the systems being considered. But these questions and several more all can be characterized as sensitivity analysis problems analyzable by means of operations research applied game theory studies. When these questions are asked in context about a specific system, assuming all other factors held constant there is a reasonably chance that qualitative and in some instances quantitative answers rather than allegories can be supplied.

In the debate on appropriations for weapons systems, the menu of what they have versus the menu of what we have is often used. This is the most elementary of military accounting systems. Richelson (1982) discusses the problems with the construction of single number static indicators. Game-theoretic analysis at the most stripped down level provides a way to ask better questions concerning the operational meaning of the differences in weapons arrays. Grotte (1980) gives a model for examining stabilizing and destabilizing changes in nuclear force posture based to some extent on the utilization of the work of Bracken, Falk, and Miercourt (1977; see also Bracken, Brooks, and Falk, 1985) on optimal weapons allocations. He encounters the immediate modeling difficulties of how to assess payoffs and how to consider damage exchange rates. Shubik and Weber (1981) in considering network defense against first strike encounter the same difficulties.

As early as the brief note by Ellsberg (1961*a*) the idea of a stability index derived from game theory analysis has been considered. O'Neill (1987) explicitly using a "stag hunt" matrix game illustrated in Table 4.12 has suggested an explicit measure of stability where the numbers in the matrix are based upon the type of detailed computation suggested by Bracken, Falk, and Miercourt (1977), thus the selection of this particular payoff structure is justified by consideration of the costs and payoffs for the war-peace scenario.

It is assumed that $r_1 > a_1 > 0$. O'Neill's index is given by:

$$(r_1/a_1 - 1)(r_2/a_2 - 1).$$

The index is a single number based upon a single 2×2 matrix game where the numbers are the result of a more or less elaborate accepted operations research methodology for providing damage assessment in weapons interchange. Its strength (and the strength of the Grotte [1980] work as well as the extensions of the earlier paper of Dalkey [1965] euphemistically entitled "Solvable Nuclear War Models") is that the detailed weapons evaluation and damage exchange problem is acknowledged, studied separately from the overall assessment, but connected to it. A weakness is that it is doubtful that a special small matrix game reflects enough of the problems of stability and serves as more than a parable for talking about stability.

Recent work by Jerome Bracken (1988) illustrates the importance of elabo-

TABLE 4.12   The Stag Hunt

Player A	Player B	
	1	*2*
1	(0,0)	$(-r_1,-a_2)$
2	$(-a_1,-r_2)$	$((-a_1-r^1)/2,(-a_2-r_2)/2)$

rate calculations based upon a stability index and also shows how delicately results will depend on the selection of such an index. In particular Bracken observes that even if two countries agree on a disarmament program, the actual sequencing of moves must be selected so that at any point in the process as the countries change their force structure no zones of instability develop.

In summary: (1) the idea of trying to construct stability indices, if viewed only as a methodological discipline, is probably worthwhile; (2) the need to concentrate openly and explicitly on which, if any, overall payoff or utility function is going to be employed is critical; (3) the need to understand that the technical problem of weapons and damage assessment can and should be separated from the much more complex problem of the societal evaluation of the damage is important; (4) the transparency of the models is high, and their very unreality helps to warn against misuse.[18]

There appears to be a considerable disconnection between the meant-to-be-informed public, including much of the political science community, and the military on the role and importance of formal assessment models. There has been for over 30 years a sizable industry of consultant firm model builders such as Vector, Stanford Research Institute, SAI, Logicon, and Mathematica that have been building specific assessment models that are utilized in the evaluation of weapons systems and also appear in shadow form when a major game such as the Global War Game at the Naval War College was played. When these models are used in a major game, unless the players are highly experienced professionals in the nature of the warfare being studied, their transparency is lost and the players may be willing to accept dangerously wrong results emerging from the black box as an approximation of reality.

On occasion an article designed for wide dissemination may connect the political science overview with the assessment; thus, for example, Steinbruner (1984) in a discussion of launch under attack notes a simple command and control assessment model developed by Morawski and Blair at Brookings to perform a sensitivity analysis on retaliation plans.

Two considerably different game-theoretic models are now noted. Guth (1985) uses an extensive form game with incomplete (and inconsistent) information to model the type of problem that is uppermost in the minds of many Western Europeans. The nuclear deterrence situation is modeled with three players, the Soviet Union, the United States, and the Europeans, with neither of the first two knowing the true type of the third player at the start.

Shubik (1986) has attempted to formally model the idea of differences in perception between leaders and those being led. A game-theoretic analysis points out the possibility that such a difference in perception could be used for strategic manipulation by the leaders. This point is related to, but not identical with, the observations of Jervis (1988) on misperception.

O'Neill (1988) in a perceptive paper presents a simple game where two individuals desire a prize, but each does not know if the other is strongly or weakly motivated. He then shows that at the first stage players may rationally decide to burn some resources prior to making a demand in order to signal their level of resolution. After this display the players then make their demands. If both demands add to more than the prize, they each pay a conflict penalty; otherwise they get their demanded share plus half of the remainder of the final prize. The resemblance to Potlatch behavior in establishing "face" seems to be more than casual, as O'Neill notes an important feature may be to spend on arms to signal that you are the "big man on the block," not merely have arms available.

Nalebuff and Shubik (1988), modifying the game "so long sucker" originally invented by Hausner, Nash, Shapley, and Shubik (1964), have produced a game in which the concept of revenge plays a role as a means for breaking ties. There are three players. Any player who is called on to move twice is eliminated, and the move bounces back to the person who eliminated her. A player who has the move can give the move to any other player. There is only one winner, the last survivor. The payoff for winning is 1; all others obtain 0.

The first person to move is selected at random. It is fairly easy to see that being called on to move is undesirable. If player A moves first, she must select B or C. But the game is completely symmetric, and neither wants the move. One convention is that a player announces the policy that she regards being given the move as a hostile act and will retaliate by giving the move back. If one player does this, it is highly advantageous, but this is not true if all follow this policy.

It is still an open challenge to game theory and social psychology to sort out the purely strategic components of revenge, honor, morale, and bluff from the psychological and societal factors.

Problems with Modeling Deterrence

In his book Bueno de Mesquita (1981) and in an article Bueno de Mesquita and Riker (1982) stress the expected utility model for considering war scenarios. But it is at this point that the warnings of formal game theory and of modeling are at their highest. The difficulties with attaching preferences or utility functions or payoffs (as distinct from physical outcome descriptions) to a country as a whole are considerable. One has to justify how and why one can attach a completely ordered preference structure to a nation-state. Otherwise, the payoff structure must be derived from games within the game (i.e., from a subgame representing a single country as several actors), or a much more complex representation of preferences than a complete ordering may be called for.

An array of political science scholars have attacked rational deterrence theory, saying that it does not match with their case studies, but Achen and Snidal (1989) argue that these attacks are not compelling. Lebow and Stein (1988) argue that "theories of deterrence built on better models of subjective expected utility or game theoretic analyses of strategic preferences would still suffer from crippling limitation." They argue that preferences change, misperceptions are rampant, and miscalculations abound.

From the viewpoint of game theory and its contribution to the understanding of deterrence, I find that I strongly agree and strongly disagree with both viewpoints noted above. The proponents of rational deterrence theory appear to expect too much. The opponents do not appear to have a better general theory to offer.

At this point, at best we can hope for a patchwork of limited theories that are not necessarily even consistent, but at least raise and hopefully partially answer different interesting and relevant questions.

It has been suggested here that there are many reasonable questions that can be asked for which applied game theory investigations can provide useful answers and insights. Yet when one contemplates scenarios for the start of World War III, it is hard to not envision scenarios involving a small war say in Europe, escalating through blunders, misperception, or failures in communication or in the understanding of the context and meaning of the messages being sent. Actions may be required in time spans that permit instinct or rigid programming to dominate.

The model of the rational person is a gross low-dimensional oversimplification to enable far more complex individuals with limited calculating capability to sweeten their intuitions and improve their insights. It does not provide overall operational plans on how to fight or avoid World War III.

Game-theoretic analysis has shown clearly that even throwing away all of the complications of personality and society, this simple model of the rational person does not provide us with an extension of the concept of rational behavior beyond a situation involving two parties in total opposition. Furthermore, when the players are not single individuals, or are acting as fiduciaries on behalf of others, the description of what their preferences are becomes extremely complex even without postulating limited rationality.

Coping with the immediate problems of how to think and act concerning the overhanging threat of nuclear destruction and the metaphysics of deterrence here and now can be helped by game-theoretic analysis. However, factors such as asymmetries of mindset, individual and organizational risk assessment, coping with system failure, the role of specific leaders, and control systems call for the broad array of behavioral science studies in parallel as well as modifications and complications to most of the current formal models.

Game theory does have a central role to play, but the limitations of current models as well as the strengths of rational strategic analysis must be appreciated. It is about as good a language as we have for discussing and understanding strategy. It provides an underlying methodology, a way to formalize critical questions. In particular it serves one purpose extremely well. It helps to clarify basic concepts. Thus, for example, attempts to formalize concepts of threat and deterrence have had only limited success, not because game theory has failed, but because the analysis shows that they are far more complex than most verbal treatments make them out to be. Good game-theoretic analysis serves to sort out that which can be explained by impersonal rational calculation and that which cannot.

In its role in helping to clarify concepts, game theory clearly illustrates the current limitations of formal strategic analysis. This is not a negative comment, as it illustrates where and why conceptual links have not yet been forged between the approaches of the other behavioral sciences and the utilitarian economics view of the rational agent.

The future development of strategic analysis calls for the explicit modeling of constrained or context rational behavior. This will undoubtedly happen. A way in which it will happen will be by attempting to reconcile the discrepancies between formal optimization theories and behavioral approaches, not by opting for the use of one while claiming that the other is unrealistic or irrelevant.

A Program for the Future

Where do we go from here? A few remarks are made suggesting the type of programs that may have both societal and scientific value.

History teaches that humans adjust to living next to Vesuvius or on top of the Saint Andreas fault or on a hurricane-exposed stretch of coast. When disaster strikes, they are surprised that it could happen to them. Hope, optimism, foolhardiness, and an ignoring of the suggested odds are all close cousins. Heroism and foolishness, caution and fear appear to be linked in ways we still do not understand.

Life is more than an accounting exercise, but it is often a good idea to understand the accounting even though you defy the odds. Nuclear megadeaths, greenhouse effects, or nuclear winters change after a few years from being "unthinkable" to becoming uninteresting everyday household bogeymen. They go from unthinkable to boring and unfundable. The idea that one could even dream of spending the cost of a nuclear carrier task force on basic research appears to be foreign to the administrative mind in particular and to the public in general.

Throwing money at a problem is by no means a guaranteed way to solve it (as the Nixon administration's attack on cancer indicates). The availability of talent and trained personnel is critical. The Vietnam War destroyed several generations of analysts. They can and must be replaced and reinforced. Institutional support, money, and long-term educational programs can help. A program for the future is noted at three levels: (1) education and training; (2) research and basic theory development and experimentation; and (3) policy, operations, and current procedures.

University and Military Education

In particular, good interdisciplinary work is difficult to carry out successfully. Yet the start made at RAND in the 1950s does not appear to have been surpassed by the 1980s. The nature of many defense problems calls for a blend of understanding involving political science, economics, social psychology, and game theory.[19]

There is a danger that one can fall into the trap of romanticizing the past. Often the call is to re-create Camelot, ignoring the change in time and circumstances. This discussion is based on the premise that not only is it not possible to re-create the past (except in near parody such as towns like Williamsburg), but it is also usually not desirable to do so. The call is not for a RAND of the 1980s or 1990s, but for a program that will be as successful or more successful than the research establishment was in the 1950s and early 1960s.

The choice in education is often presented as though it were a choice between being literate or numerate but not both. If you know the classics, you are not a customer for calculus. Yet the very essence of good conversational game theory and good model building in general is an appreciation of both. The numbers are recognized and used. But it is not what the numbers are that counts—it is what they mean. In order to understand what they mean it is necessary to be able to do a certain amount of calculation, but it is also critical to be able to set them in context.

Conversational game theory backed up with a decent knowledge and mastery of the basic concepts of formal game theory could improve the intermix of historical literacy with formal concepts of strategic analysis. Such a course (possibly combined with a liberal number of small operational and experimental games) could and should be given at every academy, war college, and major university. The languages of game theory open up a level of strategic literacy and discourse that serves as a basis to test both essays on strategy and formal models. The level envisioned calls for an intermix of the writings of Kahn (1961), Schelling (1960, 1984), Ellsberg (1961*a* & *b*), Rapoport (1960), Shubik (1975a,b), and others together with a rigorous but basically elementary text on game theory for the political scientist.

The understanding of the rigor of formal model building combined with a skepticism of models produces individuals who are able to avoid the demands for spurious realism and detail that often are the earmark of the operator who lacks the formal training to seek fruitful abstraction.

The type of intermixed operational, experimental, and theoretical course given by Raiffa (1982) on bargaining can easily be modified to concentrate more on diplomatic and military contexts.

The Need for Experimental, Educational, and Operational Gaming

The study of strategy calls for the use of several different techniques. Of varying importance to the problems at hand are: (1) the essay (including conversational game theory); (2) free-form operational gaming; (3) semirigid operational gaming; (4) simulation; (5) experimental gaming; and (6) rigid rule gaming and analysis (including formal game theory).

A reasonably detailed discussion of the history and purposes of gaming and simulation has been given elsewhere (Shubik, 1975*a* & *b*; and Brewer and Shubik, 1979) and is not repeated here. The uses of operational and educational gaming have been recognized by every major military establishment in the world. An example of the value attached to the importance of gaming is the size of the war gaming department at the Center for Naval Warfare Studies at the United States Naval War College.[20] But the gap between basic game theory research, the results of social psychology and experimental gaming, and military operational and teaching gaming is probably larger now than it was in the 1950s and 1960s. At that time the Systems Development Corporation was spun off from RAND to perform much of the activities in gaming and systems design while RAND still maintained a high level of activity in both experimental gaming and game theory.

Despite the presence of a war gaming department with between 60 and 80 members, even the Naval War College does not have an experimental gaming and game theory component that at a bare minimum would supply the connections for the flow of insights and understanding between operational gaming and theory and experimentation.

A group of between 7 and 10 professionals at the Ph.D. level could be of considerable worth. It would consist roughly of 2 game theorists, 2 experimental social psychologists, 1 or 2 statisticians; 1 or 2 quantitative political scientists, and 1 or 2 engineer-physicists with broad weapons systems understanding. Bureaucratic and administrative problems in adequately funding such a group to attract first-class professionals may present problems. But it is a group of this variety that is needed to provide the interlink between the universities and defense education and the mathematics and hard and soft sciences approach to defense problems.

Fashion changes. After the seminal work of Goldhamer and Speir (1961) there was an interlude when the Political Military Exercise (PME) flourished as an art form. In the past 10 or 15 years the sweep of fashion carried in with it the all-computer simulation, expert systems, and the dream of artificial intelligence. It is possible that the current trend is somewhat back in the direction of the PME and free-form game. But regardless of sponsorship or lack of sponsorship, the hard questions have hardly been asked, let alone answered. Is the experience generalizable beyond the game? What are the purposes served? Was anything actually learned from the work of Guetzkow et al. (1963) on Internations Simulation and its relatives? Did the PMEs of Bloomfield (1960) leave lasting results? Were the ingenious small and more mechanized games of Paxson (1972) of lasting value?

An even more important set of questions is, did any of this work interface with and influence the development of game theory and experimental gaming and vice versa? We do not have to be in the loop where not knowing history dooms us to living it again. It can be established that at least the work on formal game theory has been cumulative. We know considerably more than we did 20 or 30 years ago. It is not that clear that the work on conversational game theory, applied strategic analysis, operational gaming, or even experimental gaming has been consistently cumulative. Cute portrayals of paradoxes, clever examples, and even profound insights are certainly better than nothing, but they do not constitute a unified and growing body of knowledge.

At this time we have enough trained personnel, but we are missing the focus and the institutional will and means to direct sufficient organizational and other assets to fundamental applied research in bargaining, negotiation, deterrence, experimental psychology, gaming, and game theory. Yet the size of funding required is a fraction of the amount we are willing to expend on a broad array of hardware improvements for communications and weapons systems that at best offer only marginal tactical improvements.

A few specific items concerning experimental gaming are noted: (1) When does a war game go nuclear? (2) What do we know about gaming and the relationship between real-time operations and game time operations? (3) What do we know about gaming, briefing, and start point and end point effects in trying to model ongoing phenomena?

It is more or less accepted in the war gaming community that war games do not go nuclear with ease. An in-depth study of the evidence of war game plays by different national groups—investigating what percentage went nuclear and why—would merit support.

An all-encompassing problem for gaming, game theory, and their applications to war is, do we need to make allowances for the interplay between attitude toward risk and culture? Would a Japan of today still find the Kamikaze volunteers that it found 45 years ago? Are risk perceptions and attitudes toward risk taking to a good first approximation culture free, or is this an important point at which we should abandon the assumption of external symmetry?

What Does Game Theory Have to Contribute That Is Operationally Useful Concerning Deterrence?

Not one but many problems are posed by trying to understand deterrence. There are many disciplines required to investigate the highly different but related parts. Yet whether looking at the political process, the command and control system, arms control bargaining, the hardening of silos, or first- and second-strike scenarios, a component of individualistic conscious interlinked strategic decision making is present.

Game theory provides an underlying set of languages and methodology for the study of conflict and cooperation. It is an organizing device and not a substitute for substantive knowledge and understanding of context. Its strengths highlight its limitations. By forcing us to understand the logical implications of trying to push the model of the individual goal-oriented rational intelligent actor in multiperson interaction, it highlights the need to consider models with limited rationality, and constraints on data processing. The behavioral models of political science are in general not necessarily incompatible with game-theoretic thought on dynamics.

"Has game theory lived up to its promise?" This particular rhetorical sentence can be used equally well for a session in self-congratulation or criticism. The more proper qualification is "promise to whom?" With this in mind I close on a moderately optimistic note. The concepts of game-theoretic analysis were one of the major new conceptual insights of the twentieth century. The acceptance of new insights is a social process. About half a century is not inordinately long for basically new ideas to make their way into commonly accepted knowledge. When newspapers and popular writers start to talk of the "zero-sum problem" or the Prisoners' Dilemma and when conversational game theory examples proliferate, these serve as an indication that the basic concepts have made their way into the thinking of society as a whole.

The early proponents of "a revolution in thought" often misestimate the straight technical difficulties in modeling and mathematics in providing specific answers to burning (and often ill-defined complex) questions. Game theory per se will not solve many of the problems in deterrence. It has not even solved many of the problems in the economics of oligopoly theory (a subject at which it was first aimed). But it has provided considerable insights and a clarification of the problems. The mere fact that work is proceeding on all three levels (conversational, low church, and high church) is a sign of progress.

The gap between the acceptance of conversational theorizing in the social sciences and the appreciation of the formal concepts and difficulties encountered in game theory, models of limited rationality, and artificial intelligence is important. It needs to be narrowed if the flow of valuable ideas between those with substantive concerns and methodologists is to be increased. Although this is by no means the best of all possible worlds, there are indications that this gap is closing. More stress on the appropriate educational programs could speed up this process.

There are enough low church problems that are sufficiently well defined and are directly relevant to defense problems that support of them is merited (to some extent on an ad hoc basis).

Basic research and new ideas require the growth and backing of a cadre of researchers. But although increased funding is a necessary, it is not always a sufficient condition; the talent has to be available. It is possible that some of the talent that is currently going into law and finance (in accord with Willy Sutton's law)[21] could be redirected. However, extra resources spent on basic research, even if they help to bring forth excellent work, may only contribute tangentially to the specific problems of policy advice on deterrence now.

A good overall strategy requires the simultaneous study of the operational problems at hand with the means at hand and the willingness and foresight to sponsor and pay for the educational and research programs required, without unrealistic stress on magic solutions that rarely, if ever, come directly from basic research, but that in the long run feed off it much as a healthy tree feeds off the soil in which it is planted.

Notes

The original work was supported in part by the Department of the Navy, Contract N00014-77-C-0518, and in part by the National Research Council. Support for the extensive revisions and new version has been from the Pew Foundation.

1. The recent publication by Davis and Stan (1984) indicates that Soviet and U.S. views of deterrence differ.

2. See Shubik (1982:38) for an estimate.

3. There is a minor technical distinction to be made between the class of two-person zero-sum games and two-person constant-sum games. However, they are strategically equivalent, and the distinction is not developed here (see Shubik, 1982:chap 8).

4. Technically the maximin calls for the utilization of a mixed strategy.

5. See Shubik (1982:chap. 9)

6. There are many other solutions that have been suggested and analyzed to some degree. These include the stable set, the bargaining set, and the kernel (see Shubik, 1982:chaps. 6, 7, and 11).

7. See Shubik (1982) and Shubik (1984:chaps. 8 and 12).

8. For a discussion of alternative ways for portraying multistage games see Shubik (1982:chap. 3).

9. Harsanyi (1982) has for many years worked on constructing a theory that selects a unique special equilibrium point for all games, even though they may have a profusion of plain Nash equilibria.

10. Barry O'Neill, in discussion, has suggested the term proto-game theory, which he uses instead of conversational game theory.

11. This list has been developed in some detail elsewhere (Shubik, 1983b) in the context of corporate planning, but although some important modifications must be made in accounting for differences in long-range defense planning and corporate planning, there is a considerable overlap in planning needs. Schelling's (1966) observations on modeling, abstraction, and empirical content are closely related to this approach.

12. By strong ordering we mean that ties are ruled out in the description of preferences. If ties are included, then the number of different cases, as counted and classified by Powers (1986), turns out to be 726.

13. The game is named after a scenario originally supplied concerning the cross-examination of two suspects who might give evidence against each other.

14. A paper by Shubik and Weber (1981) provides examples. The first part is aimed strictly at application and computation (albeit at a relatively formal level) concerning real problems in network defense and target hardening. The second aspect relates the mathematics of the defense problem to a pure game-theoretic problem in understanding the connection between the noncooperative equilibrium solution to one game and the value solution to a related game.

15. An interesting treatment of this question is provided by L.J. Cohen (1981), who observes: "The object of this paper is to show why recent research in the psychology of deductive and probabilistic reasoning does not have 'bleak implications for human rationality' as has sometimes been supposed."

16. The stable set and the bargaining set provide two examples.

17. The more recent work of Rubinstein (1986) is related to the approach of Stahl.

18. Even though it was written over 20 years ago, the compendium of misapplication of game theory noted by Wohlstetter (1964) still merits rereading. The article by Intriligator (1982) also provides a useful (but not critical) classification of the role of mathematical models research on conflict theory.

19. As well as backup understanding of the relevant aspects of engineering, physics, mathematics, operations research, management science, and computer science.

20. See the Annual Report 1985–1986, United States Naval War College, Center for Naval Warfare Studies.

21. Q. Mr. Sutton, why do you rob banks? A. Because that's where the money is.

References

Achen, C.H., and D. Snidal. 1989. Rational deterrence theory and comparative case studies. *World Politics* 41:143–169.

Arrow, K.J. 1985. The economics of agency. In J.W. Pratt and R. Zeckhauser, eds., *Agency: The Structure of Business*. Cambridge, Mass.: Harvard Business School Press.

Aumann, R.J., and M. Maschler. 1967. Repeated games with incomplete information: A survey of recent results. In *Report to the U.S. Arms Control and Disarmament*, pp. 287–403. Princeton, N.J.: Mathematica Policy Research, Inc.

Axelrod, R. 1984. *The Evolution of Cooperation*. New York: Basic Books.

Beer, F.A. 1986. Games and metaphors. *Conflict Resolution* 30:171–191.

Benoit, J.-P., and V. Krishna. 1988. *Renegotiation in Finitely Repeated Games*. Cambridge, Mass.: Harvard Business School.

Binmore, K. 1986. Modeling rational players. DP86/133, London School of Economics.

Blair, B.G. 1985. *Strategic Command and Control*. Washington, D.C.: Brookings Institution.

Bloomfield, L.P. 1960. Political gaming. *U.S. Naval Institute Proceedings* 86:57–64.

Bracken, J. 1988. Stable transitions from mutual assured destruction to mutual assured survival. Not yet published, available from the author.

Bracken, J., P.S. Brooks, and J.E. Falk. 1985. Robust preallocated preferential defense. *IDA Paper P-1816*. Institute for Defense Analysis, Alexandria, Virginia.

Bracken, J., J.E. Falk, and F.A. Miercourt. 1977. A strategic weapons exchange allocation model. *Operations Research* 25:968–976.

Bracken, P. 1983. *The Command and Control of Nuclear Forces*. New Haven, Conn.: Yale University Press.

Brams, S.J. 1984. *Superpower Games*. New Haven, Conn.: Yale University Press.

Brams, S.J., and M.P. Hessel. 1984. Threat power in sequential games. *International Studies Quarterly* 28:23–44.

Brams, S.J., and D. Wittman. 1981. Nonmyopic equilibria in 2 x 2 games. *Conflict Management and Peace Science* 6:39–62.

Brewer, G., and M. Shubik. 1979. *The War Game*. Cambridge, Mass.: Harvard University Press.

Bueno de Mesquita, B. 1981. *The War Trap*. New Haven, Conn.: Yale University Press.

Bueno de Mesquita, B., and W.H. Riker. 1982. An assessment of the merits of selective nuclear proliferation. *Conflict Resolution* 26:283–306.

Cohen, L.J. 1981. Model of strategic behavior and nuclear deterrence. *The Behavioral and Brain Sciences* 4:317–370.

Cournot, A.A. [1838] 1897. *Researches into the Mathematical Principles of the Theory of Wealth*. Reprint. New York: Macmillan.

Cross, J.G. 1969. *The Economics of Bargaining*. New York: Basic Books.

Dalkey, N. 1965. Solvable nuclear war models. *Management Science* 11:783–791.

Davis, P.K., and P.J.E. Stan. 1984. Concepts and models of escalation. RAND R-3235, Santa Monica, Calif.: RAND Corporation.

Diekmann, A., and P. Mitter, eds. 1986. *Paradoxical Effects of Social Behavior*. Heidelberg and Vienna: Physica-Verlag.

Dubey, P., and L.S. Shapley. 1979. Mathematical properties of the Banzhaf power index. *Mathematics of Operations Research* 4:99–131.

Ellsberg, D. 1961*a*. The crude analysis of strategic choices. *American Economic Review, Proceedings* 51:472–478.

———. 1961*b*. Risk ambiguity and the savage axioms. *Quarterly Journal of Economics* 75:643–669.

Foster, J.L. 1978. Essential equivalence: What is it and how should it be measured? *The Fifth National Security Affairs Conference, Proceedings* 23–51.

George, A.L., and R. Smoke. 1974. *Deterrence in American Foreign Policy: Theory and Practice*. New York: Columbia University Press.

Goldhamer, H., and H. Speier. 1959. Some observations on political gaming. *World Politics* 12(1):71–83.

Grotte, J.H. 1980. Measuring strategic stability with two strike nuclear exchange models. *Conflict Resolution* 24:213–239.

Guetzkow, H., C.F. Alger, C.F. Brody, R.D. Noel, and R.C. Snyder. 1963. *Simulation in International Relations*. Englewood Cliffs, N.J.: Prentice-Hall.

Guth, W. 1985. An extensive game approach to model the nuclear deterrence debate. *Zeitschrift fur die gesamte Staatswissenschaft* 140:525–538.

Harsanyi, J.C. 1959. A bargaining model for the cooperative n-person game. In A.W. Tucker and D.R. Luce, eds., *Contributions to the Theory of Games*, vol. 4. Princeton, N.J.: Princeton University Press.

———. 1967. Games with incomplete information played by "Bayesian" players, I: The basic model. *Management Science* 14:159–182.

———. 1968*a*. Games with incomplete information played by "Bayesian" players, II: Bayesian equilibrium points. *Management Science* 14:320–334.

———. 1968*b*. Games with incomplete information played by "Bayesian" players, III: The basic probability distribution of the game. *Management Science* 14:486–502.

———. 1982. *Papers in Game Theory*. Dordrecht, Holland: Reidel.

Hausner, M., J. Nash, L.S. Shapley, and M. Shubik. 1964. So long sucker a four-person game. In M. Shubik, ed., *Game Theory and Related Approaches to Social Behavior*, pp. 359–361. New York: Wiley.

Ikle, F.C. 1971. *Every War Must End*. New York: Columbia University Press.

Intriligator, M.D. 1967. *Strategy in a Missile War*. Security Studies Project, University of Los Angeles.

————. 1982. Research on conflict theory. *Conflict Resolution* 26:307–327.

Intriligator, M.D., and D.L. Brito. 1984. Can arms races lead to the outbreak of war? *Conflict Resolution* 28:63–84.

Jervis, R. 1988. War and misperception. *Journal of Interdisciplinary History* 18:675–700.

Jomini, A.-H. 1947. *Summary of the Art of War: A Condensed Version*. Ed. J.D. Little. Harrisburg, Pa.: Military Service Publishing Company (original, 1838).

Kahn, H. 1961. *On Thermonuclear War*. Princeton, N.J.: Princeton University Press.

————. 1962. *Thinking About the Unthinkable*. New York: Avon.

Kreps, D.M., and R. Wilson. 1982b. Sequential equilibria. *Econometrica* 50:863–894.

————. 1982a. Reputation and imperfect information. *Journal of Economic Theory* 27:280–312.

Lanchester, F.W. 1916. *Aircraft in Warfare: The Dawn of the Fourth Arm*. London: Constable and Co.

Lebow, R.N., and J.G. Stein. 1988. Rational Deterrence Theory: I Think, Therefore I Deter. Available from the authors.

Mayer, T.F. 1986. Arms races and war initiation. *Conflict Resolution* 30:3–28.

Miller, G.A. 1956. The magic number seven, plus or minus two: Some limits on our capacity for processing information. *Psychological Review* 63:81–97.

Nalebuff, B., and M. Shubik. 1988. Revenge and rational play. Preliminary paper mimeographed. Available from authors.

Nash, J.F., Jr. 1950. The bargaining problem. *Econometrica* 18:155–162.

————. 1953. Two-person cooperative games. *Econometrica* 21:128–140.

O'Neill, B. 1986. International escalation and the dollar auction. *Conflict Resolution* 30:33–50.

————. 1987. A measure for crisis instability with an application to space-based antimissile systems. *Conflict Resolution* 31:632–672.

————. 1988. Stockpiling nuclear weapons as deliberate self-damage. Mimeographed. University of Maryland, prepared for ISAC conference on Deterrence, Yale University, October.

Paxson, E.W. 1972. Computers and national security. In H. Sackman and H. Borko, eds., *Computers and the Problems of Society*. Montvale, N.J.: American Federation of Information Processing Societies Press.

Powers, I. 1986. A taxonomy of 2 × 2 games with weakly ordered preferences. Part of Ph.D. thesis, School of Organization and Management, Yale University, New Haven, Conn.

Raiffa, H. 1982. *The Art and Science of Negotiation*. Cambridge, Mass.: Belknap/Harvard.

Rapoport, A. 1960. *Fights, Games and Debates*. Ann Arbor, Mich.: University of Michigan Press.

————. 1964. *Strategy and Conscience*. New York: Harper and Row.

Rapoport, A., M.J. Guyer, and D.G. Gordon. 1976. *The 2 × 2 Game*. Ann Arbor, Mich.: University of Michigan Press.

Richardson, L.F. 1960. *Arms and Insecurity*. Chicago: Quadrangle Books.

Richelson, J.T. 1982. Static indicators and the ranking of strategic forces. *Conflict Resolution* 26:265–282.

Roth, A.E. 1979. *Axiomatic Models of Bargaining*. Berlin: Springer-Verlag.

Rubinstein, A. 1986. Finite automata play the prisoner's dilemma. *Journal of Economic Theory* 39:83–96.

Schelling, T.C. 1960. *The Strategy of Conflict*. Cambridge, Mass.: Harvard University Press.

————. 1966. *Arms and Influence*. New Haven, Conn.: Yale University Press.

————. 1976. A framework for evaluating arms proposals. In M. Pfaff, ed., *Frontiers in Social Thought*, pp. 283–305. New York: North-Holland.

————. 1984. *Choice and Consequence*. Cambridge, Mass.: Harvard University Press.

Selten, R. 1975. Reexamination of the perfectness concept for equilibrium points in extensive form games. *International Journal of Game Theory* 4:25–55.

————. 1978. The chain store paradox. *Theory and Decision* 9:127–159.

Shapley, L.S. 1953. A value for n-person games. In H. Quhn and A.W. Tucker, eds., *Contributing to the Theory of Games*, vol. 2, pp. 307–317. Princeton, N.J.: Princeton University Press.

Shubik, M. 1964. *Game Theory and Related Approaches to Social Behavior*. New York: Wiley.

————. 1968. On the study of disarmament and escalation. *Journal of Conflict Resolution* 12:83–101.

————. 1971. The dollar auction game: A paradox in noncooperative behavior and escalation. *Journal of Conflict Resolution* 15:109–111.

————. 1975a. *Games for Society, Business and War*. Amsterdam: Elsevier.

————. 1975b. *The Uses and Methods of Gaming*. New York: Elsevier.

————. 1982. *Game Theory in the Social Sciences*, Vol. 1. Cambridge, Mass.: MIT Press.

————. 1983a. *The Mathematics of Conflict*. Amsterdam: North-Holland.

————. 1983b. The strategic audit: A game theoretic approach to corporate competitive strategy. *Managerial and Decision Economics* 4(3):160–171.

————. 1984. *Game Theory in the Social Sciences*, Vol. 2. Cambridge Mass.: MIT Press.

————. 1986. Games with perceptive commanders but with indoctrinated or less perceptive subordinates. In A. Diekmann and P. Mitter, eds., *Paradoxical Effects of Social Behavior*, pp. 209–222. Heidelberg and Vienna: Physica-Verlag.

Shubik, M., and R.J. Weber. 1981. Systems defense games: Colonel Blotto, command and control. *Naval Research Logistics Quarterly* 28(2):281–287.

Simon, R.I. 1967. The effects of different encodings on complex problem solving.

Ph.D. thesis, Department of Administrative Science, Yale University, New Haven, Conn.

Stahl, I. 1972. *Bargaining Theory*. The Economic Research Institute, EFI Stockholm.

Steinbruner, J. 1984. Launch under attack. *Scientific American* 250:37–47.

Teger, A. 1980. *Too Much Invested to Quit*. New York: Pergamon.

Van Damme, E.E.C. 1983. Refinements of the Nash equilibrium concept. Doctoral diss. Eindhoven, the Netherlands.

von Neumann, J., and O. Morgenstern. 1944. *Theory of Games and Economic Behavior*. Princeton, N.J.: Princeton University Press.

Weiss, H. 1983. Requirements for a theory of combat. In M. Shubik, ed., *The Mathematics of Conflict*. Amsterdam: North Holland (original, 1953).

Wohlstetter, A. 1964. Sin and games in America. In M. Shubik, ed., *Game Theory and Related Approaches to Social Behavior*, pp. 209–225. New York: Wiley.

Zagare, F. 1981. Nonmyopic equilibria and the Middle East crisis of 1967. *Conflict Management and Peace Science* 5:139–162.

Governments, Economic Interdependence, and International Cooperation

ARTHUR A. STEIN

Introduction

Figuratively, the world has become smaller during the last two centuries. Revolutions in transportation and communication have made it possible to traverse great distances quickly and have allowed instantaneous contact between most points on the globe. Large numbers of people and enormous quantities of goods now move around the world quickly and easily. Since the Second World War, international commerce and exchange have expanded especially rapidly, faster even than global production and reaching ever new heights. Vast sums of money now flow speedily from country to country, and a global around-the-clock capital market is almost at hand. These changes have led to the growth, too, of forecasts that this burgeoning international commerce would bring peace as well as prosperity. This optimism, a direct descendant of predictions made throughout the last two centuries, grows from the proposition that greater interdependence would bind nations so closely that they would cooperate rather than fight.

These hopes voiced during the last two centuries by proponents of a link between commerce and peace have other modern echoes as well. Since World War II, the belief that European economic interdependence and integration would lead to political cooperation and perhaps even political integration has appeared episodically. Similarly, the possibility that the nations of the Communist bloc would join international economic institutions such as the International Monetary Fund (IMF) has recently raised expectations of more extensive economic ties between East and West and of the potential, therefore, for more peaceful relations.[1] In the last two decades, the rapid growth of international exchange, the relative decline of American economic power, and the growing impact of other nations' behavior on the U.S. economy have led American scholars to shift to a more explicit focus on international economic interdependence.[2]

Yet concomitant with the expansion of international commerce and economic interdependence has been the growth of economic conflict. Friction between trading partners has increased, and fears about the rise of a new protectionism, even of renewed economic warfare, have also been heard. Ironically, it almost appears that a new mercantilism has arisen alongside the new interdependence.

Scholarly enterprise, not surprisingly, has followed history. For some 15 years now we have analyzed the crises brought on by interdependence, heard dire warnings about the imminent collapse of the international economic order, and worried a great deal about the economic conflicts among some of the advanced industrial societies.

In this chapter, I review the various links made between international commerce and economic interdependence and international cooperation. I briefly cover early arguments, not only because of their analytic ties to modern propositions, but also because they represent alternative formulations that must be kept in mind when assessing empirical studies of the implications of interdependence for cooperation. I specifically distinguish *political liberalism* (and its subvariant, *republican liberalism*), *financial liberalism, neutralizing commercial liberalism, binding commercial liberalism*, and *sociological liberalism*. After assessing the assumptions underlying the various propositions, both early and recent, that link trade, interdependence, and cooperation, I discuss empirical work on the link between economic interdependence and international cooperation and address methodological issues associated with measuring interdependence.

Finally, I develop an argument about the ramifications of interdependence. I begin by delineating the nature of state interests and the relationship between state and society in order to establish the basis of a government's supply of protection. I hold that protectionism has been a price for liberalization (both internationally in getting nations to accept certain liberal arrangements and domestically in buying off those opposed to liberalization), that successful liberalization generates both protectionist and antiprotectionist interests, and that the process of negotiating trade liberalization generates protectionist bargaining chips necessary for achieving reciprocity in agreements. Finally, I argue that successful liberalization and increases in economic interdependence have generated new areas of conflict. Specifically, incongruent domestic policies and practices have emerged as the central components of trade disputes in a world of low tariffs. And resolving such conflicts requires, in turn, ever greater levels of cooperation.

Political Liberalism: Commerce, Governments, and Peace

In its modern form, the argument linking peace with international commerce and economic interdependence dates from the late eighteenth century. The original argument was rich and multifaceted. For many, it represented not merely an analytic argument, but a political agenda.

The earliest proponents of the proposition that trade leads to peace were responding both to widespread mercantilist practices in the seventeenth and eighteenth centuries and to seemingly constant wars. Their concerns were international and domestic, economic and political. They advocated an end to mercantilist practices that included domestic economic monopolies and the exclusion of foreign goods.[3]

The key element linking all these ideas was a particular set of views of the nature of people and of government. Theorists held that individuals in the state of nature managed to get along and work out mutually acceptable exchanges but that coercive governments then corrupted this idyll. Wars did not stem from rivalries between people. Rather, states coerced their citizens, and states fought wars. This distinction between intergovernmental and international relations is nicely captured in the words of free trade advocate Richard Cobden, who called for "as little connection as possible between governments, as much connection as possible between the nations of the world" (Hinsley, 1963:97). Holding that there existed "a natural disharmony between governments and states," liberals believed in "a natural harmony between nations and societies" (Hinsley, 1963:111).

This argument, a form of *political liberalism*, was part of a political agenda, at the heart of which was an assault on state power. Unconstrained monarchs engaged in self-serving ventures such as wars and imperialism, which only enriched the few and were not in the interests of the many. And unfettered commerce, in this view, would serve to constrain the arbitrary exercise of state authority.[4]

The nineteenth-century advocacy of free trade represented an attack on domestic as well as foreign policy. Among others, a new elite demanded an end to the concession of trading monopolies, and therefore it challenged the privileged classes who benefited from these bestowals (Jones, 1987). Moreover, dismantling such mercantilistic practices would entail constraining the power of the state and recognizing a variety of individual rights. In short, liberalism in the early part of the nineteenth century conjoined the call for international free trade with one for laissez-faire domestic policies.

Republican liberalism, whose advocates pressed for replacing monarchies with republics, constituted one variant of political liberalism.[5] To Tom Paine, monarchy represented no less than "the enemy of mankind and the source of misery." If, throughout Europe, sovereignty were to be restored "to its natural and original place, the nation," then "the cause of war would be taken away" (quoted in Waltz, 1959:101). Kant and Rousseau, too, believed that because princes waged war in their own interests rather than in those of their people, representative governments would not wage wars.[6]

A central assumption in this line of argument was that war destroyed wealth and prosperity and was, therefore, not in the interests of individuals. At best, war benefited the few; it never helped the nation as a whole (Silberner, 1946:280).[7] Thus, when intergovernmental relations "became relations between nations or peoples—war, which was materially profitless and absurd and morally wrong, would be replaced by free and peaceful economic competitions" (Hinsley, 1963:111).[8]

In contrast, commerce created a wealth and prosperity that could be widely enjoyed and which therefore created an interest in peace. As John Stuart Mill put it, commerce was "rapidly rendering war obsolete, by strengthening and multiplying the personal interests which are in natural opposition to it" (quoted in Silberner, 1946:66). Governments constrained by the wealth-seeking interests of individuals would not engage in materially destructive wars.

This conclusion relied on additional assumptions about the nature of and relationship between economics and politics. First, it presumed an individual interest in wealth and prosperity. Second, it presumed that wealth and prosperity were provided by exchange. Third, such commerce required the existence of domestic economic freedoms, which in turn rested on political ones. Hence, the very adoption of free trade necessarily entailed curtailing state power and making it responsive to the economic interests of individuals. And fourth, truly representative states would not be able to finance their wars through taxation, for the newly empowered citizenry would not approve of costly and unnecessary fighting.

In short, political liberalism held that governments would not wage wars because their constituents had no interest in doing so. Commerce, unfettered at home and abroad, would serve to constrain the actions of rulers. And this argument depended critically on the assumption that wars were invariably destructive of wealth and prosperity, which were the primary interests of the citizenry.

By the end of the nineteenth century, however, the argument's interlocking components had all come into question. Observers began to reappraise the relationships between representative governments, international commerce, free trade, and peace and war. As a result, the benefits of a liberal world order no longer seemed indubitable.

First, it had become clear that democracies fought wars and engaged in imperial adventures. The British, for example, during the high point of domestic liberalism, fought in the Crimean War in the middle of the nineteenth century. Moreover, the democracies, like monarchies and autocracies, engaged in imperialism at the end of the nineteenth century.[9]

The links between representative governments, the absence of domestic regulation, and free trade also appeared to be problematic as liberals discovered that democracies were all too capable of imposing domestic regulations and trade restrictions. The original argument had held that since the vast majority of citizens benefited from unencumbered trade, whereas only a minority did so from mercantilism, representative governments would not restrict domestic or international exchanges. But in nineteenth-century Britain, a whole system of state intervention accompanied laissez faire (Koot, 1987:8). And in the twentieth century, the argument has been made that the workings of representative governments leave them open to the pressures of organized particularistic interests for protection rather than the unorganized general interest in unfettered trade.[10]

Moreover, the link between free trade and prosperity came to be questioned. If representative governments attended to their constituents' interest in wealth, then they would pursue those policies that ensured economic development and growth. And it came to be argued that nations that industrialized late could only do so through interventionist state policies, for the ability to trade on comparable terms required protection rather than free trade.[11] In the nineteenth century, for example, the use of tariffs had allowed new industries to develop in the United States. This success then strengthened the claims made on behalf of protection and state intervention.[12]

In the twentieth century, proponents of state coercion expanded their position to hold that only those nonindustrial nations with governments capable of coercive direction could successfully obtain the material benefits of extensive trade. Only state power could keep labor costs down, restrain consumer demand, and ensure international competitiveness. The title of an essay by the economist Carlos Diaz Alejandro (1981), "Open Economy, Closed Polity?" captures the painful irony inherent in this position.

In short, the original liberal formulation was turned on its head, and coercive interventionist governance was argued to be consistent with, if not necessary to, growing international commerce. Friedrich List (1841) argued that protectionism was a prerequisite to free trade, because only protection would permit industrialization, itself a requirement for liberal commerce to occur.

After more countries modernized, then free trade between a set of industrial nations could replace the international monopoly of one such country, England.

Finally, the links drawn between the desire for wealth, commerce, and international cooperation also came under attack. German nationalists, epitomized by List (1841), argued in the middle of the nineteenth century that wars need not always be destructive but had, in fact, proved beneficial. Thus, an interest in maximizing wealth was consistent with engaging in war. Moreover, they averred, protectionism was not only a product of the desire for prosperity, but also a consequence both of war and of the hostile trade policies of other nations.

In short, by the end of the nineteenth century, each of the links in the original argument of political liberalism had been challenged. A national interest in prosperity could lead to protectionism. Even wars, the most extreme forms of international conflict, could be supported by the broad mass of citizens on grounds of self-interest. And representative states did interfere in international commerce, either because they, like monarchies, could reflect narrow interests or because such interference was deemed in the interests of the nation as a whole.

By the end of the nineteenth century, as it became increasingly obvious that the links between representative governments and both war and trade had proved historically tenuous, a new liberal formulation came to replace the original set of arguments. Still committed to free trade, the new liberalism abandoned the vision of domestic laissez faire in favor of a positive role for the state. In England, the very home of laissez-faire liberalism, the extension of the franchise had engendered working-class demands for social reform. It had become increasingly clear that individuals wanted government assistance as well as liberties and rights. A representative state became redefined as one that did more than simply protect property and provide security.[13] By the end of the nineteenth century, English liberals had anticipated Keynes and other twentieth-century theorists and politicians in developing arguments on behalf of a positive role for government in domestic economy and society.[14] Indeed, nineteenth-century liberals saw that monopolies and oligopolies could be a product not only of state direction, as had been true earlier, but of market concentration as well. Hence, they came to advocate a role for the state in combating economic centralization and so assuring competition.[15]

Neutralizing Commercial Liberalism: Economics and Conflict

A second strain of liberal thought stressed a different set of causal links between free trade and cooperation. According to this other logic, which also dated from the early nineteenth century, unfettered commerce would bring peace by removing economic causes of international conflict. From the belief that war was born of economic competition and rivalry, theorists came to the conclusion that free trade would undercut these roots of hostility.[16] If states went to war to enrich themselves through plunder and conquest, or in response to barriers established by others to protect those other nations' markets, then eliminating these reasons for conflict would do away with its existence altogether. And indeed, liberals held, colonial competitions, imperial wars, and trade disputes had all been fostered by the existence of trade barriers and rivalries.[17] On the other hand, they posited, nations would not fight over trade if all had access to the others' domestic and colonial markets. Likewise, the ability to buy raw materials and goods would make colonialism and imperialism unnecessary. Some of the causes of war would be eliminated.

This particular strand of liberalism, a *neutralizing commercial liberalism*, focused on the economic bases of conflict.[18] It presumed that conquest and plunder could enrich a nation as a whole, and so war was indeed a purposive self-interested activity pursued by nation-states. It held, too, that nations had, in the interest of self-defense, a reason for maintaining trade barriers in response to the actions of other states. In short, all of these constituted economic bases for international conflict.

In this view, free trade undercut the economic bases of conflict. Commercial liberalism neutralized these roots of discord. All the economic benefits to be obtained by conquest, plunder, and market control (using barriers to control a market, at home or in a colony) could be obtained by commerce. Exchange, not conquest, would secure the needs of the people without any of conflict's attendant costs.[19] Even if imperialism paid, commerce was cheaper. Thus, unfettered commercial access would do away with some of the roots of war.

In the 1930s, a revised version of this perspective was used to explain the apparent drift toward another European war. The great powers had created economic blocs from which they excluded their trading rivals.[20] These restrictive practices led to the formation of political blocs, and since political and economic disputes were held to reinforce one another, war appeared the likely result.[21] When World War II did, in fact, occur, the argument linking economic and military conflict provided one interpretation of its origins. Wanting to create a new postwar world, those who adhered to this view worked to prevent the reemergence of economic blocs (Gardner, 1956).

Today, in light of changing world circumstances, the proposition has been revamped yet again. Although states may no longer plunder for wealth, they may still need raw materials available only in other nations. In the wake of the oil crisis of the 1970s, the political implications of resource dependency reemerged as a source of concern. Countries with large populations, high levels of industrialization, and insufficient domestic supplies need access to other nations' raw materials. They experience "lateral pressure" and become active participants in the international arena. They can obtain what they need by conquest or through trade. Hence, the most recent version of this perspective describes a world of nations with free access to needed resources as inherently more peaceful than one without it. [22]

This hypothesis about the route to international cooperation is formulated only as the negation of one about the origins of international conflict. The key proposition posits that economic scarcity leads to conflict and war. The presumed negation avers that eliminating the causes of conflict will ensure cooperation. Unfortunately, the hypothesis that x causes y cannot be used to infer that the absence of x means the absence of y. The reason, of course, is that other causes of y may also exist. [23] And since no statement necessarily logically implies its negation, one can find scholars who hold both views and those who accept only one or the other.

Sociological Liberalism: Commerce as Communication

A third element of liberal thought links commerce with international cooperation as a function of interaction. [24] Rather than focusing either on state power and the need to constrain it or on eliminating economics as a cause of conflict and war, this line of reasoning rests on a view of trade as nothing more than one form of interaction and communication between peoples. The focus is not on the political or economic consequences of exchange, but on its immediate sociological consequences.

For *sociological liberalism*, free trade brings an increase in commercial links between peoples, and such ties are deemed to be inherently pacific. Hirschman (1977) demonstrates that such arguments were made on behalf of capitalism and against passions in the eighteenth century. In 1748, Montesquieu wrote that "wherever there is commerce, there the ways of men are gentle" (quoted in Hirschman, 1977:60). And William Robertson, writing in 1769, said, "Commerce tends to wear off those prejudices which maintain distinctions and animosity between nations. It softens and polishes the manners of men" (quoted in Hirschman, 1977:61). Others argued that exchange promoted peace because it led to the development of shared interests among peoples. But their emphasis was not on the development of common economic interests in trade. Rather, their logic held that the simple act of communication paves the way to international cooperation by increasing each people's knowledge of others and their ways, customs, practices, and concerns. The greater this familiarity, the more likely cooperation becomes. John Stuart Mill, for example, believed that contact with foreigners constituted a source not only of technical but also of moral progress and that trade provided such contact (Silberner, 1946:66).[25]

The view that trade, as a form of interaction, improves the prospects for peace received heightened attention as the nineteenth century's revolutions in the means of communication and travel sped and expanded the scope of international contact. Railroads, steamships, and telegraph lines increasingly linked far parts of the world. These changes all seemed to promise improved prospects for peace. For, as the prominent British author Henry Thomas Buckle wrote, "the greater the contact, the greater the respect." Referring more specifically to British-French relations, he declared that "every new railroad which is laid down, and every fresh steamer which crosses the Channel, are additional guarantees for the preservation of that long and unbroken peace which, during forty years, has knit together the fortunes and the interests of the two most civilised nations of the earth" (quoted in Blainey, 1973:20).[26] Even in 1921, in the wake of the First World War, which occurred despite high levels of contact and interaction in Europe, one author could write that

> friendship between the people of two nations is woven out of innumerable transactions, large and small, between individuals in which both parties have benefited and which they desire to renew. And not withstanding all that is said to the contrary, in the vast majority of cases the parties to the transactions learn to respect each other's qualities—their uprightness, their shrewdness, their energy, and often also their forbearance and generosity.
>
> This fabric of individual relationship is one element in the power of commerce to promote peace between nations. (Bosanquet, 1924:152–153)

Much like the early liberal advocacy of free trade as a means to peace, new recommendations flowed from these assumptions about the ramifications of improved communication and increased understanding among peoples. Both government policies and private programs tried to expand the scope of interaction between the citizens of different countries. The nineteenth century saw the convocation of conferences of every kind, the proliferation of international exhibitions and world fairs, and, in 1896, the establishment of the modern Olympic Games.[27]

So strong was the belief in the power of contact to prevent hostilities that not even the outbreak of World War I discredited the ability of these proliferating meetings to encourage peace. On the contrary, some proponents of interaction blamed not the inefficacy of contact, but the lack of communication between the leaders of the disputing nations. More opportunity for them to have discussed their concerns, this logic held, would have made the difference. The solution for the future would be to establish a mechanism to ensure such talks, and the League of Nations was born.

This faith in communication as a means to understanding, and therefore to cooperation, continued. Although the League could not stop World War II, a new organization, the United Nations, was established to facilitate international dialogue. The postwar era has been replete with institutionalized and ad hoc summits intended to bring national leaders face to face.[28] Not only political contact among governments, but also cultural and scientific exchanges among peoples have been promoted.

The modern version of the argument that communication leads to cooperation is associated with the seminal scholarly work in the fields of international relations and comparative politics done by Karl Deutsch and his students. Deutsch argues that interaction does more than improve understanding; it also generates community. He believes it essential to the development of a group consciousness and argues that the extent of social interaction defines the bounds of the community. Equating integration with interdependence, and both with transaction flows, he suggests that the growing relative importance of international commerce would lead not merely to international cooperation, but to the emergence of a new, integrated community of nations. Deutsch and his students focus on secular trends in transactions and on the relative levels of internal versus external communications. Their aim is to assess whether integration (here understood as the equivalent of interdependence) was declining or rising, especially as regarded the prospects for Western European integration in the 1950s and 1960s.[29]

Although Deutsch considers changes in the absolute values of interchange to be of some importance, he especially emphasizes the importance of the relative role of international to domestic flows of communication. Presuming actors to have a fixed or finite ability to focus attention and to communicate and interact, Deutsch argues that the ratio of foreign to domestic transaction is critical. A declining ratio signals increasing self-preoccupation, insulation, and nationalism. In contrast, growing levels of international to domestic transactions create cosmopolitanism, integration, and international interdependence.

In an array of studies, Deutsch and his students come to bleak conclusions about relations among the Western allies. Deutsch's own analyses show that industrialization led to a concentration on internal communication and transaction and to a relative decline in international transactions (Deutsch and Eckstein, 1961, among others). Thus, after an initial flurry in which it appeared that there was some movement toward European integration, the data suggest that the trend toward integration appeared to be leveling off. An analysis of interactions between the United States and Britain shows that these nations, too, were becoming less responsive to each other (Russett, 1963b).

There are two key problems with emphasizing the direct value of interactions, however. Familiarity can, of course, bring comprehension; but it can also breed contempt.[30] To know more about others is not always to like them better. And even understanding another's position need not lead to sympathy for it. Further, there is no logical reason to expect knowledge and familiarity either to generate common interests or to reduce conflicts of interest. If familiarity and knowledge were at the heart of cooperation, then families would not feud, couples would not divorce, and war would not be most common among states that share borders (Wilkinson, 1980:chap. 5). In fact, some interaction is required for conflicts of interest to occur. Just as actors who do not interact cannot cooperate, so they cannot fight (Stein, 1990:13–14).

Financial Liberalism: Mobile Wealth and Constrained Government

Still another argument about commerce and government and war can best be characterized as *financial liberalism*. This argument hinges on the growth of money and bills of exchange, which represent "movable wealth" (Hirschman, 1977:72–77, 81–88). Such wealth is invisible and can move quickly. And because of its mobility and fungibility, such wealth can elude the grip of greedy and capricious rulers. In Montesquieu's words, bills of exchange allowed commerce to "elude violence, and maintain itself everywhere," and as a result "rulers have been compelled to govern with greater wisdom than they themselves might have intended" (quoted in Hirschman, 1977:72).[31] Moreover, the ability to exchange currencies also constrained princes from foolish policies, or made them self-defeating; as Montesquieu put it, "[foreign exchange] operations have done away with the great and sudden arbitrary actions of the sovereign or at least with their success" (quoted in Hirschman, 1977:74).

International transactions entail the exchange of currencies, which represent a form of mobile wealth that eludes the ready grasp of rulers. Movable capital thus constrains capricious rule in a way that fixed capital does not. The ability of individuals to shift their funds means that rulers have to be responsive to the concerns of owners of capital.

As movable capital is invested overseas, its owners develop broader interests. Someone "whose business interests are confined" is "parochial in his sympathies and outlook." But investment generates a "stake" and an interest in the policies pursued within other nations (quotes from 1911 work of J.A.

Hobson, quoted in Hall, 1987:131). Similarly, a modern variant of liberalism, one that recognizes the role of finance and capital flows, argues that high levels of investment preclude conflict, which destroys wealth and impedes the commerce that generates the income to repay loans. And the concomitant domestic argument is that bankers and financiers oppose war because it destroys the commercial underpinnings of finance as well as affects the confidence that financial systems require for their maintenance.[32]

Binding Commercial Liberalism: Commerce and Interdependence

Finally, classical liberal thought provides one last argument about the peaceful implications of economic exchange. Adam Smith and especially David Ricardo argued that mercantilist policies did not enrich nations but free trade did. A nation would become wealthier by buying from abroad what others could produce more cheaply and by exporting what it could produce more cheaply itself. Increased wealth flowed not from self-sufficiency but from exchanges based on specialization. Exactly such a process had occurred within nations and would, the two economists predicted, occur between them. Commerce would lead to a division of labor with each nation exploiting its comparative advantage. All countries would serve and rely on one another, and peace would follow.

This conclusion is not unrelated to the other four strains of liberal analysis. It holds that economic exchange fosters not only mutual reliance but also awareness, especially the recognition of joint interests. Most basically, nations come to recognize that their own prosperity is dependent upon another's. In the words of John Stuart Mill, "commerce first taught nations to see with good will the wealth and prosperity of one another" (quoted in Silberner, 1946:66). The self-interest of states, and of the people within them, becomes tied to commerce rather than war.

To the extent that this has occurred, indicators of economic interchange do more than capture the simple fact of interaction between parties; they also reflect a degree of mutual reliance. They show the extent to which a nation is open and sensitive to external influences, even the degree to which it is vulnerable to others. They measure economic interdependence.

From this perspective, conflict and war between interdependent nations becomes unthinkable and therefore impossible. War destroys commerce and is, even independent of the price of arms and soldiers, too costly to wage. In any war, the burden of conflict can come to include the damage wrought upon the entire nation's standard of living. But in a world of interdependent nations, war may also be impossible because such states rely upon others for important goods. With the acquiescence of their trading partners, they may still battle countries with which they do not trade, but they may simply be incapable of fighting those upon whom they rely for the requirements of life and, perhaps, even for the essentials for waging war.

This fifth argument implicitly characterizes interdependence in two different ways. Although both presume it to be one consequence of unhindered commerce, the salient characteristic of the international relationship differs. On the one hand, a nation's increasing involvement in international transactions is seen as reflecting its greater openness to the international economy and therefore its heightened sensitivity to changes in the external environment. Alternatively, when described as the mutual dependence that comes from a division of labor, interdependence is viewed as the vulnerability of no longer self-sufficient states.[33]

As interdependence grows, not only do nations become more sensitive to developments in other countries, but industrialists, traders, and financiers come to rely upon international exchange as well. This represents a domestic variant of the argument linking interdependence to cooperation. International commerce creates domestic interests in its maintenance. Exporters do not want their markets to disappear. Importers do not want their supplies to diminish. Foreign investors do not want to have their holdings confiscated. Bankers want trade and capital flows to be sustained so that loans will be repaid. In addition, since financiers know that war destroys the value of their assets (property) without affecting their liabilities, they consider conflict destructive (Withers, 1916:chap. 5).[34] For all these reasons, interdependence is understood to generate a powerful case for its own maintenance.

Assumptions

The five classic liberal views about the relationship of interdependence and peace all assume that the interactions between states are mutual and symmetrical. This is implicit, for example, in the argument about the cooperative ramifications of communication, an inherently two-way phenomenon. Tourists journeying from one country to another affect both nations' perceptions of the other. Those traveling not only observe a foreign country but are also seen by those whom they visit. Hence, there is no reason to assess imbalances in communication. The direction of mail flows or of other forms of traffic do not matter, for communication inherently involves interchange that affects both sender and receiver. The economic arguments also depend on an assumption of reciprocity. Their advocates, who developed them in response to mercantilism, understood that exchange could involve exploitation. They assumed, however, that unfettered trade would not generate exploitive relationships devoid of mutuality and symmetry. Their view assumes, again implicitly, that open exchange creates not dependence, but interdependence.

The four arguments that focus on the importance of commerce as such (and not as a form of communication) also assume the importance of wealth.[35] They take as given that people and states care about economic welfare. Although their emphasis on the material appears to echo mercantilism, it differs in being conjoined with the belief that unfettered exchange maximizes prosperity. Hence, a concern with prosperity is believed to play a role in redirecting international politics away from conflict and war and into the cooperative realm of commerce and exchange.[36]

This focus on wealth is conjoined with an emphasis on cost. Whatever the specific links drawn by different causal arguments, and whether they emphasize that commerce breeds cooperation or merely reduces the incentives for war, all the arguments that focus on commerce and exchange contain an emphasis on relative costs and benefits. War is costly, and exchange is beneficial. The prospects of commerce increase the costs associated with war, and the development of commerce creates a constituency to press the case for peace. As governments become more representative, the greater the degree to which those costs come to be included in political calculations and decisions and to be reflected in the political system.

Empirical Work

Ironically, despite longstanding interest in the relationship between economic interdependence and peace, there have been few direct tests of this link. Testing the various propositions that describe how interdependence actually generates international cooperation requires confronting problems of measurement and specification. In fact, studying this question empirically illuminates analytic and conceptual issues to which the theoretical literature does not provide a very good guide. As a result, empirical analyses have generated new distinctions and conceptualizations and often disagree strongly with one another.[37]

Only a few studies look directly at the relationship between commerce and cooperation—most just describe the evolution of international exchange. Presuming the consequences that flow from commerce, many scholars have done no more than assess exchange trends as indications forecasting the probable future of shifts in international cooperation. For if growing international trade necessarily implies a developing division of labor, which in turn increases the burden of withdrawing from commerce, then these trends directly capture the opportunity costs of conflict. Those who define community as communication have done similar studies, but rather than looking at trade patterns, they have investigated changes in relative communication as direct manifestations of community development.[38]

Market Integration or Concentration

Confronting the issues of what and how to measure has raised a variety of conceptual and definitional issues. Most basically, although scholars agree that interdependence grows along with increases in international commerce, they argue about whether all exchanges entail interdependence.

For some, the most important cooperative impact of economic interdependence is the development of a global market in which all nations specialize and global wealth is maximized.[39] No nation could cut itself off from the market without experiencing some cost. Every nation would be linked to and dependent upon this market. This is a *market-integration view of economic interdependence* and is reflected in the arguments made about integrating largely autarkic nations, such as the former Soviet Union, into the world economy. Integration into a larger market itself generates incentives for international cooperation. And indeed, integration into a larger market requires that states reach agreements and cooperate about various matters, generating rules and regulations for commercial exchange.

For others, market integration does not represent an interdependence that generates international cooperation. If integrated markets were truly competitive, no individual nation would be specifically dependent on any other nation, for it could invariably find alternative suppliers and consumers. Thus, although no country might be able to cut itself completely off from all others, it could conflict with any particular nation with impunity. Indeed, international cooperation and conflict could fully reflect political calculations and could be made irrespective of economic calculations. At the same time, the market would be depoliticized in that it would not reflect politics or have any political implications. Hence, whereas some scholars would view the development of a competitive international marketplace as representing economic integration and interdependence, others would consider a truly competitive international marketplace, in which exchanges were both mutually beneficial and easily replaceable, as signifying a world with *no* interdependence.[40]

In contrast with a market-integration view, others offer a *market-concentration view of economic interdependence*. For them, international exchange represents interdependence only if the international marketplace is closer to an oligopoly or monopoly. Indeed, interdependence actually depends on the existence of reciprocally costly oligopolies, because in such a world, nations have no alternative sources for their necessary purchases, prospects exist for extortion, and the exchanges themselves already constitute an exploitive relationship. Only in an oligopolistic world of small numbers does such mutual interdependence obtain and necessitate international cooperation. States must cooperate with others on whom they are economically dependent, and those others must reciprocate for the same reason. This view builds directly upon the argument that war is too costly in a world with commercial exchange; here, however, the costliness derives from the absence of a perfectly competitive market.[41]

Level and Unit of Analysis

There also exist core disagreements in the literature on interdependence concerning the proper level and unit of analysis for study. This dispute grows largely from the existence of varying conceptualizations of economic interdependence and international exchange. And each perspective suggests a different focus of attention.

Interdependence can be an international characteristic. When world trade increases faster than world production, global interdependence also increases.[42] And increasing global interdependence can be argued to lead to increasing global cooperation.

Alternatively, interdependence can be seen as inherently dyadic, as the mutual dependence of pairs of nations. States integrated into the world economy but not part of a bilateral relationship of mutual reliance are not, in this view, interdependent and are also not, therefore, pressed to cooperate with one another. For in a competitive world market, states could be deeply involved in global commerce without being bound to any particular nation or set of nations. They could always find alternative consumers and suppliers, and so bilateral political conflicts would in no way be constrained or inhibited by the existence of extensive commercial links between the feuding nations. Just as anyone can risk offending a storekeeper when other merchants sell at comparable prices, nations would in no way be constrained by their commercial ties. Cooperation is the result of the interdependence that characterizes the strategic interaction of dyads.[43]

Most typically, interdependence is conceptualized as a national characteristic derived from international commercial exchange. Nations that export higher proportions of their GNPs are understood to be more open to the world economy—more interdependent—than those selling less abroad.[44] They are part of an international division of labor. And interdependence characterizes the nation.

Finally, interdependence can be conceptualized as a national characteristic derived from economic relationships that entail potential costs, that make a nation sensitive, even vulnerable, to developments in, and actions of, other nations. Using this definition requires more than that exports and imports constitute a high proportion of GNP before a nation can be called interdependent. Rather, this understanding of interdependence emphasizes the concentration of both production and consumption. The economies of states that export a large variety of goods are hardly dependent on any particular product or on any specific trading partner. They may be linked to the world economy, but their diversification minimizes their vulnerability and even their sensitivity to external influences. To the extent that interdependence entails dependence, a concentration of exchange of a small set of goods with a small number of trading partners entails such reliance in a way that diversification does not. Indeed, the workings of comparative advantage in an open trading world would result in domestic specialization and an international division of labor.

What to Measure

The appropriate measurement of interdependence varies for these alternative conceptualizations. Those who focus on interdependence as an economic phenomenon limit their attention to trade and capital movements. In contrast, those who argue that cooperation grows from communication, of which commerce is but one form, look not only at overtly economic links, but at such indicators as mail and tourist flows as well.

Even among scholars who share a view of interdependence as a narrowly economic phenomenon, disagreement persists about what to measure. Those who define interdependence as sensitivity to the world economy consider most, if not all, exchanges to be salient. For in this view, since all trade improves the welfare of the parties involved, everyone loses when the transactions disappear. Moreover, since all exchange leads both to some domestic specialization and to the partial reliance of the trading partners upon one another, breaking the relationship can prove costly.

Others do not see all exchanges as comparable. They define interdependence as mutual dependence, the reliance of nations on one another for something they cannot do without. Yet not all goods are necessarily critical. Nations can do without some goods more readily than others. Some imports constitute inputs essential to the functioning of the economy, others do not.[45] A dependence on others for videocassette recorders is not the same as one for oil or computer chips.

Still others define interdependence as mutual dependence that creates mutual vulnerability, and this entails the absence of alternative suppliers.[46] Although a nation may purchase a critical commodity from one other country, the good may be available from other suppliers. Despite the Soviets' reliance on the United States for a disproportionate percentage of essential wheat imports in the middle 1970s, it had no trouble finding alternative sources of grain when the United States imposed an embargo. For scholars who adopt this view, therefore, interdependence must be measured by the exchange, within a mutual relationship, of critical goods for which there are no substitutes and that are available exclusively from a small set of trading partners.[47]

More specifically, interdependence can be viewed as a function of growth in the relative importance of a nation's foreign transactions, of increases in the concentration of those transactions, or of both. For some scholars, therefore, interdependence increases as a state's imports and exports come to constitute a larger proportion of GNP. As this occurs, the country becomes more oriented toward the international economy and more sensitive to foreign developments. For others, the degree of a nation's interdependence is signaled by the concentration both of the products and of exchange partners involved in the full range of its foreign commerce; dyadic interdependence increases, then, when such concentration marks the trade between specific pairs or sets of nations.

Increasingly in modern times, as financial flows have grown in importance, they, too, can be measured as indicators of interdependence. In the development of commerce and economic thought, trade preceded and determined international monetary exchange. Foreign reserves were held to ensure necessary imports. Foreign investment flowed to ensure necessary raw material inputs and to maintain overseas markets. But increasingly, international capital flows have dwarfed commercial transactions and are now seen as determinants of them. The American trade deficit with Japan, for example, is seen as the by-product of the large Japanese capital inflows necessitated by the American budget deficit. And all the same arguments about appropriate measures of interdependence, between those who stress the generalized integration of financial markets versus specific dyadic financial links, can be sustained.

Yet interdependence can also be measured not in terms of the magnitude of flows, but in terms of its presumptive market consequences. Since interdependence is associated with the growth of exchange and the development of a division of labor, it is possible to measure it directly by looking not at transaction flows, but at their economic consequences.[48] One ramification of relative openness, for example, is the development of an integrated market with equal factor prices.[49] Greater financial openness, with its concomitant increase in capital flows, leads to the emergence of an integrated international capital market. The effect should be to equalize interest rates.[50] And indeed, the sensitivity and mutual responsiveness of capital and equity markets in advanced industrial societies have grown markedly, and these can be deemed to be measures of economic interdependence.

Benchmarks: How to Measure

The variety of ways in which scholars manipulate trade statistics clearly illuminates the conceptualization and measurement problems inherent in assessing integration and interdependence. Trade figures have been gathered and recorded longer than many other measures of economic, political, and social phenomena. Considered important in and of themselves, they have been used to measure a range of different concepts. Changes in trade between nations, for example, are taken to be indicative of changes in their relationship, of alterations in the division of labor between them. Hence, indices of trade are used in virtually all studies of economic interdependence and regional integration.[51]

Most scholars interested in the relative importance of trade to a national economy use a ratio of foreign trade (exports and imports) to national income as a measure of interdependence. By such measures, economic openness and interdependence were high during the middle of the last century and prior to World War I and then declined markedly. Following the Second World War, such ratios again rose, in many cases reaching or exceeding earlier levels by the 1970s.[52]

Yet a ratio of foreign trade to national income does not capture a bilateral view of interdependence. Such relationships can be indicated, however, by dividing the two nations' joint trade by the gross national product of one. Generating two such separate measures of interdependence from the same numerator provides comparable assessments of the importance of the bilateral trade relative to each nation's economy. An alternative measure of interdependence assesses trade between two nations relative to the total trade of each, again generating separate measures for the two states. In short, trade figures can be made relative to different benchmarks, and in some circumstances, different measures generate divergent assessments of interdependence, its growth, and its decline.[53] Moreover, just as there are different measures of central tendency and variance, so there are different ways of assessing concentration.[54]

Assessing historical trends requires the use of temporally comparable data. In studies of foreign investment, for example, different definitions and conceptualizations can have dramatic consequences for assessing change over time. Analyses of foreign investment typically distinguish between direct and portfolio investment. The former involves direct control of subsidiaries rather than the mere ownership of stock. The issue of managerial control is central to an assessment of the implications of investment as generating economic interdependence, yet managerial control is difficult to assess, and there has been a good deal of historical debate about the bases of control, the distinction between direct and portfolio investment, and the relative magnitudes involved. Recent scholarship has shown that nineteenth-century corporations were often able to conduct their overseas business through unincorporated branches, and that diffuse stock ownership often coexisted with extensive management control by a small group of partners. These findings have generated quite different estimates of the relative importance of foreign direct investment in the period before World War I.[55]

Dimensionality

Some of the conceptual and methodological problems in the study of interdependence arise simply from the existence of different kinds of transaction flows. The most basic issue is the dimensionality of interdependence.[56] It can, on the one hand, be seen as a unidimensional concept that has multiple indicators, which can be combined into a single metric that characterizes the degree of interdependence.

On the other hand, interdependence can have different, clearly distinct dimensions.[57] The term can be used to characterize one market or many, and the many may be characterized by different degrees of interdependence. Examples abound. Capital markets are much more integrated than labor markets. States can open their markets to international trade while still encumbering international flows of capital.[58] More important, low barriers to trade and to capital flows are not currently matched by equally low barriers to the movement of people (labor).[59] If these different aspects of openness always grew together, or in tandem, then there would be little conceptual difficulty in combining multiple indicators into one measure of interdependence.[60] But when they do not, then conceptual and measurement problems interact.[61] In addition, certain kinds of transactions may vary inversely when, for example, they are substitutes for one another.[62] Moreover, the relationship between the movements of different kinds of exchange can vary under different regimes. Capital mobility has different consequences under fixed than under floating exchange rates, for example.

In short, the existence of different factors of production, characterized by different degrees of international mobility, and the existence of markets characterized by different degrees of openness generate conceptual and measurement problems for assessing interdependence and its consequences. There may be different degrees of interdependence along these different dimensions. And given the existence of varying arguments about the bases of interdependence, and of such distinctions as that between sensitivity and vulnerability, it becomes possible to distinguish interdependence by type and domain (sensitive financial interdependence but vulnerable-goods interdependence with no labor-market interdependence, etc.). Different indicators may be appropriate as measures of different kinds and facets of interdependence. And a good deal of theoretical development will be necessary if the political implications vary with the particular constellation of interdependencies.

But if interdependence generates cooperation because it changes the cost-benefit balance between cooperation and conflict, then any of the measures of interdependence may be appropriate, and they can even be used conjunctively. All of the measures capture the benefits of commerce and the costs of its disruption. And if what distinguishes them is the extent to which they measure cost, then the strength of the relationship between economic interdependence and international cooperation should grow with measures of interdependence that capture increasing cost.[63] Thus, we should expect the weakest relationship for general measures of trade growth, and that relationship should strengthen as measures capture higher costs and benefits of trade. Thus, dyadic indicators and assessments, for example, should generate a larger estimate of the impact of economic interdependence.[64]

Economic Interdependence and Cooperation

There are few studies that directly assess the link between economic interdependence and international cooperation. Moreover, they generate still more conceptual and measurement issues, and they generate contradictory findings.

Analyses of pairs of nations in the postwar era point to a significant relationship between trade and net cooperation—between, that is, total imports and exports and the frequency of cooperative events minus the frequency of conflictual ones (Polachek, 1980; Gasiorowski and Polachek, 1982).[65] But these studies also find that the nature of the good and the elasticity of demand are also important, for the exchange of some goods can be associated with conflict. Nations that import greater amounts of oil from Saudi Arabia direct less hostility toward it than those buying less; the more substantial the purchases, the lower the degree of conflict directed toward the producer of this essential good. In contrast, however, Saudi Arabia directs more hostility at those nations to which it exports more (Polachek, 1980).[66]

Domke (1988) tests a national, as opposed to dyadic, argument about interdependence and finds that there is sometimes an inverse relationship between trade, measured as a ratio of exports to gross national product, and a state's involvement in war.[67] Unfortunately, the empirical analysis works backward, assessing only years in which wars occurred and then determining whether belligerents tended to export less of their national product than those not involved in the same war. Although there is some support for the hypothesis, there are some wars, including both World Wars I and II, in which there is no relationship between trade ratios and involvement in these wars.[68]

Studies of the impact of interdependence find that it, too, can increase conflict. Puchala (1970), in a study of Franco-German relations between 1954 and 1965, analyzes changes in indicators of bilateral trade, trust, and amity, all of which increased linearly through the decade. Cooperation, however, followed a different pattern. Whereas much of the period evinced dyadic cooperation, the years from 1963 to 1965 saw a growth in conflict. Puchala argues that this resulted from an increased "strain" or "load," which this new and fragile relationship could not yet sustain. Implicit in this post hoc explanation for the unexpected result is the possibility that the growing ties between the two nations might be responsible for the increase in conflict.

A study by Gasiorowski (1986a) is notable for recognizing not only the possibility that interdependence increases cooperation and reduces conflict but also the converse. Although he does not investigate whether interdependence has both effects (nor does he develop a logic for how and why it could have both effects), he does find that different measures of interdependence show opposite effects from one another. Some measures, such as import-price elasticity (used to assess the impact of domestic-price sensitivity) and long-term capital flows (relative to gross national product), show no effect on the degree of conflict directed at a nation's trading partners.[69] Others, however, are associated with growing conflict. Three measures of concentration of trade (of import partners, of export partners, and of export commodities) directly affect the level of conflictual behavior (each is significant when it is the only one of the three included in the equation). Similarly, short-term capital flows (controlled for GNP) also directly affect conflict. By contrast, trade as a percentage of GNP has an inverse affect: it increases cooperation. That is, nations direct more hostility toward those with whom their trade is highly concentrated and toward those to which they are linked by extensive short-term capital flows. But the same equation also shows exactly the opposite result: the higher the ratio of a nation's trade to its national product, the less conflict it displays toward its trading partners. As a result, Gasiorowski concludes, as he hypothesizes, that interdependence can indeed increase both cooperation and conflict.[70]

The developers of the GLOBUS models also consider the dual impact of interdependence in their development of a complex multi-equation model intended to simulate global processes. The model includes one equation linking cooperation between pairs of states to their bilateral trade (their dyadic exports and imports as a percent of one's trade) and another linking conflict to a bilateral trade imbalance (the product of the ratio of bilateral imports to exports weighted by the ratio of one nation's total imports to total exports) (Smith, 1987:616, 618). The latter equation posits, in other words, that the more one nation imports from another, relative to what it exports to that other, then the more conflict it directs at the other country. That conflict is either mitigated as a function of the first state's overall trade surplus or magnified as a function of its overall trade deficit. In short, trade increases cooperation, but trade imbalances increase conflict. If an increase in trade results in an increase in one nation's trade deficit, then either an increase in cooperation or conflict is possible as a function of the relative effects.

The implications of these dual effects are captured in a simulation of the ramifications on U.S.–Mexican relations of an American provision of tariff preferences to third-world nations (Pollins and Brecke, 1987:524–531). The tariff concessions lead to a growth in trade that increases cooperation between the two nations. In the simulation, however, interdependence engenders conflict. This occurs because the growth of U.S. trade with Mexico, a result of the preferences, also increases the U.S. trade deficit with Mexico, and this increases hostility toward Mexico. A third equation in the model links hostility from one nation to a reciprocal response by the country toward which it is directed. So despite the positive effects on cooperation of the increasing dyadic trade and the improving Mexican trade balance with the United States, Mexico responds to increased American hostility. The positive impact of increased trade on cooperation is not only canceled out, but fully overwhelmed by the conflict resulting from the trade imbalance and subsequent reciprocation.

These studies illustrate the complexity of the hypothesis-testing exercise. Disagreements about the nature of the dependent variable and how to measure it build on extant disputes about how to assess interdependence. Moreover, the results are mixed, suggesting that economic interdependence can have dual effects. Indeed, it can increase conflict and cooperation simultaneously. Finally, the existence of numerous explanations of international conflict and cooperation suggests the importance of assessing the implications of interdependence while controlling for plausible rival hypotheses. Indeed, there is one rival explanation that can lay claim to explaining both cooperation and trade: hegemonic stability theory. In the early 1970s, scholars began a debate over the proposition that a hegemonic distribution of power leads to the creation of liberal international orders. This rival argument suggests not that economic interdependence generates cooperation, but that a hegemonic power creates an international order characterized by increases in trade, economic interdependence, and international cooperation. Although the theory has many variants and has come under a variety of assaults, it still poses a problem for arguments about economic interdependence.[71] At the very least, empirical studies about the pacific implications of interdependence should control for this rival hypothesis and include both hegemonic and nonhegemonic periods.

Moreover, it is especially important to control for noneconomic bases of international cooperation and conflict. After all, the argument that economic ties reduce conflict and increase cooperation presumes the importance of the marginal changes in a cost/benefit calculus. And it may be that the existence of economic interdependence increases the costs of conflict. But there may be situations in which the presumed benefits are perceived to be so great that even the increased costs associated with an interdependent relationship do not outweigh them. And it may be that individuals and nations pursue prosperity, but that other national objectives outweigh them in specific circumstances.[72] Hence, economic interdependence may be very important at the margins and so, at times, critical overall.

Finally, it is important (and this is discussed further below) to assess the significance of the reverse relationship, of the impact of international cooperation on commerce. There is, after all, the reverse argument that "trade follows the flag."[73] In this case, the existence of economic interdependence already presupposes international cooperation.

The net consequence of the foregoing discussion of measurement and empirical work is to suggest a need to assess theoretically the political implications of commerce. Without an understanding of the mechanics, of the process by which private economic transactions are related to political decisions, no understanding of the relationship between economic interdependence and international cooperation is possible. Indeed, this suggests a pressing need to assess international economic relations in the context of the international political strategies of states.[74]

Governments and Interdependence

The analytic link between economic interdependence and international cooperation necessarily depends upon assumptions about the causes and consequences of economic exchanges, about the nature of state interests, and about the relationship between state and society. International cooperation reflects relations between governments and thus requires some assessment about the nature of state interests. And since commercial transactions involve societal actors (individuals and firms), linking these with international cooperation requires the elucidation of the relationship between state and society.

The nature of the relationship between state and society is central to arguments about the political implications of trade and finance. The importance of this link is implicit in some of the propositions about commerce and cooperation and quite explicit in others. It rests on the simple fact that economic interdependence, because it entails commercial transactions, typically involves private actors.[75] Unlike these individual economic ties, however, international cooperation exists between governments. The international links that develop from commercial exchange might have no effect on intergovernmental relations were states fully autonomous from society and unconcerned with issues of material welfare. Fluctuations in the business cycle, for example, had far less of an impact on international politics when the state was not charged with maintaining the health of the economy than in modern times, after that responsibility developed.[76]

Below, I develop a set of arguments essential to understanding the link between economic interdependence and international cooperation. First, I argue that economic interdependence is a product of state policy and not an autonomous and independent development. Second, interdependence generates societal and governmental pressures both for its limitation and for its continued growth. And third, interdependence therefore generates new kinds of conflict and necessitates ever greater levels of international cooperation if it is to be maintained. In essence, I argue that the development of a division of labor between nations generates conflicts that states must manage in order to sustain and continue the process of global specialization and exchange.

International Cooperation as Prerequisite to Economic Interdependence

One of the state's most basic powers rests in its ability to control access to its domestic society. Even weak governments have some ability to limit the movement of goods and services across borders. Governments not strong enough to extract income taxes can still collect customs duties on imports.[77]

There is an immense variety in the actual forms of control that states both can and have exercised over cross-border movements. They can regulate the entry of goods, capital, technology, information, and people. They can discriminate by categories of items as well as by their source. They can restrict the entry not only of capital and goods, but also of people; indeed, all nations have immigration laws. And although states most typically restrict what enters their borders, they sometimes put important controls upon what can leave. They can define allowable destinations for both their exports and their citizens. In the early part of the nineteenth century, for example, Britain attempted to limit the export of equipment and even the emigration of artisans who knew the secrets of the industrial revolution (Jeremy, 1977). In much the same way, the United States imposed bans on selling high technology to the Soviet Union during the Cold War.

Given that states have the ability to regulate entry and exit for goods and people, the growth of international commerce and exchange depends, at a minimum, on the acquiescence of governments.[78] A necessary condition for international trade is the absence of prohibitive barriers to exchange.

In addition, the very existence of international exchange, especially on any sizable scale, necessitates not only that governments accept imports and permit exports, but that there be concrete cooperative arrangements between states as well. Trade between countries, in virtually all cases, presupposes the existence of commercial agreements between their governments.[79] Moreover, states find it necessary to establish (or to join already extant) bilateral or multilateral arrangements to facilitate commerce and the transportation and communication upon which it depends. The delivery of mail across borders relies on the existence of an International Postal Union. The ability to make cross-border telephone calls necessitates not only the adoption of a standardized technology, but also the actual decision by countries to take part in this international network.[80] Railroad travel between nations requires use of a common track gauge. Also important are the existence of exchangeable currencies and state guarantees of property rights.[81] In short, since states can control entry into and exit from their nations, the existence of commercial links and economic interdependence reflects political decisions and the development of agreements and institutions that facilitate those links.[82] Hence, any assessment of the political implications of commerce must necessarily take into account the cooperative underpinnings of trade.[83]

The fact that commercial links depend on extant agreements between governments means that international economic transactions are often rooted in international politics. Indeed, governments often encourage traders and investors to move into particular areas. States also prevent their capital from funding others' investments, especially by constraining the ability of foreign governments to float bonds in their domestic capital markets. In one analysis, Eugene Staley (1935:55) finds numerous instances of investments being used as "the tools of diplomacy." When there exists international friction, he finds, investments tend to be the "servants," rather than the "masters," of diplomacy. Among the many instances he cites of governments influencing foreign investment are examples of direct participation, subsidies, guarantees, and the less concrete means of persuasion and inducement.[84]

In some cases, states develop economic links to consolidate interests rooted in security considerations.[85] Indeed, the political component of exchange underlies the evolution of the postwar economic order and of ties among the

Western Europeans, between Western Europe and the United States, and among Japan, Korea, Taiwan, and the United States. American leaders self-consciously sought to use commercial ties to forge an anti-Communist West. At the same time, they wanted to cut the links between Western Europe and the Soviet bloc and to sever the economic relationship between Japan and the Communist Chinese. Hence, the United States predicated its bestowal of foreign aid on the eradication of certain economic barriers and the acceptance of critical liberal economic principles.[86]

Governments and the Supply of Protection and Liberalization

Central to an understanding of liberalization and protection is the recognition that they are government policies. The nature of government policy and of the changing role of government are essential to an explanation of governments' supply of both liberalization and protection.

Government policy inherently raises the prospect of protection because it creates cartelized international trade where a competitive market would otherwise exist. State actions may serve to transform their nations' discrete producers into cartels. National policies may impose a uniformity, one that deviates from the expected market outcome, upon atomistic and unorganized individuals and firms. An excellent example is provided by agricultural policies, which turn an inherently competitive market involving millions of scattered producers and consumers into a cartel. Thus, what would be a competitive global market becomes an oligopolistic one in which nations, a relatively small group, speak for vast numbers of individual consumers and producers.

Moreover, modern governments have a larger role than that which troubled those who pressed for laissez-faire policies at the beginning of the nineteenth century. And with the greater role for government have come more reasons for states to limit economic interdependence and to control trade, even at the cost of conflict with other nations.

Well before the twentieth century, governments took a conscious responsibility to promote economic development. Governments rationalized the protection of infant industries as necessary for national growth. Policymakers came to see tariffs as more than revenue-raising measures and as more than acts intended to increase the material wealth of the state. They stressed instead the role of tariffs in national economic development, a role that could be guided by the government. Trade policy was thus subordinated to other governmental programs intended to foster development and generate growth.

But in contrast with earlier eras, when cycles of boom and bust were accepted as natural phenomena that governments could not affect, the twentieth century has seen the adoption of a perspective that holds states responsible for their nations' economic well-being. Governments are expected to ensure economic growth, combat recession and depression, hold down unemployment, maintain price stability, and even take care of specific groups of citizens who need help.[87] The problems in an economy are deemed national problems: the nation's unemployment, the nation's inflation rate, and the nation's weakness in international competition (Fisk, 1989:195). And in response, the development of the welfare state has entailed the provision of a safety net to catch and support those individuals buffeted by the winds of economic competition.[88]

As a result, governments react to the domestic effects of growing economic interdependence. Increasing involvement in international exchange leads to domestic adjustment, the shifting of resources from the production of some goods to others. In response, state policies have addressed the concomitant loss of investments and jobs and the other problems of community dislocation. One result has been the provision of adjustment assistance, including programs to retrain and retool workers, as one element of the safety net. In addition, however, governments have provided some protection for industries suffering from foreign competition.[89]

This need to help those hurt by market forces is reinforced in societies with representative governments. Electoral pressures lead legislators to propose policies in response to requests for protection from foreign competition.[90] Or, as a Democratic senator succinctly described this aspect of representation in 1883, "I am a protectionist for every interest which I am sent here by my constituents to protect" (quoted in Blackford and Kerr, 1990:206). Especially during recessions, governments are pressed to provide economic assistance, including relief from the vagaries of the global economy.[91]

Critical to this argument that representative governments are particularly likely to provide assistance is an assumption that those who seek protection organize and mobilize, but that those who benefit by maintaining and expanding interdependence do not. The current conventional wisdom holds that those who actively seek governmental relief get concentrated benefits, which make bearing the costs of organization worthwhile. By contrast, the expense of paying for the assistance to that injured subset of the population is diffused throughout the entire society, so there is little incentive for anyone to assume the concentrated costs of opposing protection. The direct conclusion, therefore, is that the specific group desirous of protection will always succeed in obtaining it, whereas the broader population interested in promoting trade and interdependence, unable to solve the collective action problem, will always lose.[92]

But governments supply protection even when there is no societal demand for it. One reason is to encourage the development of infant industries. Another, however, derives from concerns about national security.[93] States do not want international specialization to proceed to the point that they become dependent on another nation's producers for critical goods.[94] In other cases, the desire to preserve national prestige has led to policies intended to maintain a productive presence in a particular arena.[95] In other words, states do not just respond to demands that they protect declining industries threatened by imports; they assist emerging and even thriving ones as well.[96]

Governments even use liberal economic arguments on behalf of protectionism, sometimes as rationalization, but sometimes as quite legitimate explanations of procompetitive protectionism.[97] Economic theory can provide a basis for domestic antitrust policies. But the international arena has no central authority to prevent the emergence of monopolies and so guarantee competition. Hence, the Europeans argue, their support for Airbus Industries represents no more than an attempt to ensure that Boeing does not develop a monopoly in the commercial aircraft industry.[98] Indeed, such governmental interventions can actually serve to maintain a competitive free market.

Governments not only adopt measures to limit penetration of the domestic market by imports, but they also use policies to create a competitive advantage. This is the basis of some nations' complaints about others' use of industrial policies to target and create export industries.[99] The comparative advantages of modern industrial societies are increasingly a product of governmental policy rather than natural endowments.[100] The Japanese government, for example, decided in the early 1950s to develop a steel industry even though the country had no modern plants and few experts and lacked two basic material inputs, iron ore and coal (Gold, 1979). In effect, state policies that create comparative advantage make the government a critical factor of production and make government policy a subject of trade disputes.

For a number of reasons, therefore, international economic competition between producers will continue to involve their governments and so remain a cause of international political conflict. Moreover, modern governments will invariably pursue some mercantilistic policies, even in the absence of interest group pressures for them. *Governments sometimes supply protection in the absence of any societal demand for it.* The protection of infant and critical defense industries, and of industries that contribute to national prestige, suggests that such policies are rooted in the nature and role of government, even absent societal pressure.

Yet the increasing role of government in the economy during the twentieth century is a two-edged sword; it need not necessarily lead to greater protectionism. That modern governments are held responsible for assuring economic growth and social stability, as well as for providing a safety net, may in many instances represent a force pressing them to liberalize trade and to obtain those gains that accrue from increased efficiency. Their commitment to generating wealth means that they also pursue policies to ensure export competitiveness.[101] And since states with export-dependent economies typically try to ensure the maintenance of competitive export sectors, international trade disputes now focus not only on classically protectionist policies, but on programs to aid exporters as well.[102]

States pursue liberalization and protection in both good times and bad. Yet even in bad times, governments typically accommodate protectionists only at the margins. They do not want the aid given to those hurt by imports to come at the expense of exporters. In recessions, governments are concerned with restarting the engines of growth and so fear protectionism even as they find themselves lured by it.[103] Moreover, some of their protectionist policies are intended to help their exports.

Liberalization and Protectionism

Protectionism as a Price for Liberalization

One implication of the evolving role of government is that protectionism is always likely to be present, to some degree, in one form or another. Thus protectionism has been part of the post–World War II liberal order from the beginning. In that sense, the so-called "new protectionism" is not new. And second, acceptance of some forms and degree of protectionism was the price for governmental acceptance of trade liberalization.

Many have pointed to a new protectionism and see dangers in the patterns of current international exchanges and extant interdependence.[104] Yet such arguments do not recall that fears of protectionism have repeatedly punctuated the growing interdependence of the postwar period. In the 1940s, liberals worried about the residual trade barriers of the 1930s. In the 1950s and 1960s, they were troubled by the protectionist policies of the newly created European Economic Community. In the early 1970s, attention shifted to the rise of nontariff barriers (NTBs) and to the ramifications of the devaluation of the dollar and the oil price shock. In the late 1970s and early 1980s, alarm about growing protectionism stemmed from concern about the policies states might pursue in a prolonged global recession. The global recovery from the recession of the early 1980s offered no respite from worries about rising protectionism. The point here is twofold: the fear of protectionism is time-honored, and "free trade" never wholly prevailed during the postwar years. Rather, anxiety about potential departures from free trade principles and actual departures themselves have both been common.

From the very beginning of the postwar era, in fact, the international agreements to liberalize trade have entailed the acceptance of some protectionism. The United States accepted, for example, the British system of imperial preferences, which it had opposed since that system's inception in the early 1930s. The United States also accepted European quantitative restrictions on the importation of American goods, and in exchange the Europeans dropped such restrictions against one another. The logic of the American position derived from a belief that the Continent's ability to recover from World War II depended upon the renewal of intra-European trade and the development of an integrated market in Western Europe. Other exceptions to liberal trade principles included permitting customs unions and accepting various barriers intended to encourage economic development and deal with balance of payments problems.

In short, the postwar trading order legitimated protectionism from the outset. It accepted the protection of infant industries as an element of economic development. It allowed regional protectionism by permitting the existence of customs unions. It accepted protectionism to spur recovery in the form of special allowances made for Europe and Japan.[105] It also permitted protectionist practices in cases of domestic injury. Although the essentially liberal elements of the postwar order involved a commitment to free trade, that commitment was in principle only. The new order constrained, but did not abolish, protectionist practices.

Protection in certain cases was accepted as part of the international order because states had a variety of objectives they wanted to pursue. They also recognized that the development of an international division of labor would entail adjustment costs and would generate immense internal pressures. Without the provision of acceptable forms of relief from those pressures, there would be no chance that states would lower barriers to trade and capital movements and so allow unfettered economic exchanges. *The postwar era's movement toward liberalization was, therefore, tied to an acceptance of some limitations on interdependence.*

Successful Liberalization and New Protectionism

Not only did post–World War II liberalization depend on acceptance of some protection, the very success of that liberalization has itself generated protection. The postwar order that promoted liberalization while accepting some protection did lead to the growth of international exchange. International trade has grown very rapidly, in most years surpassing the growth in global product (Rosecrance and Stein, 1973; Katzenstein, 1975). This spectacular growth in world trade, precisely what those who fashioned the world economic order in the late forties intended their work to accomplish, has meant a concomitant growth in most countries' proportion of national product involved in international transactions. Exports and imports now account for twice the proportions of American GNP that they did 20 years ago. Exports, which accounted for 4.4 percent of gross domestic product (GDP) in 1970, made up 8.5 percent of GDP in 1980; imports were 4.3 percent of GDP in 1970 and 9.9 percent in 1980. Other industrial nations also experienced an increase in openness (measured as exports and imports as a percentage of national product) during the decade of the 1970s.

Yet *increasing interdependence may generate increased pressure for protection.* Unless imported goods only represent inputs for production or are goods not produced domestically, the higher the ratio of imports to national product, the greater the pressure on domestic industries. Even if domestic economic growth is sufficiently rapid for no industries to feel material injury, increasing import penetration still hurts the relative position (market share) of domestic producers. Rising import levels pose no problem only when a country imports goods that are not indigenously available. When those goods are produced in the importing nation, however, the increasing penetration of foreign goods means a decline in the market shares of domestic producers. In other words, when a country imports goods that are produced domestically at a rate faster than its domestic economic growth, then domestic manufacturers of those products, although not experiencing any material injury, lose some of their domestic market share.

Of course, economic growth may also serve to dampen protectionist pressures, and the greatest protectionist challenges are most likely to arise in prolonged and severe recessions. *Yet virtually all the protectionist pressures evident in the late 1980s predated the 1982 recession and continued unabated after recovery began.* Even in good times, increased interdependence itself increases the demand for protection. As long as higher levels of imports include goods also produced at home, the growth in trade will create a need to adjust and, not surprisingly, will elicit protectionist pressures from those affected.[106]

International exchange generates pressures for domestic adjustment, which is painful and often resisted. But the protection that flows from this resistance to adjustment reflects the very success of liberalization and the growth of international commerce. In other words, *the very accomplishment of increased global trade is one cause of increased demands for protection.*

Successful Liberalization and the "New Antiprotectionism"

The same pressures that increase requests for protection, however, also swell the demand for continued and greater openness. As societies become more open, they also have a greater stake in international commerce, for more firms and jobs come to depend on exports. In other words, growing interdependence increases a nation's dependence on its exports and heightens the need to maintain access to foreign markets. The larger volume of transactions that constitutes increased interdependence also leads to a greater interest in international trade on the part of the financial community, which profits by intermediating these transactions and whose international loans can be repaid only if the value of international exchanges at least remains steady. Finally, imports themselves come to be linked with the health of the domestic economy. As the nation imports more, there are more and more people whose employment and wealth are associated with the sale and distribution of imported goods. And they have an interest in opposing protectionism.[107]

If there is an asymmetry between protectionists and internationalists, it is in their incentives to organize in order to bring pressure to bear upon the national government. Industries hurt by import competition invariably lobby for relief. Such interest group pressure is a standard explanation of and excuse for the enactment of protectionist policies (Baldwin, 1982, 1984; Frey, 1985). In comparison, the widespread interest in lower tariffs and increased trade is thought to be so diffuse that these interests do not organize and mobilize to fight protectionism. Hence, this standard argument only predicts protection; it cannot adequately explain trade liberalization.

Yet antiprotectionist forces do mobilize. It may be true that consumers who want to purchase cheap high-quality goods do not organize to oppose protection, but others, with more concentrated interests, those for whom the costs are not diffuse, do mobilize. Indeed, the number of firms and individuals that could be mobilized on behalf of freer trade expands as more of the national product is exported.[108] Firms that export extensively, especially multinational ones that use intrafirm exchanges to provide components to divisions located in other nations, have an interest in liberalized trade (Allen and Walter, 1971; Helleiner, 1977; Pugel and Walter, 1985; Milner, 1987, 1988). Farmers, for example, emerged in the late 1970s as major supporters of American free trade policies. Perceiving their livelihood to be linked to exports, they have opposed protectionist legislation. Soybean farmers led the opposition to protection for cars, steel, and textiles (Auerbach, 1986), and corn farmers mounted an extensive campaign against domestic content legislation, which was strongly supported by organized labor (Auerbach, 1984). Again, *interest in continued openness grows simultaneously with interest in greater protection.*[109]

These twin effects of interdependence in heightening the desires for both openness and protection mark state as well as society. Specific interest groups lobby on behalf of and in opposition to protection.[110] But the state also finds itself torn. On the one hand, it can secure political gains by slowing and easing the costs of adjustment and can reap, as well, the potential benefits of some mercantilistic practices (if it can get away with them). On the other hand, it can ensure improvements in the nation's welfare through improved efficiency.

Liberalization and Protectionist Buy-outs

Not only did postwar liberalization depend on accepting some forms of protection, but the very process of advancing interdependence often requires some protection as well. After all, if postwar liberalization initially depended on some toleration of protectionism, and if the success of liberalization also generates protectionist pressures, then the ability to press for further liberalization depends critically on buying off those who could defeat domestically attempts at further liberalization. The historical record of trade liberalization provides an excellent example.

Postwar trade liberalization has been accomplished by a successive series of negotiating rounds intended to lower further barriers to trade. Yet each such international agreement entails more domestic adjustment. Those already hurt by foreign competition and those who fear that their competitive margin might be negotiated away both have an incentive to mobilize politically in an attempt to forestall further liberalization. The need for governments to develop winning coalitions in favor of new agreements and greater interdependence can therefore necessitate their buying off protectionist elements.

Many new forms of trade restraint developed in the postwar period precisely because of this need to buy off protectionists in order to maintain momentum on behalf of trade liberalization. Rather than control imports by raising tariffs or imposing quotas, for example, nations have devised voluntary export restraints (VERs) to give the importing nation some relief without actually raising classical barriers to trade (tariffs). The exporting nation obtains the windfall from the higher prices it can secure for the sale of a limited number of goods. Typically, domestic producers, as a group, lose no ground, and foreign ones, also as a group, maintain their market share.[111] VERs have, in fact, paved the way for trade liberalization (Bergsten, 1975:171). Beginning in the late 1950s, such arrangements were necessary to quiet the American textile industry's demands for protection. In 1957, the first VER with Japan made possible an extension of the Reciprocal Trade Agreement Act (RTAA) and the Dillon Round of trade negotiations that followed. The negotiation of the Long-Term Arrangement on Cotton Textiles (LTA) in 1962 made possible the Trade Expansion Act and the subsequent Kennedy Round. An expansion of the LTA to wool and other fibers, in the Multifiber Arrangement of December 1973, was required to ensure passage of the Trade Act of 1974, which authorized the U.S. president to proceed with the Tokyo Round negotiations.[112] In the late 1970s, steel was added to textiles as an industry that needed to be bought off.

Not only has the U.S. government had to buy off specific industries in order to ensure continued liberalization, but each new American trade bill has also entailed either tightening extant procedures or devising new ones to help those hurt by trade competition.[113] Indeed, American trade policy did not, until 1962, officially recognize that tariff liberalization could proceed beyond the point at which imports could compete with American products. American trade policy was predicated on the concept of tariff reductions, but not to that point at which American producers might be displaced in the American market. Only in the Trade Expansion Act of 1962 was there official recognition and acceptance of the fact that liberalization brought adjustments that involved the displacement of American producers in certain fields. In fact, the 1962 act included provisions for adjustment assistance, rather than protection, as a way of helping affected firms and workers. Although some ways of providing relief involve erecting barriers and others provide financial assistance to help the dislocated adjust to other productive activities, the enactment of any relief measure points to the necessity for representative governments to shield firms and individuals from having to fully face the consequences of foreign competition.

Thus, what many see as the creeping growth of protectionism simply represents the side payments necessary to sustain and continue the degree of openness that has already been achieved.[114] Certainly such measures slow the process of adjustment. But they also provide the compensation required if firms and workers are to accept the kinds of dislocations that come with the growth of an international division of labor.

In the postwar era, the growth of protectionism in tandem with trade illuminates that there are different kinds of mercantilistic practices. Some are intended entirely to prevent exchange between societies. During the Cold War, even as the United States pressed for increased interdependence among Western nations, it maintained an embargo on the export of certain high-technology items to the Soviet Union. But other mercantilist practices actually presume the existence of exchange and interdependence. Here, too, policymakers' intentions can vary. In some cases, states try to ensure asymmetric dependence. In others, they want to increase the relative gains from trade. And in still others, they hope to limit the pace and scope of adjustment. In this last instance, mercantilism is a defensive reaction to the growth of interdependence rather than an offensive action intended to cause harm.[115] Hence, its use can be consistent with continued growth in trade and can direct and channel the growth and evolution of economic interdependence.

Since World War II, tariff levels, especially among industrial nations, have continually declined, particularly as applied to the goods whose manufacture is marked by low cost differences. Indeed, the growth of world commerce has been dominated by the exchange of similar goods between developed countries.[116] At the same time, as tariffs have declined, other barriers to trade and other practices distorting commerce have clearly become manifest and have increased in number. International agreements now control trade in textiles, steel, and automobiles, among other products. Yet states whose industries suffer material injury have typically acted to freeze levels of imports and so contain pressures for adjustment rather than protect their industries more fully by keeping out foreign goods altogether. *States have sought not to reduce trade, but to manage its growth and consequences.* Moreover, protection to an injured industry (in whatever form, even as adjustment assistance) has been used as a side payment in order to make continued liberalization possible in other areas.[117] As a result, international trade has continued to grow even in the presence of such practices. Given the levels of global trade and the nature of current protectionist practices, the alternative to a vision of unfettered free trade and a global division of labor is not autarky (no trade), but managed or organized trade.

Protectionism and Negotiating Trade Liberalization

Some protection, then, has represented a domestic side payment for increased liberalization. But the very process of negotiating international agreements to liberalize trade is itself fraught with protectionist pressures. The growth of commerce and interdependence depends on negotiated agreements between states, and such agreements come at a price, one that often includes protection.

The strategy pursued during the postwar period to increase trade has been to obtain agreements dealing with extant problems. Early negotiating rounds dealt with tariff levels. But even as tariffs came down, new issues arose. The Kennedy Round of trade talks in the 1960s was specifically intended to deal with the new problem posed by the emergence of a European customs union (the European Economic Community, EEC). The Trade Expansion Act of 1962, the basis for American negotiating authority in the Kennedy Round, was intended to restructure America's economic relationship with the EEC. Yet almost immediately upon completion of these discussions, the United States began to plan for still another set of talks, this time in order to deal with nontariff barriers and those issues left unresolved in the Kennedy Round. The United States wanted negotiations to focus on such domestic practices as government procurement and customs-valuation procedures. Similarly, disappointment in the results of the Tokyo Round became apparent in the early 1980s, even before the 1979 agreements had been fully implemented, when the United States shifted its focus to a new set of issues, including trade in services, trade in high technology, agricultural trade, and trade-related investment criteria. Despite the accords reached and the liberalization achieved since World War II, therefore, concern about the state of the trading order remains constant, for there are always issues to be added to the agenda.

In addition to liberalizing commerce and increasing interdependence, these negotiating rounds have served a number of other important purposes. First, they have produced agreements substantially liberalizing trade. Second, they have been useful devices for forestalling the domestic advocates of protectionism. Ex ante, governments have been able to argue that instituting new protectionist measures should be postponed while nations await the results of ongoing talks. Ex post, governments have been able to maintain that establishing specific protectionist measures would violate various international agreements.

But the negotiating rounds also pose problems. Each successive set of discussions has taken longer than the previous one, has lasted until just before the expiration of legislatively granted negotiating authority, and has invariably been marked by crises. Although such conferences do allow technicians to hammer out the details of new agreements, they also serve to politicize trade and transform certain issues into matters of major national concern. Moreover, legislation authorizing the negotiations has provided a focal point for the concerns and efforts of protectionists. In the United States, for example, Congress has strengthened the ability of domestic industries to seek and obtain relief each time it has authorized the president to enter negotiations and offer trade concessions (Goldstein, 1983). Indeed, the trade talks generate as much protectionist fervor as they do commitment to liberalization. Ironically, this consequence stems also from the negotiating positions of governments, which, in order to obtain the best deal possible, have an incentive to stress their need to assuage domestic protectionists.

Further, the emphasis on reciprocity in trade negotiations, even as it helps move adherents toward freer trade, also engenders protectionism.[118] Reciprocity, a hallmark of international trade talks since the United States reintroduced the concept in the Reciprocal Trading Act of 1934, is a two-edged sword. A nation that unilaterally disarms itself economically is in no position to bargain and obtain concessions from others. Great Britain discovered this in the middle of the nineteenth century, when it offered to all nations the concessions it had just made to France in the Cobden-Chevalier Treaty of 1860. Having nothing more to offer other states, Britain, not surprisingly, found it quite difficult to negotiate subsequent trade agreements (Stein,

1984).[119] So, not surprisingly, nations arm themselves with protective tariffs that can be negotiated away and, in the hope that they will never be used, adopt restrictive measures contingent on the failure of others to liberalize further.[120]

Yet bargaining chips raise problems for every erstwhile free trader. The very process by which legislatures provide them in anticipation of negotiations brings protectionists out of the woodwork and can help to legitimize their arguments. It also commits legislators to a position from which they may find it difficult to extricate themselves. Moreover, not only can the actual use of bargaining chips poison the negotiating atmosphere, but a nation can also be stuck with them if the attempt to bargain them away does not succeed.[121]

The classical economists who advocated free trade recognized that it would make sense to retaliate against the protectionist practices of other nations in order to open up their markets. As Adam Smith argued in *The Wealth of Nations*, "There may be good policy in retaliations of this kind, when there is a probability that they will procure the repeal of the high duties or prohibitions complained of" (Smith, 1979:468). After all, the gains from the openness to be obtained in the future would more than compensate for the higher costs of goods in the interim. But whether retaliation and closure made sense depended on the probability of securing the desired changes in others' practices.[122]

Some governments may actually have a comparative negotiating advantage if they can turn domestic protectionist forces on and off. Governments that are too committed to free trade, or whose people are, may find that they negotiate inferior bargains.[123] A perennial problem for the American government is its difficulty in convincing typically skeptical foreigners that the demands of its domestic protectionists are real and that only concessions by other countries can prevent the United States from adopting protectionist policies and practices. At the same time, of course, foreign governments, not wanting to be perceived by their own societies as giving in to American demands, prefer to wait until the last minute before completing a new agreement. This way, they can explain to their home audiences that whatever concessions they made were necessary to forestall American protectionism. As a result, the United States has typically been forced to the brink of instituting new protectionist measures before successfully completing new trade agreements.

The problem, of course, is that such routinized theatrics involve a fair amount of discord, and politicians require tremendous skill in crisis management in order to avoid disaster. Access to its home market is a nation's most powerful negotiating lever for securing access for its exporters to foreign shores.[124] But threatening a trade war in order to get others to open their borders more fully runs the risk that one might actually occur.[125] Nonetheless, *economic brinkmanship intended to maintain economic deterrence and sustain progress in trade liberalization is the historical norm.*

Government, Domestic Policies, and International Economic Conflicts

Not only have protectionism and economic conflict been elements of the processes of liberalization and increasing economic interdependence, but the growth of interdependence has itself brought new conflicts to the fore. Progressive liberalization has led to new disputes and a substantially altered agenda for subsequent negotiation. Typically, these new conflicts are also related to the role of government in the economy.

The most important fact of twentieth-century political life is the increased size and role of government, including its intervention in the workings of the marketplace. Classical trade theory was developed in an era in which tariffs provided the basic economic policy lever for central governments. Free traders argued that doing away with the distorting effects of tariffs would lead to the maximization of global economic welfare as nations came to specialize in certain products, used their resources optimally, and exchanged goods and services freely. In other words, the abolition of tariffs would allow competition in a free and undistorted marketplace. Yet in the twentieth century, the range of government distortions of the marketplace has been as great as the range of government policy itself, and as governments have grown, so has the spectrum of distortion. As a result of the success of liberalization and the growth of interdependence, the entire array of national economic policies has become the basis for economic conflicts among nations.

As tariffs declined with successive rounds of negotiations during the postwar era, the agenda for trade liberalization shifted. In the past, advocates of free trade saw their task as eliminating tariffs and discriminatory trade treaties. Liberalization was accomplished through successive efforts to reduce tariffs; nondiscrimination was achieved by constructing an ever growing network of states linked with trade treaties that included unconditional most-favored-nation (MFN) clauses (Stein, 1984). But as tariff levels came down, the focus of trade negotiations shifted to so-called nontariff barriers (NTBs) (Olechowski and Sampson, 1980).[126] *Governments' domestic programs had become the critical issue of trade politics.*

By generating both negative and positive externalities for producers, government policy changes the nature of doing business in a myriad of ways. Governments can increase the cost of doing business by making producers internalize the costs of what had been externalities. They can, for example, require that producers bear the costs of eliminating pollution. Alternatively, governments can lower the expenses associated with production through policies that externalize private costs and make the public bear them. And by altering the costs of doing business, governments can affect international competitiveness and shape the nature and extent of international trade.

The advanced industrial nations, having largely done away with tariffs, increasingly find themselves embroiled in trade disputes that result from incongruent domestic policies.[127] More and more often, industries confronting foreign competition point to domestic policies as the cause of their problems. They argue that they are harmed by their own government's policies, while foreign companies benefit from the policies of their governments. The resolution of such disputes lies in the coordination, concertation, or harmonization of the wide range of government programs that affect the costs of producing traded goods and services.[128] For this reason, scholars distinguish between such negative steps as the removal of barriers and restrictions and such positive ones as establishing institutions for developing common policies (Tinbergen, 1959; Pelkmans, 1979).

Incongruent Domestic Policies

MACROECONOMIC POLICIES

The incongruent domestic policies that generate international economic conflicts include macroeconomic policies, which affect the exchange rate and therefore relative trade competitiveness.[129] Not surprisingly, the impact of currency appreciation in increasing imports and reducing exports generates protectionist pressures.[130] It can also lead states to urge others to change policy in order to relieve both the exchange rate problem and the trade conflict it engenders. In the 1980s, for example, the net impact of the combined macroeconomic policies of the advanced industrial nations was, for many years, a very highly valued dollar and an enormous U.S. trade deficit. As a result, a group of advanced industrial nations complained about the American budget deficit. The United States, on the other hand, pressed Germany and Japan to pursue more expansionary domestic policies. Economists and politicians have advocated macroeconomic policy coordination as a means of dealing with the problems of divergent macroeconomic policies.[131]

TAX POLICIES

International economic conflicts derive not only from the effects of macroeconomic policy on exchange rates, but also from the direct consequences of fiscal and monetary policies on relative competitiveness. The differences between one nation's tax code and others' revenue policies, for example, can cause international friction. The original General Agreement on Tariffs and Trade (GATT) agreement of 1947 distinguished between direct taxes, which governments can neither assess on imports nor rebate to their own nation's exporters, and indirect taxes, which can be rebated on exports and levied on imports. The United States relies primarily on direct taxes; Japan and many European states use indirect ones. This places the United States at a dual disadvantage. American exports to other countries often cost more than other nations' products for two reasons: because pricing must cover U.S. taxes, which are not rebated, and because an indirect tax is assessed upon the goods when they enter the foreign market. On the other hand, imports to the American market are often cheaper than domestic goods because their home-country taxes are rebated to the producing firms and because the United States does not assess an indirect tax on imports. These tax practices explain a great deal of the price differential between Japanese and American cars in their respective markets (Nevin, 1983).

Concern about incongruent tax codes focuses not only on the treatment of internationally traded goods, but also on how countries tax different domestic industries and sectors. National tax codes are giant mazes of incentives and disincentives, all of which channel investment. The effective tax rates on American industries vary widely (Jorgenson and Sullivan, 1981; Batten and Ott, 1985), and every proposed tax reform brings forth lobbyists concerned with maintaining specific tax preferences. American heavy industry was the major beneficiary of the 1981 Reagan tax bill, whereas the 1986 tax act favored high-tech over heavy industry, and the Sun Belt over the Rust Belt (Drew, 1985; see also Klott, 1985). Differential tax treatment can favor some industries and regions at the expense of others in much the same ways that tariffs and subsidies can affect the relative competitiveness of industries between as well as within nations (Bond and Guisinger, 1985).[132]

MICROECONOMIC POLICIES

International economic disputes have been rooted also in incongruent microeconomic policies. Government regulations, for example, change the costs of doing business and so can affect international competitiveness. And incongruent policies, whether the regulations differ or whether one nation regulates what another does not, can generate frictions.[133]

The emergence of pollution as one major issue in the advanced industrial societies has come to affect international economic and political relations. As a result of environmental concerns, governments in the developed nations adopted policies intended not only to clean up extant pollution, but also to prevent as much as possible from occurring in the first place. Such programs increase the costs of production, and firms operating under environmental regulations operate at a competitive disadvantage. Developing countries, whose companies have the advantage of no such requirements, see environmentalism as a luxury of the already rich. They interpret the call for broader environmental protection as an attempt to constrain third-world industrialization and growth.[134] The resolution of such disputes through the harmonization of environmental standards has proven difficult given different nations' varying levels of industrialization, tolerances for pollution, social priorities, and physical circumstances.[135]

Solving international economic disputes rooted in different regulatory policies such as those involving environmental pollution entails not only harmonizing standards but also agreement on the means of allocating the costs. Pollution, like other externalities, is a problem whose consequences are not part of a manufacturer's calculus. Governments can deal with such problems by socializing some proportion of the cost, or they can force producers to internalize the expense and bear the burden. Countries can have common pollution standards and still end up in economic disputes if they allocate the financial burden in different ways. In the case of environmental policy, and as part of dealing with different practices, the Organization for Economic Cooperation and Development (OECD) adopted the "polluter pays principle" (Rubin and Graham, 1982).

Although the incongruent domestic policies that can give rise to international economic disputes may not have been adopted with a protectionist or distortionary intention, states may disagree nonetheless about the consequences of the programs in question.[136] The agricultural dispute between the United States and Europe has focused on European export subsidies and American price supports. But the range of governmental practices in the United States that affect competitiveness includes, for example, the entire American system of university agricultural extension. Similarly, the United States has complained about industrial policies in Western Europe and Japan, but it does not recognize its own military budget, which many Americans view as an unreasonable burden for a nation whose allies spend less on mutual security, as an industrial subsidy.[137] Others do.

Unintentionally protectionist programs may be rooted in social philosophies or public goals. The United States, for example, prohibits the use of child labor, and AFL-CIO president Lane Kirkland has argued that American workers should not be asked to compete on equal terms with firms in nations that allow them to use child labor ("This Week with David Brinkley," ABC-TV, 4 September 1988).[138] Resolving international economic conflicts rooted in such different social philosophies has proven difficult.

Political Structures and Incongruent Domestic Policies

Differences in the structures of governments can also create difficulties that did not arise during the era that tariffs constituted the major agenda item of those trying to liberalize trade.[139] Tariffs, which circumscribe a national market, are almost always an element of central government policy.[140] But as incongruent domestic policies create international economic conflicts and become the focus of international efforts at harmonization and trade liberalization, the practices of subnational governments become increasingly salient. This complicates negotiations between nation-states with different governmental arrangements. Harmonizing procurement policies by providing access to foreign bidders, for example, is complicated by the autonomy of state and local governments and their protectionist practices. Most American states, for example, have "Buy American" requirements, which give preference to domestic producers (Weidenbaum, 1983:25–27).[141] In short, when differences in governmental structure generate policies that affect relative competitiveness and access, they can become the basis for hard-to-resolve international economic disputes.[142]

Internal political arrangements can have international ramifications and can lead to conflict between different political systems. The differential ability of federal and centralized systems to control subnational governments provides an illustration. In the middle 1980s, President Reagan responded to foreign pressure and announced his support for legislation that would force states to abolish certain accounting practices if they would not voluntarily reform them. At issue was California's use of the unitary method of taxation. Foreign governments had bitterly complained about, and threatened to retaliate against, California's use of this method, which required affiliated corporations that operated as a unit to report their worldwide business income. California then taxed that proportion of a firm's worldwide income deemed to be California-related. As of the middle 1980s, California was the only major taxing jurisdiction in the world to use this method, and foreign governments, especially Great Britain, had threatened sanctions in response. California finally reformed its tax code by allowing corporations to make a "water's edge election," in which they only had to report their income in the United States rather than worldwide.[143] The United States (and Germany, too) has found it necessary to restrict the role of subnational governments in order to resolve international economic disputes.[144]

Even absent structural differences, variations in national views about the proper role of government in the domestic economy can also pose problems for the harmonization of policies. Governments can be distinguished by the degree to which they intervene in the marketplace and in their nation's economic development.[145] The range of such state behaviors is evident in industrial policy, regulation, and the provision of subsidies.[146] And because governments have historically played different roles, they are more or less capable of pursuing certain policies. Although government is an inherently inefficient instrument, some are less inefficient than others and may possess a comparative advantage in the pursuit of specific policies. The Japanese government, for example, targets certain industries for special treatment in order to foster their growth. Calls for an American industrial policy represent implicit demands for harmonization.[147] Because the nature of American government and society is not particularly conducive to planning and direction, however, the United States might still be left at a comparative disadvantage in the pursuit of such programs. Moreover, any American attempt to establish central direction might undercut its extant comparative advantages that lie in the innovation and rapid transformation that come from a mobile, freewheeling, individualistic society (Badaracco and Yoffie, 1983).

Society, Culture, and International Economic Conflicts

International economic conflicts also emerge from different social and cultural practices, and resolving such disputes through harmonization is still more difficult. Again, U.S.–Japanese trade relations provide an example. Although Japan maintains very low tariffs, foreigners have a difficult time selling there, in part because Japanese business relations are built upon a very tight network that outsiders have rarely successfully breached. As a result, the substantial liberalization of Japanese trade policy, much of it accomplished through American government pressure, has done little to improve sales of foreign goods and has therefore affected gross trade flows only slightly. Changes in government policy do not necessarily translate into changes in business practices or consumer behavior, and Japanese consumers strongly prefer to buy from domestic producers. Like government policy, cultural and social practices and habits can also become the basis for trade disagreements in a world of low tariffs.[148]

As a result, attempts to harmonize the different practices that affect competitiveness have led to international pressures on governments to change many of their nations' normal practices. Adherence to a philosophy of *senyu koraku* (struggle first, enjoy later), for example, is evident in the longer working hours and fewer vacation days of Japanese than of American workers.[149] The scope of societal variations that can affect trade and cause friction is so great that some American officials have even suggested that Japan needs to change its culture. And in one attempt to resolve trade conflicts with the United States, the Japanese Labor Ministry actually began a campaign to bring Japanese work practices into line with American ones (Jameson, 1985a; Rowen, 1986; Jameson, 1985b). Ironically, those working in the Leisure Development Center charged with encouraging Japanese employees to make greater use of leisure time were themselves working overtime on that job (Wysocki, 1986). The Japanese have also pressed the United States to change its ways. A report that emerged from U.S.–Japanese discussions about each nation's structural impediments to trade, for example, called upon the United States to upgrade its educational system.[150]

Economic interdependence and policy harmonization may have profound implications for cultural differences. The desire to maintain cultural distinctiveness was the basis for Canadian demands to exclude cultural industries (such as publishing) from a free trade agreement with the United States.[151] And the likely impact of a free trade agreement on Canadian society (rather than economy) was central to the ratification debate in Canada. As harmonization comes to encompass the whole range of public policies, cultural sensitivities will become increasingly important.

Customs Unions and Incongruent Domestic Policies

The nature and range of the economic conflicts that can arise in the wake of tariff reductions and the problems inherent in harmonizing domestic economic policies in the modern world are exemplified by the experience of the European Economic Community (EEC). The formation of the EEC—the acceptance of a common external tariff—represented a commitment to reducing internal barriers to trade and placed a premium on the harmonization of domestic policies. The desirability and necessity of maintaining the EEC put tariffs and quotas out of bounds as appropriate means for dealing with domestic economic problems. Nevertheless, a complicated arrangement of accepted subsidies was built into the EEC in order to cement the union.

Moreover, the formation and evolution of the EEC led to the disappearance neither of nontariff barriers nor of incongruent domestic policies. The Community has a central institution with a bureaucracy and some legitimacy in a context of states having adopted a common tariff barrier. Yet the European Community Commission and the European Council have both expressed concern about such barriers as continue to exist within the EEC (Korn, 1981; also see Page, 1980). The dream of a unified European marketplace has remained unfulfilled, and the problem of incongruent domestic policies plagues the Community, despite the permanent institutional arrangements available to promote harmonization.[152] Current plans finally and fully to integrate Europe into one market by 1992 entail the elimination of thousands of national statutes (*Economist*, 1988).[153]

Interdependence, competition, the vagaries of the market, and the role of government combine to ensure that economic conflict remains. Even a customs union focuses attention on the source of the most serious economic problems that plague the international exchanges between its members. More important, it generates pressures on its members to harmonize their policies, and it creates an institutional backstop to prevent them from slipping back down the road of classical trade barriers.

Theory and Policy

The foregoing analysis of the implications of economic interdependence provides an understanding of both the course of recent events and the consequences of different policy paths. It does not generate unambiguous policy imperatives, although it does provide insight into the course of future events.[154]

One policy implication of the foregoing analysis is that it is difficult to make net assessments of trends toward liberalization or protection. Because liberalization and protection are conjoined, both can be present, and there will typically be a debate about whether the glass is half full or whether it is half empty. Because liberalization itself entails some protectionism, and because successful liberalization generates new areas of trade conflict, scholars have had a difficult time pointing to a single trend and have even seen opposing ones. Some see the liberal order as threatened and endangered. They point to increasing protectionist buy-outs and the rise of nontariff barriers. Yet others emphasize the continued growth in trade and the successes of past negotiating rounds, each of which has tackled progressively more difficult issues. And in assessing the negotiating rounds, scholars cannot decide whether to emphasize the creation of new rules in areas previously unaffected by international trade agreements or to emphasize the conflicts during the negotiations, the loopholes in the rules, and the areas still left untouched (Krasner, 1979).[155]

This simultaneous growth of both liberalization and protection is not merely a global phenomenon; it can be found in the policies of individual states. The seemingly contradictory policies pursued by the United States, for example, also become understandable in light of the foregoing analysis. During the 1980s, the United States both adopted protectionist measures and pressed nations to pursue free trade. It retaliated against others' protectionist practices in the name of liberalizing trade, even as others castigated its own slide into protectionism. All of these are the logical results of the conflicts created by interdependence. The American desire for liberalization is genuine. And liberalization requires negotiated agreement that in turn requires reciprocity and compromise. Without closure or the threat of closure, mutual openness cannot be achieved. And without side payments to buy off domestic opponents, trade liberalization in a representative polity is difficult to achieve.

Moreover, even as the United States pursued such multilateral avenues as trade negotiations, it also negotiated bilateral free trade agreements, which were often castigated by free traders as discriminatory arrangements that undercut the prospects for multilateral liberalization. Yet liberal trade is the product of bilateral arrangements. The free trade era of the 1860s began with the Cobden-Chevalier Treaty. What prevented this bilateral agreement from being a classic mercantilist instrument was the inclusion of an unconditional most-favored-nation clause and the fact that both Britain and France proceeded to sign such agreements with other states. The result was a network of states linked by bilateral treaties that all included MFN clauses.[156] New adherents joined because it was in their interest to trade with these nations on the best terms available. In effect, the discrimination against outsiders (i.e., the least favored nations) provided the impetus for negotiating such agreements. The requirement of reciprocity in such treaties meant that each new agreement liberalized the entire network of trade relationships.

The first GATT negotiating round in 1947 was really a set of bilateral agreements between 22 countries. Its unique feature was that the negotiations were pursued simultaneously in one place and that all the bilateral agreements included the same set of initial articles as well as unconditional MFN clauses.[157] Since then, the negotiating rounds have become more multilateral, but the key negotiations remain bilateral.

It is not surprising, therefore, that nations have gone outside GATT both to resolve trade problems and to further the cause of trade liberalization. Measures such as the VERs discussed above have been negotiated bilaterally, outside GATT. And free trade areas, such as that between Canada and the United States, have also been negotiated outside GATT. The slowness in working out a new international agreement on trade in services has also led to negotiated bilateral agreements.

The foregoing analysis provides no new prescription, only an understanding that discriminatory practices are not necessarily threats to the prospect of liberal trade. Rather, they are the necessary requisites for trade liberalization. Bilateral and small-group agreements that can establish a critical mass and create an incentive for new adherents are important mechanisms for liberalizing international commerce.[158] And discrimination, in the form of customs unions, free trade areas, and preferential arrangements, has continued to be an accepted means of trade liberalization. That is the history of the evolution of GATT and the EEC.[159]

Both the growth of commerce and the resolution of economic conflicts rooted in economic interdependence require international cooperation. Such cooperation need not be multilateral, it need not involve international institutions such as GATT, and it need not require agreement on broad liberal principles. And achieving the requisite cooperation and agreement to resolve conflicts sometimes requires threats and retaliation. And this makes possible an understanding of the existence of illiberal practices in the service of liberalism.

In addition, the analysis here of economic interdependence and international cooperation also holds implications for understanding the relations between the West and the Soviet Union. Historically, two arguments have been made regarding optimal American policy toward the Soviet Union during the Cold War. First, George Kennan's original vision of containment laid out a defensive policy limited to economic and political means. Kennan argued that the United States could increase the costs and strains to Soviet society and the Soviet empire by sustaining economic and political pressures against the Soviet Union.[160] Yet the reverse argument, that contact and openness should replace containment, underlay the policy of détente.[161] Openness, increasing commercial contact (and for a Deutschian, human contact), would moderate the Soviet Union and increasingly integrate it with others.

The arguments made for both economic containment and détente contain problematic assertions yet can claim ultimate vindication. The argument for economic containment was clearly wrong in its forecast that containment would lead to Soviet collapse within a decade to one generation. And its correctness after four and a half decades must be tempered with the confounding consequences of the pursuit of détente.

The détente argument is problematic, for Soviet economic openness did not do away with Soviet adventurism and the presumed economic burden did not deter Soviet entry into Afghanistan.[162] And yet Gorbachev's domestic and international actions were entirely consistent with the requisites of developing economic exchange on a substantial scale. The development of extensive commerce required both a political transformation, the international cooperation that underlies the development of economic interdependence, and an internal economic transformation of Soviet policies and practices.

But the foregoing analysis of the implications of the growth of economic interdependence also makes clear the painful challenges that lie in the path of Soviet integration into the global economy.[163] Any substantial growth of trade with the West will require a wholesale transformation of Soviet society and polity as well as economy. This will be painful, and it is likely to be resisted. As important, the adoption of markets and the growth of market exchange will generate numerous pressures for adjustment, which in a more representative political system will create pressures to manage and control the pace of integration into the world economy. And although the need to harmonize will initially lead to the adoption of Western models and mimicry of the West (Soviet institutions and practices have little legitimacy, as they are widely perceived to be inefficient failures), it is likely that there will be increasing opposition and resentment within the Soviet Union. It may be necessary in the short term, as it was with Western Europe and Japan after the war, to allow the Soviets to avoid certain reciprocal commitments and for the West to accept some degree of Soviet protectionism. But the process of their economic integration will be long and difficult and will itself lead to economic conflicts with the West. Moreover, the Soviets' need to conjoin liberalization with protection in order to control the nature and pace of adjustment will make it difficult to ascertain the course of Soviet policy. Just as there are disagreements about continued liberalization among Western nations, and just as the United States follows contradictory policies, so, too, will the Soviets simultaneously pursue market liberalization and what will appear to be socialist protection. Some will see a Soviet trend toward liberalization, while others will point to protective practices and doubt both the Soviets' commitment to liberalization and their ability to adopt appropriate policies. Such vacillation is part and parcel of the implications of economic interdependence.

Conclusion

Economic exchange and interdependence presuppose international agreement on minimally required rules of the game, generate direct benefits, and create domestic groups interested in the maintenance and growth of international commerce. Although this does not ensure peace, it does mean that the presumed benefits to be derived from conflict must be so great as to outweigh its costs, including the foregone gains from trade. Commerce and interdependence do make war less likely.

Yet economic interdependence serves also to generate international economic conflict. The very success in lowering tariffs among nations and the resultant growth in world trade raise new areas of conflict and eventually bring the problem of incongruent government policies to the fore. When nations' domestic policies diverge, it is possible to have "unencumbered trade" that is not free trade, that many in the society find unfair, and that can become the basis of international conflict. Success in lowering tariffs thus places the burden on states to harmonize those policies that affect the production of traded goods. Further liberalization entails the never-ending process of harmonizing domestic policies.

Yet the increasing liberalization of international exchange and the corollary growth of economic interdependence also generate pressures for heightened cooperation, for there are enormous economic costs in allowing trade disputes to become trade wars and in allowing economic competition to spill over into political and military competition. Hence, states deal with conflicts either by negotiating protectionism in order to manage trade cooperatively or by reaching new international agreements designed to coordinate or harmonize domestic practices. Although the former may represent a limitation on continued liberalization and domestic adjustment, and although the latter may be preferable from the standpoint of economic efficiency, both represent increases in international cooperation. And indeed, negotiated protection in some sectors has been one element of continuing liberalization in others. Thus, world trade has continued to grow, and governments have embarked on new agreements and negotiations, even as certain forms of protection have survived.

The increasing interdependence of advanced industrial societies brings not only growing intimacy, but a greater potential for discord as well. Nations are not unlike couples, who can only fight about how to squeeze a toothpaste tube if they are living together. Fights about educating and raising children occur only after a couple has conceived a child. Couples intimate enough to have had children can still get divorced. Resolving the disputes that grow from familiarity generates higher levels of intimacy and interdependence. Indeed, the economic problems and conflicts that plague relationships among the major trading nations are, in part, a reflection of those states' very successes in establishing an open world economic order and strengthening interdependence. *Increasing interdependence between nations, like increasing intimacy between individuals, brings new conflict and requires greater adjustments and accommodations.* Growing interdependence generates conflicts, and resolving them entails greater cooperation.

Notes

My appreciation to Amy Davis, Robert Keohane, Deborah Larson, Paul Papayoanou, Ronald Rogowski, Lars Skalnes, and two anonymous referees for their comments, and to Elizabeth Bailey, Mark Brawley, Alan Kessler, and Tammy Tonucci for research assistance. An earlier version of this paper was presented at the Program on International Politics, Economics and Security (PIPES) at the University of Chicago in May 1989. My thanks to all the participants, especially Duncan Snidal and Daniel Verdier, for the discussion. The paper makes use of material first included in an unclassified memorandum written in January 1983 for the director of the Policy Planning Staff of the U.S. Department of State. The arguments presented here are solely my own. I am also grateful to the Council on Foreign Relations for an International Affairs Fellowship that made possible my stay at Policy Planning. My thanks also to the Brookings Institution, where I developed these and other ideas while decompressing from the experience of government service. The methodological and conceptual issues were the focus of an earlier paper presented at the National Academy of Sciences in January 1988. The first draft of this paper was completed in October 1988, and final copy was completed in October 1990. Finally, my thanks to the UCLA Academic Senate for financial support.

1. Belief in the cooperative ramifications of economic links provided one of the underpinnings of Nixon and Kissinger's pursuit of détente, for example. Still more recently, scholars have even argued about the value of commercial exchanges and their implications for developing "vested interests in peace" among the participants in the Arab-Israeli conflict (Arad and Hirsch, 1981; Hirsch 1981; Arad, Hirsch, and Tovias, 1983).

2. The set of works associated with the reemergence of the topic includes Cooper (1968, 1972), Morse (1970, 1972), Rosecrance and Stein (1973), Waltz (1970), and Young (1969). Work in the middle and latter part of the decade includes Katzenstein (1975), Keohane and Nye (1977), Little and McKinlay (1978), Reynolds and McKinlay (1979), and Rosecrance, Alexandroff, Koehler, Kroll, Lacqueur, and Stocker (1977). For more recent evaluations, see Jones (1984) and Little (1984). Most of these works are characterized by an emphasis on economic considerations. Some evolved from earlier studies of international organizations and regional integration.

3. For the view of mercantilism as an integrated doctrine with perspectives on both domestic and international political order, see Buck (1942). Many liberals also advocated an end to imperialism and colonialism and favored reductions in military spending, if not outright disarmament.

4. For Hirschman (1977), this represented an argument on behalf of interests as constraining the passions of rulers.

5. The phrase "republican liberalism" comes from Keohane (1990); Nye (1988) refers to this as "democratic liberalism." I consider republican liberalism to be a variant of political liberalism, for some saw commerce as constraining state power and the arbitrary use of state authority independent of the particular form of government. In other words, they understood commerce to constrain even nonrepresentative governments.

6. For works on Kant's views of international relations, see, among others, Doyle (1983a & b, 1986), Gallie (1978), Hinsley (1963), Hoffmann (1965), and Waltz (1959, 1962).

7. This view was maintained most eloquently in the early twentieth century by Angell (1913, 1921).

8. Some, such as David Ricardo, James Mill, John Ramsay MacCulloch, John Stuart Mill, Michel Chevalier, Henri Baudrillart, and Gustave de Molinari, thought that free trade would make war less likely; others, including Jean-Baptiste Say, Richard Cobden, Frederic Bastiat, and Charles Dunoyer, believed that it would end war altogether (Silberner, 1946).

9. The impact of political systems on the propensity for war has been extensively studied. For a starting point for tracing the literature see Doyle (1986).

10. This literature has been dubbed the endogenous tariff literature. Entry into the field can be obtained through essays by Baldwin (1982, 1984), Frey (1985), and the superb critical survey by Nelson (1988).

11. The decisive importance of state intervention in assuring industrialization for latecomers is stressed by Gerschenkron (1962).

12. The great German mercantilist, List, discussed briefly below, developed his protectionist ideas in the United States, where he published a book on the American political economy (List, 1827).

13. The famous distinction between negative and positive liberty is made by Berlin (1969).

14. Ruggie (1982) dubs the conjunction of domestic interference in the market with international free trade "embedded liberalism."

15. Mill (1873) epitomized this liberal shift away from laissez-faire doctrines. This changed perspective is evident also in the works of T.H. Green, D.G. Ritchie, J.A. Hobson, and L.T. Hobhouse (Bullock and Shock, 1956:xlii ff., and part 5).

16. Here, they did not contrast free trade with the alternative of autarky and self-sufficiency, but with imperialism and colonialism.

17. One of the reasons given, for example, for the resumption of war between Britain and France in 1803, following their having signed a peace treaty at Amiens in 1802, was the absence of any commercial agreement in the peace treaty (Bosanquet, 1924:24–26). For a Marxist such as Lenin (1917), imperialism was rooted not in mercantilistic practices, but in capitalist competition.

18. The phrase "commercial liberalism" comes from Keohane (1990). He uses it to encompass the general view that commerce promotes cooperation, and he distinguishes a sophisticated from a naive variant of the argument. I argue here that there are different arguments made by liberals as to why commerce would induce cooperation or reduce conflict, and so I distinguish between a neutralizing and a binding variant of commercial liberalism, as well as offer an argument that emphasizes the role of finance.

19. Richard Rosecrance (1986) argues that some governments have adopted the strategy of being "a trading state."

20. Echoing List, Keynes pointed out that protection in self-defense made sense: "Separate economic blocs, and all the friction and loss of friendship they bring with them, are expedients to which one may be driven in a hostile world where trade has ceased, over wide areas, to be cooperative and peaceful and where are forgotten the healthy rules of mutual advantage and equal treatment. But," he went on, "it is surely crazy to prefer that" (quoted in Eichengreen, 1984, 373; also see Gerrard, 1988; Willoughby, 1982b).

21. This view was held by American secretary of state Cordell Hull. For a sophisticated 1930s version of this argument, see Staley (1939).

22. Lateral pressure is a concept developed by Robert North (Choucri and North, 1975). A fuller development of his argument is in North (1977). For other discussions of the conflictual impact of resource scarcity in the modern world, see Orr (1977) and Russett (1981–82).

23. This problem, discussed further below, plagues the literature linking commerce

and war. Hall (1987) argues that "liberalism can only survive if it takes geopolitics seriously" (p. 134), which entails a recognition that the "state system continue[s] to be able to generate social conflict in its own right" (p. 137).

24. Nye (1988) refers to this as sociological liberalism.

25. The critical implication of this perspective for an understanding of the causes of war is that it implicitly treats conflict as an inherent product of misunderstanding or misperception. When familiarity and knowledge of others exist, conflict can be avoided and cooperation assured. If conflicts of interest arise, they must be rooted in inaccurate perception or misunderstanding. Further, this argument bears some relationship to the view in economics that self-interested actors with full information consummate all Pareto-improving exchanges, leading to a world in equilibrium, with no actor having a unilateral interest in changing position. For modern neoclassical economists, the basis of conflict lies in imperfect information. For a discussion of the centrality of misperception to liberal arguments about international relations, see Stein (1990).

26. Blainey (1973:20) points out that Buckle, who "thought foreign travel was the greatest of all educations as well as a spur to peace," died of the typhoid that he contracted while traveling in the Middle East.

27. The view that communication was essential even led to the invention of new languages intended to be truly universal and not reflective of any nationality. A German priest, J.M. Schleyer, developed Volapuk in 1880. Within a decade, it had both a million students and a rival, Esperanto, which was invented in 1887 by a Russian who hoped it would reduce the feuding between the Polish, German, Yiddish, and Russian speakers of his region. It was not long before supporters of the two universal languages were feuding with one another (Blainey, 1973:22–23).

28. There are, for example, European Community (EC), economic, Arab, and American-Soviet summits, among others. In the 1984 U.S. presidential campaign, Democratic candidate Walter Mondale proposed annual American-Soviet summits on the model of the economic ones. Mondale was attacking President Reagan's failure to have met even once during his first term with the Soviet leader. Ironically, President Reagan proceeded in his second term to meet annually with his Soviet counterpart.

29. In their work, trade and investment are just two of the indicators used for interaction and communication. They also gathered and assessed an array of others, including mail flows, telephone calls, and migration. Deutsch's own work focuses on a range of issues: the role of communications (Deutsch, 1966b, 1968), transactions in general (Deutsch, 1960, 1964), and trade in particular (Deutsch, Bliss, and Eckstein, 1962; Deutsch and Eckstein, 1961). Key works by his students on these same issues include those by Alker and Puchala (1968), Katzenstein (1976), Puchala (1970), and Russett (1963b, 1971). For a critique by a Deutsch student, see Young (1969). For the work of another Deutsch student that epitomizes the link between Deutsch on integration and the focus on interdependence in the 1970s, see Katzenstein (1975). For a formalization of Deutsch's argument, see Zinnes and Muncaster (1987). For the interest of Deutsch and his students in an array of indicators, see Russett, Alker, Deutsch, and Lasswell (1964).

30. Deutsch is aware of this. Hence, he sometimes emphasizes that there must be

value compatibility as well as a multiplicity of interactions (Deutsch, 1969:103–104). On more and less contact as the bases of different kinds of war, see Wright (1965b:381).

31. Hirschman (1977) points out that before Montesquieu, Spinoza also had emphasized the importance between different kinds of wealth. This section draws upon Hirschman's analysis.

32. An alternative formulation also exists. Liberals argued, and Marxists adopted some of these arguments, that foreign investment leads to conflict and generates intervention in other nations and war between capital-exporting nations. It does so not because it is in the interests of the nation as a whole, but because it is in the interests of a particular segment of the business and financial community, which usurps the control of state power for private gain. The anti-Semitic variant of this argument refers to the role of "international Jewish finance capital" (Hall, 1987:132). Finally, one can also make the argument that the fungibility and mobility of capital can make financial interests indifferent to political conflict because of its ability to move to safe havens.

33. Given the indirect nature of economic competition, a nation linked to the international economy can be affected by events in countries with which it does not trade. Two states that produce and export the same commodity, for example, are sensitive to the other's fortunes, as when the prices obtained by American farmers reflect the harvests in other major agricultural exporting nations.

34. Historical lore is full of contrasting characterizations of particularistic interests that favor war because it improves their economic circumstances.

35. Even more basically, they assume the existence of market exchange and of money (Gilpin, 1977).

36. This argument can be conjoined with one holding that modernization necessarily entails an emphasis on the accumulation of wealth by both individuals and governments (Morse, 1976b). Modernization itself leads to a concern with material welfare and a resulting shift in political priorities from the "high politics" of national security issues to what is often taken to be, at least by diplomats and statesmen, the "low politics" of trade and investment (Morse, 1970).

37. Moreover, given the variety of analytic links in the assorted arguments discussed above, virtually any empirical work relevant to one perspective is irrelevant to another. Indeed, given that some of the arguments linking commerce with cooperation are really negations of propositions linking scarcity to closure and conflict, there are assessments, not discussed here, that have focused entirely on this latter link.

38. Given the multiplicity of indicators of communication, scholars paid a good deal of attention to the issue of their covariation and pioneered the use of factor analysis in international relations. Some of their empirical studies also focused on issues of less direct concern to the question of interdependence, such as whether elite attitudes covary with aggregate measures.

39. Olson (1982) refers to the formation of an economic and political union as "jurisdictional integration."

40. The argument is comparable to that made about relations between firms. Companies, too, are interdependent in the sense that they interact in a competitive market

and are affected by changes in market conditions. Yet they are not interdependent in that they do not interact strategically with one another and remain unaffected by the decisions of any specific competitor.

41. Even in a perfectly competitive market in which there are alternative suppliers and consumers, some costs may remain either in the process of shifting commercial partners or from the shrinking size of the market that international conflict might bring.

42. This phenomenon of trade increasing faster than production is necessarily matched for at least one of the nations involved. Note that the inverse relationship is not necessarily true. The trade openness of individual nations can increase without a concomitant increase in the openness of the international system as a whole.

43. This view of interdependence is consistent with a game-theoretic conceptualization. Tetreault (1980:431–433) distinguishes between systemic interdependence and bilateral interdependence. For a general argument that strategic interaction should be seen as another level of analysis, see Stein (1990).

44. Some discuss openness without linking it to the concept of interdependence; see Grassman (1980), Beenstock and Warburton (1983), and Kar (1983). Still others distinguish the interconnectedness implied by transactions from the reciprocal costs implied by only some transactions (Keohane and Nye, 1977). Since exchange implies some division of labor, transactions themselves can be seen as capturing a dimension of interdependence, which Rosecrance, Alexandroff, Koehler, Kroll, Lacqueur, and Stocker (1977) refer to as horizontal interdependence.

45. The same kind of question arises about asymmetries in trade balances, about whether creditors and debtors will be comparably affected by conflict and whether, therefore, they are equally free to threaten to disrupt the relationship.

46. Keohane and Nye (1977:9), for example, define what they call sensitivity interdependence as responsiveness to external changes but do not see all exchanges as entailing the reciprocal costs that they see as underlying interdependence. For Keohane and Nye, exchange that entails reciprocal costs is a prerequisite not to vulnerability but to sensitivity interdependence. Where sensitivity entails responsiveness, they see vulnerability as entailing an inability to reduce externally imposed costs through a change in policies. Their distinction is not precise enough to recommend an unambiguous measurement strategy. Moreover, their conceptualization of complex interdependence differs from their discussion of economic interdependence. The former is a political construct that presumes the international political consequences of the latter.

47. Kenneth Waltz (1970, 1979) is the strongest and most consistent exponent of the view that there is no interdependence in the modern world. He advocates a conceptualization of interdependence as vulnerability and mutual dependence, and he criticizes those who view it as sensitivity. In keeping with this view, he analyzes data measuring nations' reliance on critical raw material imports such as oil. But Waltz (1979) also adopts a definitional analytic argument holding that great powers in an anarchic international system, because they are functionally equivalent units between which there cannot have developed a division of labor, cannot possibly be interdependent. Were they to be interdependent, they would no longer be great powers.

48. Many economists assume the existence of interdependence and focus on the

international transmission of macroeconomic policies under different exchange rate regimes. For a review, see Helliwell and Padmore (1985).

49. More generally, under those conditions in which free exchange should result in the equalization of factor prices, price comparability is a good measure of interdependence. For Rosecrance, Alexandroff, Koehler, Kroll, Lacqueur, and Stocker (1977), transactions measure horizontal interdependence, whereas cross-national responsiveness to changes in factor prices constitutes vertical interdependence. For Gasiorowski (1986b), horizontal interdependence applies to countries with similar levels of development and factor endowments, whereas vertical interdependence refers to relationships between nations at quite different levels of development and with different factor endowments. For discussions of factor price equalization and European integration, see Tovias (1982), Gremmen (1985), and van Mourik (1987). Also see Mokhtari and Rassekh (1989).

50. For studies by political scientists, see Rosecrance, Alexandroff, Koehler, Kroll, Lacqueur, and Stocker (1977) and the subsequent exchange about it (Tetreault, 1980; Rosecrance and Gutowitz, 1981; Tetreault, 1981). For work by economists, see the review essay by Obstfeld (1986). Also see Cumby and Mishkin (1986), Cumby and Obstfeld (1984), von Furstenberg (1983), Glick (1987), and Mishkin (1984). Note that even so specific an empirical emphasis as the consequences of openness can be assessed in different ways. It is possible to analyze the consequences of capital mobility, and so to assess changes in capital mobility itself, by comparing either asset yields (interest rates) across countries or the relationship between savings and investment. The latter approach originated in an important paper by Feldstein and Horioka (1980).

51. Indices of financial and monetary interdependence are less widely used, largely because of the paucity of good data, especially for the years prior to World War II. Kar (1983) argues that a measure of financial openness is the ratio of gross financial flows (inflows and outflows) to national income. This captures the importance of external financial transactions relative to the size of the domestic economy and is quite similar to the ratio of international exchange (imports and exports) to national income, a measure that is used to measure trade openness. Kar criticized Grassman (1980), who, for reasons of data availability, instead used a ratio of net (rather than gross) capital flows (i.e., the current account balance) to national income.

52. Writing a decade and a half after the end of World War II, Deutsch and Eckstein (1961) emphasized the declining importance of foreign trade. More than 10 years later, Rosecrance and Stein (1973) and Katzenstein (1975) found that ratios of trade to income had continued to grow after the war and had reached new heights. Grassman (1980) fit trend lines to the century-long pattern of decline and growth and found no unambiguous trends. All these studies used a ratio of trade to national income. Beenstock and Warburton (1983) suggested that "real openness" should be measured by a ratio of trade to national income and that the ratio should be adjusted for price movements. This, they demonstrated, unambiguously shows that by the 1970s, openness exceeded earlier levels.

53. For a discussion of this regarding Western European trade and integration, see Clark and Welch (1972).

54. The measures developed to assess inequality and concentration are similar. In fact, the Gini inequality measure is also known as the Gini concentration ratio. There are many articles and books comparing such measures. See Cowell (1977) and the works cited therein. In addition, also see Alker and Russett (1966), Caporaso (1974), Gastwirth (1975), Gini (1921), Morris (1972), and Woytinsky (1943).

55. See the discussion of this issue by Jones (1987).

56. This differs from the discussion above, in which different conceptualizations (called dimensions by some) of interdependence are described as the functions of different ways of looking at one aspect of interaction. The issue here derives from the existence of different kinds of transaction flows.

57. This issue arose in the study of regional integration (Bernstein, 1972; Lindberg, 1970; Puchala, 1970).

58. Trade openness and financial openness were not especially highly correlated in the 1960s (Whitman, 1969). It may be that trade openness cannot necessarily be sustained past some level without concomitant financial openness. If so, one would lag behind the other.

59. By contrast, during the last century, when neither passports nor work permits were required, there was immense migration in and from Europe.

60. There might be disputes, however, between proponents of different aggregation and clustering procedures entailing different conceptual logics.

61. The same situation exists within nations as well. Capital mobility within the United States is not matched by labor mobility. Yet if regions are clearly seen as segments of an integrated national market, then it is possible to have interdependence without complete factor mobility and without complete equalization of factor prices.

62. Direct foreign investment can be seen as a substitute for exports. The issue of transaction substitution also arises when market exchanges can be internalized as intrafirm ones. A literature on transactions cost economics focuses on such internalization to explain the growth of firms, including the development of multinational enterprises. For a review, see Teece (1986).

63. This is one way to differentiate between scholars who stress the relative political importance of sensitivity interdependence and those who emphasize vulnerability interdependence. Those who hold that sensitivity interdependence increases cooperation are arguing, in effect, that even the marginal benefits of such links tip the political calculus toward cooperation. On the other hand, those who hold that only vulnerability interdependence generates cooperation are arguing, in effect, that the cost/benefit consequences of such links must be much greater in order for them to affect the political calculus of states.

64. To my knowledge, no one has attempted this, and the parameter estimates (and their variances) from extant studies cannot be compared.

65. These studies do not adjust the value of trade for the size of the economy, nor do they weigh cooperative and conflictual events by any measure of intensity. Further, despite developing a conceptualization of interdependence as a bilateral phenomenon, they employ no measures of trade-partner concentration.

66. Similarly, trade had more of an affect on the conflict behavior of the Warsaw

Pact toward the United States than vice versa, presumably because the Warsaw Pact nations benefitted more from the trade (Gasiorowski and Polachek, 1982).

67. Domke (1988) also uses two other measures, both of which predict less well a nation's likelihood of being involved in war at any particular time. One of these is the change in the proportion of exports to GNP; the other is the residual observation from a regression of export proportion onto GNP. This latter variable is intended to control for the fact that great powers tend to have large economies and, in general, trade proportionately less of their GNPs than small powers.

68. Domke's (1988) analytic discussion is richer than his empirical analysis. He develops three links between commerce and war, but the data and analysis are insufficiently precise to capture the subtlety of the various arguments he delineates linking trade decisions to war.

69. Here, the data on conflict behavior is weighted for both intensity and the percentage a country's trade conducted with the target nation.

70. A study by Sayrs (1989) separately regresses the amount of cooperation and the amount of conflict on measures of trade and finds that trade can affect one without affecting the other. The study is also notable for controlling for plausible rival explanations, for disaggregating and separately estimating effects on economic as distinguished from military cooperation, and for separately estimating relationships for high- and low-volume traders. Yet the analyses are not well rooted theoretically.

71. A good place to begin entry into the literature is through the discussions by Snidal (1985) and Conybeare (1987).

72. Rosecrance (1973:chaps. 14 and 15) develops a hierarchical model of national interests in which security and ideology are pursued as objectives ahead of material wealth. See also the discussion of lexicographic preferences in Stein (1990:chap. 4).

73. For recent empirical work that finds such a relationship, see Pollins (1989*a* & *b*). Also see Summary (1989).

74. For an explanation of foreign economic policy, including trade, investment, and foreign aid, in the context of a state's grand strategy, see Skalnes (in progress). For an argument that the implications of economic interdependence vary with the degree of threat in the international system, see Papayoanou (in progress).

75. The exceptions provided by state enterprises and government loans are so marginal as not to matter.

76. Conversely, the absence of a link between state and society might mean that links between two governments would have no repercussions on either's society or domestic economy. International political accommodation achieved by a royal marriage, for example, would not affect the divisions between the two societies. A domestic version of this phenomenon is evident in consociational democracies, in which elites reach agreements that have no fundamental repercussions on divisions within the society.

77. Not surprisingly, reliance on import taxes is more prevalent among developing countries than among developed countries (Stein, 1984). Moreover, one implication of lower tariffs is higher domestic taxes (Rousslang, 1987).

78. Border control can, of course, be imperfect; smugglers can always evade it. On

the other hand, the scope of smuggling cannot be the basis for any substantial growth of exchange and interdependence.

79. There were cases, especially in the nineteenth century, when commercial openness was coerced rather than achieved voluntarily (Stein, 1984).

80. During the economic crisis of 1981–1982, the Polish government declared martial law and, for a time, unplugged from the international phone system so that information about its domestic problems would not reach the West.

81. The overall argument being made here is akin to that made about the existence of a market presupposing a minimal government that provides and enforces a structure of property rights and enforces contracts. Stein (1990:chap. 2) discusses the role of regimes in providing coordination, especially in areas that facilitate transportation and exchange.

82. Keohane (1990) characterizes arguments that recognize the importance of rules and institutions for international relations as "regulatory liberalism." He argues that this is separate from liberal arguments about the effect of trade, which he dubs "commercial liberalism." He calls the synthesis of these two "sophisticated liberalism." The argument I make here is that commerce depends on an institutional political infrastructure.

83. The conjuncture of this view with an argument that commerce and exchange require political stability and certainty can lead to the conclusion that peace generates trade, rather than the other way around. Yet the commerce generated by peace, or cooperative bilateral relationships, is itself consequential in changing subsequent calculations of the costs and benefits to be derived from cooperative or conflictual policies.

84. The global debt crisis of the 1980s illuminated the political basis of capital flows as it became clear that the exposures of national banks varied. The Europeans held more Eastern European debt; the United States had lent more to Latin America. If capital flowed only on the basis of rates of return, such a pattern would not have been likely to occur. It may be that such a pattern reflects differential information, but then this, too, reflects the past history of political (and geopolitical) links and ties. The basic political links between nations, together with government encouragement of banks to make certain loans, largely explain the distribution of exposure.

85. See the analysis in Skalnes (in progress). In fact, studies show that economic links do play a role in deterring attacks on one's allies (Russett, 1963a; Fink, 1965; Huth and Russett, 1984; Papayoanou, in progress). Convincing one's opponent (not to mention one's populace) of the strategic importance of another nation or area often entails developing a broad array of other ties with that country. Wright (1965a) shows that conflicts with higher costs are less likely to escalate.

86. For an example of American views, see Gardner (1956) and Pollard (1985). For a history of economic links and the forging of the Pacific alliance, see Borden (1984). For a general discussion and postwar examples of trade being subordinated to security, see Holsti (1986). For nineteenth-century examples as well as more recent ones, see Stein (1984).

87. For an intellectual history of evolving conceptions of unemployment, see Garraty (1978).

88. This responsibility exists virtually independent of the form of government, and it increases with the degree of industrialization and economic development. Indeed, one can imagine a modern explanation for authoritarian governments in precisely these terms. Whereas in earlier times monarchies could avoid numerous responsibilities, the very range of modern governmental responsibilities seems to require authoritarian solutions. If a government is to be held responsible for maintaining employment, then there exists a logic for its grabbing control of aspects of the means of production and politicizing decisions about resource allocation by removing some of them from private hands.

89. Adam Smith recognized that opening a domestic market to foreign competition would lead to suffering, especially by the owners of fixed capital, who could not dispose of such wealth without substantial losses. He argued, therefore, that such changes "should never be introduced suddenly, but slowly, gradually, and after a very long warning" (Smith, 1979:471).

90. One implication is that political enfranchisement and increasing political participation had important consequences for trade policy during the nineteenth century (Milward, 1981).

91. For articles linking protection with the business cycle, see Gallarotti (1985), Gourevitch (1986), McKeown (1984), and Cassing, McKeown, and Ochs (1986). The implication of the argument in this entire section is that protection is manifest even in good times and even absent a societal demand for it.

92. That politicians are more responsive to specific electoral threats than to potential electoral promise can also be explained with the psychological findings that losses loom larger than gains (Kahneman and Tversky, 1979).

93. In the late 1980s, a Pentagon study urged government support for the semiconductor industry on just such grounds (Sanger, 1987). An economic basis exists for such support in some cases (Thompson, 1979).

94. Although NATO was formed in 1949, its member nations still duplicated one another's defense industries in 1990. They have been willing to outspend the Warsaw Pact on conventional forces and to allow duplication, but have been unwilling to standardize equipment and allow specialization and interdependence. Trade liberalization has even been suggested as a means to weapons standardization (Wolf and Leebaert, 1978).

95. South Korea used quotas on the importation of foreign movies in an attempt to ensure the development and survival of a domestic film industry. Companies were allowed to import one film for every four they produced. In response to American complaints, the Koreans replaced this requirement with one that importers contribute to a fund for the promotion of domestic film production (Jameson, 1984; see also Pagano, 1985). French and Japanese industrial policies aimed at ensuring the existence and survival of native producers of certain goods provide other examples. Johnson (1965) develops a theory of protection by positing a "preference for industrial production."

96. Even though the market for microelectronic applications is growing, governments have become concerned with the market share of foreign producers and with the risks of relying on others for such products. The United States and Western Europe

have responded with a variety of measures. The European reaction is described in Becker (1983).

97. Indeed, there is a long-standing recognition in economic theory of a logic for some degree of protection. But most economists nonetheless opposed protection on practical and political grounds (Humphrey, 1987). A modern example of an economic basis for protectionism is provided by strategic trade policy; for reviews see Stegemann (1989) and Richardson (1990).

98. They argued that their subsidization of research and development at Airbus was equivalent to Pentagon military contracts awarded to U.S. civilian aircraft manufacturers.

99. There is a massive literature on industrial policy. For discussions of different kinds of national industrial policies, see Diebold (1980), Katzenstein (1985), McKay and Grant (1983, and the rest of this special issue of the journal), and Pinder (1982). On Japan, see Wheeler, Janow, and Pepper (1982) and especially Johnson (1982), who argues that the role of the Japanese state has been similar to that of other late industrializers, that of a "developmental state" taking on "developmental functions."

100. Cooper (1987:250–251) points out that many factors can influence comparative advantage: "It would be absurd to pretend otherwise and to treat each geographic area as a tabula rasa with natural endowments but with no social or political system."

101. Much the same is true of foreign investment. States want foreign investment yet regulate it. For a typology of regulation, see Reich (1989).

102. Such programs include export credit arrangements. For a discussion of the competition among industrial nations in providing export credits, and their tortuous path to an agreement, see Moravcsik (1989).

103. These observations are as true of weak as of strong states. Political scientists have recently distinguished between states strong and autonomous enough to impose their views of their nations' interests on society and those unable to do so. Implicit in this literature is the view that weak states pursue protectionism because they cannot resist the demands of domestic protectionist forces, whereas strong states can impose adjustment. Yet there are research traditions that emphasize state strength relative to market forces rather than to domestic interest groups. Strong states can then be seen not as ones strong enough to impose adjustment but as ones strong enough to resist market forces in a way that weak penetrated states cannot. Dependency theorists, for example, emphasize this kind of weakness and argue that some third-world states are so weak that they cannot resist market adjustment. Analytically, there is no reason to expect any systematic relationship between the strength of a state and its choice of particular policies. Strong states are likely to be more interventionist and activist, but this can be to ensure the competitiveness of exports. Weak states can be penetrated by exporters as well as by domestic firms whose products compete with imports.

104. The literature on the new protectionism is vast. For examples, see Balassa (1978), Krauss (1978), and Salvatore (1987). Concern about the trading order is evinced by, among others, Aho and Bayard (1982), Long (1978), and Tumlir (1978–1979). For a review of the revival of protectionist thinking in Europe, see Kahler (1985).

105. This discussion makes clear why there is no consistent correlation between

hegemony and openness. A hegemonic United States could not impose openness; in fact, it acceded to many departures from liberal principles. Yet slow liberalization did accompany a rapid growth in trade. The decline of American hegemony has not meant either the return to closure or the end of efforts at further liberalization, for the relative economic decline of the United States does not change the fact that there remain benefits to be gained from further liberalization and costs from closure.

106. Demands for protection are sector- and industry-specific and therefore vary with the economic performance of particular industries. Some industries, of course, can perform poorly even in periods of general growth, whereas others can do well during recessions. Overall, however, the business cycle matters in that the performance of most industries varies with it. For a discussion that links the business cycle to old versus new regions, see Cassing, McKeown, and Ochs (1986). The demand by labor for protection may also vary with such circumstances as whether, for example, the work force is growing and the demand for labor exceeds union membership (Wallerstein, 1987).

107. Even as auto workers and producers pressed for import constraints in the 1980s, dealers and distributors of imported cars opposed them. An association of foreign car dealers organized against such protectionism. In developing countries, also, domestic interests with ties to imports have opposed protection (Amelung, 1989).

108. Governments that want to fend off protectionist demands can also encourage efforts on behalf of free trade. The Reagan administration did this during its battle against domestic content legislation. For an analysis of antiprotectionism and American foreign trade policy, see Destler and Odell (1987).

109. Much the same case can be made about the liberalization of capital markets. Some interests oppose foreign investment; others encourage it. Encarnation and Mason (1990) argue that capital liberalization in Japan cannot be understood as a product of American pressure, but that its timing and substance were dictated by local oligopolists with an interest in technologies controlled by foreign firms.

110. Frieden (1988) argues that American foreign economic policy in the 1930s reflected the struggle between those domestic economic actors with preferences for internationalist policies and those favoring isolationism.

111. Unlike a tariff, which provides the increased domestic price of goods to the importing nation's government as revenue, a VER, which also raises the domestic price, allows the exporting companies to pocket the difference.

112. For a discussion of the international politics of textiles, see Aggarwal (1985).

113. Ironically, though, the protection provided often tends to be illusory. Each extension of the original RTAA and each passage of an entirely new trade act have entailed tightening old procedures or instituting new mechanisms to provide relief from imports. Yet once the trade bill has been passed, the procedures for obtaining relief have tended to work slowly and even to stall without providing any (Goldstein, 1983, 1986). An even broader argument holds that national crises have tended to generate expansions in government's power to regulate trade (Twight, 1985).

114. Such side payments can be argued to reflect the redistribution necessary for liberalization to represent a Pareto-superior improvement.

115. For an alternative characterization of state adjustment strategies, see Ikenberry (1986).

116. Recognition of this fact led to the development of an entire literature devoted to explaining intra-industry trade (Grubel and Lloyd, 1975; Giersch, 1979).

117. The need for protectionist buy-outs, and their economic and political costs, will vary as a function of political systems, the strength and insulation of ruling elites, and the access of societal interests to the political system.

118. For the development of an important distinction between diffuse and specific reciprocity, see Keohane (1986).

119. Indeed, the major pieces of tariff legislation that scholars consider elements of the return to protection in the last quarter of the nineteenth century were enacted prior to renegotiations of trade agreements (Stein, 1984).

120. Hence, exporting firms that depend on openness can support threatening closure in the hope of increasing market access (Milner and Yoffie, 1989).

121. This almost occurred in 1970, when Wilbur Mills championed protectionist legislation only in order to provide ammunition to the White House in its negotiations for a textile agreement with Japan. When talks broke down and the White House decided to support the bill, Mills feared the measure might actually pass. It did not, but Mills still found himself trapped by a commitment he had made to textile producers to seek quotas if no agreement was reached. Opposed to such legislation except in order to provide a bargaining chip, and believing that the administration had botched the trade talks, Mills went to Japan himself in order to secure an agreement that would assuage the textile lobby and so ensure that no quotas came into being (Destler, Fukui, and Sato, 1979).

122. Other economists also recognized the possibility of pursuing trade reciprocity (Humphrey, 1987).

123. This point does not apply to states that are so tiny that their markets do not matter to others and that cannot, therefore, further undercut their nonexistent bargaining leverage.

124. For an empirical examination of the utility of reciprocity in trade liberalization, see Rhodes (1989), as well as Gadbaw (1982).

125. The famous trade wars of the late nineteenth century were all fought as part of the renegotiations of expired trade agreements (Stein, 1984). They were very much like strikes that occur during labor-management negotiations.

126. In the Tokyo Round, negotiators concluded a number of agreements concerning NTBs. Among the issues involved were opening government procurement to foreign bidders and notification of new product standards (Krasner, 1979).

127. Migue (1982) argues that government regulations and the bureaucratic supply of goods have the same effects as trade barriers.

128. For discussions of harmonization, see Johnson (1968) and Liesner (1971). On coordination, see Buiter and Marston (1985).

129. Indeed, the impact of changes in exchange rates can quickly dwarf alterations in tariff levels. Further, the views of economists about the causal direction between

trade and capital flows have shifted dramatically. In the past, they held that trade imbalances determined capital flows and exchange rate movements. The current conventional wisdom is that capital flows drive trade imbalances.

130. Bergsten (1975) argues that an overvalued dollar better predicts protectionist pressures in the United States than does the business cycle.

131. Economists emphasize the reduced ability of domestic macroeconomic policy to affect outcomes in an economy open to external economic forces (Cooper, 1973; Lindbeck, 1978). My own emphasis is less on the state's loss of autonomy than on the international economic and political impact of divergent policies and practices in a host of domains. Dissenting economists have noted that coordination can sometimes be counterproductive (Rogoff, 1985) and can depend critically on adequate knowledge of the economic links between economies (Frankel and Rockett, 1988).

132. Japanese business leaders have campaigned for reductions in corporate tax rates, pointing out that in 1982 and 1983, Japanese firms paid an average of 51.3 percent of profits in corporate taxes, whereas American firms averaged 33 percent (*Los Angeles Times*, 17 September 1984:pt. 4, p. 3). Ironically, American business leaders, in campaigning for accelerated depreciation, have emphasized that the cost of capital is lower in Japan (Albertine, 1985; see also Behr, 1984). Not surprisingly, the U.S. tax reform package was followed by changes in other industrial nations' tax laws. And liberalization of capital markets in Europe was followed by pressures for tax harmonization (Isard, 1990).

133. The United States became embroiled in a dispute with Canada when it deregulated its trucking industry and the Canadians left theirs unchanged. There had been no conflict as long as both countries imposed similar trucking regulations. Similarly, problems accompanied the drive to deregulate financial markets, an effort that spread from one industrial nation to another in the 1980s and led to international efforts to coordinate banking regulations (Kapstein, 1989). Antitrust policy provides an excellent example of the impact of different national conceptions of what is legal. U.S. antitrust policy does not allow American firms to cooperate in overseas marketing. Yet Japanese traders do things in the United States that would be illegal for American companies to do abroad. This led Mike Mansfield, the American ambassador to Japan, to urge a change in America's "antiquated antitrust laws" (Jameson, 1985c). Not only do antitrust policies vary, so, too, do the prospects for judicial relief. Whereas the U.S. Supreme Court ruled that foreign governments could sue for punitive damages under American antitrust laws, Great Britain denied the request of a U.S. court for evidence related to monopolistic practices, arguing "it is axiomatic that in anti-trust matters the policy of one state may be to defend what it is the policy of another state to attack" (Tumlir, 1978–1979:63).

134. The relative cost of environmental regulations may also drive decisions about where to locate plants. The industrial-flight hypothesis argues that firms leave industrial countries because of increasingly tough environmental laws. The pollution-haven hypothesis argues that firms are drawn to underdeveloped societies with the most lax environmental laws. But empirical studies have not found much evidence of any

impact of environmental laws and policies on either firm location or general trade patterns (Leonard, 1988; Tobey, 1990).

135. The Japanese have even justified tariffs on environmental grounds. They argue that to prevent environmental problems, such as landslides, they need to nurture sturdier trees by thinning their forests. To ensure that essential thinning occurs, they argue, they must maintain a domestic market for Japanese lumber. Hence, they keep a tariff on forestry products (Jameson, 1985d).

136. Indeed, it is possible to argue that measures adopted for the purpose of protection, such as minimum quality standards or requirements that products be labeled to identify national origin, have a valuable nonprotective role for both consumers and producers (Falvey, 1989).

137. This argument can be made, for example, about a Houdaille Industries trade complaint about unfair Japanese competition in the machine tool industry. Houdaille had charged that Japan's industrial policy provided its producers with an unfair advantage. One could retort, however, that the Japanese were only compensating for the implicit industrial policy embodied in Defense Department policies that had aided the American machine tool industry during the 1950s (Holland, 1989).

138. The economist J.E. Meade points out that the United Kingdom subsidized the consumption of milk, which was produced at home, while taxing the consumption of wine, which was produced abroad. Was this "an inadmissible interference with . . . optimisation," he wonders, or "a legitimate case of social economies and diseconomies" (Robson, 1980:100–101).

139. The broad array of institutional differences can encompass such elements as the structure of labor and capital markets and the nature of government policy instruments. See Black (1982), Rybczynski (1984), Vittas (1986), and Katzenstein (1977).

140. There have been some cases of internal tariffs, tariffs within a nation. The French physiocrats supported free trade "primarily because they desired the freedom of domestic trade" (Gide and Rist, 1913:29).

141. Moreover, the existence of rampant local graft and corruption gives some indication of the difficulty of enforcing equal treatment provisions for local procurement.

142. Rogowski (1987) demonstrates that nations that trade a great deal are more likely to have systems of proportional representation because, he argues, nations that are very open to the international economy must have policy stability, continuity, and consistency—hallmarks of systems marked by proportional representation.

143. This discussion draws upon California, State Assembly (1986).

144. Problems can also arise between nations with similar political systems when each locates the authority over a particular issue at a different level of government. In the middle 1980s, a dispute broke out between the United States and Canada over lumber. At issue was the stumpage fees that lumber companies pay landowners to harvest timber. In Canada, 95 percent of the timberland is owned by provincial governments, which set the stumpage fees. In the United States, public timber forests are federally owned. The United States used different procedures for setting stumpage fees than did the provincial governments of Canada, and American lumber executives

pressed for protection against what they considered subsidized Canadian lumber exports (Martin, 1985).

145. For discussions linking ideology and national competitiveness, see Lodge and Vogel (1987).

146. For a contrast of American and British approaches to regulation, see Vogel (1986).

147. More broadly, the American preoccupation with Japanese practices of all kinds reflects these pressures for harmonization. Many American firms eagerly seek the key to Japanese success and want to duplicate it, whether it entails the nature of inventory practices (e.g., just-in-time delivery of components) or the organization of work (e.g., quality circles). Eventually, the United States may obtain national health insurance because American corporations come to oppose the American Medical Association and press for the socialization of an expense that they bear but which few of their overseas competitors do.

148. Abbott and Totman (1981) distinguish between three levels of barriers to trade. Tariffs and quotas are first-level barriers, government policies and practices are second-level barriers, and cultural patterns and social attitudes are third-level barriers.

149. The average Japanese worker works 200 hours more a year than the average American worker.

150. This provides another example, like that involving stumpage fees (see footnote 144 above), in which a national government does not have control over a policy that another country wishes to see altered. In the United States, of course, education policy is in the purview of the states, which often turn it over to local school districts.

151. The successful agreement to negotiate free trade with Canada in the late 1980s contrasts with three earlier twentieth-century efforts, all of which foundered.

152. For an analysis of the tortuous and limited movement toward fiscal harmonization in Europe, see Puchala (1984).

153. Distortionary governmental policies can be a problem even within a single country. Cities and states within the United States compete for industries and jobs by offering tax inducements and/or freer regulatory environments. States' differential tax practices affect the relative competitiveness of firms. When discussing state support for Research Triangle Park (a development intended, in part, to maintain a state presence in the computer industry), the North Carolina legislator, and future governor, James Hunt said that, in effect, North Carolina was telling the Silicon Valley that it did not intend to let the computer chips fall where they may. Just as competition continues within nations, so will it continue between nations. The economic competition between states remains bounded, however, because of the overarching power and authority of the federal government.

154. No knowledge of means-ends relationships provides policy prescriptions unless societal goals are presumed. Moreover, knowledge need not bring with it an ability to control if it is not related to the policy levers at the disposal of government, if the causal impact of policy levers is small relative to other factors, or if events are not reversible.

155. Dunn (1987) makes the same kind of case about trade in automobiles, that it

was not as liberal in the 1950s and 1960s as many think, nor as protectionist in the 1980s as some claim. For another argument that does not despair of recent events, see Strange (1985). More broadly, see Willoughby (1982a).

I would argue that a similar argument can be made about the latter part of the nineteenth century, an era that most scholars characterize as increasingly protectionist. They point to the adoption by many European states of new tariff acts that called for higher duties, to a decline in trade relative to gross national product, and to the tariff wars as epitomizing an era of closure. Yet the tariff wars broke out in the midst of trade negotiations, and most trade treaties were renegotiated when they expired and new ones were also struck. What is striking about the period is the degree of international trade that was sustained during an extended depression in which a number of the European states began to industrialize.

156. The MFN clause transformed trade, an inherently divisible private good, into a collective one (Stein 1984, 1990:208).

157. This proved to be especially fortunate when the planned International Trade Organization (ITO) was stillborn.

158. Free trade classically entailed two components, lowering or removing barriers to trade and doing away with discrimination. Yet the classic discriminatory instrument, the bilateral trade agreement, became the vehicle for nondiscrimination when unconditional most-favored-nation clauses were incorporated.

159. It may even be the story of the evolution of events in North America, as Mexico responded to the U.S.–Canadian free trade agreement by expressing its interest in similar discussions. It is also the story of various preferential arrangements, such as those that the European Community has negotiated with various countries.

160. Although he emphasized the ideological component of frustrating Soviet designs and stressed the limits of totalitarian rule, his argument contained an economic element as well.

161. The issue is more complicated, because various hybrid possibilities also existed (e.g., military containment conjoined with increasing commercial exchange).

162. Indeed, some would argue that détente was linked to a new offensive era in Soviet diplomacy.

163. Although the entire chapter, including this section, was written before the demise of the Soviet Union, the analysis holds.

References

Abbott, K.W., and C.D. Totman. 1981. "Black ships" and balance sheets: The Japanese market and U.S.–Japan relations. *Northwestern Journal of International Law and Business* 3:103–154.

Aggarwal, V.K. 1985. *Liberal Protectionism: The International Politics of Organized Textile Trade.* Berkeley, Calif.: University of California Press.

Aggarwal, V.K., R.O. Keohane, and D.B. Yoffie. 1987. The dynamics of negotiated protectionism. *American Political Science Review* 81:345–366.

Aho, C.M., and T.O. Bayard. 1982. The 1980s: Twilight of the open trading system? *World Economy* 5:379–406.

Albertine, J.M. 1985. Why stifle U.S. business competitiveness? *Los Angeles Times*, pt. 2, p. 7, 4 December.

Alker, H.R., Jr. 1973. On political capabilities in a schedule sense: Measuring power, integration, and development. In H.R. Alker, Jr., K.W. Deutsch, and A.H. Stoetzel, eds., *Mathematical Approaches to Politics*, pp. 307–375. San Francisco: Jossey-Bass Publishers.

Alker, H.R., Jr., and D. Puchala. 1968. Trends in economic partnership: The North Atlantic area, 1928–1963. In J.D. Singer, ed., *Quantitative International Politics: Insights and Evidence*, pp. 287–315. New York: Free Press.

Alker, H.R., Jr., and B.M. Russett. 1966. Indices for comparing inequality. In R.L. Merritt and S. Rokkan, eds., *Comparing Nations: The Use of Quantitative Data in Cross-national Research*, pp. 349–372. New Haven, Conn.: Yale University Press.

Allen, R.L., and I. Walter. 1971. *The Formation of United States Trade Policy: Retrospect and Prospect*. New York: New York University, Graduate School of Business Administration, Institute of Finance.

Amelung, T. 1989. The determinants of protection in developing countries: An extended interest-group approach. *Kyklos* 42(4):515–532.

Angell, N. 1913. *The Great Illusion: A Study of the Relation of Military Power to National Advantage*, 4th rev. and enl. ed. New York: Putnam's.

———. 1921. *The Fruits of Victory: A Sequel to "The Great Illusion"*. New York: The Century Co.

Angell, R. 1969. *Peace on the March: Transnational Participation*. New York: Van Nostrand.

Arad, R.W., and S. Hirsch. 1981. Peacemaking and vested interests: International economic transactions. *International Studies Quarterly* 25:439–468.

Arad, R., S. Hirsch, and A. Tovias. 1983. *The Economics of Peacemaking: Focus on the Egyptian-Israeli Situation*. New York: St. Martin's.

Auerbach, S. 1984. Corn belt champions free trade. *Los Angeles Times*, pt. 4, p. 2, 30 July.

———. 1986. Imagine, a continent of Japans. *Washington Post National Weekly Edition*, 16, 31 March.

Badaracco, J.L., Jr., and D.B. Yoffie. 1983. "Industrial policy": It can't happen here. *Harvard Business Review* (November/December):97–105.

Balassa, B. 1978. The new protectionism and the world economy. *Journal of World Trade Law* 12:409–436.

Baldwin, D.A. 1980. Interdependence and power: A conceptual analysis. *International Organization* 34:471–506.

Baldwin, R.E. 1982. The political economy of protectionism. In J.N. Bhagwati, ed., *Import Competition and Response*, pp. 263–292. Chicago: University of Chicago Press.

———. 1984. Trade policies in developed countries. In R.W. Jones and P.B. Kenen, eds., *Handbook of International Economics*, vol. 1, pp. 571–619. Amsterdam: North-Holland.

Barrera, M., and E.B. Haas. 1969. The operationalization of some variables related to regional integration: A research note. *International Organization* 23:150–160.

Batten, D.S., and M. Ott. 1985. The president's proposed corporate tax reforms: A move toward tax neutrality. *Federal Reserve Bank of St. Louis Review* 67:5–17.

Becker, J. 1983. Thinking big on microchips. *Europe* (January/February):26–27.

Beenstock, M., and P. Warburton. 1983. Long-term trends in economic openness in the United Kingdom and the United States. *Oxford Economic Papers* 35:130–135.

Behr, P. 1984. Low cost of capital gives Japanese an immense industrial advantage. *Los Angeles Times*, pt. 4, p. 3, 2 July.

Bergsten, C.F. 1975. On the non-equivalence of import quotas and "voluntary" export restraints. In *Toward a New International Economic Order: Selected Papers of C. Fred Bergsten, 1972–1974*, pp. 157–189. Lexington, Mass.: D.C. Heath and Company.

Berlin, I. 1969. Two concepts of liberty. In *Four Essays on Liberty*, pp. 118–172. New York: Oxford University Press.

Bernstein, R.A. 1972. International integration: Multidimensional or unidimensional? *Journal of Conflict Resolution* 16:403–408.

Black, C.E. 1966. *The Dynamics of Modernization*. New York: Harper and Row.

Black, S.W. 1982. *Politics Versus Markets: International Differences in Macroeconomic Policies*. Washington, D.C.: American Enterprise Institute.

Blackford, M.G., and K.A. Kerr. 1990. *Business Enterprise in American History*, 2nd ed. Boston: Houghton Mifflin.

Blainey, G. 1973. *The Causes of War*. New York: Free Press.

Bond, E.W., and S.E. Guisinger. 1985. Investment incentives as tariff substitutes: A comprehensive measure of protection. *Review of Economics and Statistics* 67:91–97.

Borden, W.S. 1984. *The Pacific Alliance: United States Foreign Economic Policy and Japanese Trade Recovery, 1947–1955*. Madison, Wis.: University of Wisconsin Press.

Bosanquet, H. 1924. *Free Trade and Peace in the Nineteenth Century*. Publications de L'Institut Nobel Norvégien, Tome VI. New York: Putnam's.

Brams, S.J. 1966a. Trade in the North Atlantic area. *Peace Research Society (International) Papers* 6:143–164.

———. 1966b. Transaction flows in the international system. *American Political Science Review* 60:880–899.

———. 1968. A note on the cosmopolitanism of world regions. *Journal of Peace Research* 5(1):87–95.

Buck, P.W. 1942. *The Politics of Mercantilism*. New York: Henry Holt and Company.

Buiter, W.H., and R.C. Marston, eds. 1985. *International Economic Policy Coordination*. Cambridge, England: Cambridge University Press.

Bullock, A., and M. Shock, eds. 1956. *The Liberal Tradition: From Fox to Keynes*. London: Adam and Charles Black.

Buzan, B. 1984. Economic structure and international security: The limits of the liberal case. *International Organization* 38(Autumn):597–624.

Cain, P.J. 1978. J.A. Hobson, Cobdenism and the development of the theory of economic imperialism. *Economic History Review* 31:565–584.

———. 1979. Capitalism, war and internationalism in the thought of Richard Cobden. *British Journal of International Studies* 5:229–247.

California, State Assembly, Committee on Revenue and Taxation. 1986. *California Unitary Reform 1986*. No. 0132-A. Sacramento: California State Assembly.

Caplow, T., and K. Finsterbusch. 1968. France and other countries: A study of international interaction. *Journal of Conflict Resolution* 12:1–15.

Caporaso, J. 1974. Methodological issues in the measurement of inequality, dependence, and exploitation. In S.J. Rosen and J.R. Kurth, eds., *Testing Theories of Economic Imperialism*, pp. 87–114. Lexington, Mass.: D.C. Heath and Company.

Cassing, J., T.J. McKeown, and J. Ochs. 1986. The political economy of the tariff cycle. *American Political Science Review* 80:843–862.

Choucri, N., and R.C. North. 1975. *Nations in Conflict: National Growth and International Violence*. San Francisco: W.H. Freeman and Company.

Clark, C., and S. Welch. 1972. Western European trade as a measure of integration: Untangling the interpretations. *Journal of Conflict Resolution* 16:363–382.

Conybeare, J.A.C. 1987. *Trade Wars: The Theory and Practice of International Commercial Rivalry*. New York: Columbia University Press.

Cooper, R.N. 1968. *The Economics of Interdependence: Economic Policy in the Atlantic Community*. New York: McGraw-Hill.

———. 1972. Economic interdependence and foreign policy in the seventies. *World Politics* 24:159–181.

———. 1973. *Economic Mobility and National Economic Policy*. Wicksell Lecture. Stockholm: Almqvist and Wicksell International.

———. 1985. Economic interdependence and coordination of economic policies. In R.W. Jones and P.B. Kenen, eds., *Handbook of International Economics*, vol. 2, pp. 1195–1239. Amsterdam: North-Holland.

———. 1987. Industrial policy and trade distortion. In D. Salvatore, ed., *The New Protectionist Threat to World Welfare*, pp. 233–265. New York: North-Holland.

Cowell, F.A. 1977. *Measuring Inequality: Techniques for the Social Sciences*. New York: Wiley.

Cumby, R.E., and F.S. Mishkin. 1986. The international linkage of real interest rates: The European–U.S. connection. *Journal of International Money and Finance* 5:5–23.

Cumby, R.E., and M. Obstfeld. 1984. International interest rate and price level linkages under flexible exchange rates: A review of recent evidence. In J.F.O. Bilson and R.C. Marston, eds., *Exchange Rate Theory and Practice*, pp. 121–151. Chicago: University of Chicago Press.

Destler, I.M., H. Fukui, and H. Sato. 1979. *The Textile Wrangle: Conflict in*

Japanese-American Relations, 1969–1971. Ithaca, N.Y.: Cornell University Press.

Destler, I.M., and J.S. Odell. 1987. *Anti-Protection: Changing Forces in United States Trade Politics.* Washington, D.C.: Institute for International Economics.

Deutsch, K.W. 1953. *Nationalism and Social Communication: An Inquiry into the Foundations of Nationality.* New York: Wiley.

―――. 1956. Shifts in the balance of communication flows: A problem of measurement in international relations. *Public Opinion Quarterly* 20:143–160.

―――. 1960. The propensity to international transactions. *Political Studies* 8:147–156.

―――. 1964. Transaction flows as indicators of political cohesion. In P.E. Jacob and J.V. Toscano, eds., *The Integration of Political Communities*, pp. 75–97. Philadelphia: Lippincott.

―――. 1966a. Integration and arms control in the European political environment: A summary report. *American Political Science Review* 60:354–365.

―――. 1966b. Power and communication in international society. In A. de Reuek and J. Knight, eds., *Conflict in Society*, pp. 300–316. Boston: Little, Brown.

―――. 1968. The impact of communications upon international relations theory. In A.A. Said, ed., *Theory of International Relations: The Crisis of Relevance*, pp. 74–92. Englewood Cliffs, N.J.: Prentice-Hall.

―――. 1969. *Nationalism and Its Alternatives.* New York: Knopf.

Deutsch, K.W., C.I. Bliss, and A. Eckstein. 1962. Population, sovereignty and the share of foreign trade. *Economic Development and Cultural Change* 10:353–366.

Deutsch, K.W., and A. Eckstein. 1961. National industrialization and the declining share of the international economic sector, 1890–1959. *World Politics* 13:267–299.

Deutsch, K.W., and B.M. Russett. 1963. International trade and political independence. *American Behavioral Scientist* 6:18–20.

Diaz Alejandro, C.F. 1981. Open economy, closed polity? *Millennium: Journal of International Studies* 10:203–219.

Diebold, W., Jr. 1980. *Industrial Policy as an International Issue.* New York: McGraw-Hill.

Domke, W.K. 1988. *War and the Changing Global System.* New Haven, Conn.: Yale University Press.

Doyle, M.W. 1983a. Kant, liberal legacies, and foreign affairs. *Philosophy and Public Affairs* 12:205–235.

―――. 1983b. Kant, liberal legacies, and foreign affairs, part 2. *Philosophy and Public Affairs* 12:323–353.

―――. 1986. Liberalism and world politics. *American Political Science Review* 80:1151–1169.

Drew, E. 1985. A reporter in Washington. *New Yorker*, 73, 5 August.

Dunn, J.A., Jr. 1987. Automobiles in international trade: Regime change or persistence? *International Organization* 41:225–252.

East, M.A., and P.M. Gregg. 1967. Factors influencing cooperation and conflict in the international system. *International Studies Quarterly* 11:244–269.

Economist. 1988. A survey of Europe's international market. 9 July.

Eichengreen, B. 1984. Keynes and protection. *Journal of Economic History* 44:363–373.

Encarnation, D.J., and M. Mason. 1990. Neither MITI nor America: The political economy of capital liberalization in Japan. *International Organization* 44:25–54.

Falvey, R.E. 1989. Trade, quality reputations and commercial policy. *International Economic Review* 30:607–622.

Feldstein, H.S. 1967. A study of transaction and political integration: Transnational labour flow within the European Economic Community. *Journal of Common Market Studies* 6:24–55.

Feldstein, M., and C. Horioka. 1980. Domestic saving and international capital flows. *Economic Journal* 90:314–329.

Fink, C.F. 1965. More calculations about deterrence. *Journal of Conflict Resolution* 9:54–65.

Fisher, W.E. 1969. An analysis of the Deutsch social-causal paradigm of political integration. *International Organization* 23:254–290.

Fisk, G.M., and P.S. Pierce. 1923. *International Commercial Policies.* New York: Macmillan.

Fisk, M. 1989. *The State and Justice: An Essay in Political Theory.* Cambridge, England: Cambridge University Press.

Flournoy, F.R. 1946. British liberal theories of international relations, 1848–1898. *Journal of the History of Ideas* 7:195–217.

Frankel, J.A., and K.E. Rockett. 1988. International macroeconomic policy coordination when policymakers do not agree on the true model. *American Economic Review* 78:318–340.

Frey, B. 1985. The political economy of protection. In D. Greenaway, ed., *Current Issues in International Trade*, pp. 139–157. New York: St. Martin's.

Frieden, J. 1988. Sectoral conflict and foreign economic policy, 1914–1940. *International Organization* 42:59–90.

Gadbaw, R.M. 1982. Reciprocity and its implications for U.S. trade policy. *Law and Policy in International Business* 14(3):691–746.

Gallarotti, G.M. 1985. Toward a business-cycle model of tariffs. *International Organization* 39:155–187.

Gallie, W.B. 1978. *Philosophers of Peace and War: Kant, Clausewitz, Marx, Engels, and Tolstoy.* Cambridge, England: Cambridge University Press.

Galtung, J. 1964. Summit meetings and international relations. *Journal of Peace Research* 1(1):36–54.

Gardner, R.N. 1956. *Sterling-Dollar Diplomacy: Anglo-American Collaboration in the Reconstruction of Multilateral Trade.* Oxford: Clarendon Press.

Garraty, J.A. 1978. *Unemployment in History: Economic Thought and Public Policy.* New York: Harper and Row.

Gasiorowski, M.J. 1985. The structure of third world economic interdependence. *International Organization* 39:331–342.

———. 1986a. Economic interdependence and international conflict: Some cross-national evidence. *International Studies Quarterly* 30:23–38.

———. 1986b. Structure and dynamics in international interdependence. In M.A. Tetreault and C.F. Abel, eds., *Dependency Theory and the Return of High Politics*, pp. 71–99. Westport, Conn.: Greenwood Press.

Gasiorowski, M., and S.W. Polachek. 1982. Conflict and interdependence: East-West trade and linkages in the era of détente. *Journal of Conflict Resolution* 26:709–729.

Gastwirth, J.L. 1975. Statistical measures of earnings differentials. *American Statistician* 29:32–35.

Gerrard, B. 1988. Keynes and the policy of practical protectionism. In J. Hillard, ed., *J.M. Keynes in Retrospect: The Legacy of the Keynesian Revolution*, pp. 153–171. Aldershot, Hants, England: Edward Elgar.

Gerschenkron, A. 1962. *Economic Backwardness in Historical Perspective*. Cambridge, Mass.: Harvard University Press.

Gide, C., and C. Rist. 1913. *A History of Economic Doctrines: From the Time of the Physiocrats to the Present Day*. Authorised translation from the 2nd revised and augmented edition of 1913. Boston: D.C. Heath.

Giersch, H., ed. 1979. *On the Economics of Intra-Industry Trade*. Tübingen, Germany: J.C.B. Mohr.

Gilpin, R. 1977. Economic interdependence and national security in historical perspective. In Klaus Knorr and Frank N. Trager, eds., *Economic Issues and National Security*, pp. 19–66. Lawrence: Regents Press of Kansas.

Gini, C. 1921. Measurement of inequality of incomes. *Economic Journal* 31:124–126.

Gleditsch, N.P. 1967. Trends in world airline patterns. *Journal of Peace Research* 4(4):366–408.

———. 1969. The international airline network: A test of the Zipf and Stouffer hypotheses. *Peace Research Society (International) Papers* 11:123–153.

Glick, R. 1987. Interest rate linkages in the Pacific Basin. *Federal Reserve Bank of San Francisco Economic Review* (Summer):31–42.

Gold, B. 1979. Advancing the technological capabilities of industry and national policies. *Research Management* (January):22, 37–41.

Goldstein, J. 1983. A Re-examination of American trade policy: An inquiry into the causes of protectionism. Ph.D. diss., Department of Political Science, University of California, Los Angeles.

———. 1986. The political economy of trade: Institutions of protection. *American Political Science Review* 80:161–184.

Gourevitch, P. 1986. *Politics in Hard Times: Comparative Responses to International Economic Crises*. Ithaca, N.Y.: Cornell University Press.

Grassman, S. 1980. Long-term trends in openness of national economies. *Oxford Economic Papers* 32:123–133.

Greenaway, D., and C. Milner. 1986. *The Economics of Intra-industry Trade*. New York: Basil Blackwell.

Gremmen, H.J. 1985. Testing the factor price equalization theorem in the EC: An alternative approach. *Journal of Common Market Studies* 23:277–286.

Grubel, H.G., and P.J. Lloyd. 1975. *Intra-industry Trade: The Theory and Measurement of International Trade in Differentiated Products*. New York: Wiley.

Guerrieri, P., and P.C. Padoan. 1986. Neomercantilism and international economic stability. *International Organization* 40:29–42.

Hall, J.A. 1987. *Liberalism: Politics, Ideology and the Market*. Chapel Hill, N.C.: University of North Carolina Press.

Harsanyi, J. 1962. The measurement of social power, opportunity costs, and the theory of two-person bargaining games. *Behavioral Science* 7:67–80.

Hart, J. 1976. Three approaches to the measurement of power in international relations. *International Organization* 30:289–305.

Heater, D. 1984. *Peace Through Education: The Contribution of the Council for Education in World Citizenship*. London: Falmer Press.

Helleiner, G.K. 1977. Transnational enterprises and the new political economy of U.S. trade policy. *Oxford Economic Papers* 29:102–127.

Helliwell, J.F., and T. Padmore. 1985. Empirical studies of macroeconomic interdependence. In R.W. Jones and P.B. Kenen, eds., *Handbook of International Economics*, vol. 2, pp. 1107–1151. Amsterdam: North-Holland.

Hinsley, F.H. 1963. *Power and the Pursuit of Peace: Theory and Practice in the History of Relations Between States*. Cambridge, England: Cambridge University Press.

Hirsch, S. 1981. Peace making and economic interdependence. *World Economy* 4:407–417.

Hirschman, A.O. 1945. *National Power and the Structure of Foreign Trade*. Berkeley, Calif.: University of California Press.

———. 1977. *The Passions and the Interests: Political Arguments for Capitalism Before Its Triumph*. Princeton, N.J.: Princeton University Press.

Hobson, J.A. 1919. *Richard Cobden, the International Man*. New York: Holt.

———. 1920. *The Moral of Economic Internationalism*. Boston: Houghton Mifflin.

Hoffmann, S. 1965. Rousseau on war and peace. In *The State of War*, pp. 45–87. New York: Praeger.

Holland, M. 1989. *When the Machine Stopped: A Cautionary Tale from Industrial America*. Boston: Harvard Business School Press.

Holsti, K.J. 1986. Politics in command: Foreign trade as national security policy. *International Organization* 40:643–671.

Hughan, J.W. 1923. *A Study in International Government*. New York: Crowell.

Humphrey, T.M. 1987. Classical and neoclassical roots of the theory of optimum tariffs. *Federal Reserve Bank of Richmond Economic Review* 73:17–28.

Huth, P., and B. Russett. 1984. What makes deterrence work? Cases from 1900 to 1980. *World Politics* 36:496–526.

Ikenberry, G.J. 1986. The state and strategies of international adjustment. *World Politics* 39:53–77.

Isard, P. 1990. Corporate tax harmonization and European monetary integration. *Kyklos* 43(1):3–24.

Jackson, J.H. 1979. United States–EEC trade relations: Constitutional problems of economic interdependence. *Common Market Law Review* 16:453–478.

Jameson, S. 1984. Korea to end film import quotas. *Los Angeles Times*, pt. 4, p. 1, 2 July.

———. 1985*a*. Change culture? Nakasone rejects idea. *Los Angeles Times*, pt. 1, p. 1, 2 August.

———. 1985*b*. Japan pushes shorter work hours. *Los Angeles Times*, pt. 4, p. 3, 20 September.

———. 1985*c*. Mansfield urges Congress, Japan to eliminate strains in trade ties. *Los Angeles Times*, pt. 1, p. 16, 13 July.

———. 1985*d*. Trees, trade and the environment. *Los Angeles Times*, pt. 4, p. 3, 21 June.

Jeremy, D.J. 1977. Damning the flood: British government efforts to check the outflow of technicians and machinery, 1780–1843. *Business History Review* 51: 1–34.

Johnson, C. 1982. *MITI and the Japanese Miracle: The Growth of Industrial Policy, 1925–1975*. Stanford, Calif.: Stanford University Press.

Johnson, H.G. 1965. An economic theory of protectionism, tariff bargaining, and the formation of customs unions. *Journal of Political Economy* 73:256–283.

———. 1968. The implications of free or freer trade for the harmonization of other policies. In H.G. Johnson, P. Wonnacott, and H. Shibata, *Harmonization of National Economic Policies Under Free Trade*, pp. 1–41. In *World Trade and Trade Policy: Comprising Three Studies of the "Canada in the Atlantic Economy" Series*. Toronto: University of Toronto Press.

Jones, C.A. 1987. *International Business in the Nineteenth Century: The Rise and Fall of a Cosmopolitan Bourgeoisie*. New York: New York University Press.

Jones, J.H. 1915. *The Economics of War and Conquest*. London: King and Son.

Jones, R.J.B. 1984. The definition and identification of interdependence. In R.J.B. Jones and P. Willetts, eds., *Interdependence on Trial: Studies in the Theory and Reality of Contemporary Interdependence*, pp. 17–63. New York: St. Martin's.

Jorgenson, D.W., and M.A. Sullivan. 1981. Inflation and corporate capital recovery. In *Tax Reduction Proposals*, pp. 445–513, part 2 of 3 hearings, U.S. Senate, Committee on Finance, 97th Congress, 1st session, 19 and 20 May.

Kahler, M. 1985. European protectionism in theory and practice. *World Politics* 37:475–502.

Kahneman, D., and A. Tversky. 1979. Prospect theory: An analysis of decisions under risk. *Econometrica* 47:263–291.

Kapstein, E.B. 1989. Resolving the regulator's dilemma: International coordination of banking regulations. *International Organization* 43:323–347.

Kar, D.K. 1983. Long-term trends in openness of national economies: Comment. *Oxford Economic Papers* 35:136–140.

Katzenstein, P.J. 1975. International interdependence: Some long-term trends and recent changes. *International Organization* 29:1021–1034.

———. 1976. *Disjoined Partners: Austria and Germany Since 1815.* Berkeley, Calif.: University of California Press.

———. 1977. Conclusion: Domestic structures and strategies of foreign economic policy. *International Organization* 31:879–920.

———. 1985. *Small States in World Markets: Industrial Policy in Europe.* Ithaca, N.Y.: Cornell University Press.

Kelley, H.H., and J.W. Thibaut. 1978. *Interpersonal Relations: A Theory of Interdependence.* New York: Wiley.

Keohane, R.O. 1986. Reciprocity in international relations. *International Organization* 40:1–27.

———. 1990. International liberalism reconsidered. In J. Dunn, ed., *The Economic Limits to Modern Politics,* pp. 165–194. Cambridge, England: Cambridge University Press.

Keohane, R.O., and J.S. Nye, eds. 1972. *Transnational Relations and World Politics.* Cambridge, Mass.: Harvard University Press.

Keohane, R.O., and J.S. Nye. 1975. International interdependence and integration. In F.I. Greenstein and N.W. Polsby, eds., *Handbook of Political Science,* vol. 8, pp. 363–414. Reading, Mass.: Addison-Wesley.

———. 1977. *Power and Interdependence: World Politics in Transition.* Boston: Little, Brown.

———. 1987. *Power and Interdependence* revisited. *International Organization* 41:725–753.

Klott, G. 1985. Tax plan: Smokestack view. *New York Times,* 31, 2 July.

Koot, G.M. 1987. *English Historical Economics, 1870–1926: The Rise of Economic History and Neomercantilism.* Cambridge, England: Cambridge University Press.

Korn, P. 1981. Increasing protectionism in Europe. *Intereconomics* 16:263–268.

Krasner, S.D. 1976. State power and the structure of foreign trade. *World Politics* 28:317–347.

———. 1979. The Tokyo Round: Particularistic interests and prospects for stability in the global trading system. *International Studies Quarterly* 23:491–531.

Krauss, M.B. 1978. *The New Protectionism: The Welfare State and International Trade.* New York: New York University Press.

Lenin, V.I. [1917] 1939. *Imperialism: The Highest Stage of Capitalism.* New York: International Publishers.

Leonard, H.J. 1988. *Pollution and the Struggle for World Product: Multinational Corporations, Environment, and International Comparative Advantage.* Cambridge, England: Cambridge University Press.

Lerner, D. 1956. French business leaders look at the EDC. *Public Opinion Quarterly* 20:212–221.

Liesner, H. 1971. Harmonisation issues under free trade. In H.G. Johnson, ed., *Trade Strategy for Rich and Poor Nations*, pp. 95–168. London: Allen and Unwin.

Lijphart, A. 1964. Tourist traffic and integration potential. *Journal of Common Market Studies* 2:251–262.

Lindbeck, A. 1978. Economic dependence and interdependence in the industrialized world. In *From Marshall Plan to Global Interdependence: New Challenges for the Industrialized Nations*, pp. 59–86. Paris: Organisation for Economic Cooperation and Development.

Lindberg, L. 1970. Political integration as a multidimensional phenomenon requiring multivariate measurement. *International Organization* 24:649–732.

List, F. 1827. *Outlines of American Political Economy*. Philadelphia: S. Parker.

————. [1841] 1856. *The National System of Political Economy*. Translated by G.A. Matile. Philadelphia, Lippincott.

Little, R. 1984. Power and interdependence: A realist critique. In R.J.B. Jones and P. Willetts, eds., *Interdependence on Trial: Studies in the Theory and Reality of Contemporary Interdependence*, pp. 111–129. New York: St. Martin's Press.

Little, R., and R.D. McKinlay. 1978. Linkage-responsiveness and the nation state: An alternative conceptualization of interdependence. *British Journal of International Studies* 4(October):209–225.

Lodge, G.C., and E.F. Vogel. 1987. *Ideology and National Competitiveness: An Analysis of Nine Countries*. Boston: Harvard Business School Press.

Long, O. 1978. International trade under threat: A constructive response. *World Economy* 1:251–262.

MacBean, A.I. 1978. How to repair the "safety net" of the international trading system. *World Economy* 1:149–161.

Machlup, F. 1977. *A History of Thought on Economic Integration*. New York: Columbia University Press.

McKay, D., and W. Grant. 1983. Industrial policies in OECD countries: An overview. *Journal of Public Policy* 3:1–12.

McKeown, T.J. 1984. Firms and tariff regime change: Explaining the demand for protection. *World Politics* 36:215–233.

Manoogian, P.R., and B. Sundelius. 1982. Transaction trends in Western Europe and the Nordic area. In R.F. Tomasson, ed., *Comparative Social Research*, vol. 5, pp. 167–192. Greenwich, Conn.: JAI Press.

Martin, D. 1985. U.S.–Canadian rift on wood exports. *New York Times*, 19, 24, 12 August.

Meade, J.E. 1953. *Problems of Economic Union*. London: Allen and Unwin.

Melko, M. 1973. *52 Peaceful Societies*. Oakville, Ontario: CPRI Press.

Migue, J.-L. 1982. Trade barriers, regulation, and bureaucratic supply as alternative instruments of wealth transfers. In J. Quinn and P. Slayton, eds., *Non-Tariff Barriers After the Tokyo Round*, pp. 103–117. Montreal: Institute for Research on Public Policy.

Mill, J.S. [1873] 1964. *Autobiography of John Stuart Mill*. Reprint. New York: New American Library.

Milner, H. 1987. Resisting the protectionist temptation: Industry and the making of trade policy in France and the United States during the 1970s. *International Organization* 41:639–665.

Milner, H.V. 1988. *Resisting Protectionism: Global Industries and the Politics of International Trade.* Princeton, N.J.: Princeton University Press.

Milner, H.V., and D.B. Yoffie. 1989. Between free trade and protectionism: Strategic trade policy and a theory of corporate trade demands. *International Organization* 43:239–272.

Milward, A. 1981. Tariffs as constitutions. In S. Strange and R. Tooze, eds., *The International Politics of Surplus Capacity: Competition for Market Shares in the World Recession*, pp. 57–66. London: Allen and Unwin.

Mishkin, F.S. 1984. Are real interest rates equal across countries? An empirical investigation of international parity conditions. *Journal of Finance* 39:1345–1358.

Modelski, G. 1961. Agraria and industria: Two models of the international system. In K. Knorr and S. Verba, eds., *The International System*, pp. 118–143. Princeton, N.J.: Princeton University Press.

Mokhtari, M., and F. Rassekh. 1989. The tendency towards price equalization among OECD countries. *Review of Economics and Statistics* 71:636–642.

Moon, P.T. 1925. *Syllabus on International Relations.* New York: Macmillan.

Moravcsik, A.M. 1989. Disciplining trade finance: The OECD export credit arrangement. *International Organization* 43:173–205.

Morley, J.M. 1881. *Life of Richard Cobden.* London: Chapman.

Morris, C. 1972. *Measures of Relative Income Inequality.* Santa Monica, Calif.: Rand Corporation, R-1026-RC.

Morse, E.L. 1969. The politics of interdependence. *International Organization* 23:311–326.

———. 1970. The transformation of foreign policies: Modernization, interdependence, and externalization. *World Politics* 22:371–392.

———. 1972. Crisis diplomacy, interdependence, and the politics of international economic relations. *World Politics* 24:123–150.

———. 1976a. Interdependence in world affairs. In J.N. Rosenau, K.W. Thompson, and G. Boyd, eds., *World Politics: An Introduction*, pp. 660–681. New York: Free Press.

———. 1976b. *Modernization and the Transformation of International Relations.* New York: Free Press.

Nagel, J.H. 1975. *The Descriptive Analysis of Power.* New Haven, Conn.: Yale University Press.

Nelson, D. 1988. Endogenous tariff theory: A critical survey. *American Journal of Political Science* 32:796–837.

Nevin, J.J. 1983. Doorstop for free trade. *Harvard Business Review* 83:88–95.

North, R.C. 1977. Toward a framework for the analysis of scarcity and conflict. *International Studies Quarterly* 21:569–591.

Nye, J.S., Jr. 1988. Neorealism and neoliberalism. *World Politics* 40:235–251.

Obstfeld, M. 1986. Capital mobility in the world economy: Theory and measurement. *Carnegie-Rochester Conference Series on Public Policy* 24:55–104.

Olechowski, A., and G. Sampson. 1980. Current trade restrictions in the EEC, the United States and Japan. *Journal of World Trade Law* 14:220–231.

Olson, M. 1982. *The Rise and Decline of Nations: Economic Growth, Stagflation, and Social Rigidities.* New Haven, Conn.: Yale University Press.

Orr, D.W. 1977. Modernization and conflict: The second image implications of scarcity. *International Studies Quarterly* 21:593–618.

Pagano, P. 1985. Studios ask U.S. to fight trade curbs. *Los Angeles Times*, pt. 4, p. 4, 11 September.

Page, S.A.B. 1980. The increasing use of trade controls by the industrial countries. *Intereconomics* 15:144–151.

Papayoanou, P. In progress. Interdependence, threat, and great power alliance strategies. Ph.D. diss., Department of Political Science, University of California, Los Angeles.

Pelkmans, J. 1979. Economic cooperation among Western countries. In R.J. Gordon and J. Pelkmans, eds., *Challenges to Interdependent Economies: The Industrial West in the Coming Decade*, pp. 69–142. New York: McGraw-Hill.

Pinder, J., ed. 1982. *National Industrial Strategy and the World Economy.* London: Croom Helm.

Polachek, S.W. 1978. Dyadic dispute: An economic perspective. *Papers of the Peace Science Society* 28:67–80.

———. 1980. Conflict and trade. *Journal of Conflict Resolution* 24:55–78.

Polak, J.J. 1981. *Coordination of National Economic Policies.* Occasional Papers No. 7. New York: Group of Thirty.

Polanyi, K. 1944. *The Great Transformation: The Political and Economic Origins of Our Time.* Boston: Beacon.

Pollard, R.A. 1985. *Economic Security and the Origins of the Cold War, 1945–1950.* New York: Columbia University Press.

Pollins, B.M. 1989a. Does trade still follow the flag? *American Political Science Review* 83:465–480.

———. 1989b. Conflict, cooperation, and commerce: The effect of international political interactions on bilateral trade flows. *American Journal of Political Science* 33:737–761.

Pollins, B.M., and P.K. Brecke. 1987. International economic processes. In S.A. Bremer, ed., *The GLOBUS Model: Computer Simulation of Worldwide Political and Economic Developments*, pp. 459–567. Boulder, Colo.: Westview Press.

Puchala, D.J. 1970. Integration and disintegration in Franco-German relations, 1954–1965. *International Organization* 24:183–208.

———. 1984. *Fiscal Harmonization in the European Communities: National Politics and International Cooperation.* London: Frances Pinter.

Pugel, T.A., and I. Walter. 1985. U.S. corporate interests and the political economy of trade policy. *Review of Economics and Statistics* 67:465–473.

Ray, E.J. 1987. Changing patterns of protectionism: The fall in tariffs and the rise in non-tariff barriers. *Northwestern Journal of International Law and Business* 8:285–327.

Reich, S. 1989. Roads to follow: Regulating direct foreign investment. *International Organization* 43:543–584.

Reinton, P.O. 1967. International structure and international integration: The case of Latin America. *Journal of Peace Research* 4(4):334–365.

Reynolds, P.A., and R.D. McKinlay. 1979. The concept of interdependence: Its uses and misuses. In K. Goldmann and G. Sjostedt, eds., *Power, Capabilities, Interdependence: Problems in the Study of International Influence*, pp. 141–166. Beverly Hills, Calif.: Sage Publications.

Rhodes, C. 1989. Reciprocity in trade: The utility of a bargaining strategy. *International Organization* 43:273–299.

Richardson, J.D. 1990. The political economy of strategic trade policy. *International Organization* 44:107–135.

Robson, P. 1980. *The Economics of International Integration*. London: Allen and Unwin.

Rogoff, K. 1985. Can international monetary policy cooperation be counterproductive? *Journal of International Economics* 18:199–217.

Rogowski, R. 1987. Trade and the variety of democratic institutions. *International Organization* 41:203–223.

Rosecrance, R. 1973. *International Relations: Peace or War?* New York: McGraw-Hill.

———. 1981. International theory revisited. *International Organization* 35:691–713.

———. 1986. *The Rise of the Trading State: Commerce and Conquest in the Modern World*. New York: Basic Books.

Rosecrance, R., A. Alexandroff, W. Koehler, J. Kroll, S. Lacqueur, and J. Stocker. 1977. Whither interdependence. *International Organization* 31:425–445.

Rosecrance, R., and W. Gutowitz. 1981. Measuring interdependence: A rejoinder. *International Organization* 35:553–560.

Rosecrance, R., and A. Stein. 1973. Interdependence: Myth or reality? *World Politics* 26:1–27.

Rousslang, D.J. 1987. The opportunity cost of import tariffs. *Kyklos* 40(1):88–102.

Rowen, H. 1986. It's the culture, not the Yen. *Washington Post National Weekly Edition* 5(16 June):5.

Rubin, S.J., and T.R. Graham, eds. 1982. *Environment and Trade: The Relation of International Trade and Environment Policy*. Totowa, N.J.: Allanheld, Osmun and Co.

Ruggie, J.G. 1982. International regimes, transactions, and change: Embedded liberalism in the postwar economic order. *International Organization* 36:379–415.

Russell, F.M. 1936. *Theories of International Relations*. New York: D. Appleton-Century Company.

Russett, B.M. 1962. International communication and legislative behavior: The Senate and the House of Commons. *Journal of Conflict Resolution* 6:291–307.

322   BEHAVIOR, SOCIETY, AND INTERNATIONAL CONFLICT

————. 1963a. The calculus of deterrence. *Journal of Conflict Resolution* 7:97–109.
————. 1963b. *Community and Contention: Britain and America in the Twentieth Century.* Cambridge, Mass.: MIT Press.
————. 1971. Transactions, community, and international political integration. *Journal of Common Market Studies* 9:224–245.
————. 1981–1982. Security and the resources scramble: Will 1984 be like 1914? *International Affairs* 58:42–58.
Russett, B., and E. Hanson. 1975. *Interest and Ideology: The Foreign Policy Beliefs of American Businessmen.* San Francisco: Freeman.
Russett, B.M., H.R. Alker, Jr., K.W. Deutsch, and H.D. Lasswell. 1964. *World Handbook of Political and Social Indicators.* New Haven, Conn.: Yale University Press.
Rybczynski, Tad M. 1984. Industrial finance system in Europe, U.S. and Japan. *Journal of Economic Behavior and Organization* 5:275–286.
Salvatore, D., ed. 1987. *The New Protectionist Threat to World Welfare.* New York: North-Holland.
Sanger, D.E. 1987. A Pentagon study urges U.S. aid for the embattled chip industry. *New York Times,* 1, 33, 13 February 13.
Sayrs, L.W. 1989. Trade and conflict revisited: Do politics matter? *International Interactions* 15(2):155–175.
Senior, N.W. 1850. *Political Economy,* 2d ed. London: J.J. Griffin and Company.
Silberner, E. 1946. *The Problem of War in Nineteenth Century Economic Thought.* Translated by A.H. Krappe. Princeton, N.J.: Princeton University Press.
Skalnes, L. In progress. Allies and rivals: Politics, markets, and grand strategy. Ph.D. diss., Department of Political Science, University of California, Los Angeles.
Smith, A. 1979. *An Inquiry into the Nature and Causes of the Wealth of Nations,* 2 vols. General editors, R.H. Campbell and A.S. Skinner. Textual editor, W.B. Todd. Oxford: Clarendon Press.
Smith, D.L. 1987. International political processes. In S.A. Bremer, ed., *The GLOBUS Model: Computer Simulation of Worldwide Political and Economic Developments,* pp. 569–721. Boulder, Colo.: Westview Press.
Smith, S. 1984. Foreign policy analysis and interdependence. In R.J.B. Jones and P. Willetts, eds., *Interdependence on Trial: Studies in the Theory and Reality of Contemporary Interdependence,* pp. 64–82. New York: St. Martin's Press.
Smoker, P. 1965. Trade, defense, and the Richardson theory of arms races: A seven nation study. *Journal of Peace Research* 2(2):161–176.
————. 1967. Nation state escalation and international integration. *Journal of Peace Research* 4(1):61–75.
Snidal, D. 1985. The limits of hegemonic stability theory. *International Organization* 39:579–614.
Staley, E. 1935. *War and the Private Investor: A Study in the Relations of International Politics and International Private Investment.* Chicago: University of Chicago Press.
————. 1939. *World Economy in Transition: Technology vs. Politics, Laissez Faire vs. Planning, Power vs. Welfare.* New York: Council on Foreign Relations.

Stegemann, K. 1989. Policy rivalry among industrial states: What can we learn from models of strategic trade policy? *International Organization* 43:73–100.

Stein, A.A. 1984. The hegemon's dilemma: Great Britain, the United States, and the international economic order. *International Organization* 38:355–386.

———. 1990. *Why Nations Cooperate: Circumstance and Choice in International Politics*. Ithaca, N.Y.: Cornell University Press.

Strange, S. 1985. Protectionism and world politics. *International Organization* 39:233–259.

Summary, R.M. 1989. A political-economic model of U.S. bilateral trade. *Review of Economics and Statistics* 71:179–182.

Surrey, S.S., and P.R. McDaniel. 1985. *Tax Expenditures*. Cambridge, Mass.: Harvard University Press.

Teece, D.J. 1986. Transactions cost economics and the multinational enterprise: An assessment. *Journal of Economic Behavior and Organization* 7:21–45.

Tetreault, M.A. 1980. Measuring interdependence. *International Organization* 34:429–443.

———. 1981. Measuring interdependence: A response. *International Organization* 35:557–560.

Thompson, E.A. 1979. An economic basis for the "national defense argument" for aiding certain industries. *Journal of Political Economy* 87:1–36.

Tinbergen, J. 1959. On the theory of economic integration. In L.H. Klaassen, L.M. Koyck, and H.J. Witteveen, eds., *Selected Papers*, pp. 138–151. Amsterdam: North-Holland, 1959.

Tobey, J.A. 1990. The effect of domestic environmental policies on patterns of world trade. *Kyklos* 43(2):191–209.

Tollison, R.D., and T.D. Willett. 1973. International integration and the interdependence of economic variables. *International Organization* 27:255–271.

Tovias, A. 1982. Testing factor price equalization in the EEC. *Journal of Common Market Studies* 20:375–388.

Tumlir, J. 1978–1979. The protectionist threat to international order. *International Journal* 34:53–63.

Twight, C. 1985. U.S. regulation of international trade: A retrospective inquiry. In R. Higgs, ed., *Emergence of the Modern Political Economy*, supplement 4, *Research in Economic History: A Research Annual*, pp. 139–195. Greenwich, Conn.: JAI Press.

van Mourik, A. 1987. Testing the factor price equalization theorem in the EC: An alternative approach: A comment. *Journal of Common Market Studies* 26:79–86.

Viallate, A. 1923. *Economic Imperialism and International Relations*. New York: Macmillan.

Vittas, D. 1986. Banks' relations with industry: An international survey. *National Westminster Bank Quarterly Review* :2–14.

Vogel, D. 1986. *National Styles of Regulation: Environmental Policy in Great Britain and the United States*. Ithaca, N.Y.: Cornell University Press.

von Furstenberg, G.M. 1983. Changes in U.S. interest rates and their effects on

324   BEHAVIOR, SOCIETY, AND INTERNATIONAL CONFLICT

European interest and exchange rates. In D. Bigman and T. Taya, eds., *Exchange Rate and Trade Instability: Causes, Consequences, and Remedies*, pp. 257–282. Cambridge, Mass.: Ballinger.

Wallerstein, M. 1987. Unemployment, collective bargaining, and the demand for protection. *American Journal of Political Science* 31:729–752.

Waltz, K.N. 1959. *Man, the State and War: A Theoretical Analysis*. New York: Columbia University Press.

———. 1962. Kant, liberalism, and war. *American Political Science Review* 56:331–340.

———. 1970. The myth of interdependence. In C.P. Kindleberger, ed., *The International Corporation*, pp. 205–223. Cambridge. Mass.: MIT Press.

———. 1979. *Theory of International Politics*. Reading, Mass.: Addison-Wesley.

Weidenbaum, M.L. 1983. *Toward a More Open Trade Policy*. St. Louis, Mo.: Washington University, Center for the Study of American Business.

Wheeler, J.W., M.E. Janow, and T. Pepper. 1982. *Japanese Industrial Development Policies in the 1980's: Implications for U.S. Trade and Investment*. Croton-on-Hudson, N.Y.: Hudson Institute.

Whitman, M. v. N. 1969. Economic openness and international financial flows. *Journal of Money, Credit, and Banking* 1:727–749.

Wilkinson, D. 1980. *Deadly Quarrels: Lewis F. Richardson and the Statistical Study of War*. Berkeley, Calif.: University of California Press.

Willoughby, J. 1982a. The changing role of protection in the world economy. *Cambridge Journal of Economics* 6:195–211.

———. 1982b. A reconsideration of the protectionist debate: Keynes and import controls. *Journal of Economic Issues* 16:555–561.

Withers, H. 1916. *International Finance*. New York: Dutton.

Wolf, C., Jr., and D. Leebaert. 1978. Trade liberalization as a path to weapons standardization in NATO. *International Security* 2:136–159.

Woytinsky, W.S. 1943. Methods of measuring inequality in individual earnings. In *Earnings and Social Security in the United States*, pp. 1–16. Washington, D.C.: Social Science Research Council, Committee on Social Security.

———. 1965a. The escalation of international conflicts. *Journal of Conflict Resolution* 9:434–449.

Wright, Q. 1965b. *A Study of War*, 2d ed. Chicago: University of Chicago Press.

Wysocki, B., Jr. 1986. Lust for labor. *Wall Street Journal*, sec. 4, p. 9D, 21 April.

Young, O.R. 1969. Interdependencies in world politics. *International Journal* 24:726–750.

Zinnes, D.A., and R.G. Muncaster. 1987. Transaction flows and integrative processes. In C. Cioffi-Revilla, R.L. Merritt, and D.A. Zinnes, eds., *Communication and Interaction in Global Politics*, pp. 23–48. Beverly Hills, Calif.: Sage Publications.

Contributors and Editors

ROBERT A. HINDE was formerly a Royal Society research professor at the University of Cambridge and is currently master of St. John's College, Cambridge. He has carried out research on the development and integration of behavior in animals and humans and has a special interest in the integration of the behavioral and social sciences. Among his recent publications are *Towards Understanding Relationships* (Academic Press, 1979); *Aggression and War* (ed. with J. Groebel; Cambridge University Press, 1989); *Cooperation and Prosocial Behaviour* (ed. with J. Groebel; Cambridge University Press, 1991); and *The Institution of War* (ed.; Macmillan, 1991). He received his B.A. from Cambridge University, B.Sc. from London University, D.Phil. from Oxford University, and Sc.D. from Cambridge University.

JO L. HUSBANDS is the staff director of the Committee on International Security and Arms Control at the National Research Council. From 1982 to 1986, she was deputy director of the Committee for National Security in Washington, D.C. Her research interests include U.S. defense policy, international negotiations, and third-world security issues such as arms transfers and nuclear proliferation. Her recent publications include *Defense Choices: Greater Security with Fewer Dollars* (with William W. Kaufman; Committee for National Security, 1986) and "The conventional arms transfer talks" (with Anne H. Cahn) in *Arms Transfers Limitation and Third World Security* (Thomas Ohlson, ed.: Oxford University Press, 1988). She received a Ph.D. in political science from the University of Minnesota.

WILLIAM W. JAROSZ is currently a Ph.D. candidate in the government department at Harvard University and a J.D. candidate at the Harvard Law School.

He is a research fellow at the Center for International Affairs at Harvard University. His dissertation applies learning theory to examine elite and institutional responses to foreign direct investment in the Soviet Union. His other research interests include theories of institutional change and international legal regimes.

ROBERT JERVIS is Adlai E. Stevenson professor of political science and a member of the Institute of War and Peace Studies at Columbia University. He is currently working on problems of psychology, decision making, and cooperation. Among his publicatons are *Perception and Misperception in International Politics* (Princeton University Press, 1976) and *The Meaning of the Nuclear Revolution* (Cornell University Press, 1989), which won the Grawemeyer Award for the best book on international peace. He received his Ph.D. in political science from the University of California at Berkeley.

RUSSELL LENG is William R. Kenan, Jr., professor of political science at Middlebury College, where he also has served as dean of sciences. His research focuses on the crisis behavior of nations, using quantitative data generated through his Behavioral Correlates of War project. His most recent work is the forthcoming *Interstate Crisis Behavior, 1916–1980* (Cambridge University Press). A summary of the findings from his previous research appears in "Militarized Interstate Crises: The BCOW Typology and Its Applications" (with J. David Singer; *International Studies Quarterly* 32, 1988). He received his Ph.D. from American University and has taught as a visiting professor at the University of Michigan.

JOSEPH S. NYE, JR., is Dillon professor of international affairs, director of the Center for International Affairs, and associate dean of arts and sciences at Harvard University. He is a fellow of the American Academy of Arts and Sciences and a senior fellow of the Aspen Institute. His most recent books are *Bound to Lead: The Changing Nature of American Power* (Basic, 1990) and *Nuclear Ethics* (Free Press, 1986). He received his B.A. from Princeton University and his Ph.D. in political science from Harvard University and did postgraduate work at Oxford University on a Rhodes Scholarship.

MARTIN SHUBIK is Seymour Knox professor of mathematical institutional economics at Yale University. His research interests are in game theory as applied to society, business, and conflict. Among his publications are *Game Theory in the Social Sciences*, Volumes 1 and 2 (MIT Press, 1982, 1984), *The Mathematics of Conflict* (Elsevier, 1983), and *Games for Society, Business and War* (Elsevier, 1975). He received his B.A. in mathematics from the University of Toronto and a Ph.D. in economics from Princeton University.

ARTHUR A. STEIN is a professor of political science at the University of California—Los Angeles. He is currently working on the bases of state interests, the nature of grand strategies, and the prospects for international cooperation. He is the author of *The Nation at War* (Johns Hopkins University Press, 1980) and *Why Nations Cooperate* (Cornell University Press, 1990). He received an A.B. from Cornell University and a Ph.D. in political science from Yale University.

PAUL C. STERN is study director of the Committee on International Conflict and Cooperation and the Committee on the Human Dimensions of Global Change at the National Research Council. His current research includes work on the formation of social attitudes on environmental policy. His publications include *Evaluating Social Science Research* (Oxford University Press, 1979) and *Global Environmental Change: Understanding the Human Dimensions* (ed. with Oran R. Young and Daniel Druckman; National Academy Press, 1992). He received a B.A. from Amherst College and M.A. and Ph.D. degrees in psychology from Clark University.

PHILIP E. TETLOCK is professor of psychology and director of the Institute of Personality Assessment and Research at the University of California at Berkeley. His major research interests include the study of international conflict, judgment and choice processes, and impression management. His recent publications include "Monitoring the Integrative Complexity of American and Soviet Foreign Policy Rhetoric: What Can Be Learned?" (*Journal of Social Issues*, 1988), *Learning in U.S. and Soviet Foreign Policy* (ed. with George Breslauer; Westview Press, 1991), and *Psychology and Social Policy* (with Peter Suedfeld; Hemisphere, 1991). He received his B.A. and M.A. degrees from the University of British Columbia and his Ph.D. in psychology from Yale University.

CHARLES TILLY is university distinguished professor at the New School for Social Research, where he directs the Center for Studies of Social Change. Most of his recent research and writing concerns large-scale social change, conflict, and collective action. His most recent books are *Strikes, Wars, and Revolutions* (Cambridge University Press, 1989) and *Coercion, Capital, and European States* (Blackwell, 1990). He received his Ph.D. in sociology from Harvard University.

Index